QuickBooks® Online for Accounting

8e

Glenn Owen

✱ Cengage

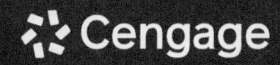

Australia • Brazil • Canada • Mexico • Singapore • United Kingdom • United States

Cengage

QuickBooks® Online For Accounting, Eighth Edition
Glenn Owen

SVP, Product: Cheryl Costantini

VP, Product: Thais Alencar

Portfolio Product Director: Joe Sabatino

Contributing Author: Robin Browning

Portfolio Product Manager: Jonathan Gross

Content Manager: Valarmathy Munuswamy, Lumina Datamatics Ltd.

Product Assistant: Flannery Cowan

Marketing Manager: Colin Kramer

Content Acquisition Analyst: Rida Syed

Content Acquisition Project Manager: Kavitha Rajasekaran, Lumina Datamatics Ltd.

Production Service: Lumina Datamatics Ltd.

Art Director and Cover Designer: Christopher Doughman

Cover Image: sittipong phokawattana/iStock /Getty Images

Copyright © 2025 Cengage Learning, Inc. ALL RIGHTS RESERVED.

WCN: 01-100-393

No part of this work covered by the copyright herein may be reproduced or distributed in any form or by any means, except as permitted by U.S. copyright law, without the prior written permission of the copyright owner.

Unless otherwise noted, all content is Copyright © Cengage Learning, Inc.

Previous edition(s): © 2024, © 2023, © 2022

For product information and technology assistance, contact us at
Cengage Customer & Sales Support, 1-800-354-9706 or
support.cengage.com.

For permission to use material from this text or product, submit all requests online at **www.cengage.com/permissions**.

Intuit and QuickBooks are trademarks and service marks of Intuit Inc., registered in the United States and other countries.

Library of Congress Control Number: 2024933574

ISBN: 978-0-357-98849-7

Cengage
5191 Natorp Boulevard
Mason, OH 45040
USA

Cengage is a leading provider of customized learning solutions. Our employees reside in nearly 40 different countries and serve digital learners in 165 countries around the world. Find your local representative at **www.cengage.com**.

To learn more about Cengage platforms and services, register or access your online learning solution, or purchase materials for your course, visit **www.cengage.com**.

Printed at CLDPC, USA, 04-24

Brief Contents

Chapter	1	An Introduction to QuickBooks Online Using the Sample Company	1
Chapter	2	An Overview of QuickBooks Online	27
Chapter	3	Setting Up a New Company: Establishing a Chart of Accounts, Beginning Balances, Customers, Vendors, and Products/Services	50
Chapter	4	Recording Operating Activities: Sales and Cash Receipts	95
Chapter	5	Recording Operating Activities: Purchases and Cash Payments	127
Chapter	6	Recording Investing and Financing Activities	161
Chapter	7	Recording Payroll	187
Chapter	8	Establishing Budgets and Preparing Bank Reconciliations	217
Chapter	9	Analysis and Recording of Adjusting Entries	247
Chapter	10	Preparing Financial Statements and Reports	266
Appendix 1		Sales Tax	292
Appendix 2		Comprehensive Case Problems	295
Appendix 3		Overview—Do I Need to Become QuickBooks Online Certified?	319
Index			320

Contents

Preface	**vii**
About the Author & Dedication	**xxi**

Chapter 1 An Introduction to QuickBooks Online Using the Sample Company — **1**

Overview	1
Begin Your Sample Company Walkthrough	1
Customers, Vendors, and Employees	3
Banking Transactions	9
Sales and Expense Transactions	12
Settings	15
Chart of Accounts	16
Lists	18
Reports	20
Company Settings	23
End Note	25
Chapter 1 Practice	26
Chapter 1 Questions	26
Chapter 1 Matching	26

Chapter 2 An Overview of QuickBooks Online — **27**

Overview	27
What Is QBO?	27
How Is QBO Similar to/Different Than the Desktop Version of QuickBooks Accountant?	28
How to Open the QBO Company You Created in the Preface	29
Navigating QBO	38
Assigning an Instructor as the Company's "Accountant"	45
Video Tutorials for QuickBooks Online (Developed and Maintained by Intuit)	46
End Note	48
Chapter 2 Practice	49
Chapter 2 Questions	49
Chapter 2 Matching	49

Chapter 3 Setting Up a New Company: Establishing a Chart of Accounts, Beginning Balances, Customers, Vendors, and Products/Services — **50**

Overview	50
Company Settings	51
Modify the Chart of Accounts and Establish Beginning Balances	53
Close Opening Balance Equity and Create a Balance Sheet	68
Trial Balance	70
Create, Print, and Export a Transaction Detail by Account	71
End Note	72
Chapter 3 Practice	73
Chapter 3 Questions	73
Chapter 3 Matching	73
Chapter 3 Cases	73
Case 1	75
Case 2	77
Case 3	80
Case 4	83
Case 5	87
Case 6	91

Chapter 4 Recording Operating Activities: Sales and Cash Receipts — **95**

Overview	95
Services, Products, and Customers	95
Sales Receipts and Invoices	100
Cash Receipts	106
Trial Balance and Transaction Detail by Account	108
End Note	110
Chapter 4 Practice	111
Chapter 4 Questions	111

Chapter 4 Matching	111
Chapter 4 Cases	111
Case 1	112
Case 2	113
Case 3	115
Case 4	117
Case 5	121
Case 6	123

Chapter 5 Recording Operating Activities: Purchases and Cash Payments   127

Overview	127
Vendors	128
Purchase Orders	129
Bills	133
Payment of Bills, Use of a Credit Card, Payments for Items other than Bills	137
Trial Balance	141
End Note	144
Chapter 5 Practice	145
Chapter 5 Questions	145
Chapter 5 Matching	145
Chapter 5 Cases	145
Case 1	146
Case 2	148
Case 3	150
Case 4	153
Case 5	155
Case 6	157

Chapter 6 Recording Investing and Financing Activities   161

Overview	161
Fixed Assets	162
Long-Term Investments	164
Equity Transactions (Common Stock, Dividends, Owner Investments, and Owner Withdrawals)	166
Long-Term Debt	168
Acquisition of a Fixed Asset in Exchange for Long-Term Debt	170
End Note	172
Chapter 6 Practice	173
Chapter 6 Questions	173
Chapter 6 Matching	173
Chapter 6 Cases	173
Case 1	174
Case 2	176
Case 3	178

Case 4	180
Case 5	181
Case 6	184

Chapter 7 Recording Payroll   187

Overview	187
Employees	188
Payroll Accounts	190
Pay Employees	191
End Note	199
Chapter 7 Practice	200
Chapter 7 Questions	200
Chapter 7 Matching	200
Chapter 7 Cases	200
Case 1	201
Case 2	203
Case 3	206
Case 4	208
Case 5	211
Case 6	214

Chapter 8 Establishing Budgets and Preparing Bank Reconciliations   217

Overview	217
Budget Creation	218
Budget Reports	221
Bank Reconciliation	226
End Note	230
Chapter 8 Practice	231
Chapter 8 Questions	231
Chapter 8 Matching	231
Chapter 8 Cases	231
Case 1	232
Case 2	234
Case 3	237
Case 4	239
Case 5	241
Case 6	244

Chapter 9 Analysis and Recording of Adjusting Entries   247

Overview	247
Trial Balance	248
Adjusting Journal Entries: Prepaid Expenses	249
Adjusting Journal Entries: Accrued Expenses	252
Adjusting Journal Entries: Unearned Revenue	253
Adjusting Journal Entries: Accruing Revenue	255
Adjusting Journal Entries: Depreciation	256

End Note	258
Chapter 9 Practice	259
Chapter 9 Questions	259
Chapter 9 Matching	259
Chapter 9 Cases	259
Case 1	260
Case 2	261
Case 3	262
Case 4	263
Case 5	263
Case 6	264

Chapter 10 Preparing Financial Statements and Reports 266

Overview	266
Income Statement	266
Balance Sheet	272
Statement of Cash Flows	275
Accounts Receivable Aging Summary	278
Accounts Payable Aging Summary	280
Inventory Valuation Summary	282

End Note	284
Chapter 10 Practice	285
Chapter 10 Questions	285
Chapter 10 Matching	285
Chapter 10 Cases	285
Case 1	286
Case 2	287
Case 3	287
Case 4	288
Case 5	289
Case 6	290

Appendix 1 Sales Tax 292

Appendix 2 Comprehensive Case Problems 295

Appendix 3 Overview—Do I Need to Become QuickBooks Online Certified? 319

Index 320

Preface

Overview

Accounting has arrived in the Cloud and its time has come. *Cloud computing* is a general term for anything that involves delivering hosted services over the Internet. According to a recent study by KPMG (a global network of professional firms), businesses—large, medium, and small—are using the Cloud to drive cost efficiencies, better enable a mobile workforce, and improve alignment with their customers and vendors.

Imagine being able to update your business's accounting information system from anywhere on any device using any operating system. That is where the global economy is going. Are you on the path?

Is This Text for You?

This text is for you if you are an instructor who desires a self-paced, self-directed environment for your students to learn the essentials of QuickBooks Online (QBO) and to review their understanding of financial accounting and reporting.

This text is for you if you are a business owner looking for a self-paced, self-directed environment for yourself to learn the essentials of QBO as well as a means to refresh your understanding of financial accounting and reporting.

This book focuses on QBO. It is not designed for users of QuickBooks Pro, Accountant, or any other desktop version of QuickBooks. In that case, Glenn Owen's QuickBooks Accountant books are a better fit. The desktop version and online versions are different, and though you can import files created in the desktop version into the online version, significant differences exist as discussed in Chapter 1.

Use of Multiple Companies

In the prior editions of this text, Intuit limited students to creating only one company. Thus, the author had to use Inuit's Sample Company to demonstrate QBO features. In this edition, with the new ability to use multiple companies (up to 4), the author has chosen to use one of those 4 to demonstrate QBO features in Chapters 3 to 10. Thus, the Sample Company is only used in Chapter 1. Later in this Preface, the instructor will be shown how to assign the Wild Water Sports company to each student. This assignment will only give the student the ability to modify a QBO file as instructed in Chapters 3 to 10. Later, the instructor can assign a second QBO company to a student so that they can complete one of 6 cases found at the end of Chapters 3 to 10. Ultimately, the instructor can only assign 4 QBO files to each student.

Directions for Instructors and Students

Intuit has finally seen the light and has agreed to give students and instructors the ability to create more than one company. They have also developed a more streamlined means to access QBO.

See overview at: https://www.intuit.com/partners/education-program/products/quickbooks/

Instructors

To give your students access to creating multiple companies:

1. First step, register yourself as a QBO Educator: Access the Educator Portal by navigating your web browser to https://www.intuit.com/partners/education-program/products/quickbooks/educator-qbo-signup/

2. Intuit will then attempt to validate you as an instructor at your educational institution.

3. After validation, navigate your web browser to https://accounts.intuit.com/index.html?redirect_url=https%3A%2F%2Feducation-portal.app.intuit.com%2Fapp%2Fdashboard&appfabric=true

4. Provide your email in the space shown in Figure Preface 1 above and then click **Sign In**.

Figure Preface 1

Sign in to the Education Portal

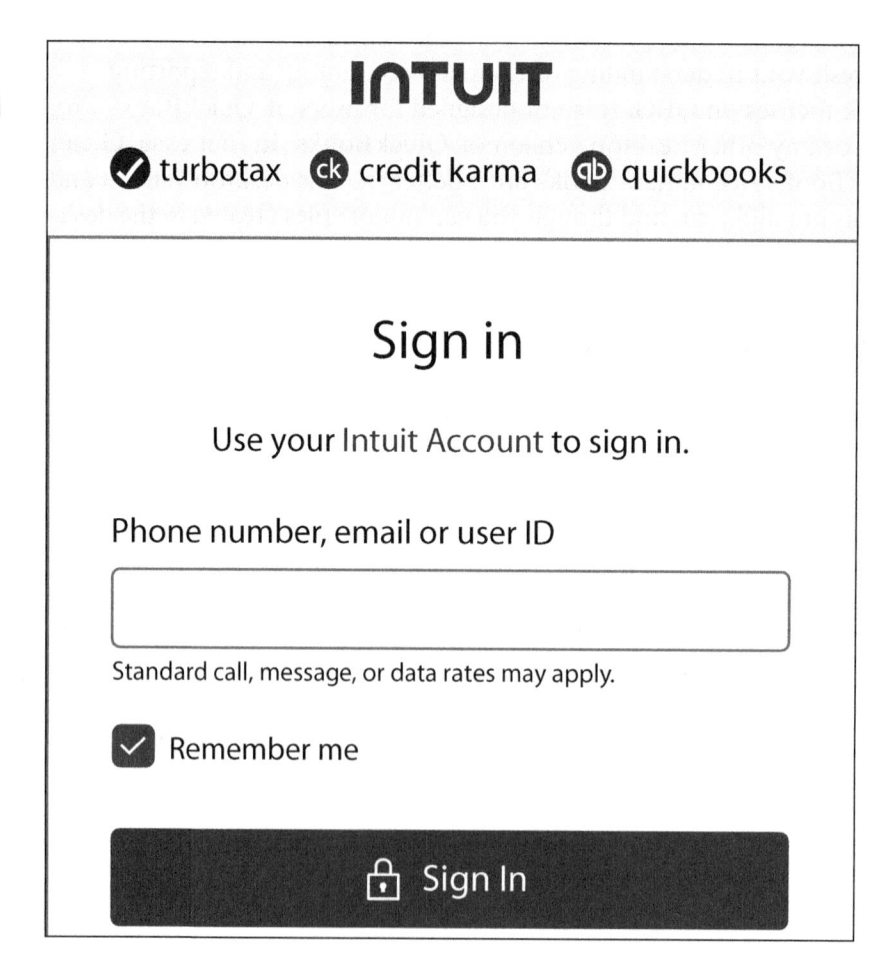

5 Provide your password in the window presented next and then click **Continue**. A Welcome to the Intuit Educator Portal window should appear as shown in Figure Preface 2.

6 Click the video box titled **How the Educator Portal Works** to see an overview of the Educator Portal.

7 To access the Sample Company this text uses in Chapter 1 to demonstrate QBO features, you will click **QuickBooks Online test drive**. Don't do this now.

8 To access QBO tutorials, you will click **Tutorials**. Don't do this now, instead proceed to the next step below.

Figure Preface 2 Welcome to the Intuit Educator Portal

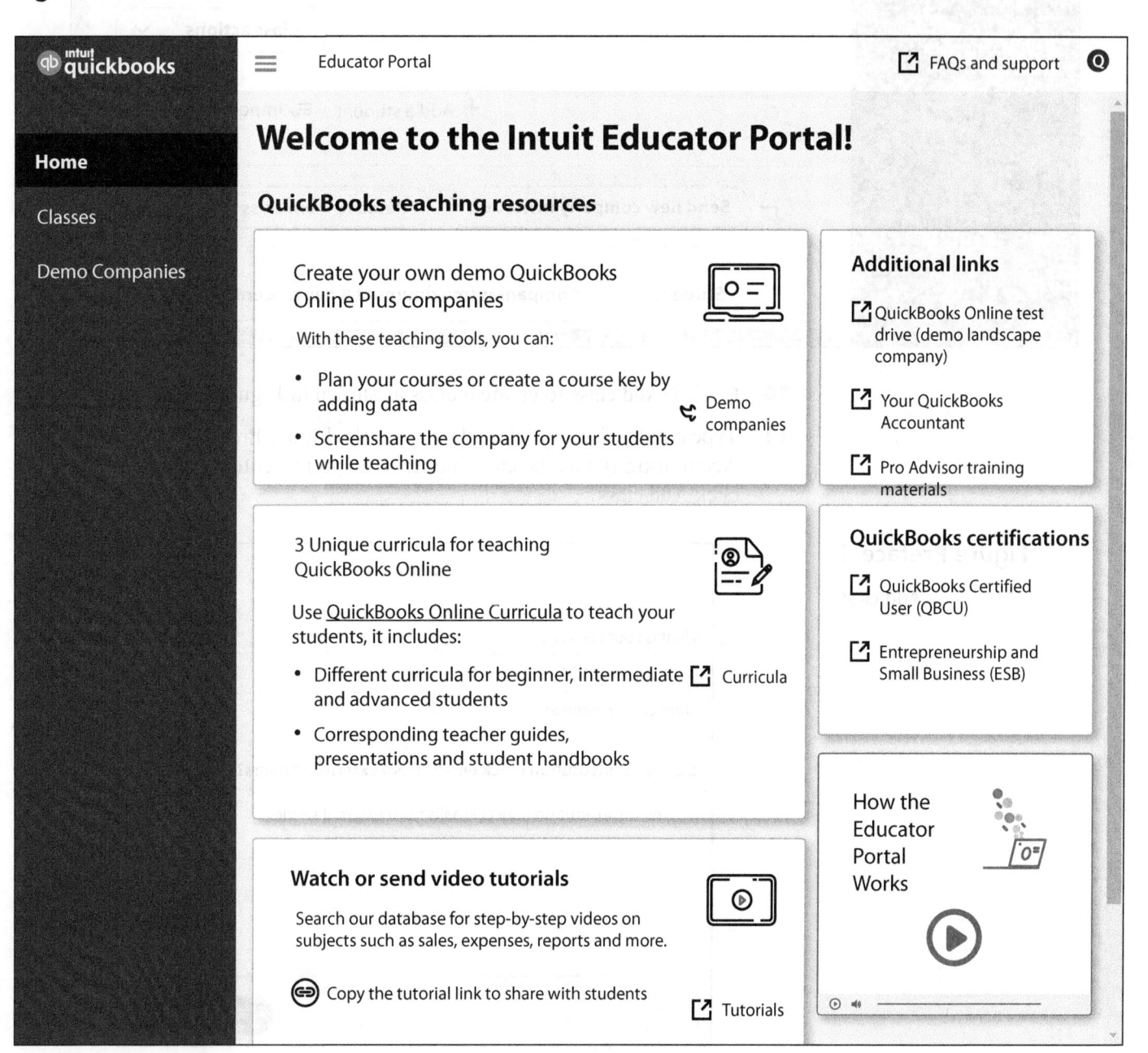

9   Click **Classes** from the navigation bar on the left to view the screen shown in Figure Preface 3. Ignore the reference to an existing Accounting 100 class. Your screen will not show the Accounting 100 class.

Figure Preface 3 Classes

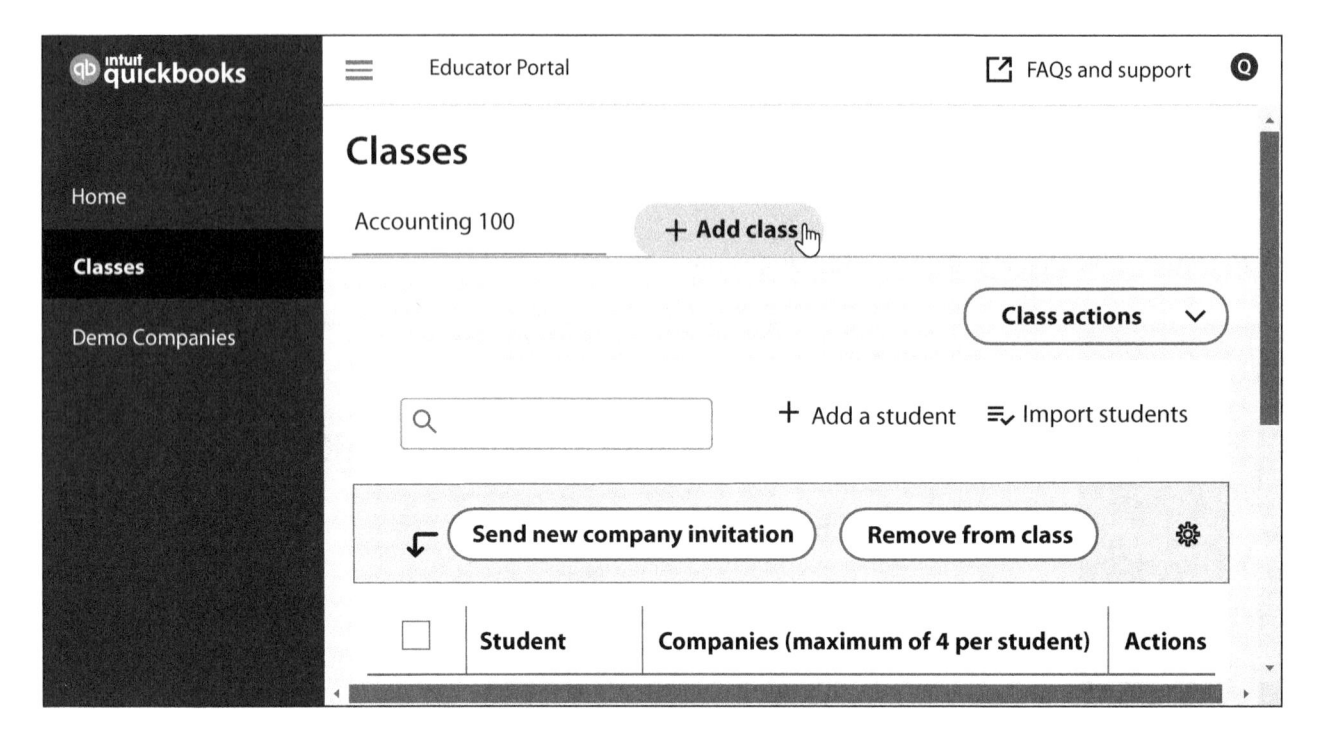

10 Click **+ Add class** to create a class as shown in Figure Preface 3.

11 Type a name for your class. For example, Figure Preface 4 shows Accounting 101 as the class name. Once you've entered a class name, click **Add class**.

Figure Preface 4

Add class

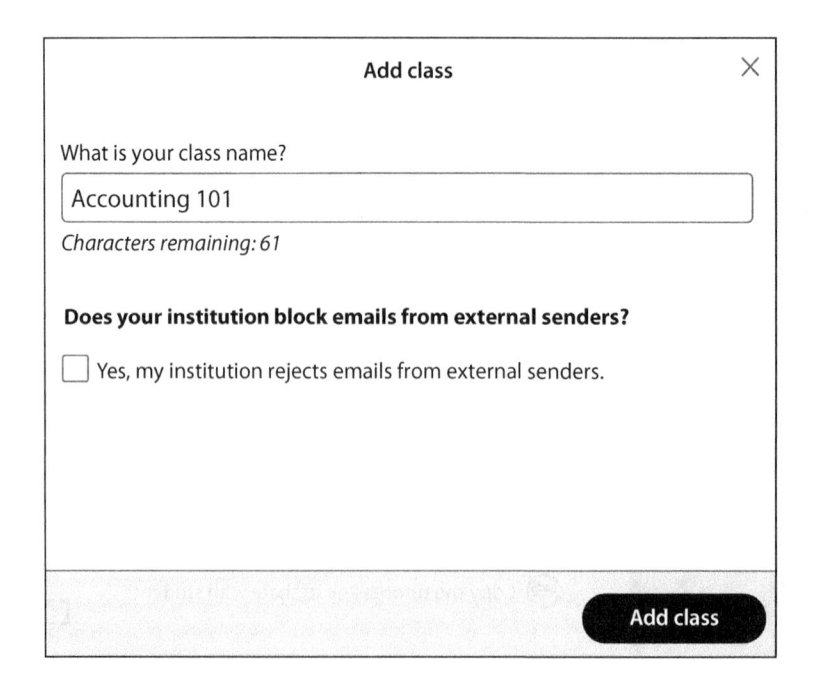

Preface xi

12 Click **Add class**. Your window should look like Figure Preface 5. Add your students to a class either by uploading a roster or clicking Add students manually.

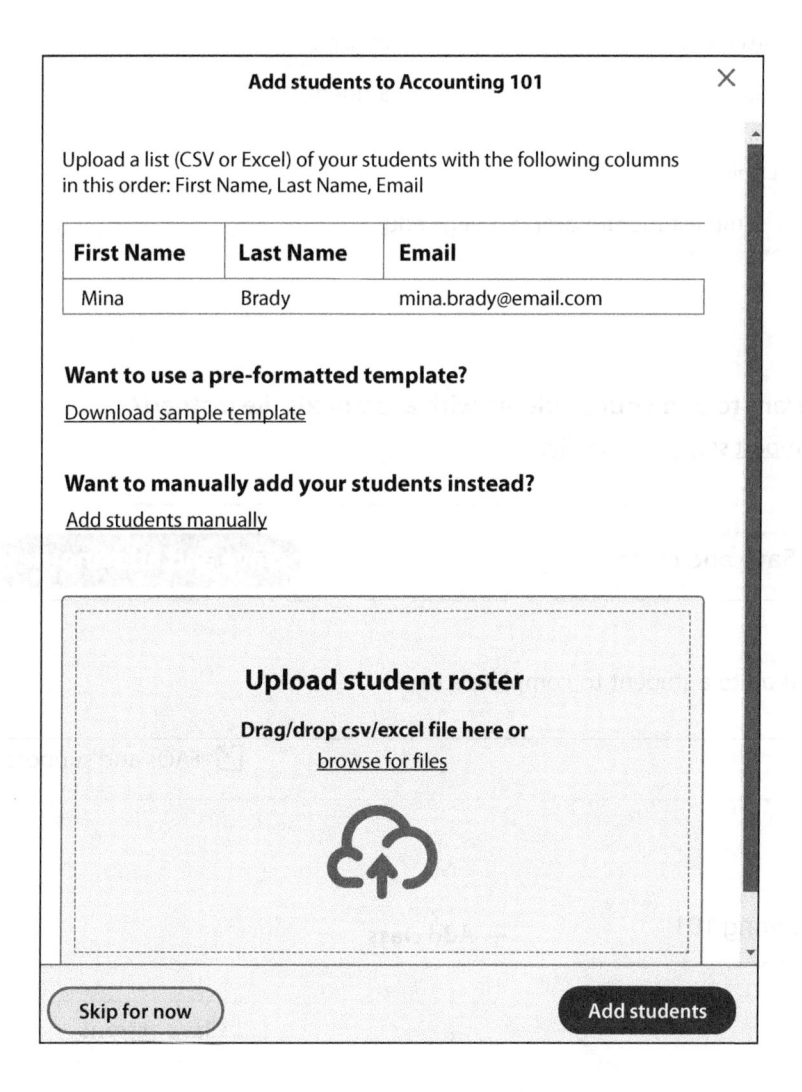

Figure Preface 5

Add students

13 In this example, click **Add students manually** to view Figure Preface 6. The student information will be empty until you perform step 14.

14 Type your student's first name, last name, and email address, then click **Save and close**. A sample student was added in this example.

15 To assign a company to a student, place a **check** next to a student's name and then click **Send new company invitation** as shown in Figure Preface 7. Below is an example of sending an invitation to one student. If you wanted to send this invitation to more students you would simply place a check next to all student names.

xii　　　　　　　　　　　　　Preface

Figure Preface 6

Adding students manually

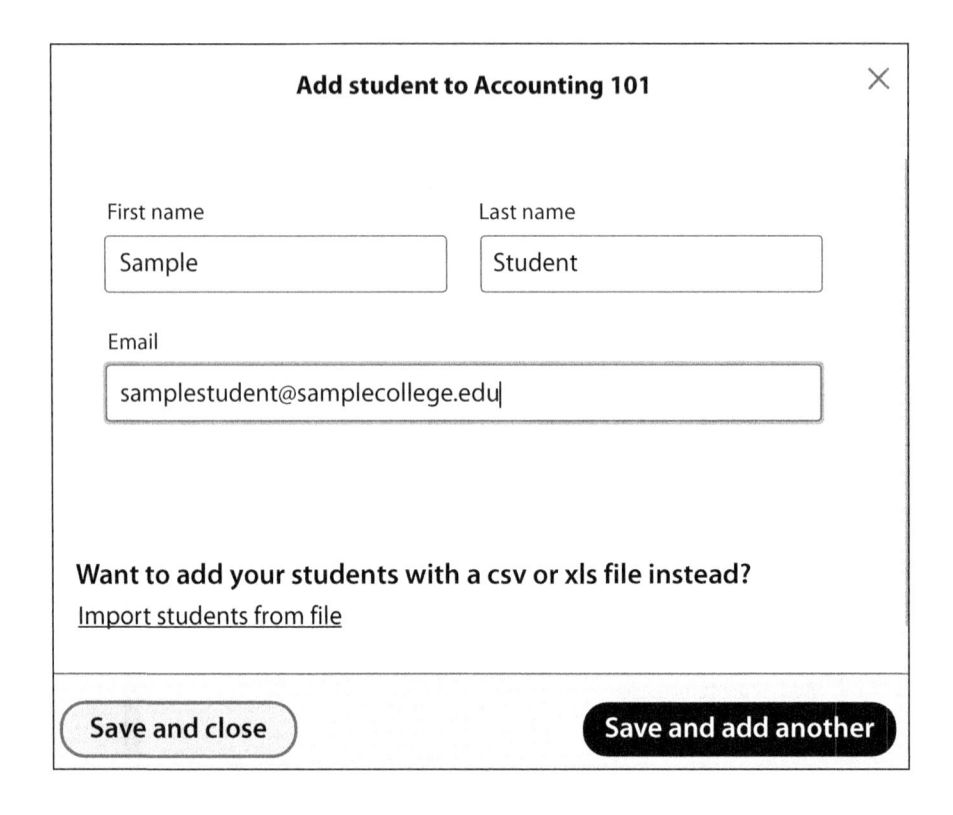

Figure Preface 7 Sending an invitation to a student to complete a case

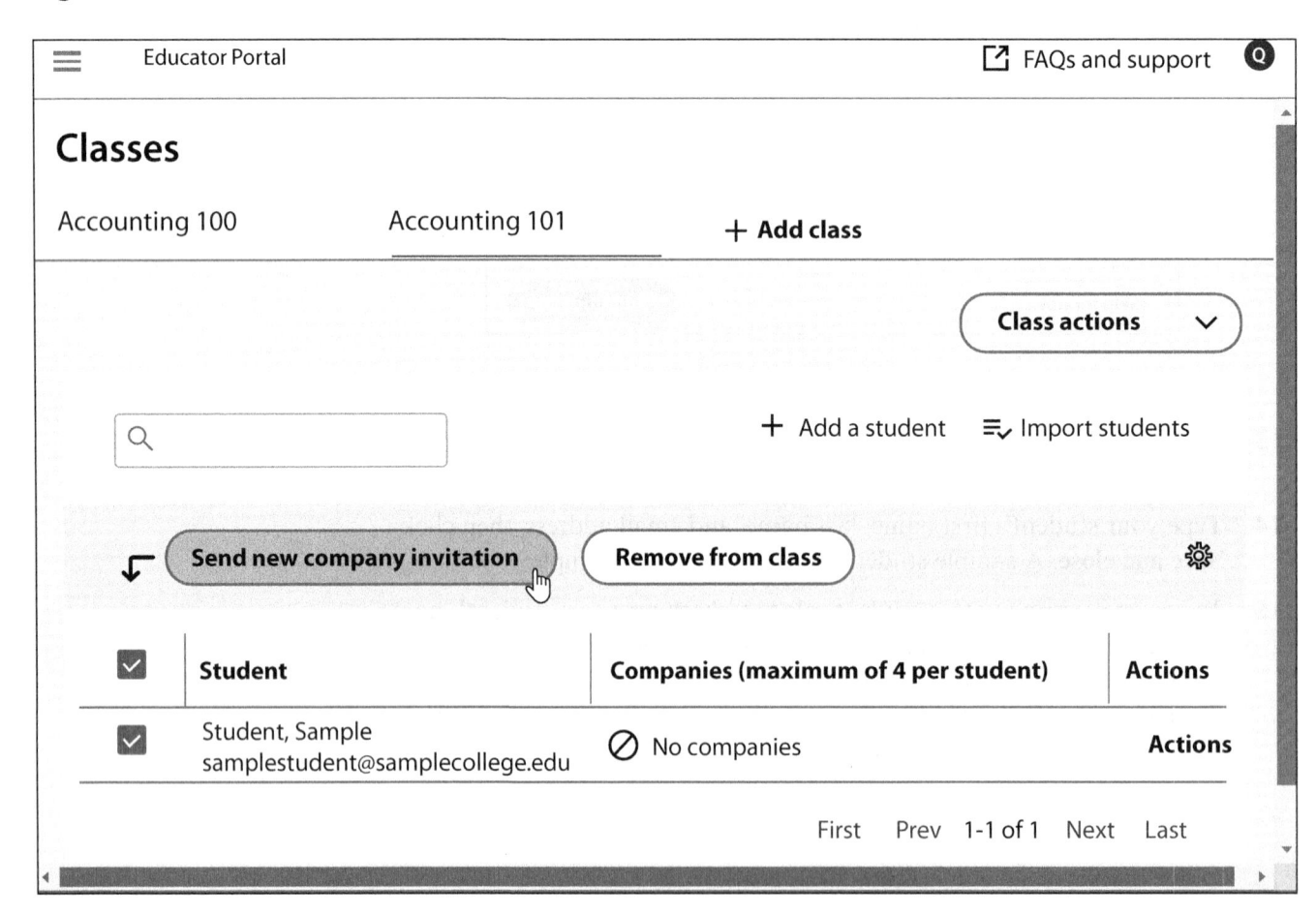

16 Type **Wild Water Sports** in the Choose a name text box as shown in Figure Preface 8. All students should be assigned the Wild Water Sports company so they can complete the chapter instructions provided by the author in Chapters 3 to 10. Later you can assign additional cases (Case 1–6) as desired up to a maximum of 4 remembering that 1 of those 4 is used up by the Wild Water Sports company. As an instructor you get to choose the name, however, it is recommended that you match the name with the case you've chosen to assign from the text (either Case 1, 2, 3, 4, 5, or 6).

Figure Preface 8

Entering a name for the company you're assigning to a student

17 Click **Next: Preview invitation** to view Figure Preface 9.

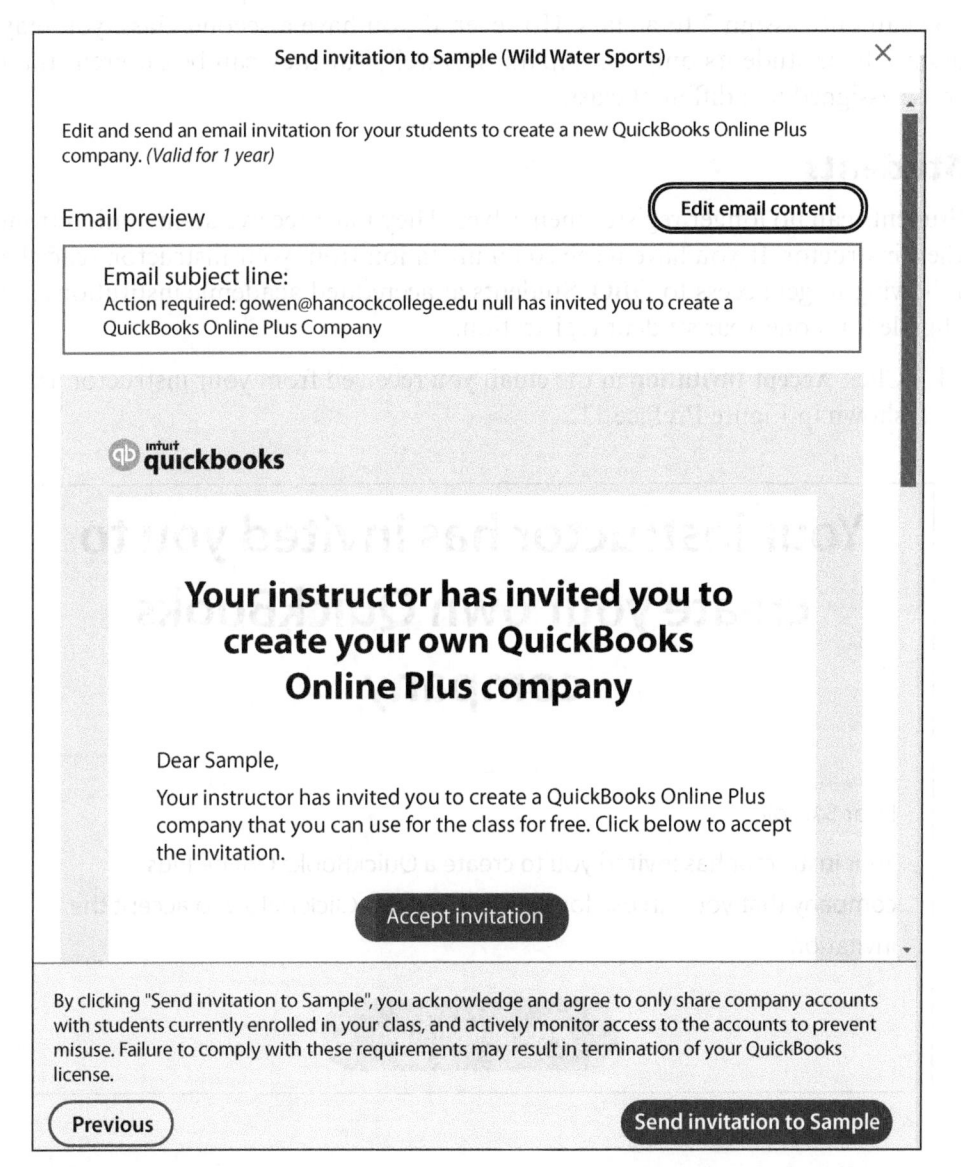

Figure Preface 9

Partial view of invitation preview

18 Click **Send invitation to Sample** (your student's first name will appear in place of Sample).

19 You should receive confirmation that your invitation was sent. Your student listing should then be updated to indicate an invitation was sent and give you the opportunity to resend the invitation if necessary. This update should look like Figure Preface 10.

Figure Preface 10

Updated student information

☐	Student	Companies (maximum of 4 per student)
☐	Student, Sample samplestudent@samplecollege.edu	⊘ Wild Water Sports: Invitation sent <u>Resend invitation</u>

20 Click your account information icon located in the upper right-hand corner of the QBO window, then click **Sign out**.

Keep in mind that you, as an instructor, may assign your class up to 3 additional companies. There are 6 cases found at the end of each chapter of this text, but you can only assign 3 to a class. However, if you have a second class, you may assign those students only 3 companies as well, but they can be different than those assigned in a different class.

Students

Students can no longer register themselves. They must receive an invitation from their instructor. If you have received an invitation from your instructor, read the following to get access to QBO. Students at accredited academic institutions are eligible for a one-year student registration.

1 Click **Accept Invitation** in the email you received from your instructor as shown in Figure Preface 11.

Figure Preface 11

Accepting an instructor's invitation to create a QBO company

> # Your instructor has invited you to create your own QuickBooks company
>
> Dear Sample,
>
> Your instructor has invited you to create a QuickBooks Online Plus company that you can use for the class for free. Click below to accept the invitation.
>
> **Accept invitation**

2. If you have already registered and been validated (see above), click **Sign In** and provide Intuit with your username and password as shown in Figure Preface 12. If you have not registered, provide your information as shown below and click **Create Account**.

Figure Preface 12

Creating a QBO account

3. Type your **email address** twice, **first name**, **last name**, **phone** (if you wish), a **password** twice, and then click **Create Account**. You should now see a QBO window like Figure Preface 13.

Figure Preface 13

QBO Welcome

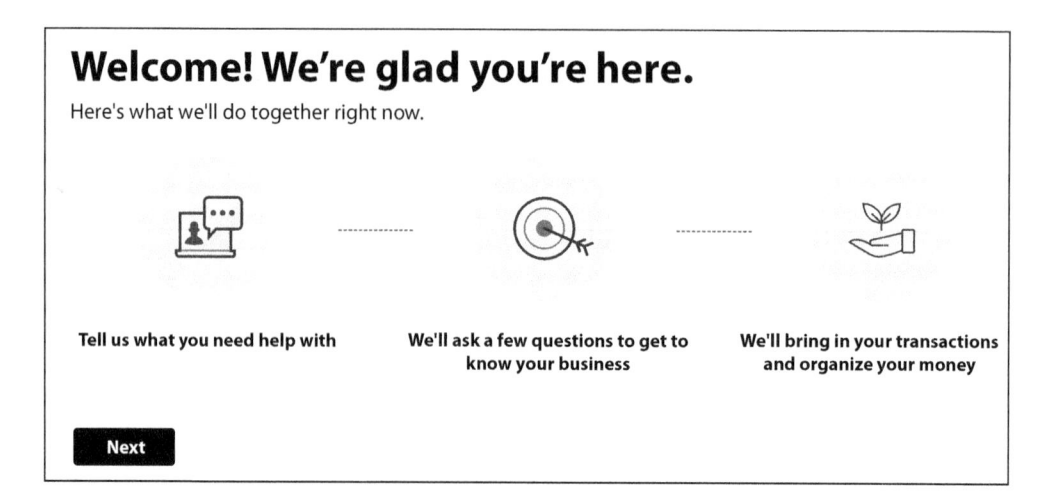

> **Welcome! We're glad you're here.**
> Here's what we'll do together right now.
>
> Tell us what you need help with — We'll ask a few questions to get to know your business — We'll bring in your transactions and organize your money
>
> [Next]

4. For now, do not click Next, instead just close the browser window. You will return to your company in Chapter 2.

Payroll

The text and related data files created for this book were constructed using QBO. In this version of QuickBooks, Intuit continues its use of a basic payroll service but has made it more accessible by having it live on its Cloud-based system. QBO initially comes with the current tax tables; however, these tables soon become outdated, and the payroll feature is disabled unless the user subscribes to the payroll service.

The author decided to use the manual payroll tax feature, which requires that students manually enter the tax deductions. This alleviates the discrepancies between the solutions manual and the students' data entry and removes the burden of having to purchase the tax table service for each copy of QBO used. Instructions on how to set up payroll for manual calculation of payroll taxes are provided in the text. For more information, see your QBO documentation.

All reports have a default feature that identifies the basis in which the report was created (e.g., accrual or cash) and the date and time the report was printed. The date and time shown on your report will, of course, be different from that shown in this text.

Instructional Design

Each chapter of this text begins with a listing of expected student learning outcomes followed by a step-by-step explanation of how to obtain those outcomes. In most chapters, the explanations utilize the Wild Water Sports company created by the student in Chapter 2 in which the author demonstrates how various operating, investing, and financing activities of a business are captured and then reported in QBO.

End-of-chapter questions, matching, and student cases follow these explanations. The questions help you to review the text-explained concepts and processes, whereas the matching section helps with terms and definitions. The student cases provide the information necessary to add data to the student's company file. Each chapter requires the student to add information to the previous chapter's rendition. Thus, for success in learning, each student must complete the previous chapter's student case before attempting the next chapter's student case.

Solutions to each chapter's student cases are provided in the instructor manual. The following is a matrix of all end-of-chapter cases that identifies key differences between cases key processes assessed. For example, Cases 1, 2, 4, and 6 are corporations, whereas Cases 3 and 5 are sole proprietors. Cases 1 and 2 do not require sales tax collections, whereas Cases 3, 4, 5, and 6 do. All cases involve business entities that sell products, provide services, and have checking accounts, customers, vendors, employees, and so on.

	Case 1	Case 2	Case 3	Case 4	Case 5	Case 6
Company Setup:						
Date company started using QBO	1/1/24	1/1/25	1/1/26	1/1/27	1/1/28	1/1/23
Location	La Jolla, CA	La Jolla, CA	La Jolla, CA	Hollywood, CA	Huntsville, AL	Sumner, WA
Company organization	Corporation	Corporation	Sole Proprietor	Corporation	Sole Proprietor	Corporation
Business	Distributor	Distributor	Retail	Sports Gym	Engineering	Automotive Dealer
Inventory products sold	Surf boards	Toys	Cell Phones	T-Shirts	Computers	Recreational Vehicle
Services provided	Consulting	Repairs	Repairs	Monthly Fees	Program Support	Repairs
Track expenses	Yes	Yes	Yes	Yes	Yes	Yes
Bill payment terms (default)	Net 30	Net 30	Net 30	Net 30	Net 30	Net 30
Hourly employees	Yes	Yes	Yes	Yes	Yes	Yes
Salary employees	Yes	Yes	Yes	Yes	Yes	Yes
Sales tax applicable	No	No	Yes	Yes	Yes	Yes
Add customers	Yes	Yes	Yes	Yes	Yes	Yes
Add employees	Yes	Yes	Yes	Yes	Yes	Yes
Add inventory items	Yes	Yes	Yes	Yes	Yes	Yes
Add service items	Yes	Yes	Yes	Yes	Yes	Yes
Add vendors	Yes	Yes	Yes	Yes	Yes	Yes
Add/delete accounts	Yes	Yes	Yes	Yes	Yes	Yes
Enter beginning balances	Yes	Yes	Yes	Yes	Yes	Yes
Accounts Used:						
Checking account	Yes	Yes	Yes	Yes	Yes	Yes
Accounts receivable	Yes	Yes	Yes	Yes	Yes	Yes
Prepaid expenses/supplies	Yes	Yes	Yes	Yes	Yes	Yes
Investments	Yes	Yes	Yes	Yes	Yes	Yes
Fixed assets	Yes	Yes	Yes	Yes	Yes	Yes
Accounts payable	Yes	Yes	Yes	Yes	Yes	Yes
Notes payable	Yes	Yes	Yes	Yes	Yes	Yes
Common stock	Yes	Yes	No	Yes	No	Yes
Owner's equity	No	No	Yes	No	Yes	No

Business Transactions:						
Record additional investment by owners	No	No	Yes	No	Yes	No
Record adjusting (accrual) entries	Yes	Yes	Yes	Yes	Yes	Yes
Record bills	Yes	Yes	Yes	Yes	Yes	Yes
Record bills received with purchase orders	Yes	Yes	Yes	Yes	Yes	Yes
Record bills received without purchase orders	Yes	Yes	Yes	Yes	Yes	Yes
Record checks	Yes	Yes	Yes	Yes	Yes	Yes
Record journal entries	Yes	Yes	Yes	Yes	Yes	Yes
Record payments made on account	Yes	Yes	Yes	Yes	Yes	Yes
Record payments received on accounts	Yes	Yes	Yes	Yes	Yes	Yes
Record payroll	Yes	Yes	Yes	Yes	Yes	Yes
Record purchase orders	Yes	Yes	Yes	Yes	Yes	Yes
Record sales invoices	Yes	Yes	Yes	Yes	Yes	Yes
Record sales receipts	Yes	Yes	Yes	Yes	Yes	Yes
Record the sale of common stock	Yes	Yes	No	Yes	No	Yes
Reports Created:						
Reports—A/P Aging Summary	Yes	Yes	Yes	Yes	Yes	Yes
Reports—A/R Aging Summary	Yes	Yes	Yes	Yes	Yes	Yes
Reports—Balance Sheet	Yes	Yes	Yes	Yes	Yes	Yes
Reports—Export Reports to Excel	Yes	Yes	Yes	No	No	Yes
Reports—Income Statement	Yes	Yes	Yes	Yes	Yes	Yes
Reports—Inventory Valuation Summary	Yes	Yes	Yes	Yes	Yes	Yes
Reports—Statement of Cash Flows	Yes	Yes	Yes	Yes	Yes	Yes
Reports—Transaction Detail by Account	Yes	Yes	Yes	Yes	Yes	Yes
Reports—Trial Balance	Yes	Yes	Yes	Yes	Yes	Yes

Comprehensive Problems

Additional transactions for Cases 1, 2, 3, 4, 5, and 6 can be found in Appendix 2. Students who have successfully completed a case in the text through Chapter 10 can be assigned these comprehensive problems. Each pick up in the month following the chapter work. For example in Case 1, chapter work occurred in January 2024, thus the comprehensive problem will describe transactions occurring in February 2024. The transactions included in February are similar in nature to those described in Chapters 3 to 10. Students assigned Case 1 would be able to complete comprehensive Case 1. Those assigned Case 2 would only be able to complete comprehensive Case 2 and the like. Ultimately your instructor can assign you up to 4 companies. All students will be assigned the Wild Water Sports company. After that your instructor can assign an additional 3 companies from the following list: Case 1, 2, 3, 4, 5, or 6.

Textbook Goals

This textbook takes a user and a preparer perspective by illustrating how accounting information is created and then used for making decisions. QBO is user-friendly and provides point-and-click simplicity and sophisticated accounting reporting and analysis tools. The textbook uses proven and successful instructional design (described earlier) to demonstrate the application's features and elicit student interaction.

The first and foremost goal of this text is to help students review fundamental accounting concepts and principles through the use of the QBO application and the analysis of business events. The content of this text complements the first course in accounting principles or financial accounting. Thus, this text should either be used concurrently with an accounting principles or financial accounting course, or be used subsequent to completion of such a course.

The second goal of this text is to teach students how to set up QBO for a business, use it to record business events, and use it to generate financial statements and reports. Acquiring these skills will help students improve their job prospects, whether the company they work for uses QuickBooks or not.

The third goal of this text is to teach students the value of a computerized accounting information system and how it can be used to communicate important information to business owners, investors, and creditors.

Date Warning

The Sample Company (created and maintained by Intuit) is used in Chapter 1 only and is used to demonstrate many aspects of QBO. The author has no control over the dates used by Intuit and those dates may change depending on when you are accessing the file online. The dates that appear in the figures supplied by the author in this text may not be the dates that appear on your screen. Instructions to generate reports in this text often suggest the user set the report period to the month before or in the month of the current system date. If you are entering data at the beginning of the month (your system date is between the 1st and the 15th of a month), you should set your report period to the month prior to your current system date. If you are entering data at the end of the month (your system date is between the 15th and the 31st of a month), you should set your report period to the current month of your current system date. For example, if you are entering data on 10/09/2024, use 10/01/2024 to 10/31/2024 as your reporting period. For example, if you are entering data on 10/21/2025, use 10/01/2025 to 10/31/2025 as your reporting period.

The student cases (Cases 1–6) are set in 2024, 2025, 2026, 2027, 2028, and 2023, respectively. If transactions are entered into the student case in other than the proper period, answers will be wrong. Be careful about entering dates into

QBO when you are working on this case. The default date when entering new transactions into QBO is the computer's system date that may or may not be in those years.

Update Warning

QBO is frequently upgraded by Intuit to provide new features, correct errors, or improve functionality. This book was written in late 2023 and early 2024, and all figures are based on how QBO looked at that time. If you are using this text in 2024 or later, Intuit may have made modifications in how QBO looks and feels or functions. Differences will occur, which are out of the author's control.

Keep in mind that sales tax rates change year to year, state to state. The solutions provided by the author for each case were based on tax rates in effect for that particular year. If a rate changes your answers for sales tax payable and related accounts may be different.

Instructor as Your Accountant

Your instructor may choose to have you assign them as your accountant so that they can see your work and progress at their convenience without having you to "send" the file. In fact, you cannot "send" your file, since all the files are on the Cloud. Instructions on how to set your instructor as your accountant are provided in Chapter 2.

Video Tutorials Developed by Intuit

Intuit, developer of QBO, and others have made video tutorials to help you get started with QBO. These tutorials can be viewed and/or sent to students from the Welcome to the Intuit Educator Portal described earlier in this text.

Instructors

To access these tutorials:

1 Login to the Educator Portal as shown in Figure Preface 1.

2 Click **Tutorials** shown at the bottom of the window to view Figure Preface 2.

3 View as many tutorials as you like and send them to students if you desire.

Students

To access these tutorials:

1 Navigate your browser to https://quickbooks.intuit.com/global/learn-and-support/video-tutorials/

2 Type a topic for a video into the text box labeled **Search for anything**.

3 View the video.

About the Author

Glenn Owen is a retired member of Allan Hancock College's Accounting and Business faculty, where he lectured on accounting and information systems from 1995 to 2016. In addition, he is a retired lecturer at the University of California at Santa Barbara, where he taught accounting and information systems courses from 1980 to 2011. His professional experience includes five years at Deloitte & Touche as well as vice president of finance positions at Westpac Resources, Inc., and ExperTelligence, Inc. Mr. Owen completed his fourth edition of Using Microsoft Excel and Access in Accounting text in 2016, which gives accounting students specific, self-paced instruction on the use of spreadsheets (Excel 2016) and database applications (Access 2016) in accounting. He has also written the 15th edition of his *Using QuickBooks Accountant for Accounting 2018* text, which is also a self-paced, case-based instruction on the use of a commercial accounting application (QuickBooks 2018). His innovative teaching style emphasizes the decision maker's perspective and encourages students to think creatively. His graduate studies in educational psychology and 41 years of business experience yield a balanced blend of theory and practice. Mr. Owen was presented the Lifetime Achievement Award in August 2016 by the Two-Year Section of the American Accounting Association.

Dedication

I would like to thank my wife Kelly, my boys Michael, Nathan, Kyle, and Casey, my grandchildren Graham, Julia, Beckett, Emelia, Oliver, Anastasia, and Kayden for their support and assistance during the creation of this and previous editions of this text. Though our boys are out of the house and pursuing their own interests, Kelly continues to listen to my often crazy ideas for new cases and experiences with college students, providing an excellent sounding board and reality check. You, the boys, their wives, and our grandchildren continue to define what life is all about.

2023 was a difficult year for the Owen family as I was diagnosed with cancer mid-summer and underwent radiation and chemotherapy treatments which rendered me unable to perform my normal duties of updating this edition. Fortunately, Robin Browning stepped into that role for me as I recovered. I owe her a great deal of appreciation for her taking on this role with little notice. I'm fully recovered now and look forward to continuing my normal role in the future. Thanks, Robin!

An Introduction to QuickBooks Online Using the Sample Company

chapter 1

Student Learning Outcomes

Upon completion of this chapter, the student will be able to do the following:

- Open the Sample Company provided by Intuit to explore QBO
- Access customer, vendor, and employee information
- Explore banking transactions
- Explore sales and expense transactions
- Explore the chart of accounts
- Explore lists
- Access reports
- Use the Gear icon to view company settings

Overview

Intuit has provided a Sample Company online to provide new users a test-drive of its QBO product. You will open this Sample Company and explore various features of QBO. In this chapter, you will be viewing the Sample Company looking at customer, vendor, and employee information. You will also be viewing banking, sales, and expense transactions and will be looking at the chart of accounts, lists, reports, and company settings. You will not be making any changes, such as adding a customer, invoice, check, and so on. That will occur in the next chapter.

The author has no control over the dates used by Intuit, and those dates may change, depending on when you are accessing the file online. The dates in the figures supplied by the author in this text may not be the dates on your screen.

Begin Your Sample Company Walkthrough

You can use this Sample Company to explore QBO as often as you like. No matter what you do to modify this Sample Company, you will be unable to save it. When you leave and later return, it will look the same as it did initially. Each time you open this Sample Company, it will retrieve your current system date (the actual date you are working on your computer) and place that date under the company name on the home page.

2   **Chapter 1**   *An Introduction to QuickBooks Online Using the Sample Company*

To open the Sample Company, do the following:

1. Open your Internet browser.

2. Type **https://qbo.intuit.com/redir/testdrive** into your browser's address text box, press **[Enter]** to view the Sample Company Dashboard shown in Figure 1.1. Transaction dates may differ on your screen from the figures shown throughout this text.

3. Click the ⬛ + New icon to view the Create menu shown in Figure 1.2.

Figure 1.1 Sample Company Dashboard

Sample Company

Craig's Design and Landscaping Services

Home   Planner

Tasks

OVERDUE
Remind your customers about 10 unpaid invoices
You're waiting for $1,525.50.   [Go]

Categorize 33 transactions
Unlock $6,951.83 in potential deductions when it comes to tax time.*   [Go]

OVERDUE
Pay 4 overdue bills
They amount to $847.67.   [Go]

Pay 1 bill due in the next week
It amounts to $755.00.   [Go]

BANK ACCOUNTS

Checking   25 to review
Bank balance   −$3,621.93
In QuickBooks $1,201.00
Updated moments ago

Savings   1 to review
Bank balance $200.00
In QuickBooks $800.00
Updated moments ago

Mastercard   7 to review
Bank balance $304.96
In QuickBooks $157.72
Updated moments ago

Visa
In QuickBooks $0

Connect accounts   Go to registers ⌄

FOR YOU   Hide
Accept online payments
Pay   VISA   MC   DISCOVER   AMEX   BANK

You're waiting for $1,525.50 in overdue invoices. Let's speed that up.
Set up auto reminders on invoices
Auto-send reminders to your customers

Quick actions

Customer   Expense   Vendor   Bank deposit   Invoice

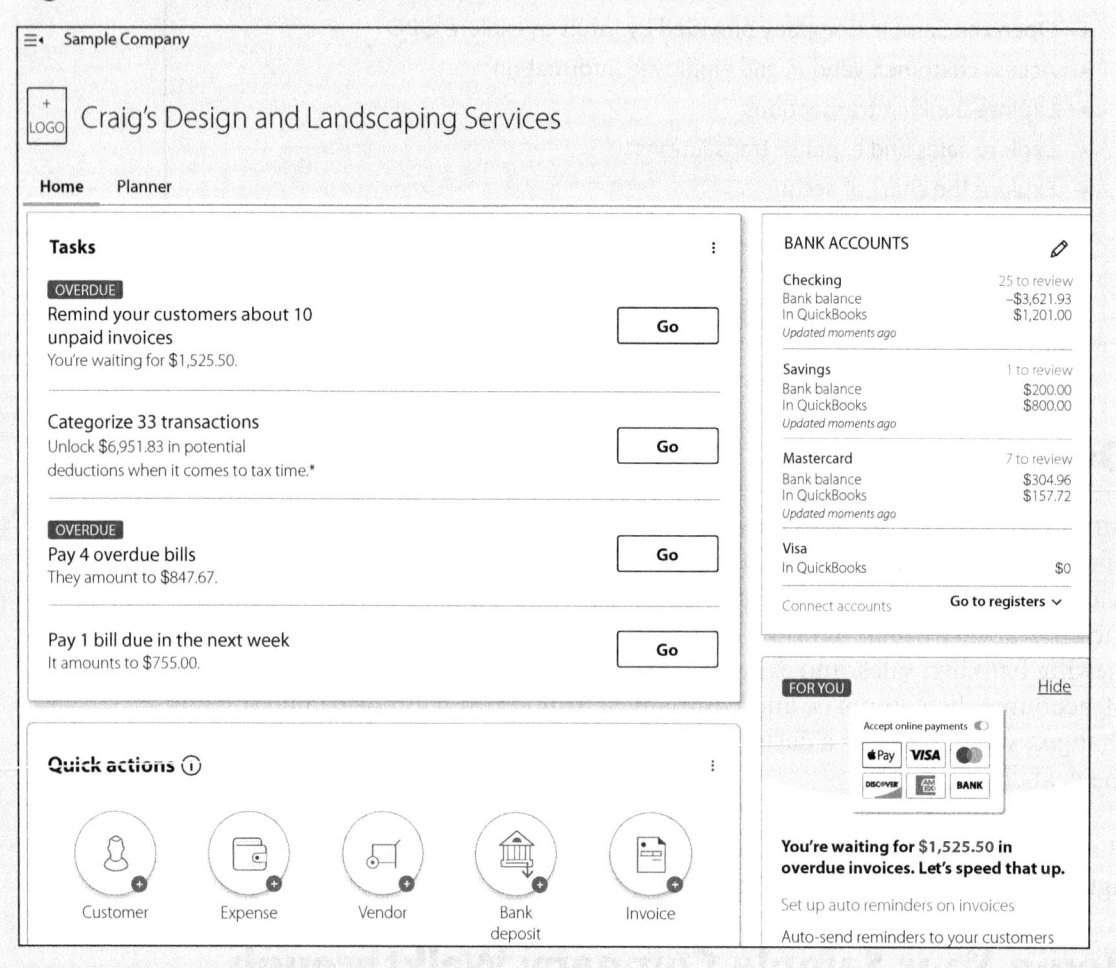

Figure 1.2 Create menu

CUSTOMERS	VENDORS	EMPLOYEES	OTHER
Invoice	Expense	Payroll ↑	Bank deposit
Receive payment	Check	Single time activity	Transfer
Estimate	Bill	Weekly timesheet	Journal entry
Credit memo	Pay bills	Add employee ↑	Statement
Sales receipt	Purchase order	Add contractor	Inventory qty adjustment
Refund receipt	Vendor credit		Pay down credit card
Delayed credit	Credit card credit		Add product/service
Delayed charge	Print checks		
Add customer	Add vendor		

Customers, Vendors, and Employees

QBO provides easy access to customer information using the navigation bar. In this section, you will open the Customers section in a new tab and drill down to a specific customer and specific transactions related to that customer.

To access customer information, do the following:

1 Click **Sales** and then click **Customers** as shown in Figure 1.3.

Trouble? If the navigation menu does not appear, click the **Show Navigation** icon located next to the words Sample Company. Clicking this icon should reveal and hide the navigation menu each time it's clicked.

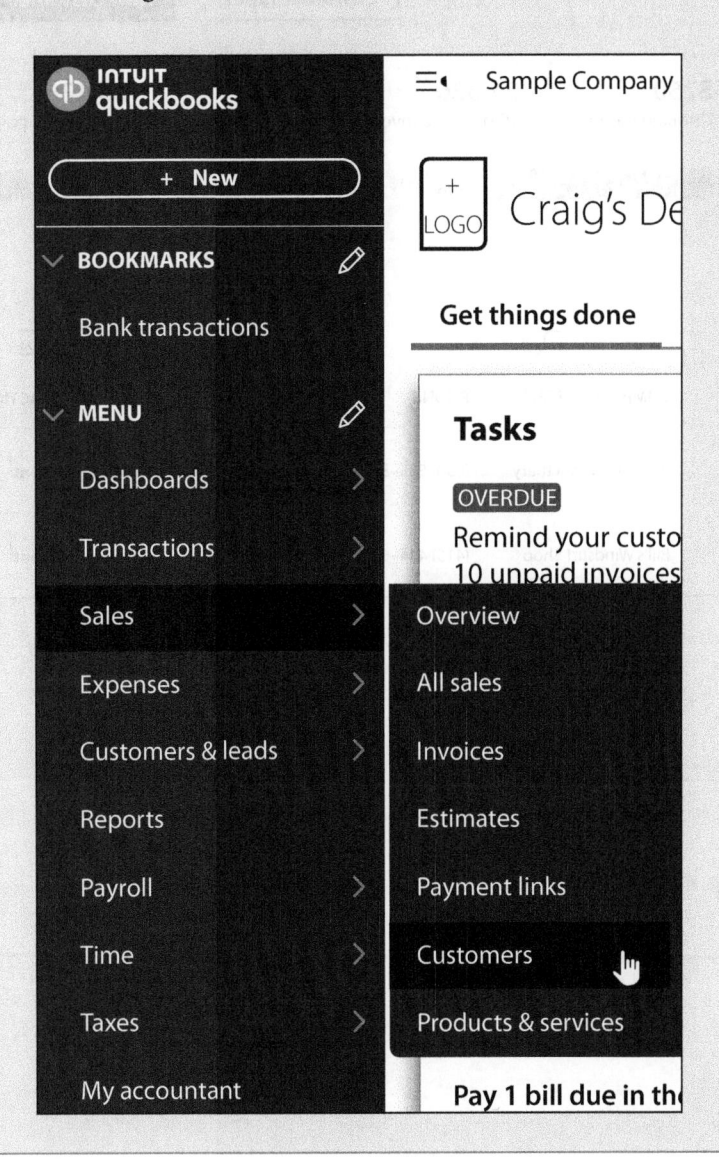

Figure 1.3 Accessing the Customers window

2 The resulting Customers window is then revealed as shown in Figure 1.4.

Figure 1.4 Customers window

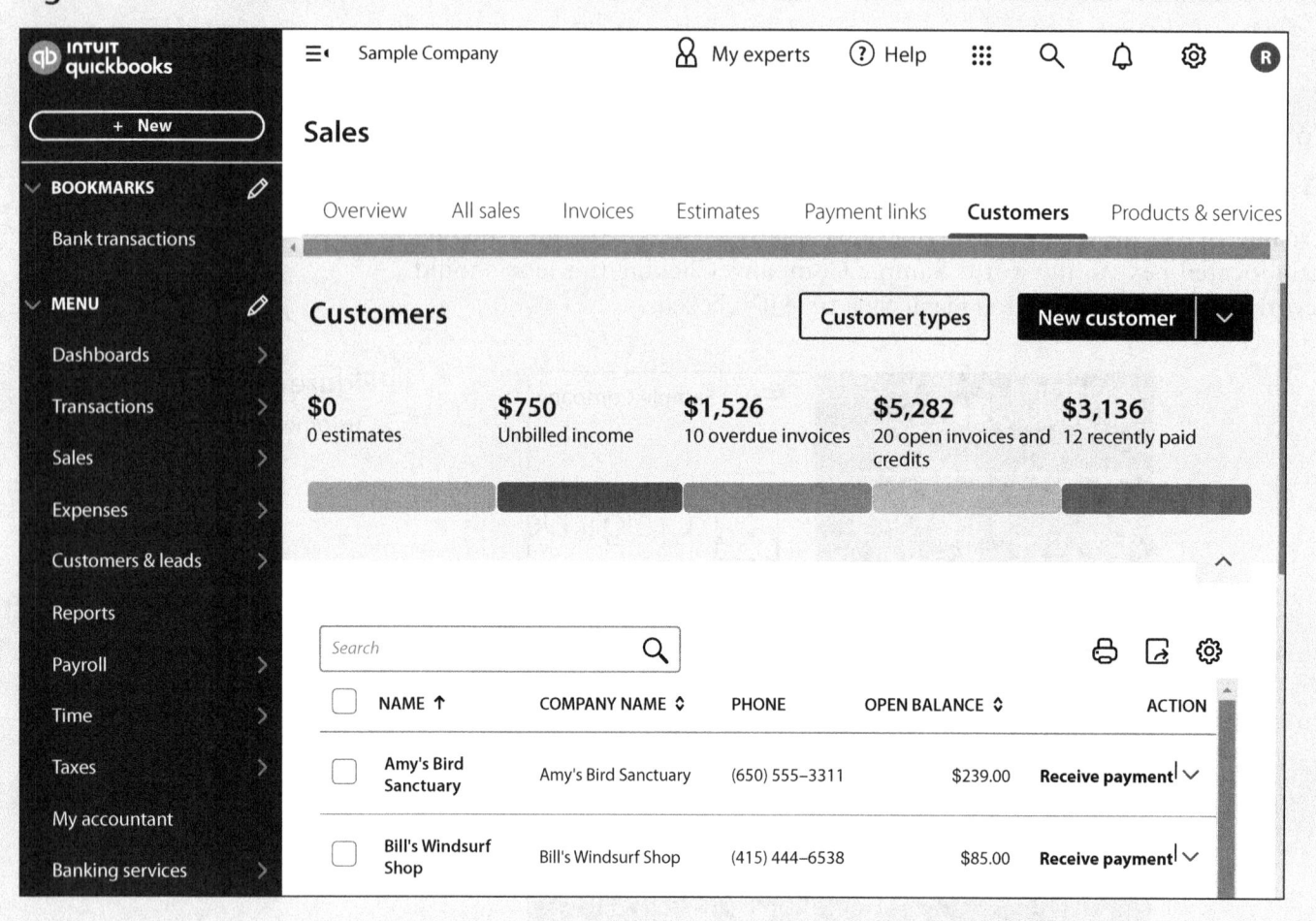

3 Click on the **Amy's Bird Sanctuary** text to view detailed transactions related to that particular customer shown in Figure 1.5.

Figure 1.5 Amy's Bird Sanctuary

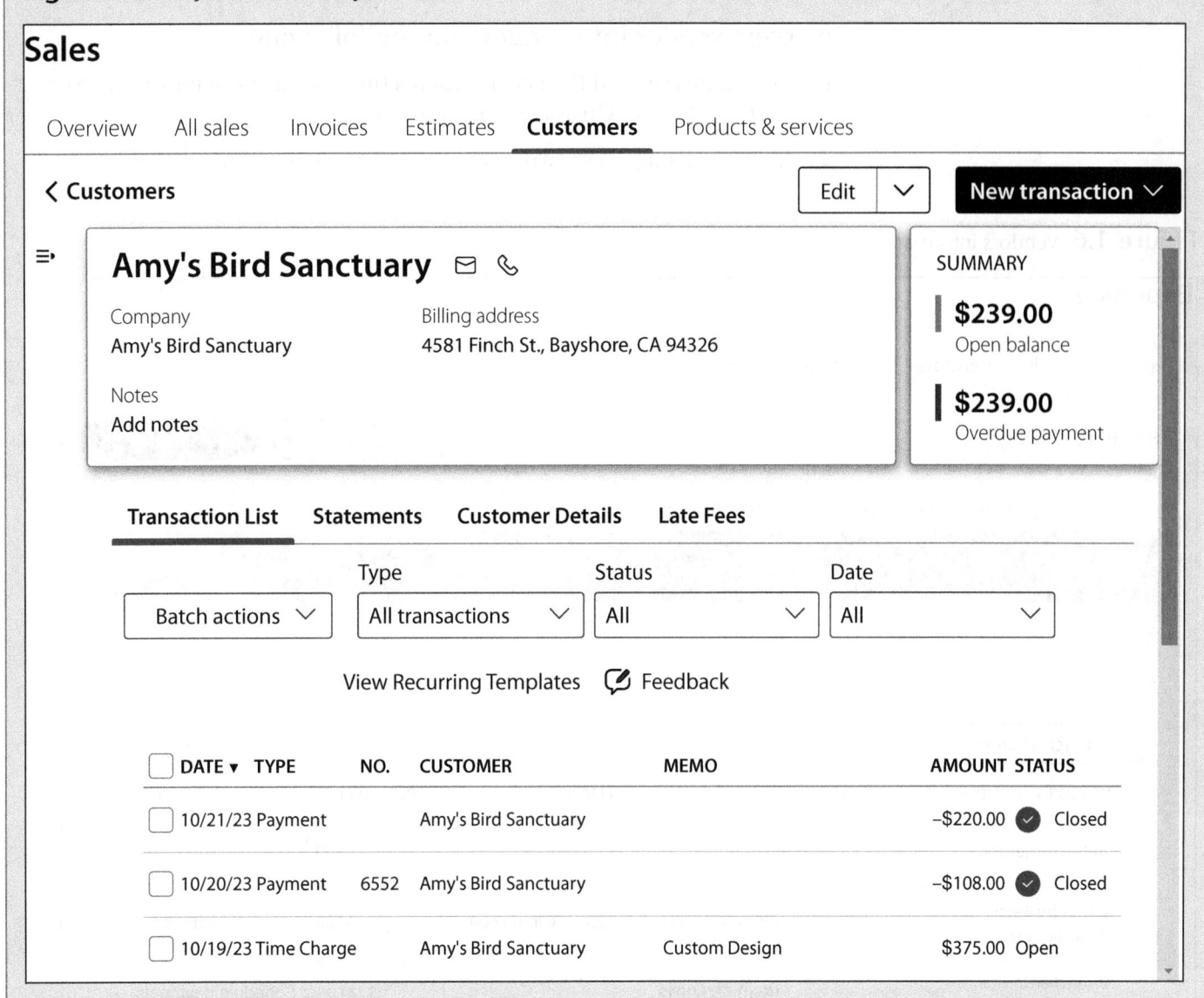

Sales

Overview   All sales   Invoices   Estimates   **Customers**   Products & services

‹ Customers   Edit ⌄   New transaction ⌄

Amy's Bird Sanctuary

Company	Billing address
Amy's Bird Sanctuary	4581 Finch St., Bayshore, CA 94326

Notes
Add notes

SUMMARY

$239.00
Open balance

$239.00
Overdue payment

Transaction List   Statements   Customer Details   Late Fees

| Batch actions ⌄ | Type: All transactions ⌄ | Status: All ⌄ | Date: All ⌄ |

View Recurring Templates   Feedback

DATE ▼	TYPE	NO.	CUSTOMER	MEMO	AMOUNT	STATUS
10/21/23	Payment		Amy's Bird Sanctuary		−$220.00	Closed
10/20/23	Payment	6552	Amy's Bird Sanctuary		−$108.00	Closed
10/19/23	Time Charge		Amy's Bird Sanctuary	Custom Design	$375.00	Open

The $239 overdue balance noted at the top of the window correlates to invoice 1021 shown near the bottom of the list. To view it, scroll down the transactions list for Amy's Bird Sanctuary. (The author has no control over the dates used by Intuit, and those dates may change depending on when you are accessing the file online. The dates, which appear in the figures supplied by the author in this text, may not match the dates that appear on your screen.)

6   **Chapter 1**   *An Introduction to QuickBooks Online Using the Sample Company*

QBO provides easy access to vendor information using the navigation bar. In this section, you will open the Vendors section in a new tab and drill down to a specific vendor and specific transactions related to that vendor.

To access vendor information, do the following:

1. Click **Expenses** and then click **Vendors** (in a manner similar to what you did for Sales and Customers previously).
2. A vendor listing as shown in Figure 1.6 should appear.

Figure 1.6 Vendors information

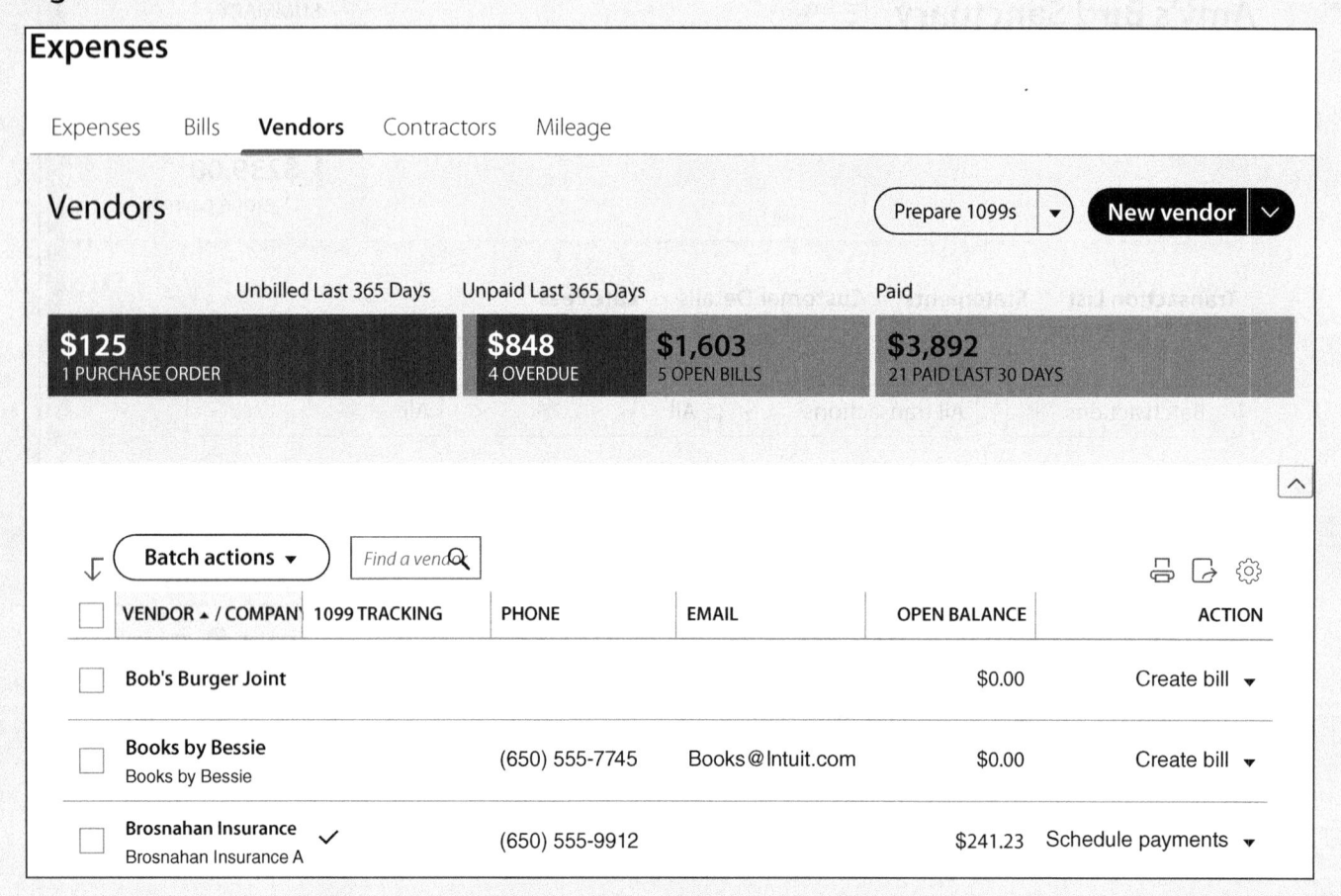

	VENDOR ▲ / COMPANY	1099 TRACKING	PHONE	EMAIL	OPEN BALANCE	ACTION
☐	Bob's Burger Joint				$0.00	Create bill ▼
☐	Books by Bessie Books by Bessie		(650) 555-7745	Books@Intuit.com	$0.00	Create bill ▼
☐	Brosnahan Insurance Brosnahan Insurance A	✓	(650) 555-9912		$241.23	Schedule payments ▼

Expenses tabs: Expenses | Bills | **Vendors** | Contractors | Mileage

- Unbilled Last 365 Days: **$125** — 1 PURCHASE ORDER
- Unpaid Last 365 Days: **$848** 4 OVERDUE / **$1,603** 5 OPEN BILLS
- Paid: **$3,892** 21 PAID LAST 30 DAYS

3. Click on the **Brosnahan Insurance Agency** text to view detailed transactions related to that particular vendor shown in Figure 1.7.
4. Click on the **$241.23** balance to view the bill received as shown in Figure 1.8.

Figure 1.7 Brosnahan Insurance Agency

| Expenses | Bills | **Vendors** | Contractors | Mileage |

Brosnahan Insurance Agency
Brosnahan Insurance Agency | P.O. Box 5, Middlefield, CA 94482
No notes available. Please click to add notes.

Edit ▾ | New transaction ▾

$241.23 OPEN
$241.23 OVERDUE

Transaction List | Vendor Details

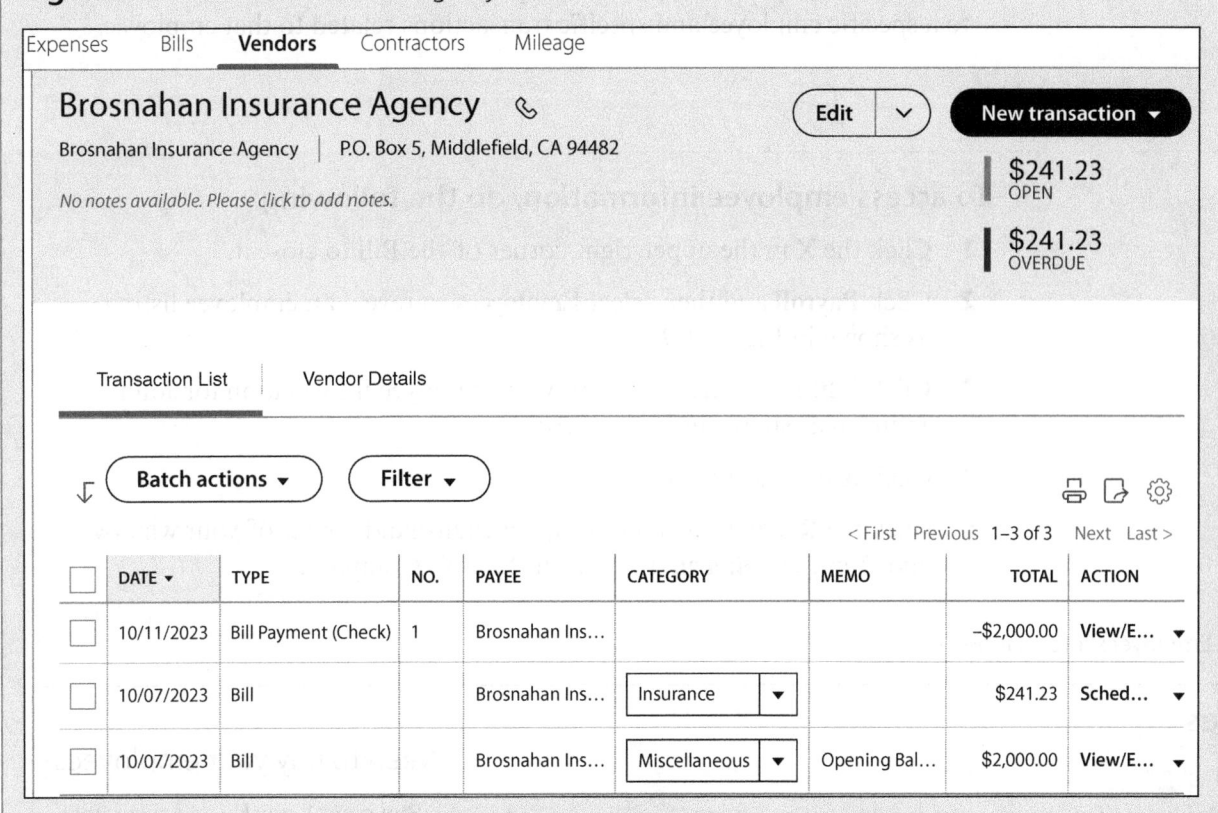

Batch actions ▾ | Filter ▾

< First   Previous   1–3 of 3   Next   Last >

	DATE ▾	TYPE	NO.	PAYEE	CATEGORY	MEMO	TOTAL	ACTION
☐	10/11/2023	Bill Payment (Check)	1	Brosnahan Ins…			−$2,000.00	View/E… ▾
☐	10/07/2023	Bill		Brosnahan Ins…	Insurance ▾		$241.23	Sched… ▾
☐	10/07/2023	Bill		Brosnahan Ins…	Miscellaneous ▾	Opening Bal…	$2,000.00	View/E… ▾

Figure 1.8 Bill from Brosnahan Insurance Agency

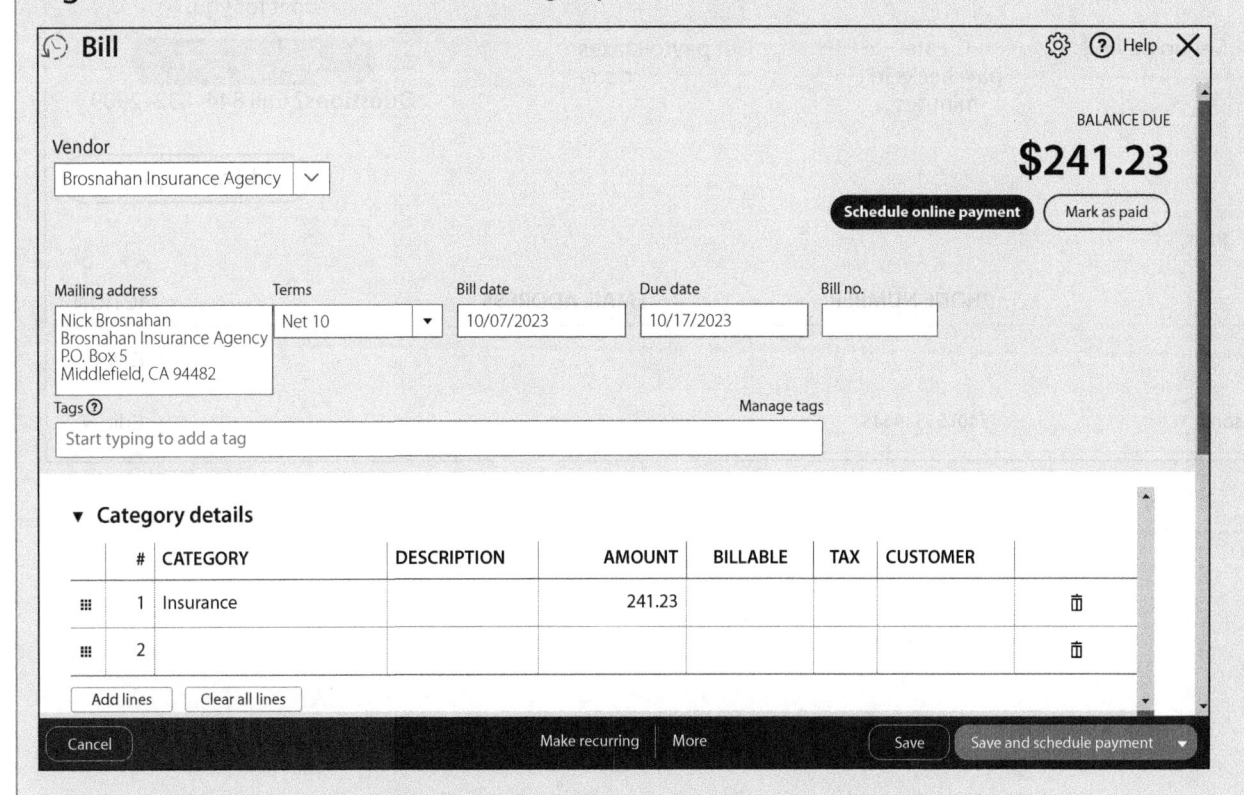

Bill   ⚙ ⓘ Help ✕

BALANCE DUE
$241.23

Schedule online payment | Mark as paid

Vendor
Brosnahan Insurance Agency ▾

Mailing address	Terms	Bill date	Due date	Bill no.
Nick Brosnahan Brosnahan Insurance Agency P.O. Box 5 Middlefield, CA 94482	Net 10 ▾	10/07/2023	10/17/2023	

Tags ⓘ   Manage tags
Start typing to add a tag

▾ **Category details**

	#	CATEGORY	DESCRIPTION	AMOUNT	BILLABLE	TAX	CUSTOMER	
⋮⋮	1	Insurance		241.23				🗑
⋮⋮	2							🗑

Add lines | Clear all lines

Cancel | Make recurring | More | Save | Save and schedule payment

The $241.23 overdue balance noted at the top of the window correlates to a bill received from an earlier month.

QBO provides easy access to employee information using the navigation bar. In this section, you will open the Employees section in a new tab and drill down to a specific employee and specific transactions related to that employee.

To access employee information, do the following:

1 Click the **X** in the upper-right corner of the Bill to close it.
2 Click **Payroll** and then select **Employees** to reveal an employee listing as shown in Figure 1.9.
3 Click **Edit** for John Johnson to view employee information for John Johnson as shown in Figure 1.10.
4 Click **X** to close this window.
5 Click the **R** icon located in the upper right-hand corner of your window, and then click **Sign out** to close the Sample Company.

Figure 1.9 Employees information

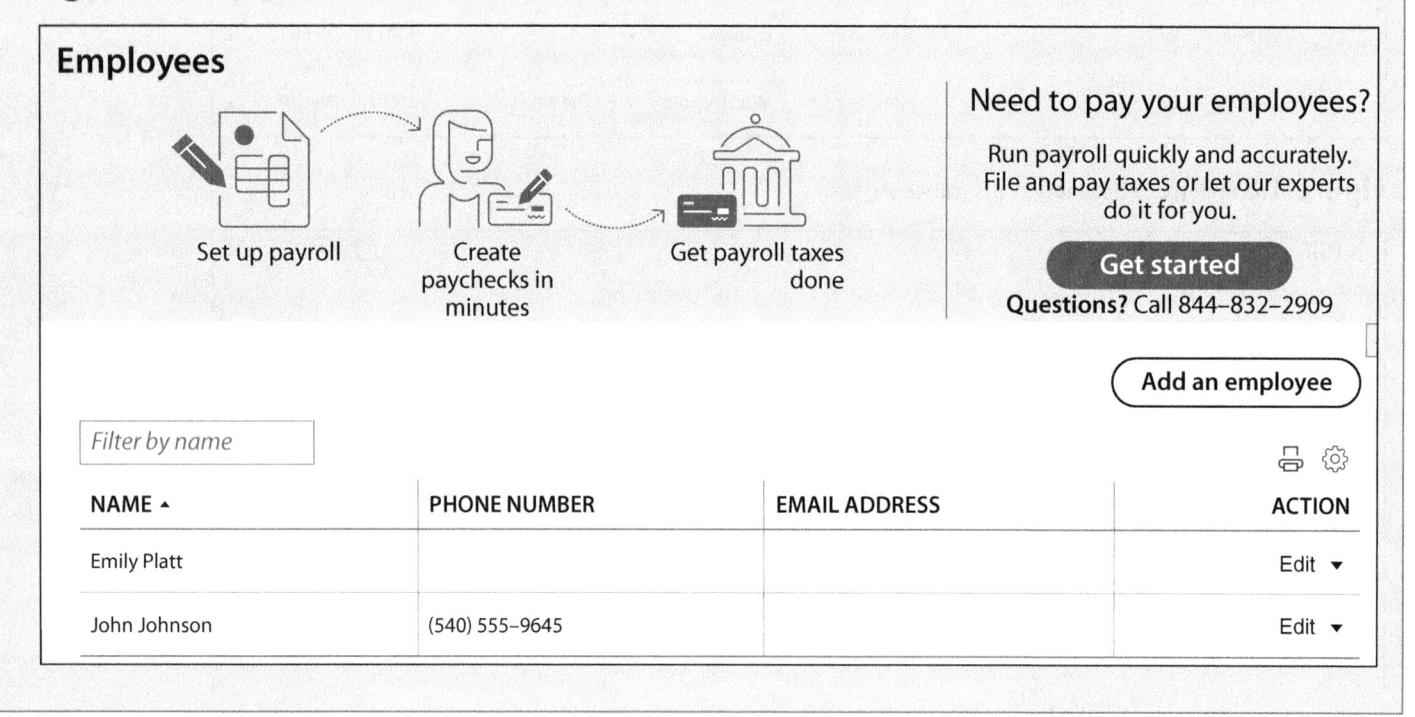

NAME ▲	PHONE NUMBER	EMAIL ADDRESS	ACTION
Emily Platt			Edit ▼
John Johnson	(540) 555-9645		Edit ▼

An Introduction to QuickBooks Online Using the Sample Company   **Chapter 1**   9

Figure 1.10 Employee Information for John Johnson

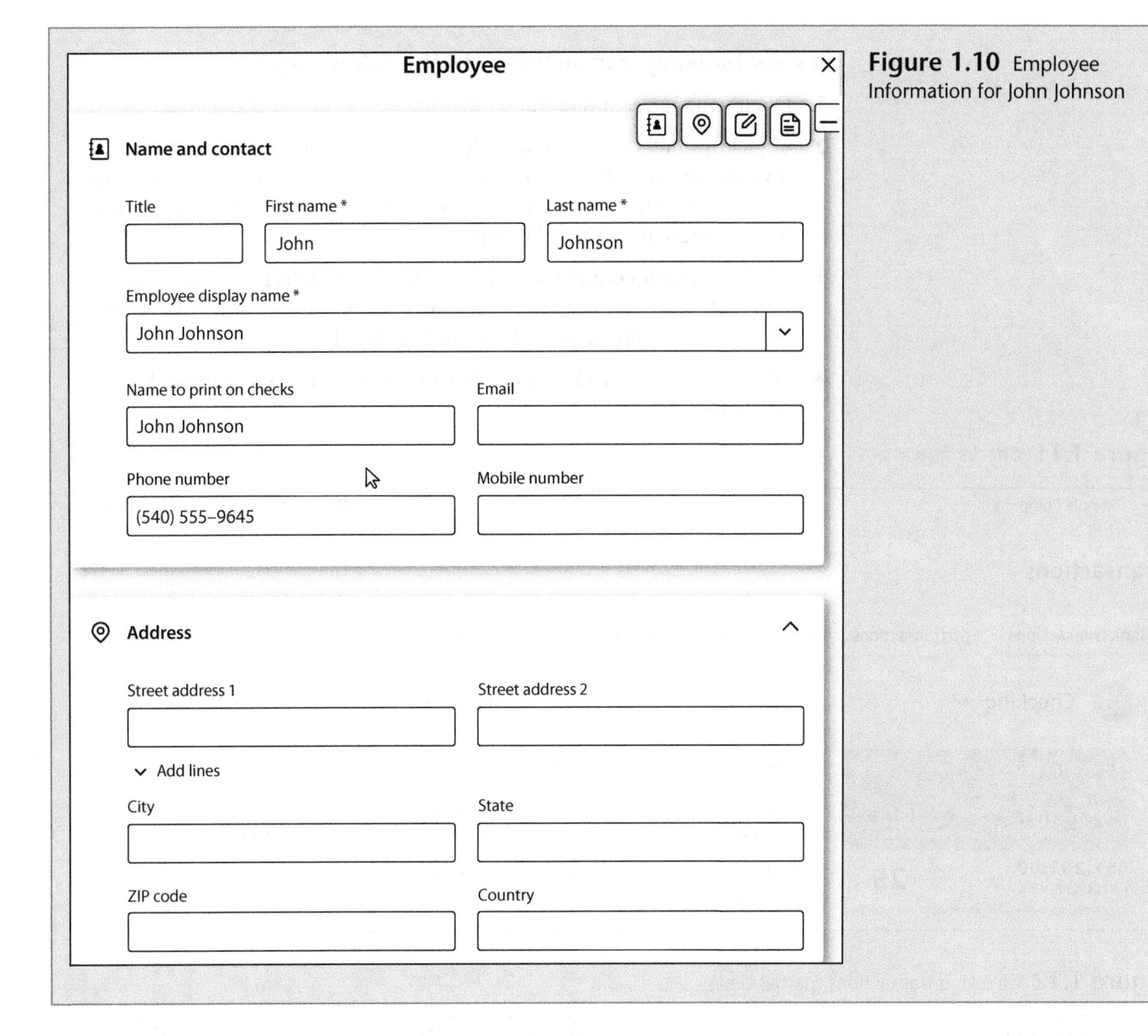

Banking Transactions

QBO has an online banking feature that lets you automatically connect to your bank and download banking-related transactions. The application automatically matches the banking transaction with a previously recorded **QBO** transaction. QBO calls this "Recognizing." This feature is briefly reviewed as this text is academically based and no "real" bank account is linked to this sample, and no "real" bank account will be linked to your student company.

To view banking transactions, do the following:

1. Open your Internet browser.
2. Type **https://qbo.intuit.com/redir/testdrive** into your browser's address text box and then press [**Enter**] to view the Sample Company home page shown in Figure 1.1. You may be asked to provide security information before proceeding. Click **Continue**.
3. Click **Transactions** and then click **Bank Transactions** from the navigation bar. Click the **X** in the Your bank connection is all set window to view the Checking page as shown in Figure 1.11.
4. Scroll down the Checking page to view banking transactions as shown in Figure 1.12.

Figure 1.11 Checking (partial view)

Sample Company			My experts	Help					

Transactions

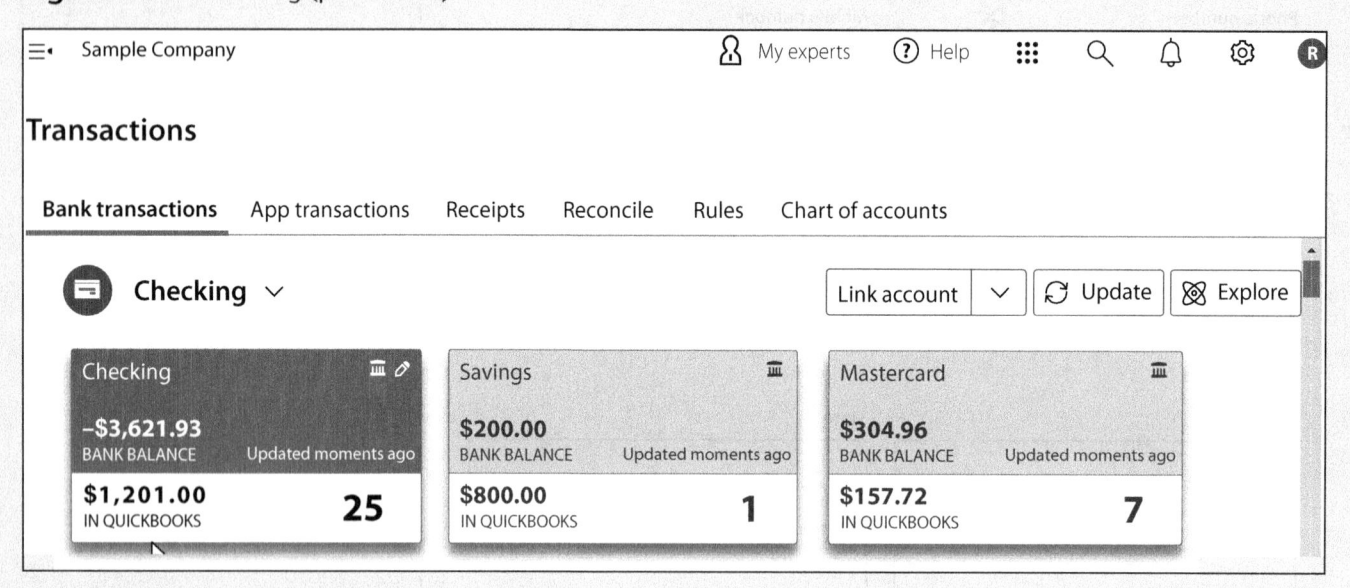

Bank transactions	App transactions	Receipts	Reconcile	Rules	Chart of accounts

Checking ⌄   Link account ⌄   Update   Explore

Checking	Savings	Mastercard
−$3,621.93	**$200.00**	**$304.96**
BANK BALANCE Updated moments ago	BANK BALANCE Updated moments ago	BANK BALANCE Updated moments ago
$1,201.00 **25**	**$800.00** **1**	**$157.72** **7**
IN QUICKBOOKS	IN QUICKBOOKS	IN QUICKBOOKS

Figure 1.12 Checking transactions (partial view)

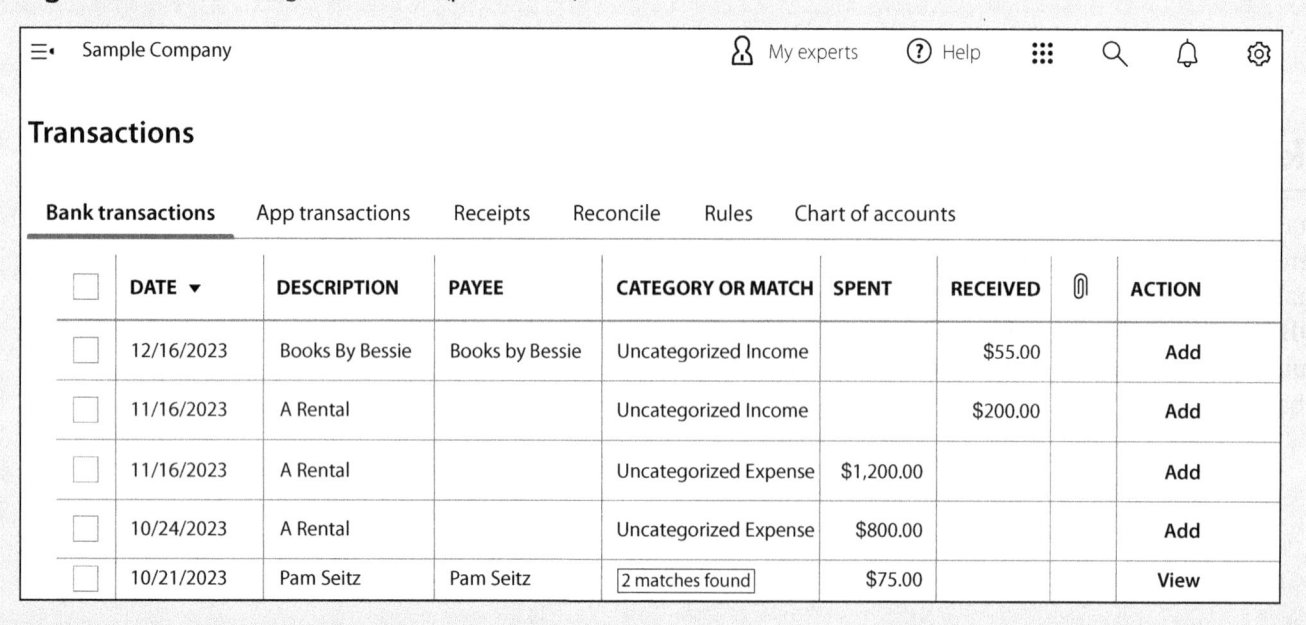

Sample Company			My experts	Help					

Transactions

Bank transactions	App transactions	Receipts	Reconcile	Rules	Chart of accounts

	DATE ▼	DESCRIPTION	PAYEE	CATEGORY OR MATCH	SPENT	RECEIVED	📎	ACTION
☐	12/16/2023	Books By Bessie	Books by Bessie	Uncategorized Income		$55.00		Add
☐	11/16/2023	A Rental		Uncategorized Income		$200.00		Add
☐	11/16/2023	A Rental		Uncategorized Expense	$1,200.00			Add
☐	10/24/2023	A Rental		Uncategorized Expense	$800.00			Add
☐	10/21/2023	Pam Seitz	Pam Seitz	2 matches found	$75.00			View

5. Scroll back up the Checking page and then click **Go to bank register** on the right to view the traditional checking account register listing each QBO-recorded check, deposit, or cash transaction affecting the checking account shown in Figure 1.13. Close any messages that may appear. You may have to enlarge your window to view the Deposit and Balance columns.

Figure 1.13 Bank Register (partial view)

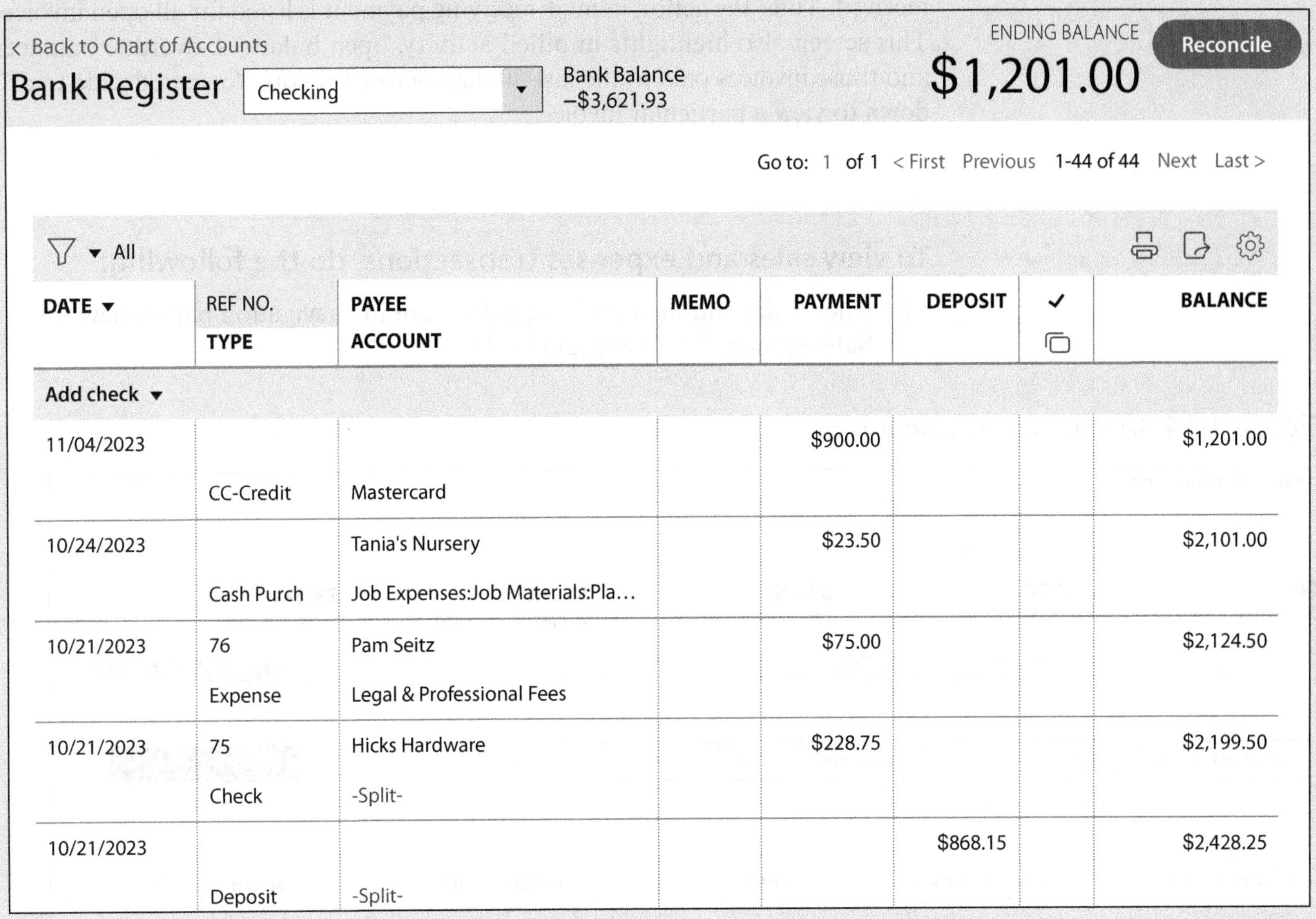

DATE	REF NO. / TYPE	PAYEE / ACCOUNT	MEMO	PAYMENT	DEPOSIT	✓	BALANCE
11/04/2023	CC-Credit	Mastercard		$900.00			$1,201.00
10/24/2023	Cash Purch	Tania's Nursery / Job Expenses:Job Materials:Pla…		$23.50			$2,101.00
10/21/2023	76 / Expense	Pam Seitz / Legal & Professional Fees		$75.00			$2,124.50
10/21/2023	75 / Check	Hicks Hardware / -Split-		$228.75			$2,199.50
10/21/2023	Deposit	-Split-			$868.15		$2,428.25

Bank Balance −$3,621.93
ENDING BALANCE $1,201.00

Bank deposits, which have not been recorded in QBO, are not recognized and are temporarily classified as Uncategorized Income. Bank charges that have not been recorded in QBO are not recognized and are temporarily classified as Uncategorized Expense.

The Bank Register seen in Figure 1.13 is similar to the general ledger account concept seen in traditional accounting without the debits and credits. The balance is shown after every increase or decrease in the account. In a bank

12 Chapter 1 *An Introduction to QuickBooks Online Using the Sample Company*

account, increases are deposits and decreases are payments. Registers exist for all assets, liabilities, and equity accounts, and they are a great way to identify and/or correct errors if they occur.

Sales and Expense Transactions

The next two choices in the navigation bar are sales and expense transactions. The Sales Transactions section provides a listing of recent sales invoices and payments: Some are closed and others are open, meaning payment has not been received. Thus, the action item of receiving payment is listed for all open invoices. This screen also highlights unbilled activity, open balances, overdue balances, and those invoices paid in the last 30 days across the top. You can decide to drill down to view a particular invoice.

To view sales and expenses transactions, do the following:

1 Click **Sales** and then click **All Sales** from the navigation bar to view the Sales section shown in Figure 1.14.

Figure 1.14 Sales Transactions (partial view)

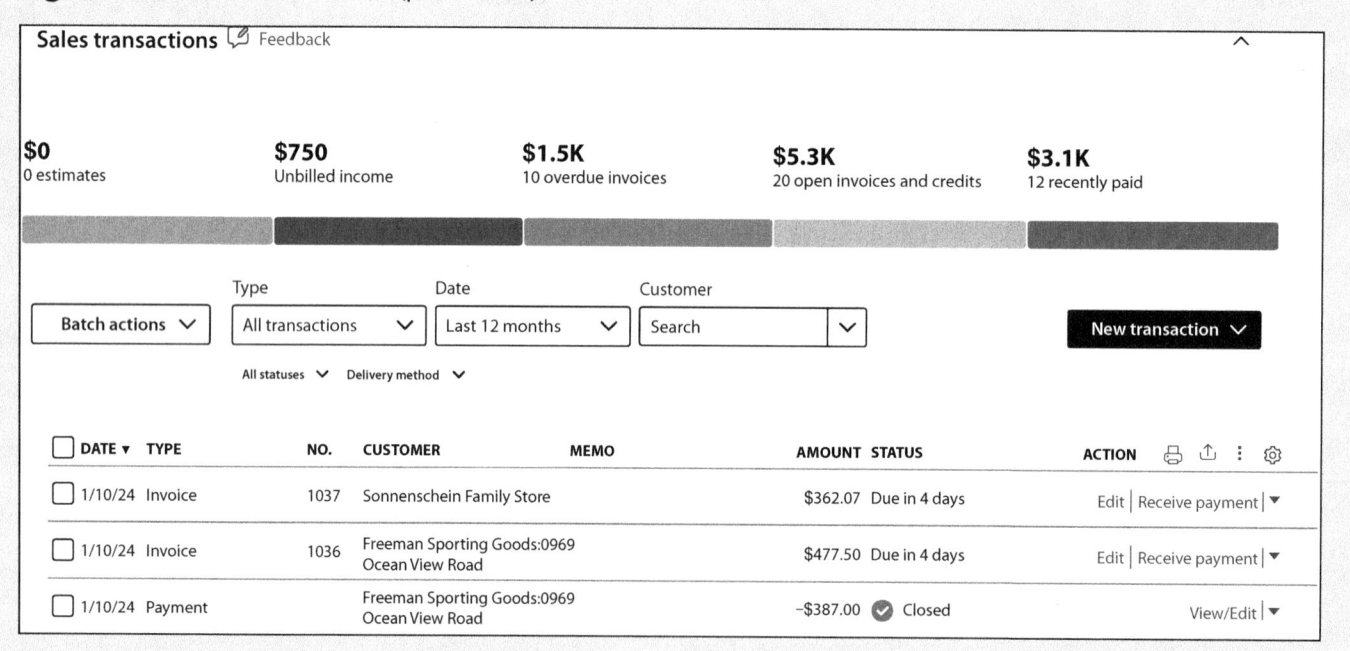

$0	**$750**	**$1.5K**	**$5.3K**	**$3.1K**
0 estimates	Unbilled income	10 overdue invoices	20 open invoices and credits	12 recently paid

DATE ▼	TYPE	NO.	CUSTOMER	MEMO	AMOUNT	STATUS	ACTION
1/10/24	Invoice	1037	Sonnenschein Family Store		$362.07	Due in 4 days	Edit | Receive payment | ▼
1/10/24	Invoice	1036	Freeman Sporting Goods:0969 Ocean View Road		$477.50	Due in 4 days	Edit | Receive payment | ▼
1/10/24	Payment		Freeman Sporting Goods:0969 Ocean View Road		-$387.00	Closed	View/Edit | ▼

2 Click on Invoice No. **1036** to reveal the activity of the invoice in a window on the right, and then click **Edit invoice** to reveal the invoice shown in Figure 1.15.

Figure 1.15 Invoice #1036

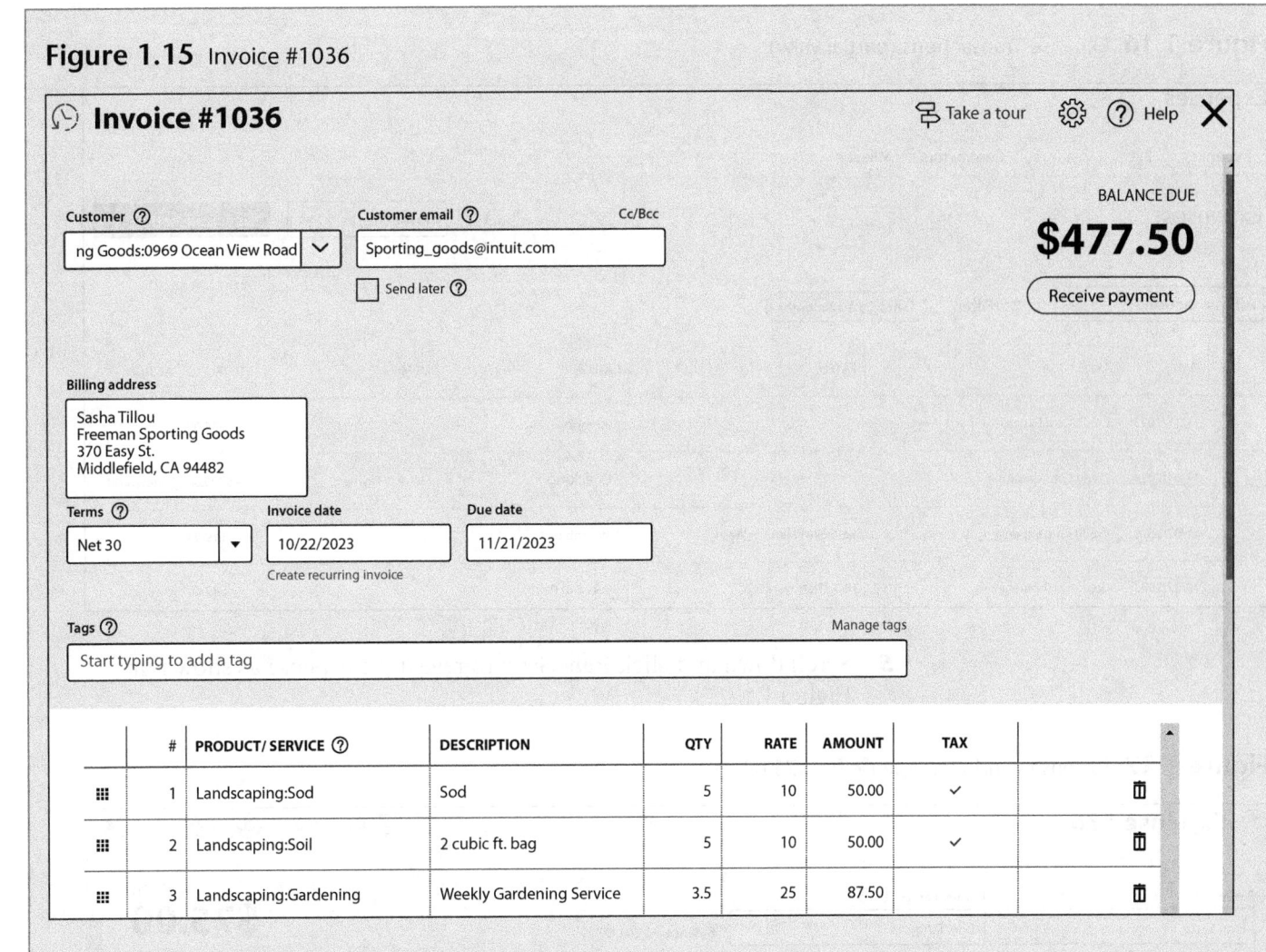

#	PRODUCT/SERVICE	DESCRIPTION	QTY	RATE	AMOUNT	TAX
1	Landscaping:Sod	Sod	5	10	50.00	✓
2	Landscaping:Soil	2 cubic ft. bag	5	10	50.00	✓
3	Landscaping:Gardening	Weekly Gardening Service	3.5	25	87.50	

3 Click **Cancel** to close Invoice No. 1036.

The Expense Transactions section will provide a listing of recent credit card charges, bills, expenses, purchase orders, checks, bill payments, and cash payments. You can decide to drill down to view a particular credit card transaction.

4 Click **Expenses** and then click **Expenses** again from the navigation bar to view the Expense Transactions section shown in Figure 1.16.

14   **Chapter 1**   *An Introduction to QuickBooks Online Using the Sample Company*

Figure 1.16 Expense Transactions (partial view)

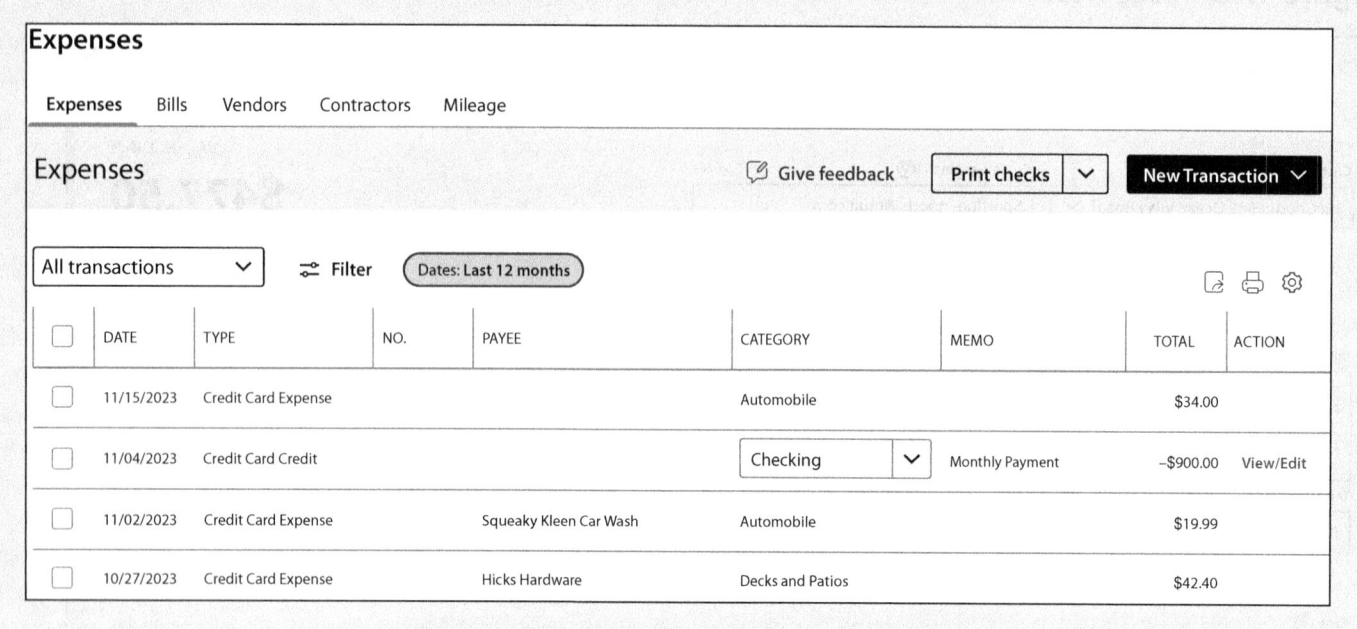

Expenses

Expenses | Bills | Vendors | Contractors | Mileage

Expenses   Give feedback   Print checks ▾   New Transaction ▾

All transactions ▾   Filter   Dates: Last 12 months

	DATE	TYPE	NO.	PAYEE	CATEGORY	MEMO	TOTAL	ACTION
☐	11/15/2023	Credit Card Expense			Automobile		$34.00	
☐	11/04/2023	Credit Card Credit			Checking ▾	Monthly Payment	–$900.00	View/Edit
☐	11/02/2023	Credit Card Expense		Squeaky Kleen Car Wash	Automobile		$19.99	
☐	10/27/2023	Credit Card Expense		Hicks Hardware	Decks and Patios		$42.40	

    5   Scroll down and click **Pam Seitz** to reveal the expense as shown in Figure 1.17.

Figure 1.17 Expense window (expense for $75.00)

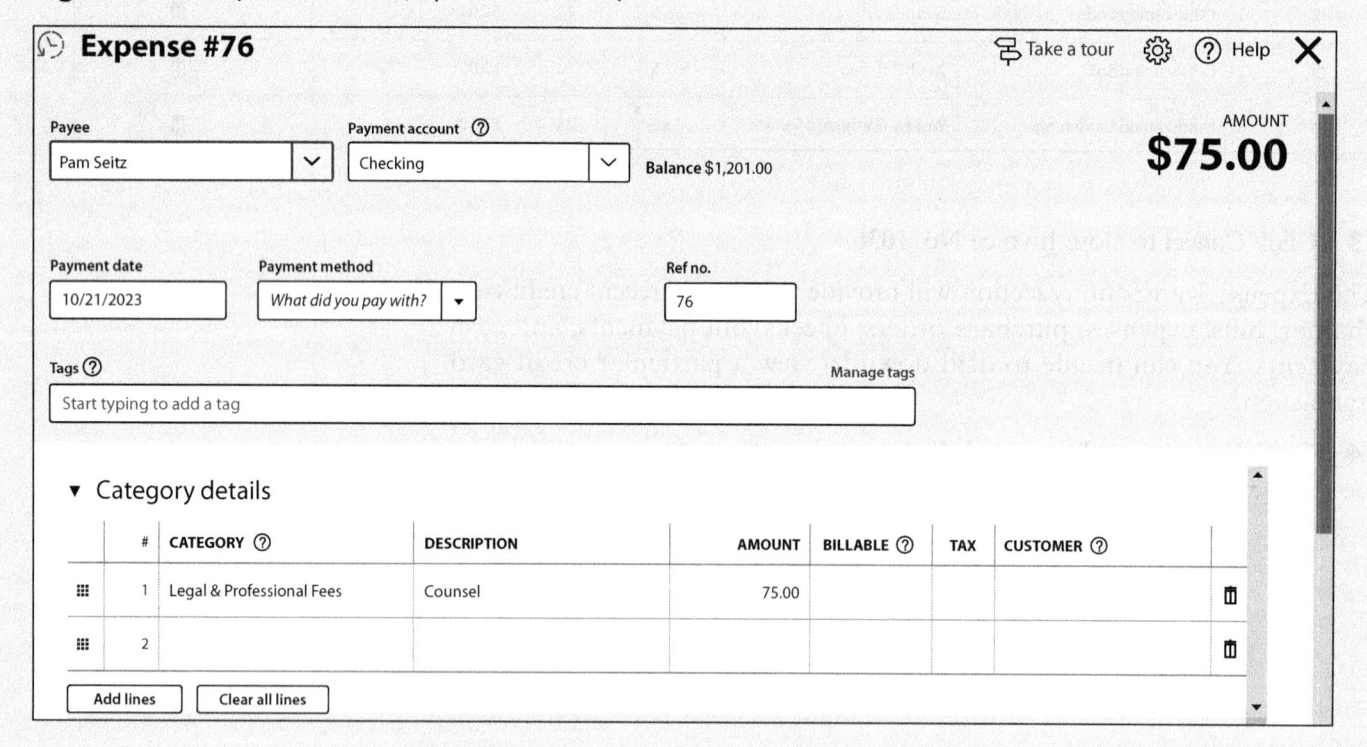

Expense #76   Take a tour   ⚙   ? Help   ✕

Payee: Pam Seitz ▾   **Payment account**: Checking ▾   Balance $1,201.00   **AMOUNT**   **$75.00**

Payment date: 10/21/2023   **Payment method**: What did you pay with? ▾   **Ref no.**: 76

Tags   Manage tags
Start typing to add a tag

▾ **Category details**

#	CATEGORY	DESCRIPTION	AMOUNT	BILLABLE	TAX	CUSTOMER	
1	Legal & Professional Fees	Counsel	75.00				🗑
2							🗑

Add lines   Clear all lines

    6   Click **Cancel** to close the expense window.

An Introduction to QuickBooks Online Using the Sample Company   **Chapter 1**   **15**

Settings

The Settings window (also known as the Gear window) is accessed by clicking the Gear icon located in the upper-right portion of the QBO window. Here you can modify your company settings, products and services, and budgets as well as reconcile bank accounts.

To view the Settings window and examine the Sample Company's settings:

1 Click the **Gear** icon as shown in Figure 1.18.

Figure 1.18 Company Settings window

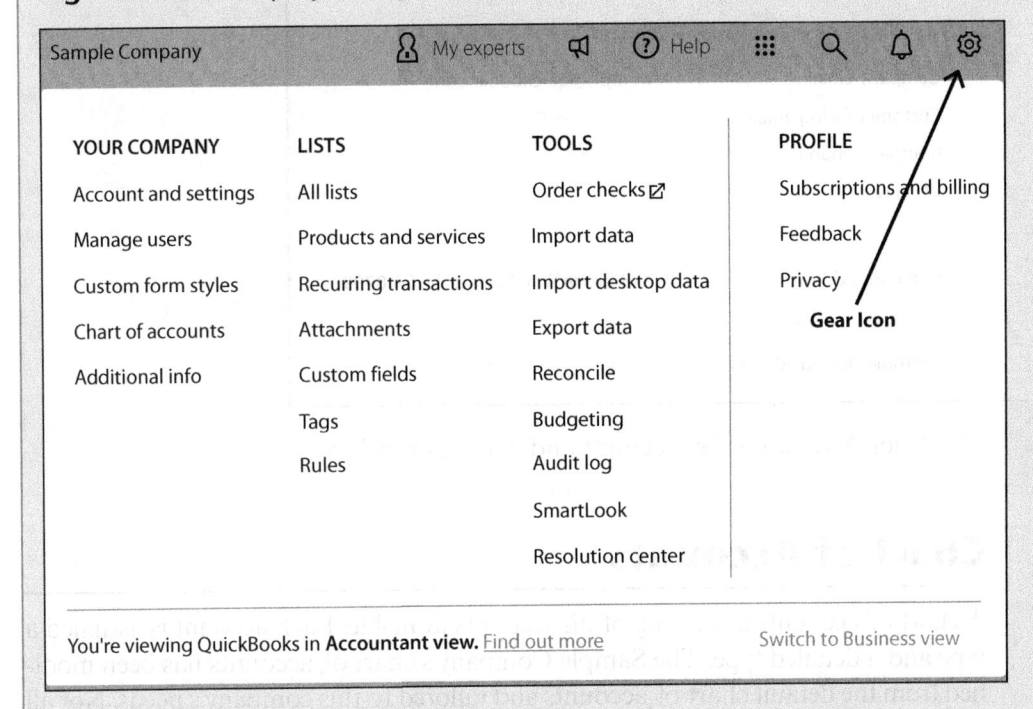

YOUR COMPANY	LISTS	TOOLS	PROFILE
Account and settings	All lists	Order checks	Subscriptions and billing
Manage users	Products and services	Import data	Feedback
Custom form styles	Recurring transactions	Import desktop data	Privacy
Chart of accounts	Attachments	Export data	
Additional info	Custom fields	Reconcile	
	Tags	Budgeting	
	Rules	Audit log	
		SmartLook	
		Resolution center	

You're viewing QuickBooks in **Accountant view.** Find out more   Switch to Business view

(Gear Icon indicated in upper-right)

2 Click **Account and settings** to view company name, type, address, and so on as shown in Figure 1.19.

Figure 1.19 Account and Settings window

Account and Settings			? Help ✕
Company	Company name		
Usage			logo
Expenses			
Time		Company name	Craig's Design and Landscaping Services
Advanced		Legal name	Same as company name
		EIN/SSN	-
	Company type	Tax form	Not sure/Other/None
		Industry	-
	Contact info	Company email	noreply@quickbooks.com
		Customer-facing email	Same as company email
		Company phone	-
		Website	-
	Address	Company address	123 Sierra Way, San Pablo, CA 87999
	Address	Customer-facing address	Same as company address

3 Click **X** to close the Account and Settings window.

Chart of Accounts

A chart of accounts is a listing of all accounts available. Each account is assigned a type and a detailed type. The Sample Company's chart of accounts has been modified from the default chart of accounts and tailored to this company's needs. Not all companies need these particular accounts, and some will need additional accounts.

To view the Sample Company's chart of accounts, do the following:

1. Click the **Gear** icon and then click **Chart of Accounts** to view the Chart of Accounts section as shown in Figure 1.20.

2. Scroll down the chart of accounts. Each asset, liability, and equity account has a View register action item listed.

3. As you scroll down, you will see that the balance in the chart of accounts for accounts payable (A/P) is $1,602.67.

4. Click **View register** on the Accounts Payable line of the chart of accounts to view the register for accounts payable shown in Figure 1.21. The ending balance in the A/P Register matches the $1,602.67

An Introduction to QuickBooks Online Using the Sample Company   **Chapter 1**   17

balance specified in the chart of accounts listing. (Remember to ignore dates in this Sample Company problem. Also click **X** to close any pop up windows that may display.)

Figure 1.20 Chart of Accounts (partial view)

Chart of accounts

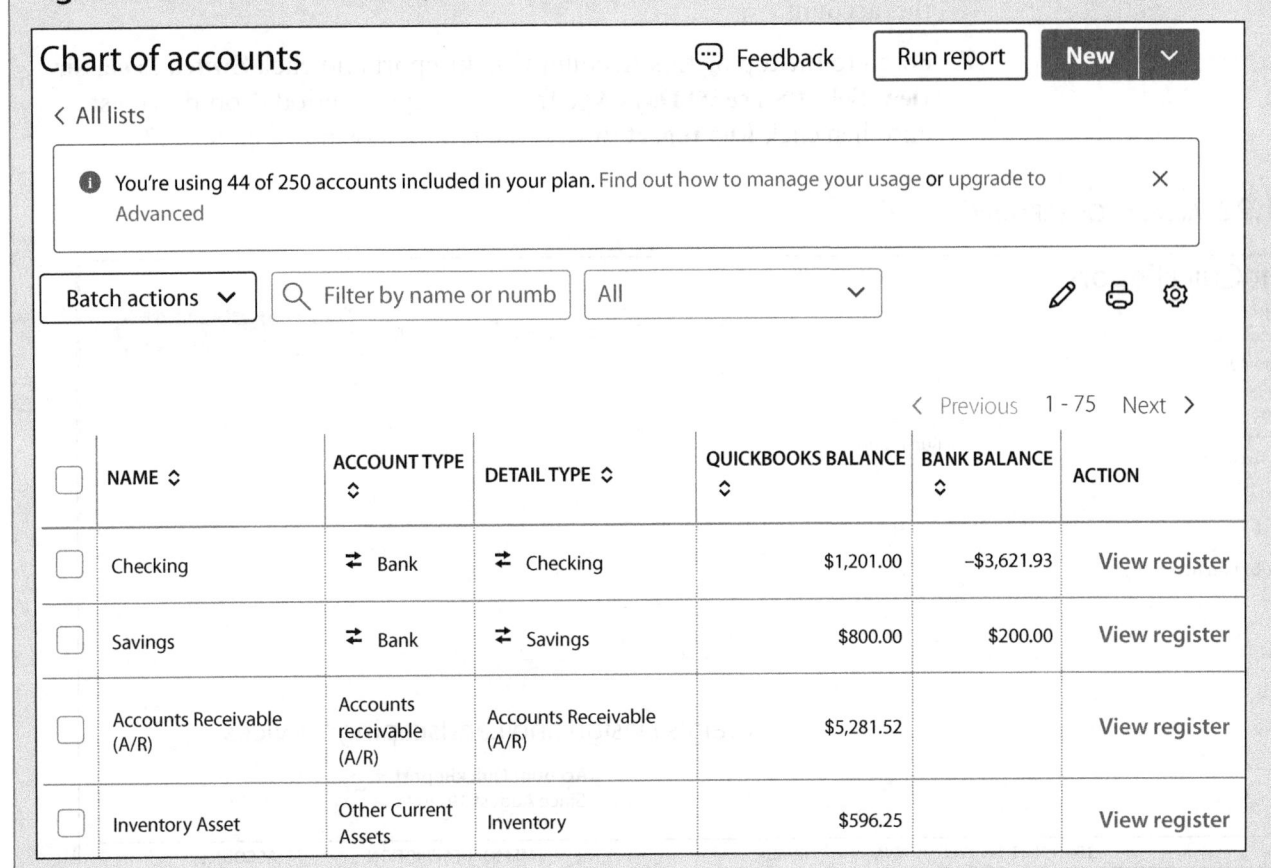

< All lists

You're using 44 of 250 accounts included in your plan. Find out how to manage your usage or upgrade to Advanced

< Previous   1 - 75   Next >

	NAME	ACCOUNT TYPE	DETAIL TYPE	QUICKBOOKS BALANCE	BANK BALANCE	ACTION
☐	Checking	Bank	Checking	$1,201.00	−$3,621.93	View register
☐	Savings	Bank	Savings	$800.00	$200.00	View register
☐	Accounts Receivable (A/R)	Accounts receivable (A/R)	Accounts Receivable (A/R)	$5,281.52		View register
☐	Inventory Asset	Other Current Assets	Inventory	$596.25		View register

Figure 1.21 A/P Register

< Back to Chart of Accounts

A/P Register   Accounts Payable (A/P) ▼

ENDING BALANCE
$1,602.67

Go to: 1 of 1   < First   Previous   1-25 of 25   Next   Last >

DATE ▼	REF NO. / TYPE	PAYEE / ACCOUNT	MEMO	DUE DATE	BILLED	PAID	OPEN BALANCE
10/22/2023		Norton Lumber and Building Materials		10/22/2023	$205.00		$205.00
	Bill	-Split-					
10/22/2023	1	Norton Lumber and Building Materials				$103.55	$0.00
	Bill Payment	Mastercard					
10/22/2023	1	Cal Telephone				$56.50	$0.00
	Bill Payment	Mastercard					
10/22/2023		Robertson & Associates		10/22/2023	$315.00		$315.00
	Bill	Legal & Professional Fees:Accounting					

5. Click **Back to Chart of Accounts** located at the top of the A/P Register.

6. Scroll down the chart of accounts to see that each revenue and expense account has a Run Report action item listed. Click **Run Report** on the Landscaping Services account line to view an Account QuickReport for this account.

7. Scroll to the top of this Account QuickReport and click **Switch to classic view**. Select **Since 90 Days Ago** from the Report period drop-down list, and then click **Run report** to view the report shown in Figure 1.22.

Figure 1.22 Account QuickReport

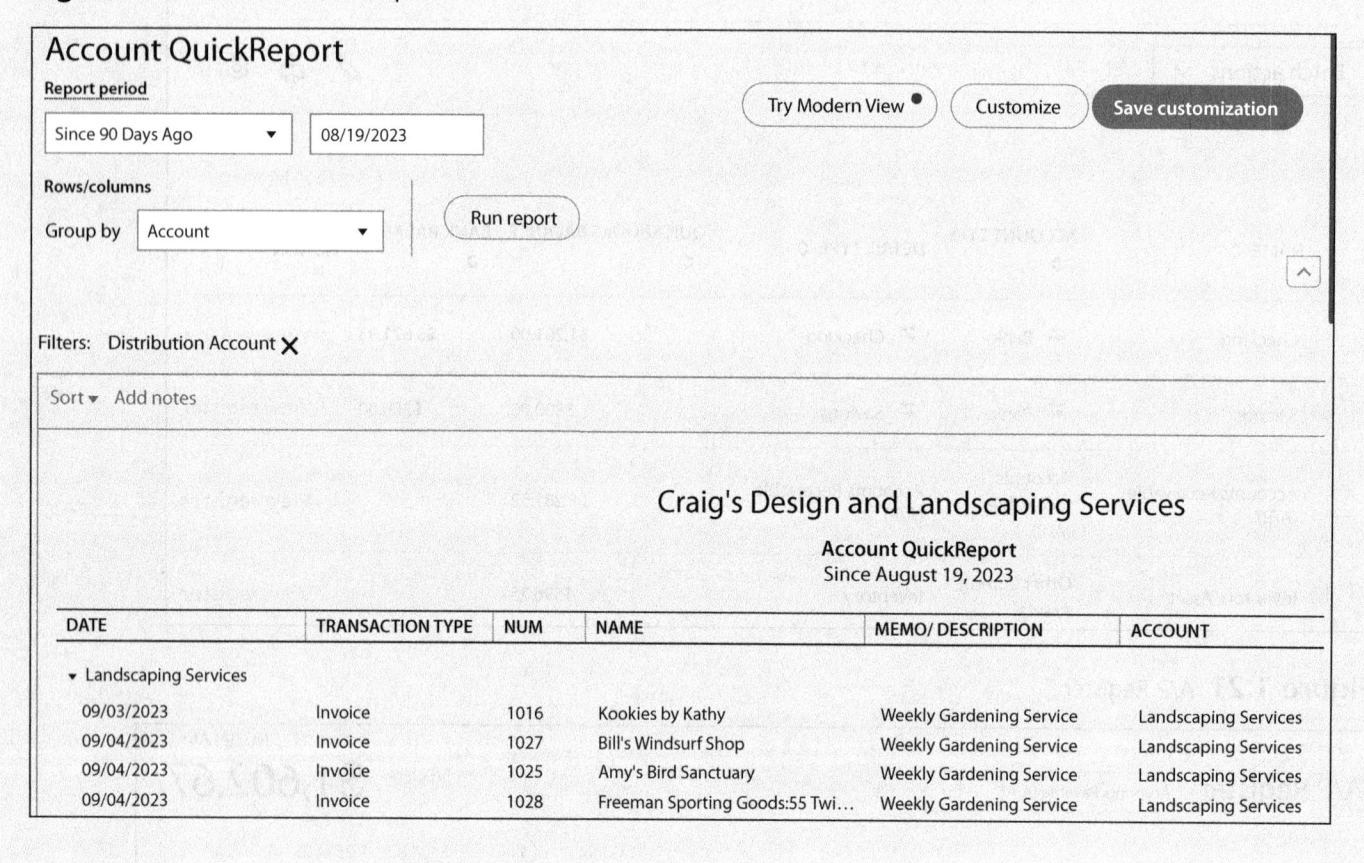

Account QuickReport

Report period
Since 90 Days Ago ▼ | 08/19/2023

Rows/columns
Group by: Account ▼   Run report

Filters: Distribution Account ✕

Sort ▼ Add notes

Craig's Design and Landscaping Services
Account QuickReport
Since August 19, 2023

DATE	TRANSACTION TYPE	NUM	NAME	MEMO/ DESCRIPTION	ACCOUNT
▼ Landscaping Services					
09/03/2023	Invoice	1016	Kookies by Kathy	Weekly Gardening Service	Landscaping Services
09/04/2023	Invoice	1027	Bill's Windsurf Shop	Weekly Gardening Service	Landscaping Services
09/04/2023	Invoice	1025	Amy's Bird Sanctuary	Weekly Gardening Service	Landscaping Services
09/04/2023	Invoice	1028	Freeman Sporting Goods:55 Twi…	Weekly Gardening Service	Landscaping Services

Lists

Lists in QBO provide you with an easy and quick way to view a collection of common items. Some of the more common lists include the chart of accounts, products and services, and terms. You can decide to view a summary of all the lists available in QBO and explore the list of terms.

To view a list of lists and the list of terms, do the following:

1 Click the **Gear** icon and then click **All Lists** to view all lists shown in Figure 1.23.

Figure 1.23 Lists

Lists

Chart of Accounts

Displays your accounts. Balance sheet accounts track your assets and liabilities, and income and expense accounts categorise your transactions. From here, you can add or edit accounts.

Recurring Transactions

Displays a list of transactions that have been saved for reuse. From here, you can schedule transactions to occur either automatically or with reminders. You can also save unscheduled transactions to use at any time.

Products and Services

Displays the products and services you sell. From here, you can edit information about a product or service, such as its description, or the rate you charge.

Product Categories

A means of classifying items that you sell to customers. Provide a way for you to quickly organise what you sell, and save you time when completing sales transaction forms.

Custom Form Styles

Customise your sales form designs, set defaults, and manage multiple templates.

Payment Methods

Displays Cash, Check, and any other ways you categorise payments you receive from customers. That way, you can print deposit slips when you deposit the payments you have received.

Terms

Displays the list of terms that determine the due dates for payments from customers, or payments to suppliers. Terms can also specify discounts for early payment. From here, you can add or edit terms.

Attachments

Displays the list of all attachments uploaded. From here, you can add, edit, download, and export your attachments. You can also see all transactions linked to a particular attachment.

Tags

Displays the list of all tags created. You can add, edit, and delete your tags here.

Custom Fields

Sort, track, and report the information that matters to you. Add custom fields to your forms so that you can capture more business-related info.

2 Click **Terms** to view the list shown in Figure 1.24.

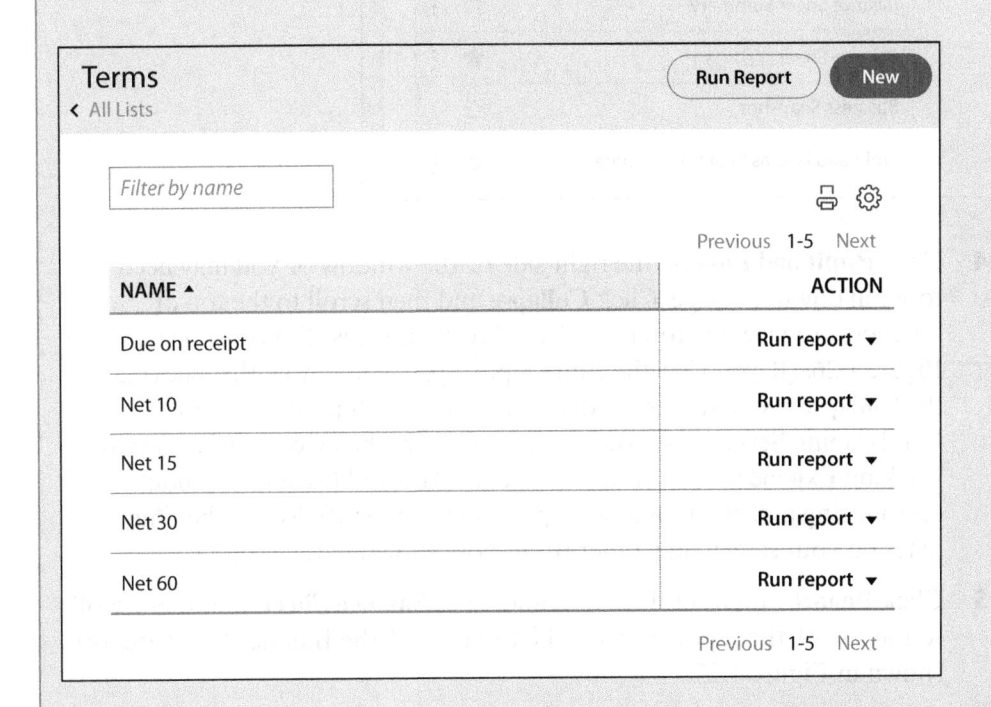

Figure 1.24 Terms

Terms
‹ All Lists

Run Report | New

Filter by name

Previous 1-5 Next

NAME ▲	ACTION
Due on receipt	Run report ▼
Net 10	Run report ▼
Net 15	Run report ▼
Net 30	Run report ▼
Net 60	Run report ▼

Previous 1-5 Next

Reports

QBO comes with many predesigned reports for use in business, all of which you can customize for your particular needs. For instance, you can decide to focus on the common financial statement reports: the Income Statement (known in QBO as the Profit and Loss report), Balance Sheet, and Statement of Cash Flows.

1. Click **Reports** from the navigation bar.
2. Click **Standard** and then click **Favorites** to hide any reports QBO had tagged as a favorite.
3. Scroll down the page to see Business overview report options shown in Figure 1.25.

Figure 1.25 Business overview reports

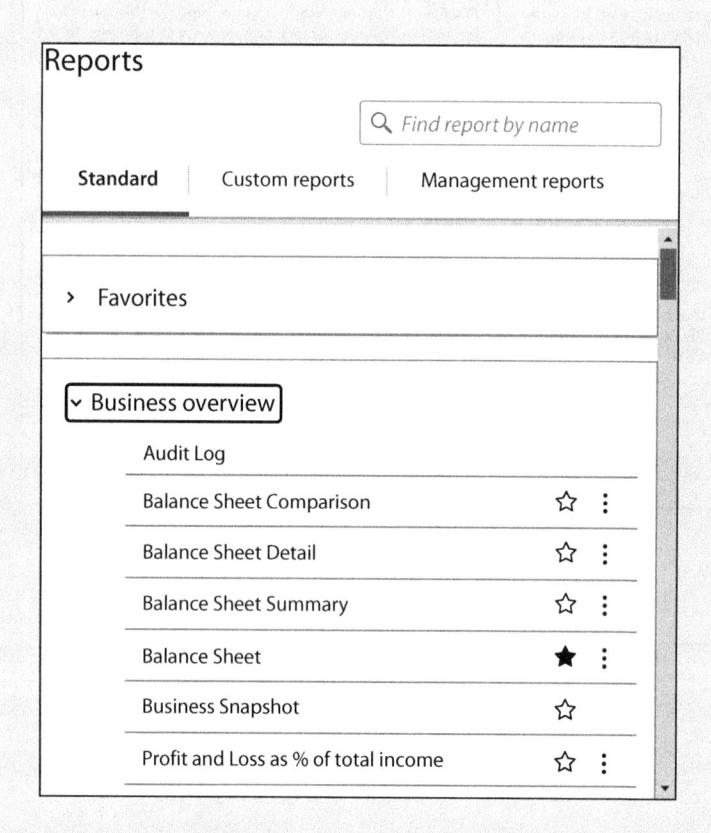

Reports
Standard · Custom reports · Management reports
> Favorites
∨ Business overview
Audit Log
Balance Sheet Comparison ☆
Balance Sheet Detail ☆
Balance Sheet Summary ☆
Balance Sheet ★
Business Snapshot ☆
Profit and Loss as % of total income ☆

4. Click **Profit and Loss** on the right side of the window or you may need to scroll down the page. Click **Collapse** and then scroll to the top of the report to view the top part of the Profit and Loss Report shown in Figure 1.26. (If you view the entire report, you would note that clicking the **Collapse** text summarizes details under a heading. For example, Landscaping Services is shown as one number when Collapse is selected. Clicking **Expand** would show more detail. You will learn more about customizing and creating other reports in Chapter 10. Remember, the dates on your screen may differ from those shown in the figure.)

5. Click **Reports**, then scroll to find and click **Balance Sheet**, and then scroll to the top of the report to view the top part of the Balance Sheet Report shown in Figure 1.27.

Figure 1.26 Profit and Loss Report (partial view)

Profit and Loss Report

Report period: This Year-to-date | 01/01/2023 to 11/16/2023

Display columns by: Total Only
Show non-zero or active only: Active rows/active columns
Compare another period: Select period
Accounting method: ○ Cash ● Accrual

[Customize] [Save customization] [Run report]

Craig's Design and Landscaping Services
Profit and Loss
January 1 - November 16, 2023

	TOTAL
▼ Income	
Design income	2,250.00
Discounts given	−89.50
Landscaping Services	6,513.97
Pest Control Services	110.00
Sales of Product Income	912.75
Services	503.55
Total Income	**$10,200.77**
▼ Cost of Goods Sold	
Cost of Goods Sold	405.00
Total Cost of Goods Sold	**$405.00**

Figure 1.27 Balance Sheet Report (partial view)

Balance Sheet Report

Report period: This Year-to-date | 01/01/2023 to 11/16/2023

Display columns by: Total Only
Show non-zero or active only: Active rows/active columns
Compare another period: Select period
Accounting method: ○ Cash ● Accrual

[Customize] [Save customization] [Run report]

Craig's Design and Landscaping Services
Balance Sheet
As of November 16, 2023

	TOTAL
▼ ASSETS	
▼ Current Assets	
▼ Bank Accounts	
Checking	1,201.00
Savings	800.00
Total Bank Accounts	**$2,001.00**

6 Click **Reports**, then scroll to find and click **Statement of Cash Flows**, and then scroll to the top of the report to view the top part of the Statement of Cash Flows Report shown in Figure 1.28.

Figure 1.28 Statement of Cash Flows Report

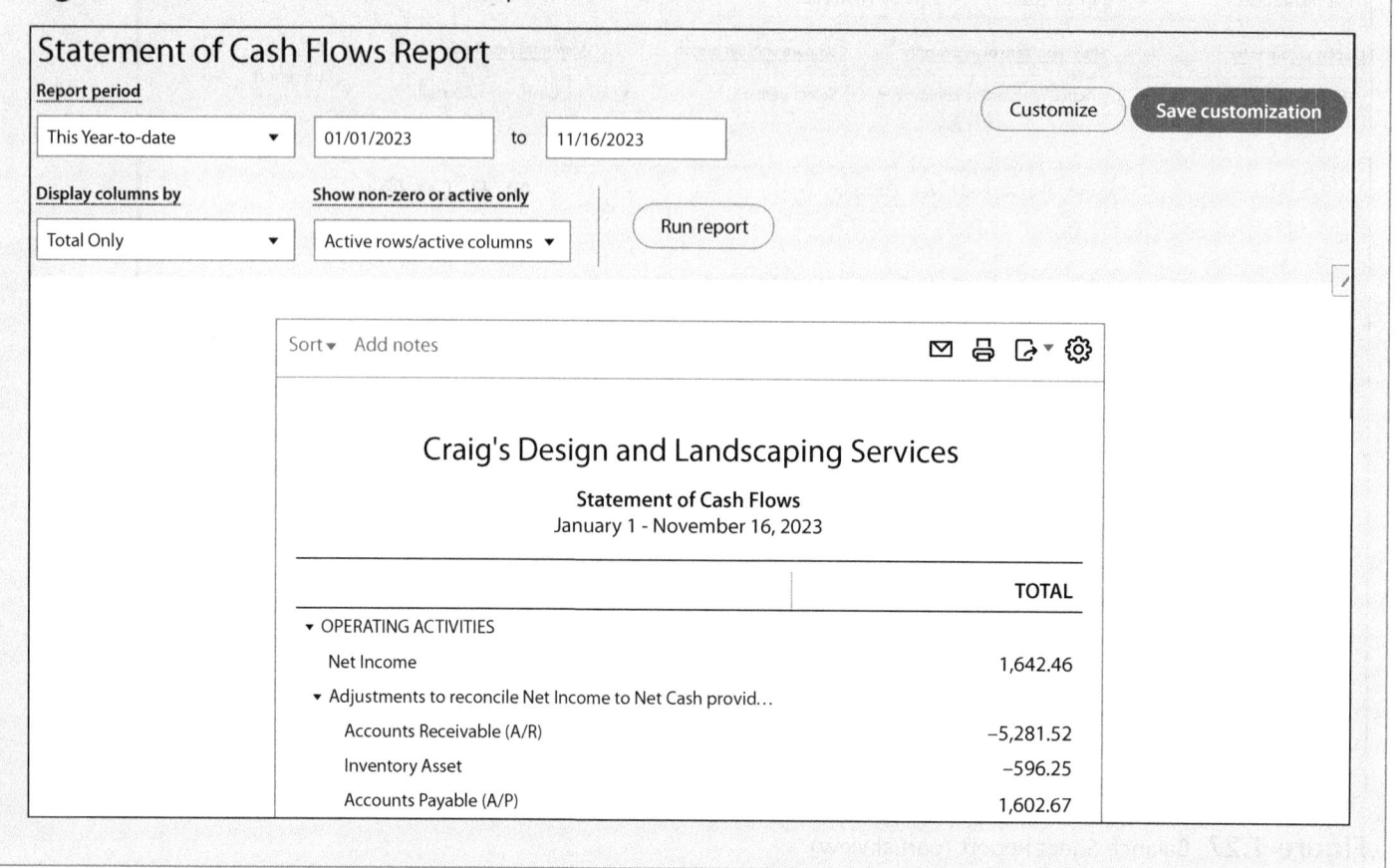

Statement of Cash Flows Report

Report period: This Year-to-date | 01/01/2023 to 11/16/2023

Display columns by: Total Only
Show non-zero or active only: Active rows/active columns

Craig's Design and Landscaping Services
Statement of Cash Flows
January 1 - November 16, 2023

	TOTAL
▼ OPERATING ACTIVITIES	
Net Income	1,642.46
▼ Adjustments to reconcile Net Income to Net Cash provid…	
Accounts Receivable (A/R)	−5,281.52
Inventory Asset	−596.25
Accounts Payable (A/P)	1,602.67

Alternatively, you can easily find a report if you know its name or part of its name. For example, if you wanted to access a report dealing with accounts receivable (A/R), you would type Accounts receivable into the report search box located in the Reports section.

To find a report related to accounts receivable, do the following:

1 Click **Reports** and type **Accounts receivable** in the Find report by name search box. Note the two reports that match your search as shown in Figure 1.29.

Figure 1.29 Reports

Reports

Standard | Custom reports | Management reports

Search: Accounts receivable
- **Accounts receivable** aging detail
- **Accounts receivable** aging summary

Company Settings

Five tabs are in the Settings section of QBO: Company, Usage, Time, Expenses, and Advanced. You can edit these by clicking on the Pencil icon to the right of each section. The settings for the Sample Company have been modified from the default settings provided when QBO first creates a company. These options in the Settings section change the way QBO appears to the user. For example, in the Time section, if time tracking is turned off, no time tracking features will be available in QBO. Also, if purchase orders are turned off in the Expenses section, no purchase orders will be available in QBO. You can decide to view each of these sections to learn more about what options you are given in QBO.

1 Click the **Gear** icon and then click **Account and settings**, and click the **Company** tab to view the Company Settings section shown in Figure 1.30.

Figure 1.30 Company settings

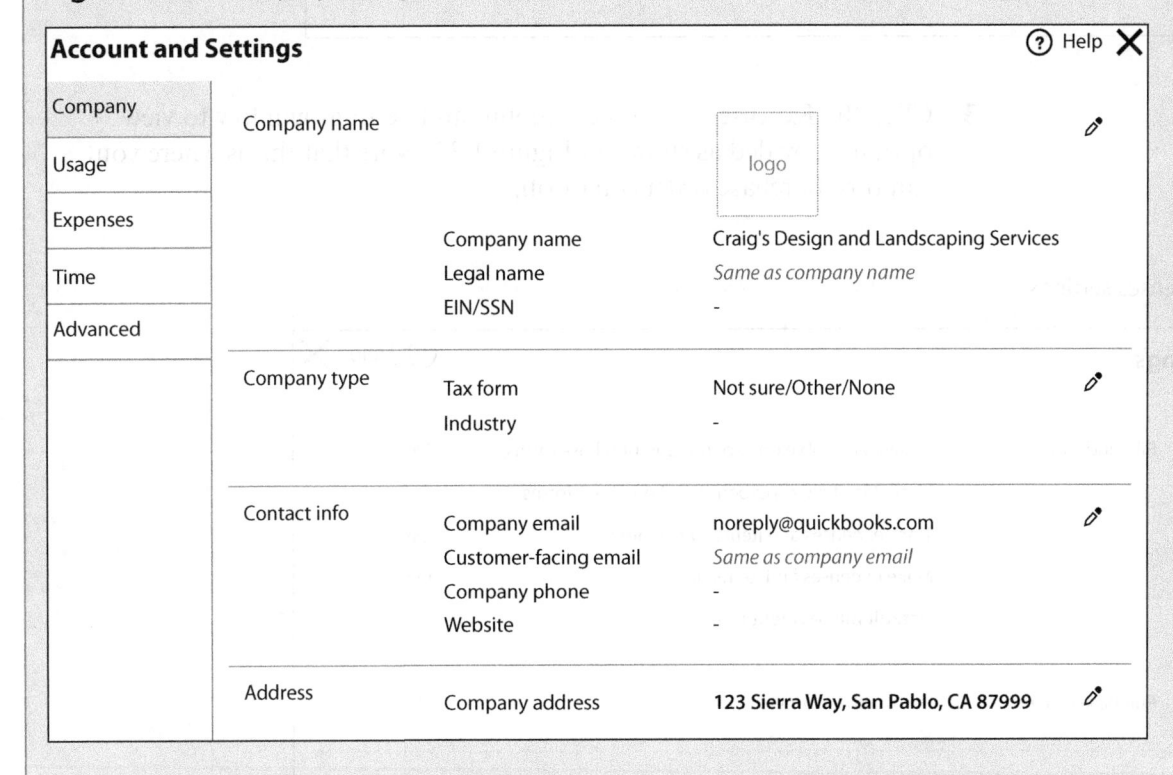

Account and Settings

Company	Company name		
Usage		logo	
Expenses			
Time	Company name	Craig's Design and Landscaping Services	
Advanced	Legal name	Same as company name	
	EIN/SSN	-	
	Company type	Tax form	Not sure/Other/None
		Industry	-
	Contact info	Company email	noreply@quickbooks.com
		Customer-facing email	Same as company email
		Company phone	-
		Website	-
	Address	Company address	123 Sierra Way, San Pablo, CA 87999

2. Click the **Time** tab in the Account and Settings window to view options provided as shown in Figure 1.31.

Figure 1.31 Time settings

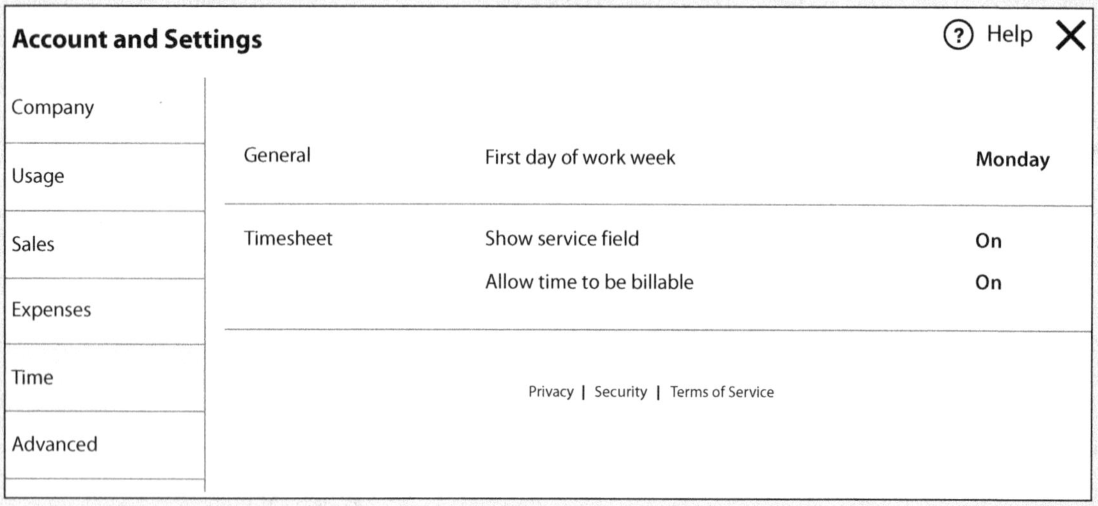

Account and Settings			? Help ✕
Company			
Usage	General	First day of work week	**Monday**
Sales	Timesheet	Show service field	On
		Allow time to be billable	On
Expenses			
Time		Privacy | Security | Terms of Service	
Advanced			

3. Click the **Expenses** tab in the Account and Settings window to view options provided as shown in Figure 1.32. Note that this is where you can turn purchase orders on or off.

Figure 1.32 Expenses settings

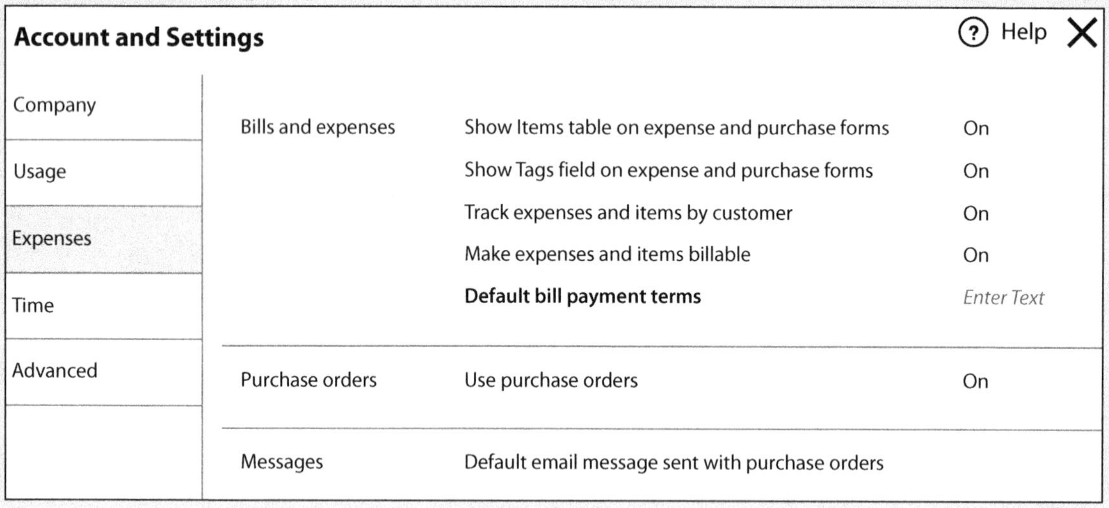

Account and Settings			? Help ✕
Company	Bills and expenses	Show Items table on expense and purchase forms	On
Usage		Show Tags field on expense and purchase forms	On
		Track expenses and items by customer	On
Expenses		Make expenses and items billable	On
		Default bill payment terms	*Enter Text*
Time			
Advanced	Purchase orders	Use purchase orders	On
	Messages	Default email message sent with purchase orders	

4 Click the **Advanced** tab in the Account and Settings window to view options provided as shown in Figure 1.33. Note that this is where you change your company type to corporation, sole proprietor, and so on.

Figure 1.33 Advanced settings

Account and Settings				Help
Company	Accounting	First month of fiscal year	January	✎
Usage		First month of income tax year	Same as fiscal year	
		Accounting method ⓘ	Accrual	
Expenses		Close the books ⓘ	Off	
Time				
	Company type	Tax form	Not sure/Other/None	✎
Advanced				
	Chart of accounts	Enable account numbers	Off	✎
		Discount account	Discounts given	
		Tips account	Enter Text	
		Billable expense income account	Billable Expense Income	
	Categories	Track classes	Off	✎
		Track locations	Off	

5 Click **Done** to close the Settings window.

End Note

In this chapter, you have used Intuit's Sample Company to practice navigating QBO. You have accessed customer, vendor, and employee information; viewed various transactions; and viewed the chart of accounts, lists, reports, and company settings. In Chapter 2, you will accept an invitation to work a case your instructor assigns you. In Chapter 3, you will use the Wild Water Sports company to learn how to modify settings, the chart of accounts, beginning balances, and products and services. In Chapters 4 through 10, you will use the Wild Water Sports company to learn how to add operating, investing, and financing activities; reconcile a bank account; create a budget; add adjusting entries; and prepare financial statements and reports.

chapter practice 1

Chapter 1 Questions

1. What steps do you take to view customer information?
2. What steps do you take to view detailed transactions related to a particular customer?
3. What steps do you take to view a specific bill from a specific vendor?
4. What steps do you take to view a specific employee's information?
5. How are bank deposits, which have not been recorded in QBO, classified?
6. How are bank charges, which have not been recorded in QBO, classified?
7. Opening the Sales Transaction section of QBO will provide a listing of _____.
8. Opening the Expense Transaction section of QBO will provide a listing of _____.
9. What lists are available in QBO?
10. What steps do you take to view all reports related to accounts payable (A/P)?

Chapter 1 Matching

a. Navigation bar
b. Amy's Bird Sanctuary
c. Brosnahan Insurance Agency
d. Recognizing
e. Uncategorized Income
f. Uncategorized Expense
g. Registers
h. John Johnson
i. Terms
j. Chart of accounts

_____ An employee in the Sample Company
_____ Bank deposits not yet recognized
_____ Exist for all asset, liability, and equity accounts
_____ Specify due dates for payment to/from vendors/customers
_____ Used to access a list of sales and expense transactions
_____ A vendor in the Sample Company
_____ A listing of all accounts available
_____ Bank charges not yet recognized
_____ A customer in the Sample Company
_____ Matching a banking transaction with a QBO transaction

An Overview of QuickBooks Online

chapter 2

Student Learning Outcomes

Upon completion of this chapter, the student will be able to do the following:

- Identify the basic features of QuickBooks Online (QBO)
- Explain how QBO is similar to and differs from the desktop version of QuickBooks
- Open the QBO company you created in the Preface to this text
- Provide information to QBO about your company
- Successfully navigate the QBO Dashboard
- Assign their instructor as their "Accountant"
- Use QBO's help feature

Overview

The focus of this chapter is to introduce you to QuickBooks Online (QBO) and get your account and company established. A description of QBO will be provided along with a brief comparison of how QBO differs from its desktop version. This text includes instructions provided by Intuit to create your own personal account with Intuit and create up to four companies. You will assign your company a name that includes your name for identification purposes. Welcome to the journey.

What Is QBO?

QBO is an online version of the popular QuickBooks accounting software developed by Intuit. The software is designed to capture common business events like purchases from and payments to vendors; sales to and collections from customers; payments and receipts to/from other operating, investing, and financing activities; period end accrual adjustments; and reports. Reports include the standard financial statements, including the income statement, statement of stockholders' equity, balance sheet, statement of cash flows, and other useful reports like accounts receivable aging. All interaction with QBO is done via an Internet connection. In other words, if you have not connected to the Internet, you will have no QBO. In other words, QBO cannot work offline.

All interaction with QBO is done online; there are no files to maintain on a computer, and everything is saved online. Thus, there is no need for backup files. The monthly fee for using QBO in its commercial (non-educational) version covers up to four companies. This text includes access to QBO for the user to create up to four companies online for a limited amount of time.

VIDEO LINK

Navigate your browser to the Video Tutorials provided by Intuit (see website address specified in the Preface to this text) and then search on how to get started in QuickBooks Online.

How Is QBO Similar to/Different Than the Desktop Version of QuickBooks Accountant?

Even though these two products share the name "QuickBooks," they are unrelated. QBO isn't a copy of QuickBooks that has been web enabled. They are different products with different database structures and approaches to solving problems even though both were developed in-house by Intuit to capture and report on accounting events.

Not all features available in QBO are available in the Windows desktop version of QuickBooks Accountant (QBDT). Likewise, not all features of QBDT are available in QBO. QBO requires an Internet connection. QBDT requires installation of software on to a computer. QBO requires a monthly fee. QBDT requires a one-time purchase and no monthly fees.

A key difference is that because QBO is online, it works on multiple operating systems (Windows, Apple, etc.) and multiple devices (desktops, laptops, smart phones, or tablets). The same cannot be said for QBDT. Intuit requires different software for QBDT to run on a Windows-based or an Apple-based computer. In this text, QBDT will always mean the Windows version of QuickBooks Accountant.

Some additional notable differences are the following:

- QBDT can be used for an unlimited number of companies; QBO limits you to four companies as assigned by your instructor. Need to manage more than four companies outside of your class using QBO? Each will cost you another monthly fee.

- QBO can automatically download bank transactions for no additional cost.

- QBDT can track inventory purchases and sales based on an average cost assumption or a first-in-first-out assumption.

- QBO can track inventory purchases and sales based only on a first-in-first-out assumption.

- QBDT can account for the receipt of inventory items (receive items function) based on a purchase order; QBO cannot and calls inventory products and services.

- QBO can automatically schedule and send invoices, whereas QBDT cannot.

- QBDT can perform manual payroll without paying Intuit a monthly payroll processing fee. QBO encourages you to sign up for its payroll service and makes manually processing payroll difficult.

- QBO can be accessed from anywhere in the world where you have access to the Internet. QBDT requires a computer with the QuickBooks application and data files installed.

- QBDT provides for profit and loss as well as balance sheet budgeting. QBO only provides for profit and loss budgeting.

- QBO operates irrespective of platform (desktop, laptop, mobile device, or tablet) or operating system (Microsoft Windows or Apple iOS). QBDT does have a version of QuickBooks for both of those operating systems, but they are different and require two separate application purchases.

An Overview of QuickBooks Online   **Chapter 2**   29

- QBDT includes a fixed asset management system, which will calculate depreciation and maintain detailed fixed asset records by individual asset, whereas QBO does not calculate depreciation and does not maintain detailed records of fixed assets.

- QBO provides automatic upgrades; this is a good and a bad feature. With QBO, you are almost always running the most current version (whether you want to or not).

How to Open the QBO Company You Created in the Preface

Instructions for both instructors and students are found in the Preface to this text. You must complete the registration process before you can proceed in this chapter.

Once you completed your QBO registration, you were presented with a QBO company shell (meaning a QBO company without any details). You were then instructed to sign out of QBO. In this section of the text, you are to return to that QBO company and add some additional information. When you return you will be presented a series of questions to set up your company in QBO. Since you exited QBO before answering questions in the Preface, QBO automatically returns you to the setup questions. Once you have completed this setup process, QBO will open your company dashboard.

To login to the company you created in the Preface to this text:

1. Type **https://qbo.intuit.com/** into your web browser.
2. Enter your User ID and password and then click **Sign In**.
3. Click **Skip for now** if asked to verify your number. Your company welcome window should now appear and look like Figure 2.1.

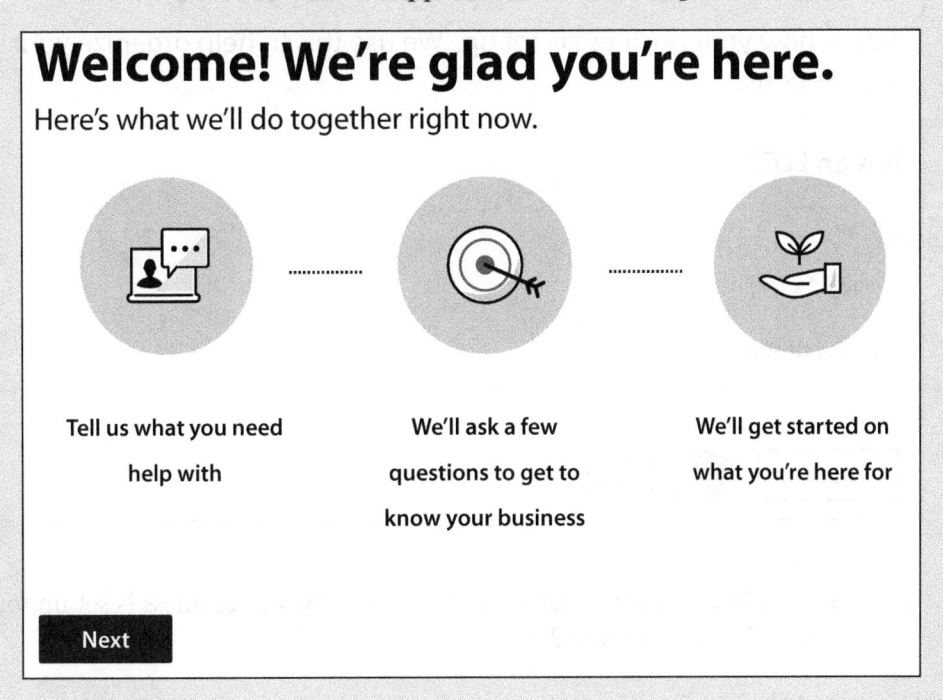

Figure 2.1

Welcome window

4. Click **Next** to answer the business name question. Type **Wild Water Sports - Student Name (ID Number)** or whatever name your instructor specifies as shown in Figure 2.2.

Figure 2.2

Business name

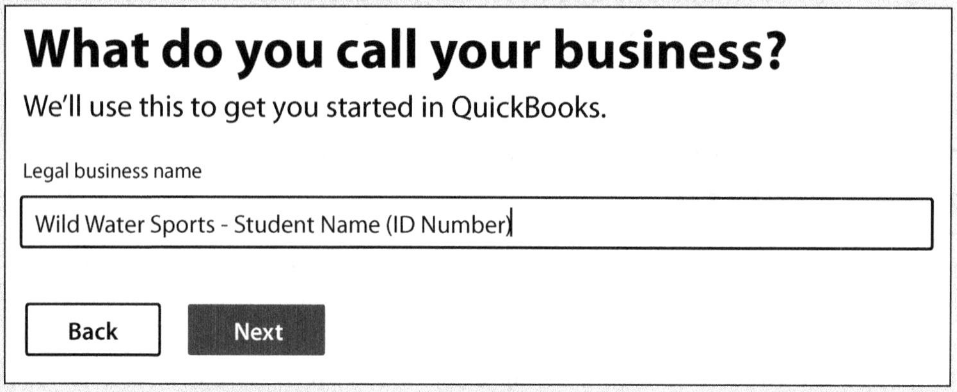

What do you call your business?

We'll use this to get you started in QuickBooks.

Legal business name

[Wild Water Sports - Student Name (ID Number)]

Back   Next

5. When asked how you have been managing your finances, click **Nothing, I'm just getting started**, then click **Next**.
6. When asked if Wild Water Sports is your main source of income, click **Skip for now**.
7. When asked how long Wild Water Sports has been in business, select **Under a year**. Click **Next**.
8. Click **Yes** to answer the type of business question as shown in Figure 2.3.

Figure 2.3

Type of business

What kind of business is this?

Tell us how your business is set up. We use this to help organize your transactions.

Is it an LLC?

○ Yes
○ No
○ I'm not sure

Back   Next

9. Click **C Corp** to answer the question about how the business is set up for taxes as shown in Figure 2.4.

An Overview of QuickBooks Online **Chapter 2** 31

Figure 2.4 How your business is set up for taxes

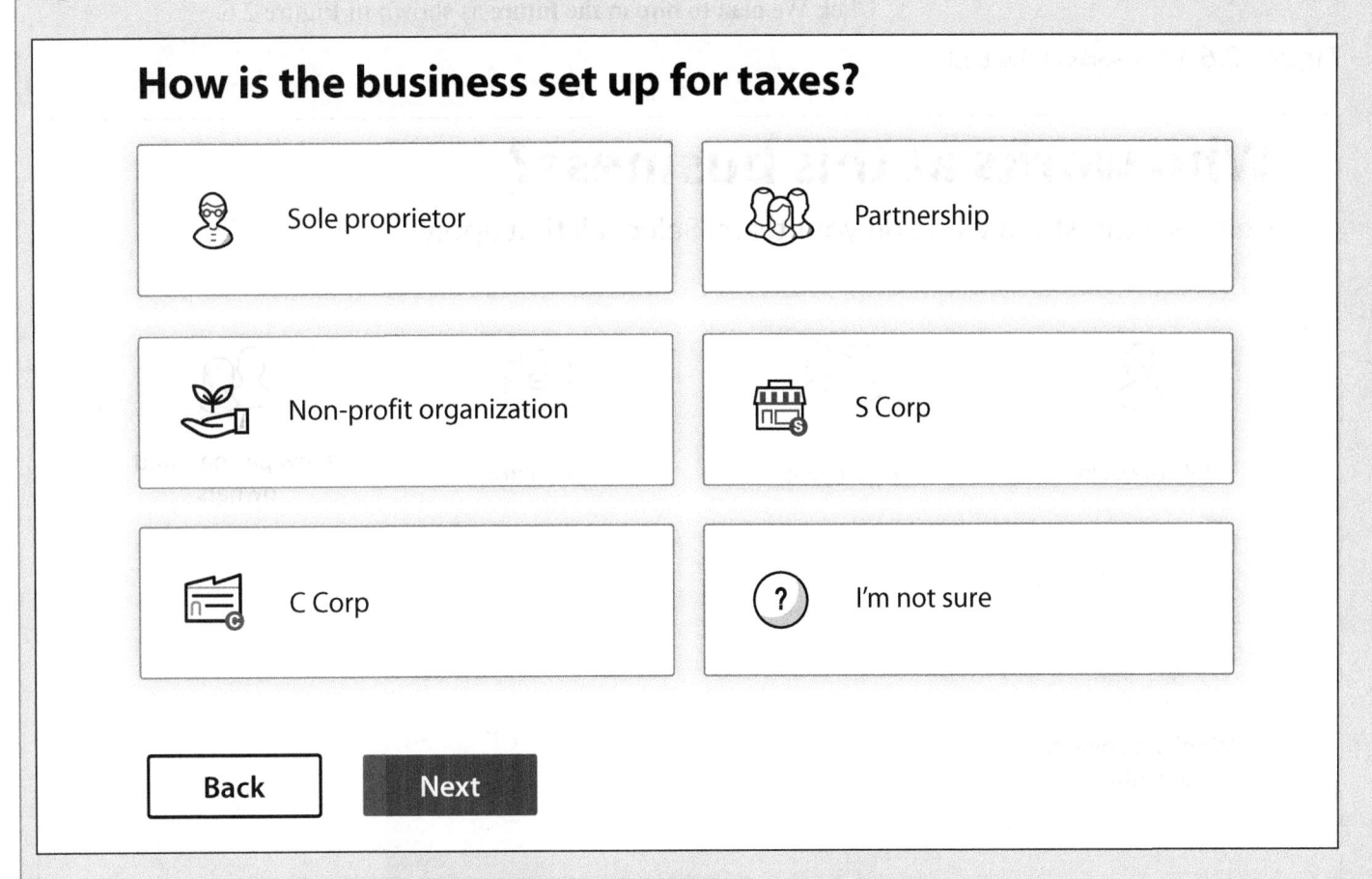

How is the business set up for taxes?

- Sole proprietor
- Partnership
- Non-profit organization
- S Corp
- C Corp
- I'm not sure

Back Next

10. Click **Next** and then click **Skip for now** when asked what's your industry. Click **Bookkeeper or accountant** as shown in Figure 2.5.

Figure 2.5 Your main role

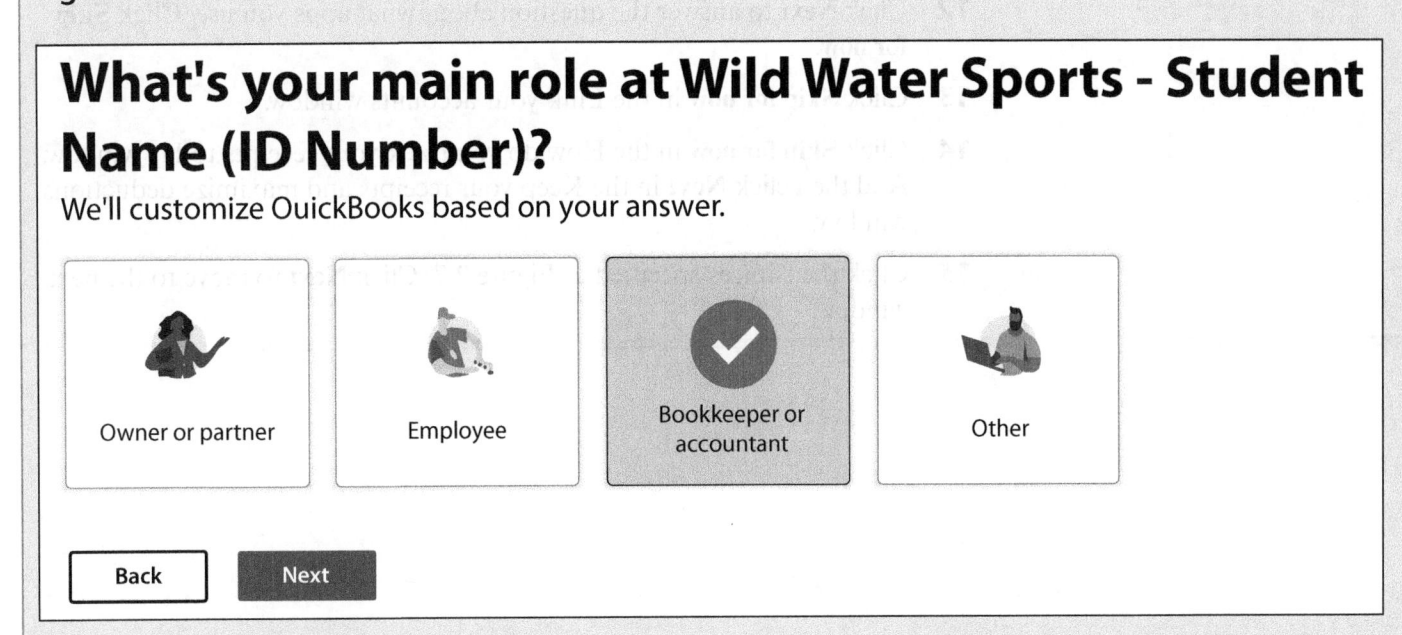

What's your main role at Wild Water Sports - Student Name (ID Number)?

We'll customize QuickBooks based on your answer.

- Owner or partner
- Employee
- Bookkeeper or accountant
- Other

Back Next

32 Chapter 2   *An Overview of QuickBooks Online*

11   Click **Next** to answer the question about who works at this business. Click **We plan to hire in the future** as shown in Figure 2.6.

Figure 2.6 Who works at this business

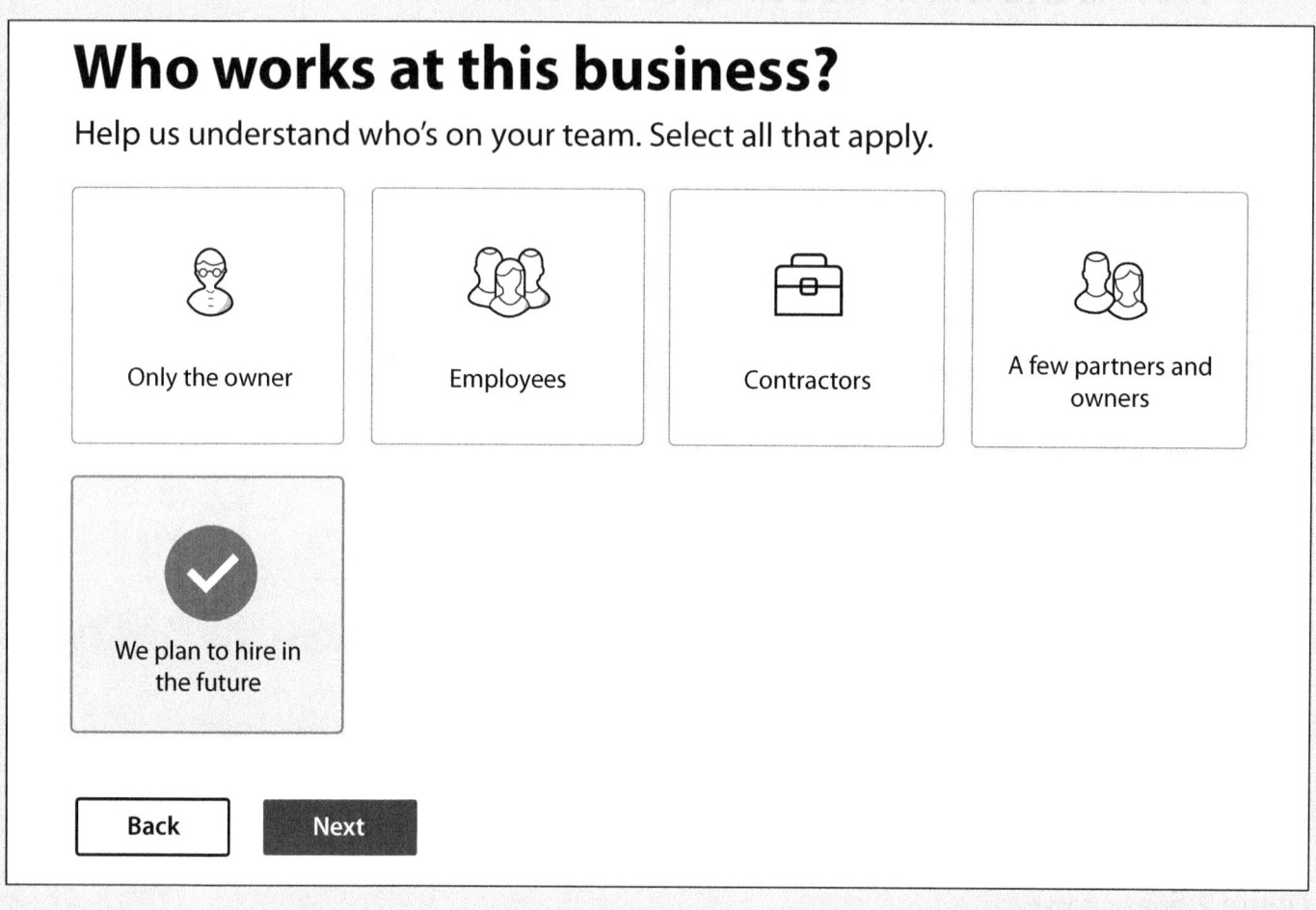

Who works at this business?
Help us understand who's on your team. Select all that apply.

| Only the owner | Employees | Contractors | A few partners and owners |

| We plan to hire in the future |

Back   Next

12   Click **Next** to answer the question about what apps you use. Click **Skip for now**.

13   Click **Skip for now** in the Link your accounts window.

14   Click **Skip for now** in the How do you track your receipts today window. And then click **Next** in the Keep your receipts and maximize deductions window.

15   Click the choices specified in Figure 2.7. Click **Next** to move to the next window.

An Overview of QuickBooks Online **Chapter 2** 33

Figure 2.7 Choices to build your setup guide

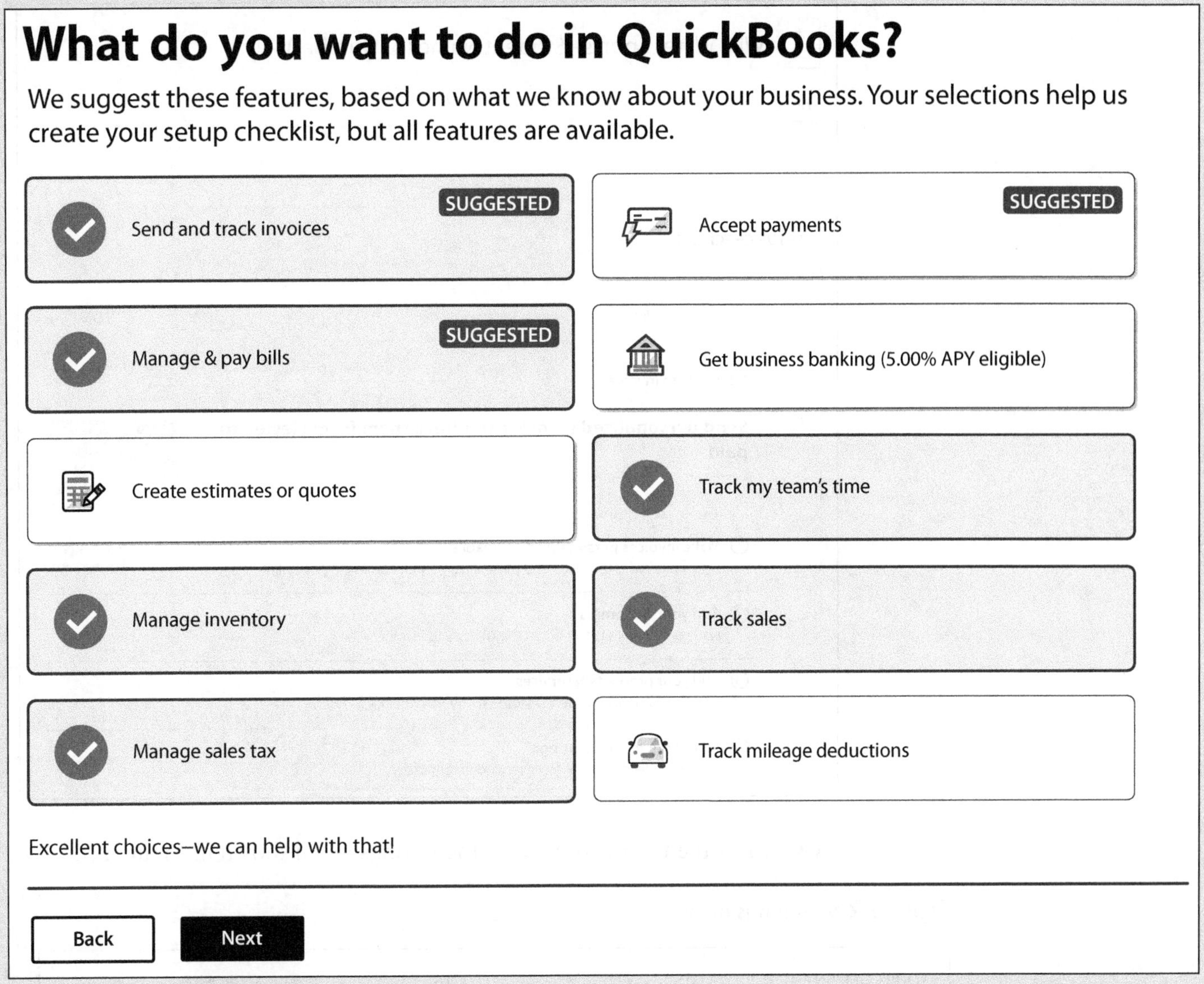

What do you want to do in QuickBooks?

We suggest these features, based on what we know about your business. Your selections help us create your setup checklist, but all features are available.

✓ Send and track invoices **SUGGESTED**	📧 Accept payments **SUGGESTED**
✓ Manage & pay bills **SUGGESTED**	🏛 Get business banking (5.00% APY eligible)
📝 Create estimates or quotes	✓ Track my team's time
✓ Manage inventory	✓ Track sales
✓ Manage sales tax	🚗 Track mileage deductions

Excellent choices—we can help with that!

[Back] [**Next**]

16. Click **Next** in the Now, we'll go over your first payment method window. And then click **Skip for now** in the Start getting paid with invoices window. Click **Next** if you get prompted to download an app.

17. Click **Let's go** to complete the setup process. At this point, click **Take a tour** or close the Welcome to QuickBooks window to view your company dashboard as shown in Figure 2.8.

34   **Chapter 2**   *An Overview of QuickBooks Online*

Figure 2.8 Company dashboard

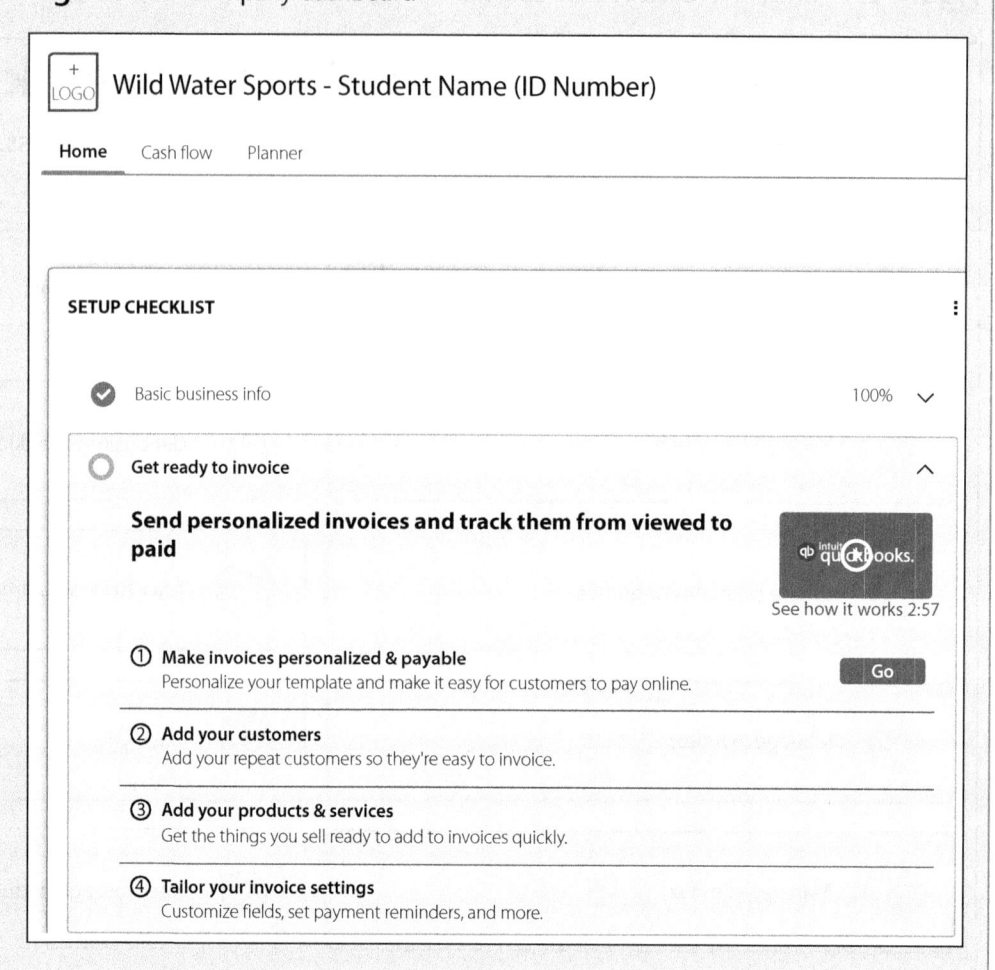

LOGO	**Wild Water Sports - Student Name (ID Number)**

Home   Cash flow   Planner

SETUP CHECKLIST

✓ Basic business info   100% ⌄

◯ Get ready to invoice   ⌃

Send personalized invoices and track them from viewed to paid

See how it works 2:57

① **Make invoices personalized & payable**
Personalize your template and make it easy for customers to pay online.   [Go]

② **Add your customers**
Add your repeat customers so they're easy to invoice.

③ **Add your products & services**
Get the things you sell ready to add to invoices quickly.

④ **Tailor your invoice settings**
Customize fields, set payment reminders, and more.

18   Click the **Gear** icon to view the settings menu shown in Figure 2.9.

Figure 2.9 Settings menu

YOUR COMPANY	LISTS	TOOLS	PROFILE
Account and settings	All lists	Order checks ↗	Subscriptions and billing
Manage users	Products and services	Import data	Feedback
Custom form styles	Recurring transactions	Import desktop data	Privacy
Chart of accounts	Attachments	Export data	
Additional info	Custom fields	Reconcile	
	Tags	Budgeting	
	Rules	Audit log	
		SmartLook	
		Resolution center	

You're viewing QuickBooks in **Accountant view.** Find out more   Switch to Business view

An Overview of QuickBooks Online   **Chapter 2**   35

19   Click **Account and settings** to view the Account and Settings section shown in Figure 2.10.

Figure 2.10   Account and Settings section

Account and Settings		
Company	Company name	
Usage		
QuickBooks Checking [NEW]		Company name
		Legal name
Sales		EIN
Expenses		
Payments	Company type	Tax form
		Industry
Time		
Advanced	Contact info	Company email
		Customer-facing email
		Company phone
		Website

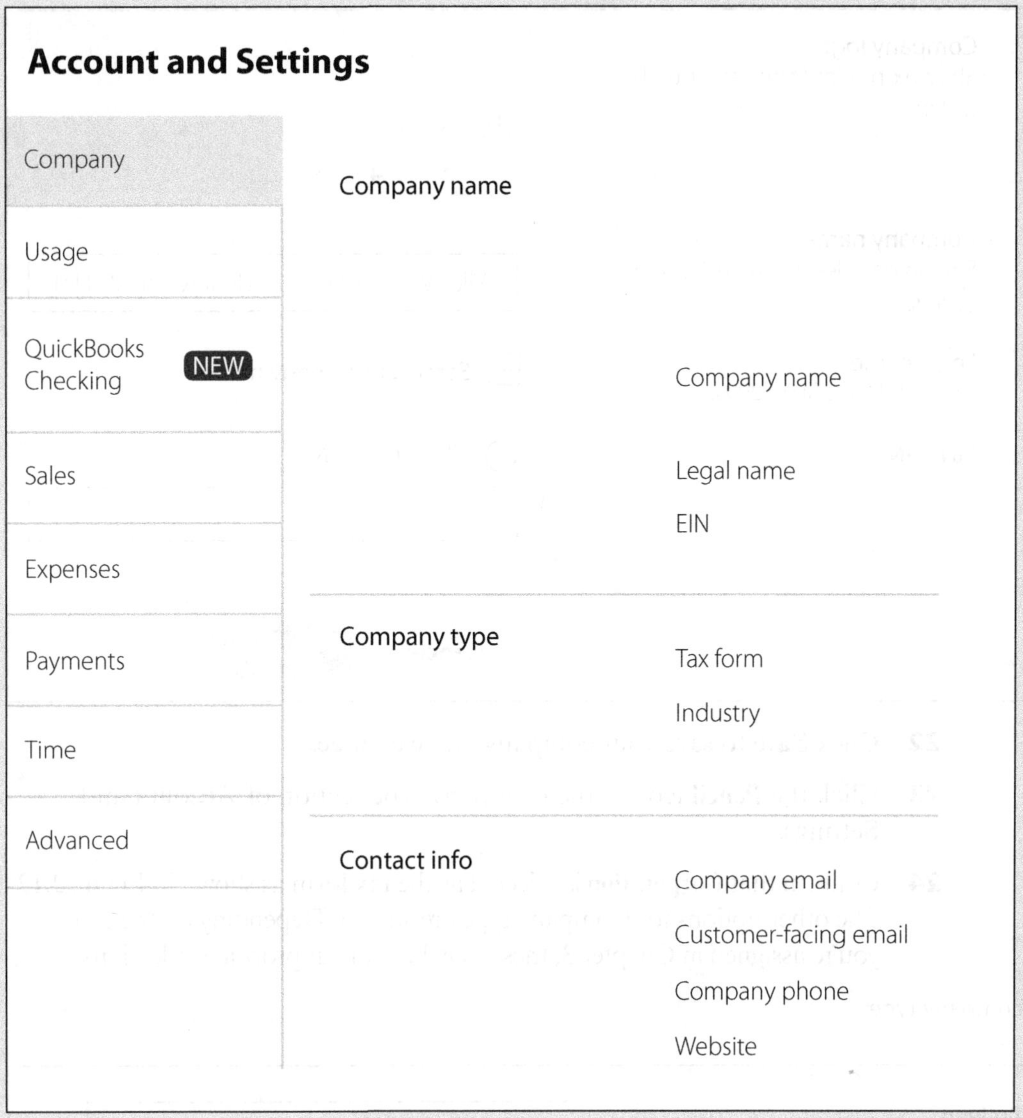

20   Click the **Company** tab and then click the **Pencil** icon in the Company name section of Account and Settings.

36 Chapter 2 *An Overview of QuickBooks Online*

21 Type **Wild Water Sports - Student Name (ID Number)** replacing Student Name with your name and ID Number in the Company Name text box and then place a check in the **Same as company name** check box as shown in Figure 2.11.

Figure 2.11 Changing your company name

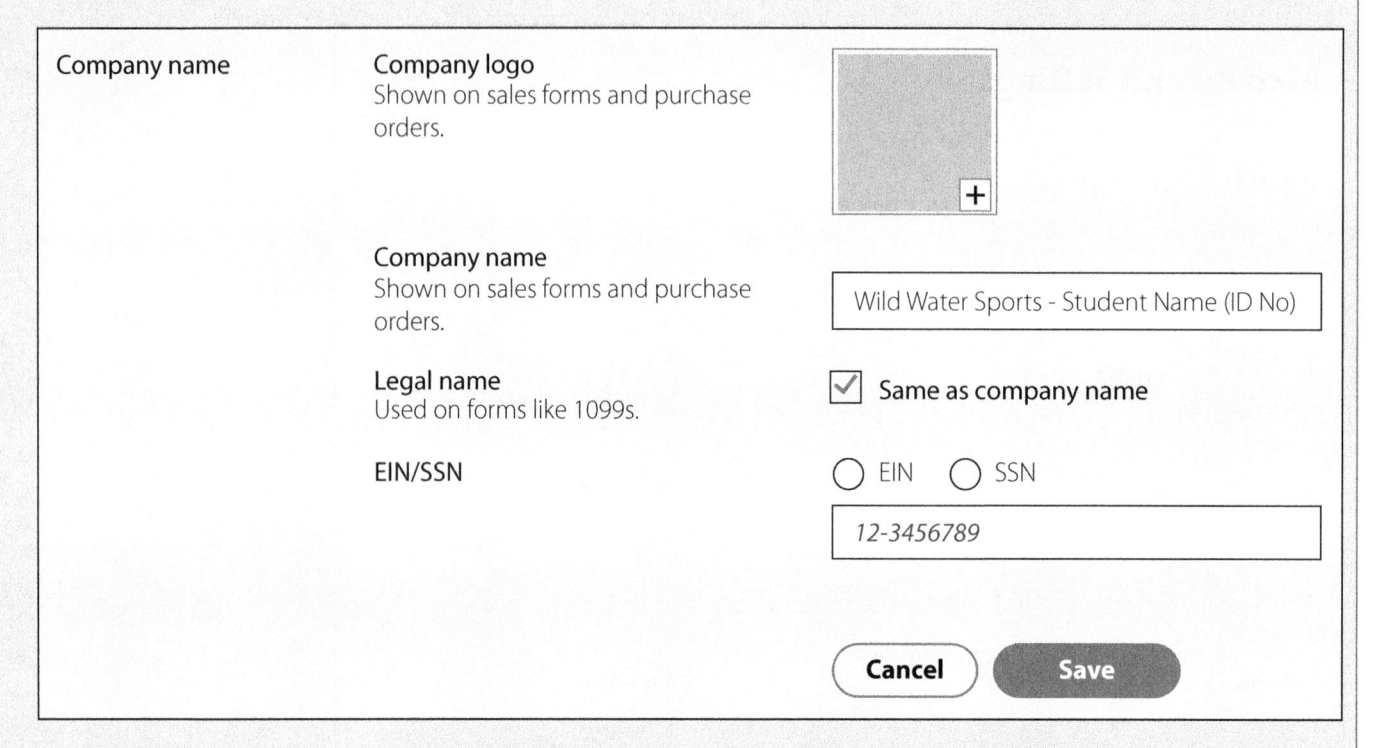

Company name		
	Company logo Shown on sales forms and purchase orders.	[+]
	Company name Shown on sales forms and purchase orders.	Wild Water Sports - Student Name (ID No)
	Legal name Used on forms like 1099s.	☑ Same as company name
	EIN/SSN	○ EIN ○ SSN 12-3456789
		Cancel Save

22 Click **Save** to save your company name change.

23 Click the **Pencil** icon in the Company type section of Account and Settings.

24 Confirm that **Corporation** is selected as the tax form as shown in Figure 2.12. The other options for Company type are shown. Depending on the case you're assigned in Chapter 3, these may be more appropriate selections.

Figure 2.12 Choosing company type

Company type		
	Tax form	Corporation, one or more shareholders (Form 1120) ▼
	Industry	Sole proprietor (Form 1040)
		Partnership or limited liability company (Form 1065)
		Small business corporation, two or more owners (Form 1120S)
		Corporation, one or more shareholders (Form 1120)
Contact info		Nonprofit organization (Form 990)
	Company email	Limited liability
	Customer-facing email	Not sure/Other/None
	Company phone	
	Website	

An Overview of QuickBooks Online **Chapter 2** **37**

25 Click **Save**.

26 Click the **Pencil** icon in the Address section of Account and Settings.

27 Type the street address shown in Figure 2.13 into the Address section of Account and Settings. Then click the full address with city, state, and zip code that displays below the street address.

Figure 2.13 Company address

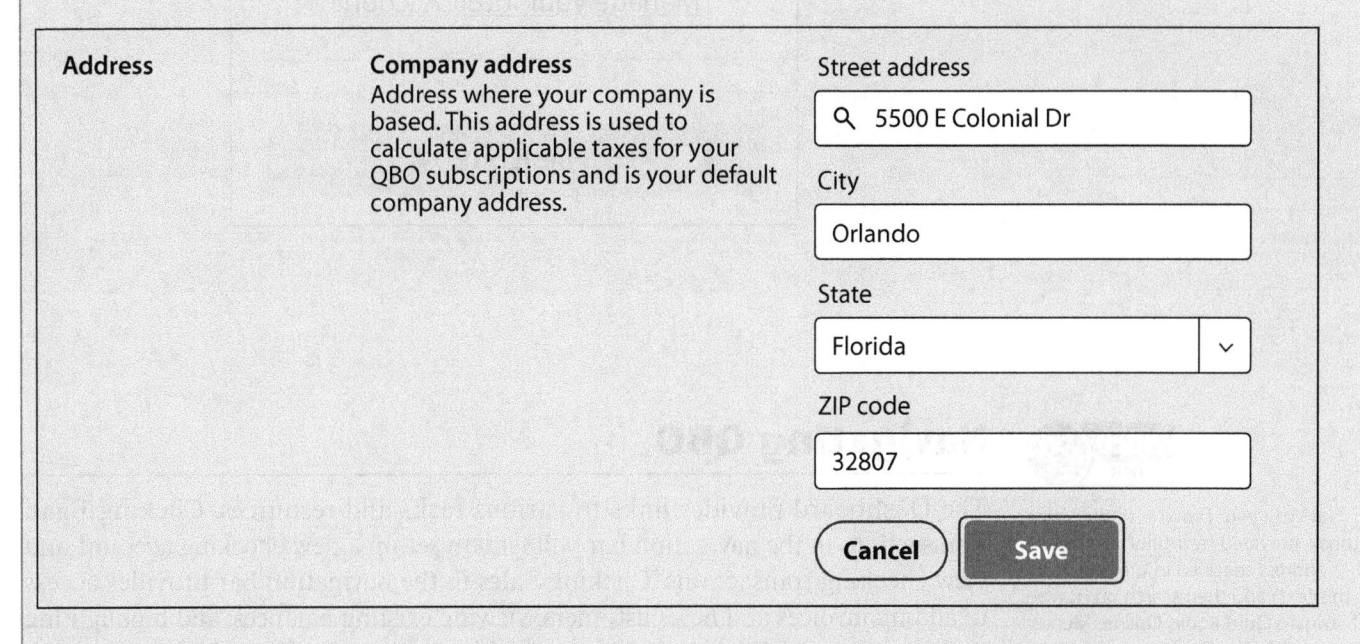

| Address | **Company address**
Address where your company is based. This address is used to calculate applicable taxes for your QBO subscriptions and is your default company address. | Street address
5500 E Colonial Dr

City
Orlando

State
Florida

ZIP code
32807

Cancel **Save** |

28 Click **Save**.

29 Click the **Sales** tab.

30 Make sure that the Preferred invoice terms are set to Net 30 in the Sales form content section and that Track inventory quantity on hand is On in the Products and services section.

31 Close the Settings window.

32 Go to Appendix 1 and complete before moving on.

33 Click **Taxes** then **Sales tax** from the Navigation bar.

34 Click **Sales Tax Settings**.

35 Click **Edit** from the Agency Action column.

36 Type **01/01/2027** in the Start date text box.

37 Click **Save** then click **Dashboard** and then **Home** from the Navigation bar.

38 Sign out of your QBO file by clicking on your account. In Figure 2.14, this is illustrated by clicking on the **S** in the upper right-hand corner of your QBO window and then clicking **Sign out**. Your window will look different.

Figure 2.14

Signing out of QBO

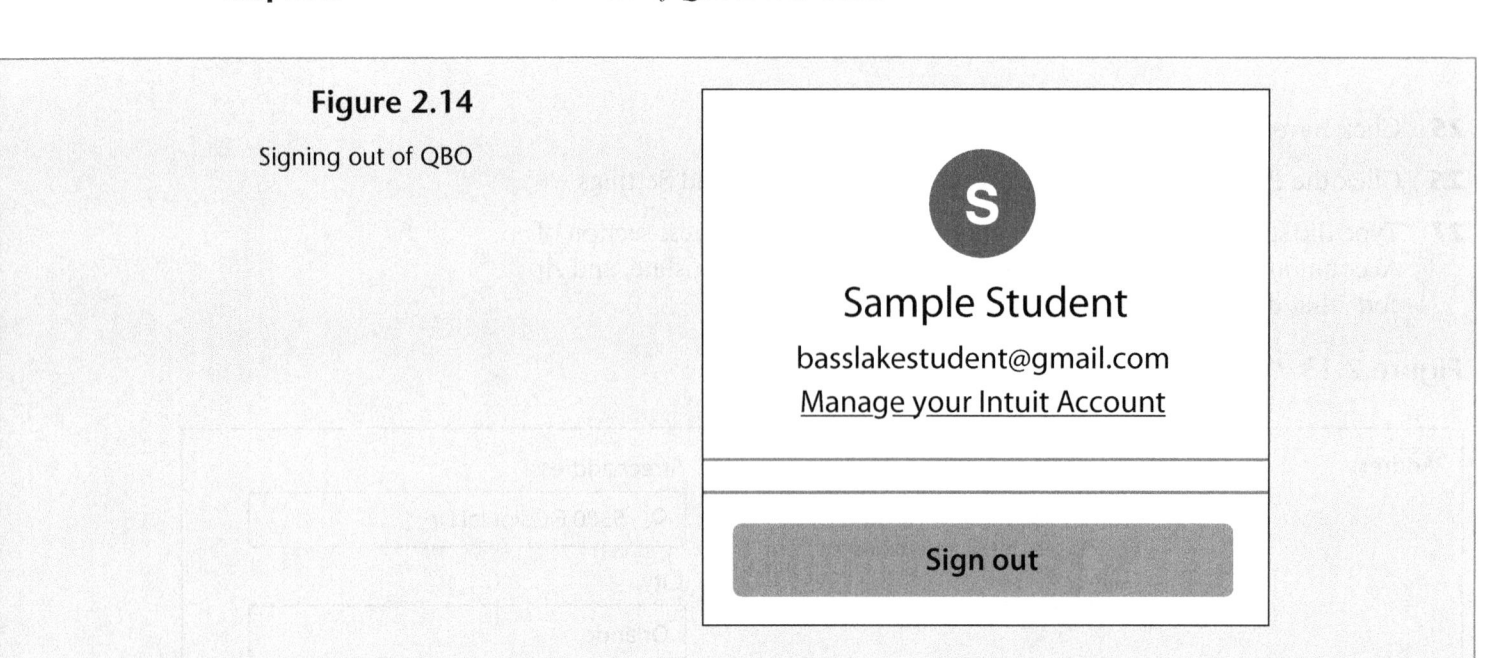

Navigating QBO

Navigate your browser to the Video Tutorials provided by Intuit (see website address specified in the Preface to this text) and then search on how to Navigate QuickBooks Online: Menus, Transactions, and Set Up.

The Dashboard provides links to various tasks and resources. Clicking **Bank Transactions** in the navigation bar will let you set up a new checking account and view checking transactions. Clicking **Sales** in the navigation bar provides access to adding invoices and new customers, viewing existing balances, and highlighting overdue accounts. Clicking **Expenses** provides access to adding new expenses, new vendors, viewing existing balances, and highlighting overdue accounts. Clicking **Payroll** provides access to adding new employees and viewing payroll information. The Transactions and Reports links will be addressed later in this text.

First you'll need to login to your account and retrieve your QBO company.

Keep in mind that in this section, you'll be navigating QBO but not making any substantial changes to your Company. Modifications to your Company will occur in Chapter 3.

To login to the case you modified earlier in this chapter:

1. Type **https://qbo.intuit.com/** into your web browser.
2. Enter your User ID and password and then click **Sign In**.
3. Click **Skip for now** if asked to verify your number.
4. Click **Dashboards** and **Getting things done**. Your window should show the QBO dashboard as shown in Figure 2.15.

An Overview of QuickBooks Online **Chapter 2** **39**

Figure 2.15 Dashboard for Wild Water Sports

[LOGO] **Wild Water Sports - Student Name (ID Number)**

Home Cash flow Planner

SETUP CHECKLIST

✓ Basic business info   100% ⌄

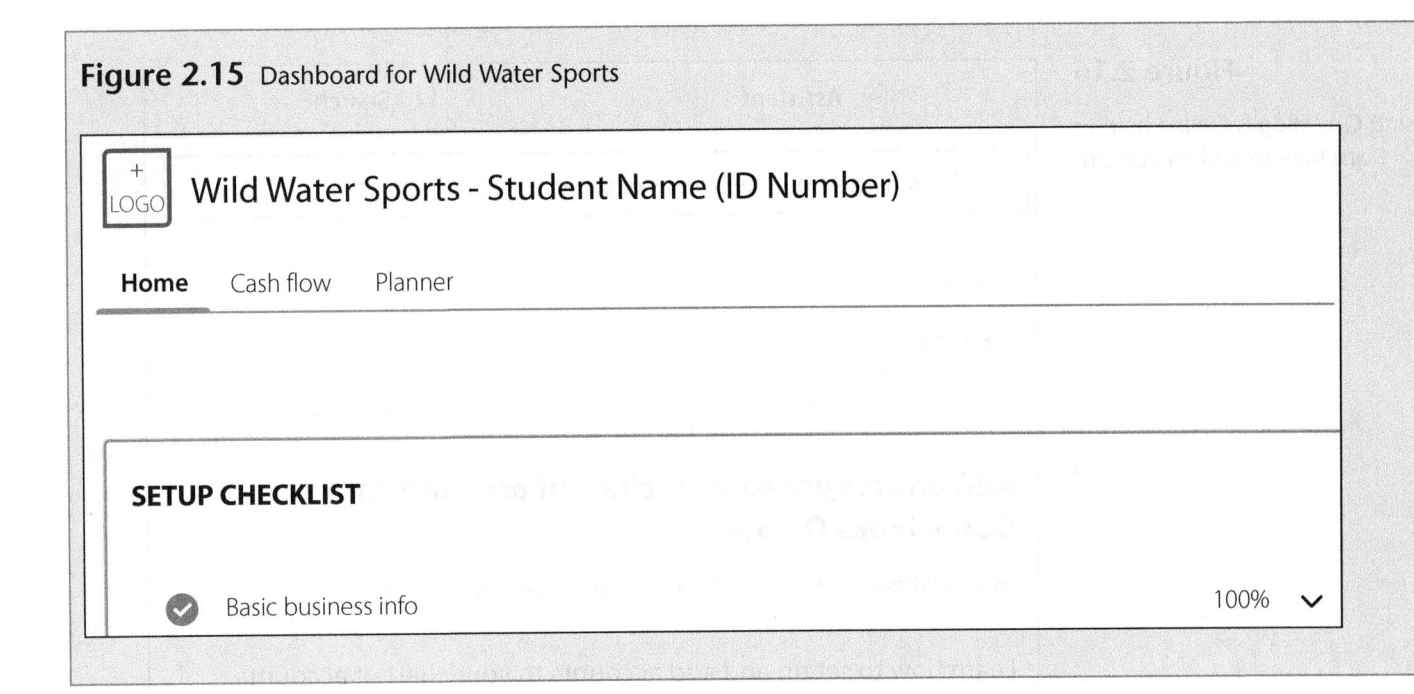

Now that you're back into your QBO Company it's time to explore QBO's help features.

To use QBO help:

1 Click the ⓘ **Help** button located in the upper-right portion of your window and then click the **Search** tab. Type **Add an account** in the Type something text box, then press **[Enter]** to view QB Assistance's response, and then click **Add an account to your Chart of accounts** to view QB Assistance's response shown in Figure 2.16.

2 Click **Back**. Type **sales tax** in the Search text box, then press **[Enter]**, and then click **Set up your sales tax** to view QB Assistance's response shown in Figure 2.17.

Figure 2.16

Using QuickBooks Online help to learn how to add an account

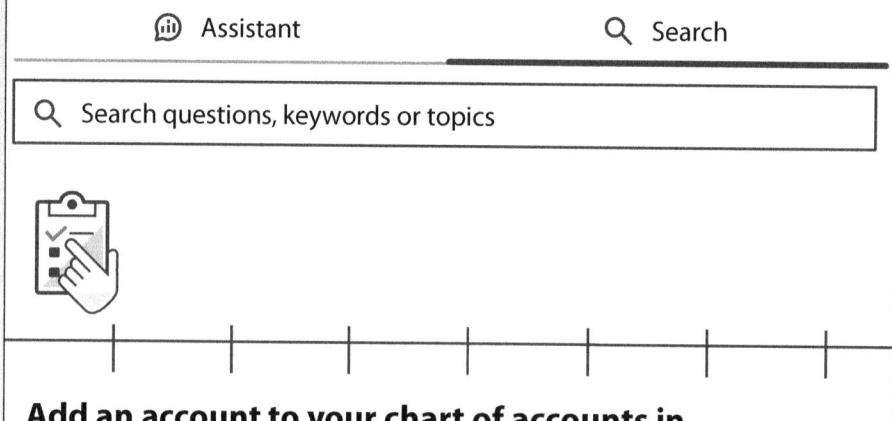

> 🔘 Assistant   🔍 Search
>
> 🔍 Search questions, keywords or topics
>
> **Add an account to your chart of accounts in QuickBooks Online**
>
> by QuickBooks • 👍 2949 • 🕒 Updated 2 weeks ago
>
> Learn how to set up and add accounts to your chart of accounts.
>
> The chart of accounts is a list of all of your accounts in QuickBooks. When you create your company file, QuickBooks automatically customizes your chart of accounts based on your business entity. Keeping your chart of accounts organized helps you when it's time to file your taxes.
>
> You can add more accounts anytime you need to track other types of transactions. Here's how to add more accounts to your chart of accounts.

Figure 2.17 Help with sales tax

> **Set up and use automated sales tax in QuickBooks Online**
>
> by QuickBooks • 👍 1827 • 🕒 Updated 3 weeks ago
>
> Learn how to set up and use the automated sales tax feature in QuickBooks Online.
>
> QuickBooks can automatically do the sales tax calculations for you on your invoices and receipts for easy and accurate filings. Then, it lets you know when your tax payment is due, so you can file on time and avoid extra fees.
>
> Here's how to set it all up and get started:

An Overview of QuickBooks Online **Chapter 2** 41

QuickBooks help is, to be frank, not very helpful. Most of what you need to be effective using QBO is outlined in this text. Now let's learn how to navigate QBO.

To navigate QBO:

1. Close the Help window, then click the [+ New] button at the top of the Dashboard to view the menu items available as shown in Figure 2.18.

Figure 2.18 The + New menu

CUSTOMERS	VENDORS	EMPLOYEES	OTHER
Invoice	Expense	Payroll ↑	Bank deposit
Receive payment	Check	Time entry	Transfer
Estimate	Bill	Add employee ↑	Journal entry
Credit memo	Pay bills	Add contractor	Statement
Sales receipt	Purchase order		Inventory qty adjustment
Refund receipt	Vendor credit		Pay down credit card
Delayed credit	Credit card credit		Add product/service
Delayed charge	Print checks		
Add customer	Add vendor		

Show less

2. Click outside the + New menu to close the + New menu, then click **Sales** from the navigation bar, and then click **Customers** as shown in Figure 2.19.

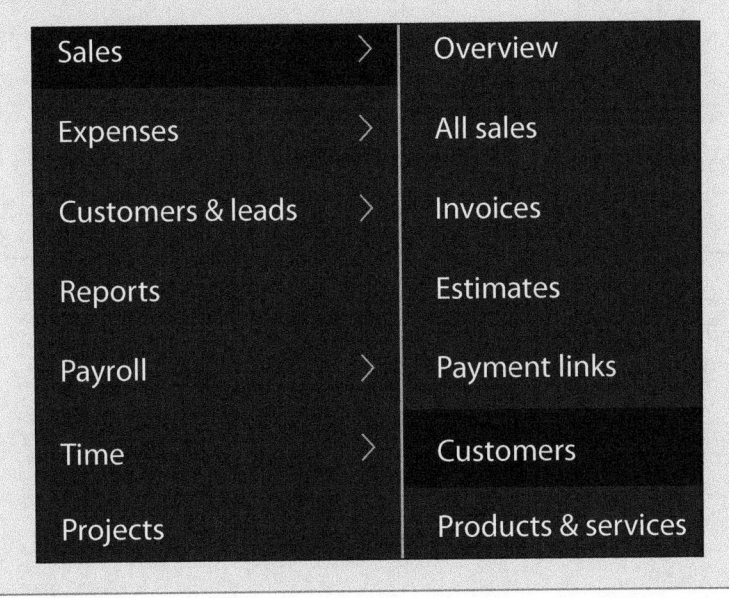

Sales >	Overview
Expenses >	All sales
Customers & leads >	Invoices
Reports	Estimates
Payroll >	Payment links
Time >	Customers
Projects	Products & services

Figure 2.19

Adding customers

3. Then click **Add customer manually** to view Figure 2.20. As you have not yet entered any customers, QBO will ask you to add your first customer. You will do this later in Chapter 3. Remember QBO is an online application, and Intuit will change it often.

Figure 2.20 Customer information window

Customer	✕

Name and contact

Title	First name	Middle name	Last name	Suffix

Company name

Customer display name *

Email

Phone number

Mobile number

Fax

Other

Website

Name to print on checks

☐ Is a sub-customer

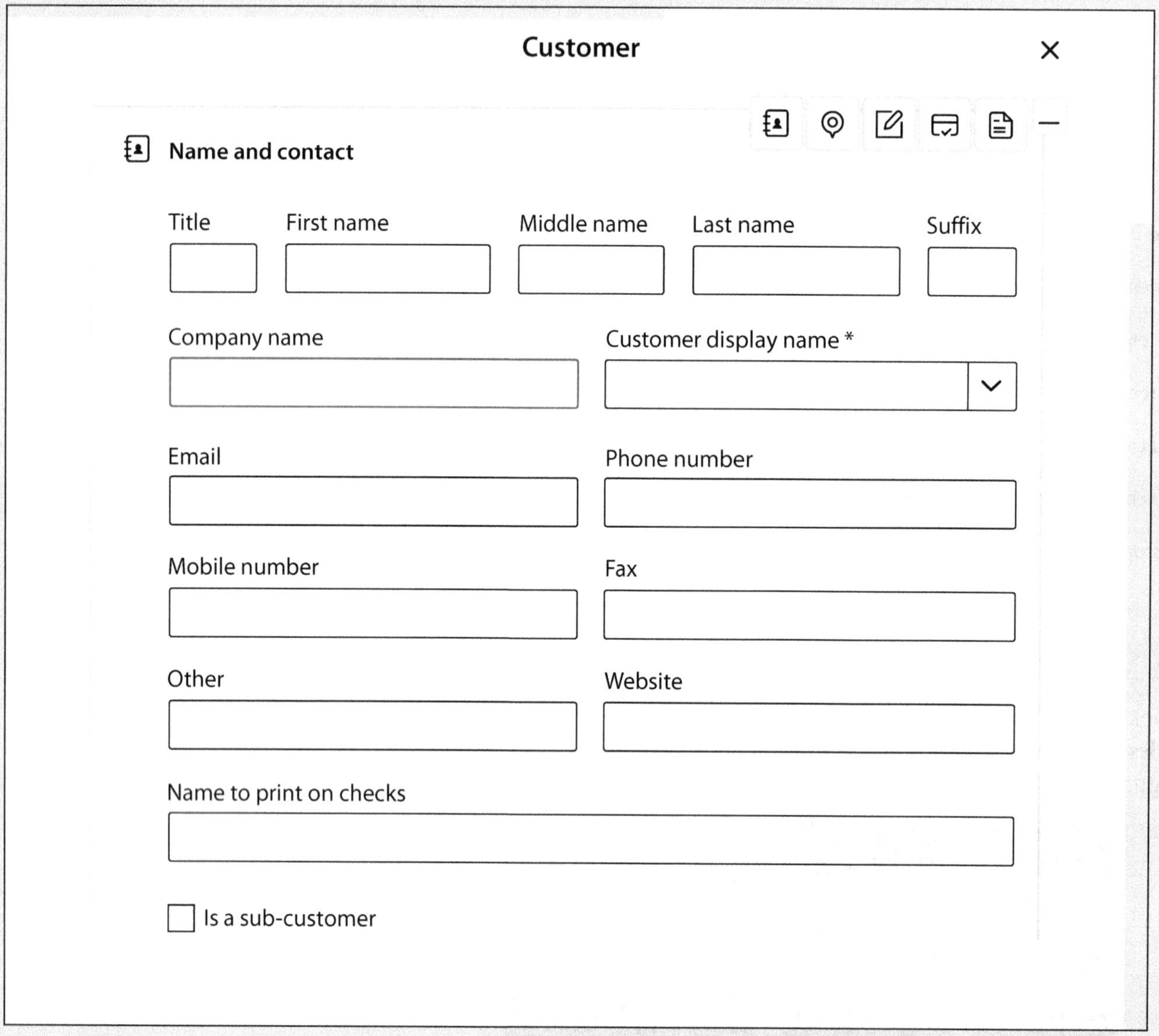

4. Click **X** from the Customer information window to close the Customer window, then click **Expenses** from the navigation bar, then click **Vendors**, and then click **Add vendor** to view Figure 2.21.

An Overview of QuickBooks Online **Chapter 2** **43**

Figure 2.21 Vendor Information window

Vendor

Name and contact

Company name

Vendor display name *

Title   First name   Middle name   Last name   Suffix

Email

Phone number

Mobile number

Fax

Other

Website

Name to print on checks

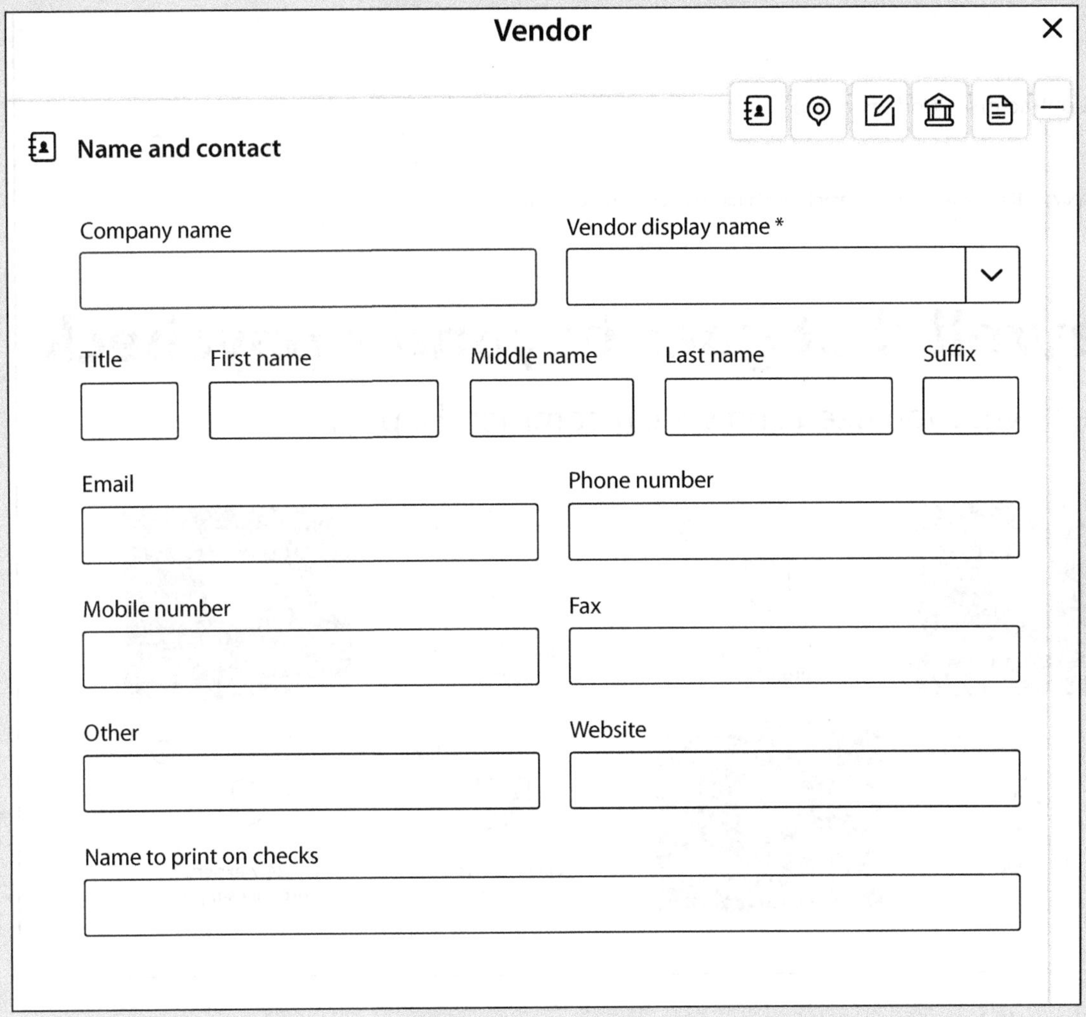

5. Click **X** to close the Vendor information window, then click **Payroll** from the navigation bar, and then click **Employees** to view Figure 2.22. In Chapter 3, you'll add employees by clicking **Add employee** located at the top of the window shown. Do not click Add employee now. Once again in this chapter, we're just showing you how to navigate QBO.

6. Click the **Gear** icon located in the upper-right corner to view Figure 2.23. This menu gives you access to details about your company, lists (such as the chart of accounts, products and services, terms, etc.), tools (such as reconciling accounts and budgeting), and your profile, which will give you the ability to switch QBO companies.

Figure 2.22 Getting started with payroll

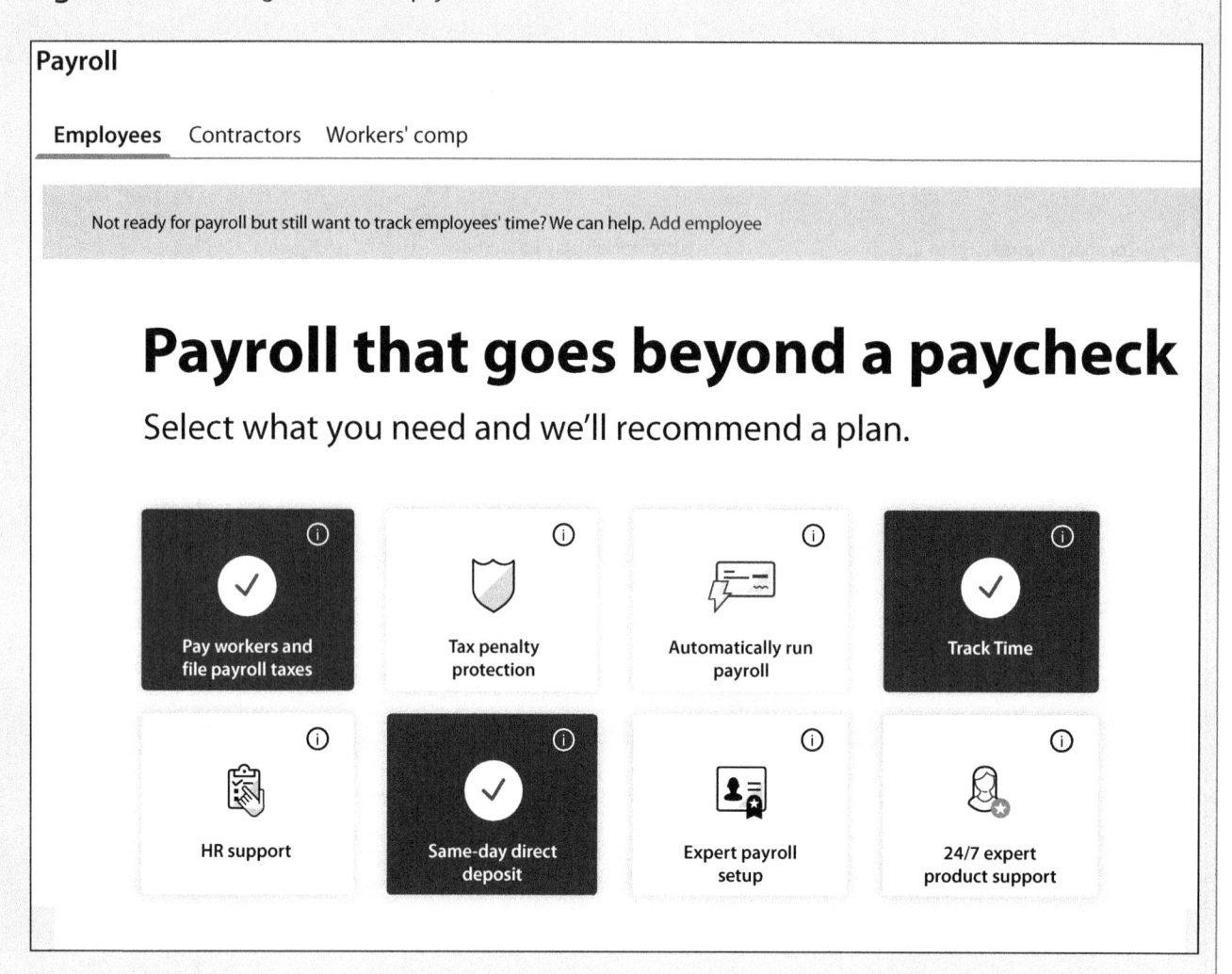

Payroll
Employees   Contractors   Workers' comp
Not ready for payroll but still want to track employees' time? We can help. Add employee
Payroll that goes beyond a paycheck
Select what you need and we'll recommend a plan.
Pay workers and file payroll taxes · Tax penalty protection · Automatically run payroll · Track Time
HR support · Same-day direct deposit · Expert payroll setup · 24/7 expert product support

Figure 2.23 Gear window

YOUR COMPANY	LISTS	TOOLS	PROFILE
Account and settings	All lists	Order checks	Subscriptions and billing
Manage users	Products and services	Import data	Feedback
Custom form styles	Recurring transactions	Import desktop data	Privacy
Chart of accounts	Attachments	Export data	Switch company
Additional info	Custom fields	Reconcile	
	Tags	Budgeting	
	Rules	Audit log	
		SmartLook	
		Resolution center	

7 If you had created more than one company you could click **Switch company** under the Profile heading to view Figure 2.24. Since you have only created one company, the Switch company text will not appear. However, if your instructor assigns you an additional case (they can assign you up to 3 more), more files will be shown such as you see in this figure. Click **Wild Water Sports** to return to your QBO company Dashboard.

Figure 2.24

Switching companies

Assigning an Instructor as the Company's "Accountant"

Your instructor may require you to assign them as your company's accountant. You do this so they, as your accountant, will always have access to your company files for grading and evaluation purposes. This will also assist the instructor in answering questions you may have about your company. The process of assigning an accountant to your company involves a brief interview in which you will provide your instructor's email address and name. Make sure you have that information before beginning this process. Your instructor will receive an email inviting them to be your accountant. Once the instructor accepts your invitation, they will have access to your company and the instructor's name will appear in the Accounting Firms section of the Manage Users page.

However, if your instructor is using the Intuit Educator Portal, you will not have to assign them as your accountant. Once they have assigned you a case, they will always be able to view your QBO file.

"How to Give Your Accountant Access to Your QuickBooks"

To assign an accountant to your company, do the following:

1. Click **My accountant** from the navigation bar.
2. Type your instructor's email address in the space provided as shown in Figure 2.25.
3. Click the **Invite** button.
4. Once your instructor accepts your QuickBooks invitation, you'll be good to go.

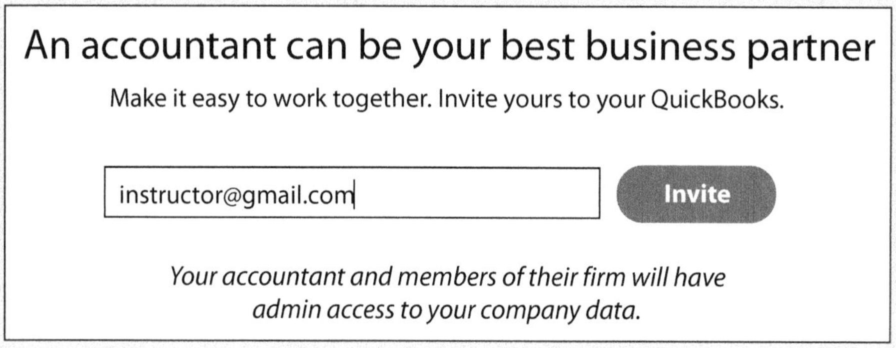

Figure 2.25
Inviting your instructor to be your accountant

An accountant can be your best business partner
Make it easy to work together. Invite yours to your QuickBooks.

instructor@gmail.com   [Invite]

Your accountant and members of their firm will have admin access to your company data.

Video Tutorials for QuickBooks Online (Developed and Maintained by Intuit)

Intuit, the developer of QBO, has made available video tutorials. The tutorials are step-by-step videos to learn your way around QuickBooks.

Throughout this text, the author will reference videos in the appropriate chapters. To view all tutorials, navigate your browser to https://quickbooks.intuit.com/global/learn-and-support/video-tutorials/.

To view two videos on QuickBooks Online, do the following:

1. Navigate your browser to the web address: https://quickbooks.intuit.com/global/learn-and-support/video-tutorials/. A partial view of that site is shown in Figure 2.26.
2. Click **Introduction to QuickBooks Online**. Your window should look like Figure 2.27.

An Overview of QuickBooks Online **Chapter 2** 47

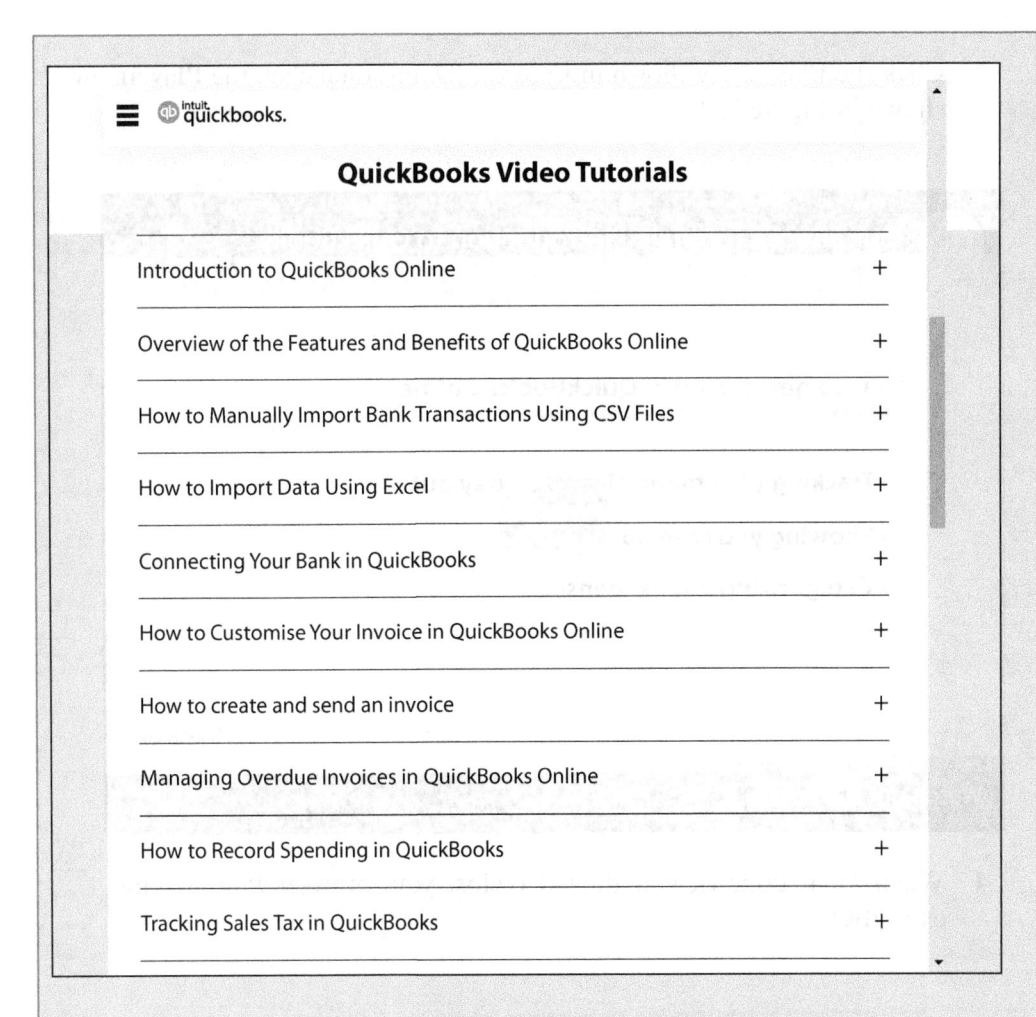

Figure 2.26

Video tutorials for QBO

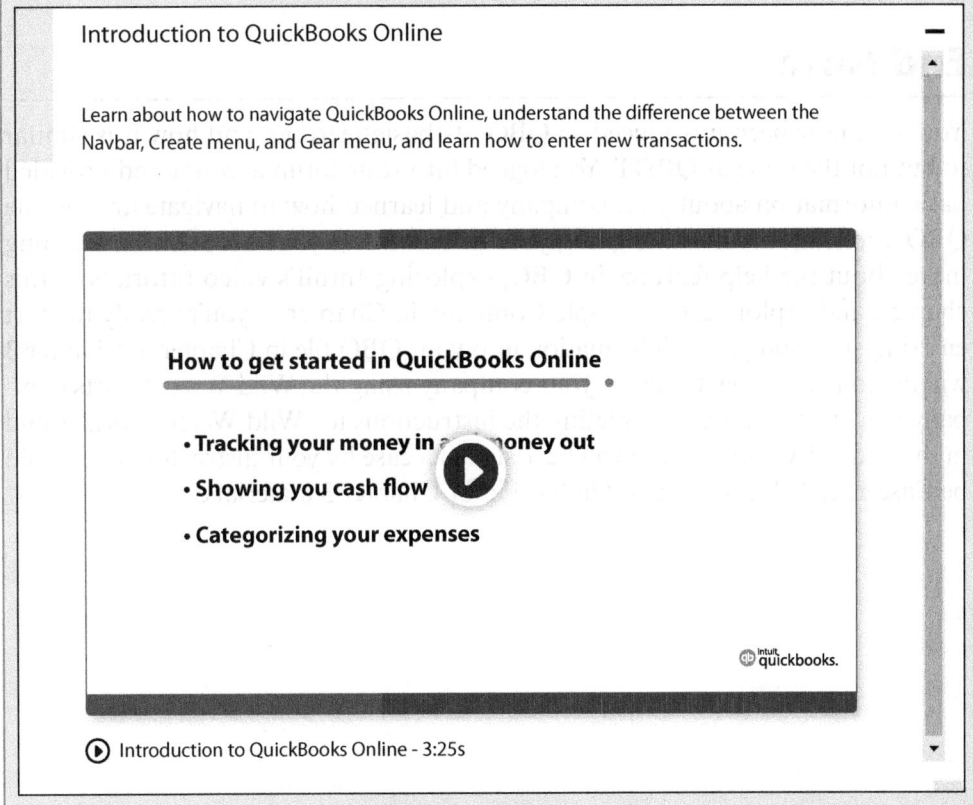

Figure 2.27

Accessing a video tutorial introducing QuickBooks Online

3 Click the **Play** arrow shown in Figure 2.27 and then click the **Play** arrow shown in Figure 2.28.

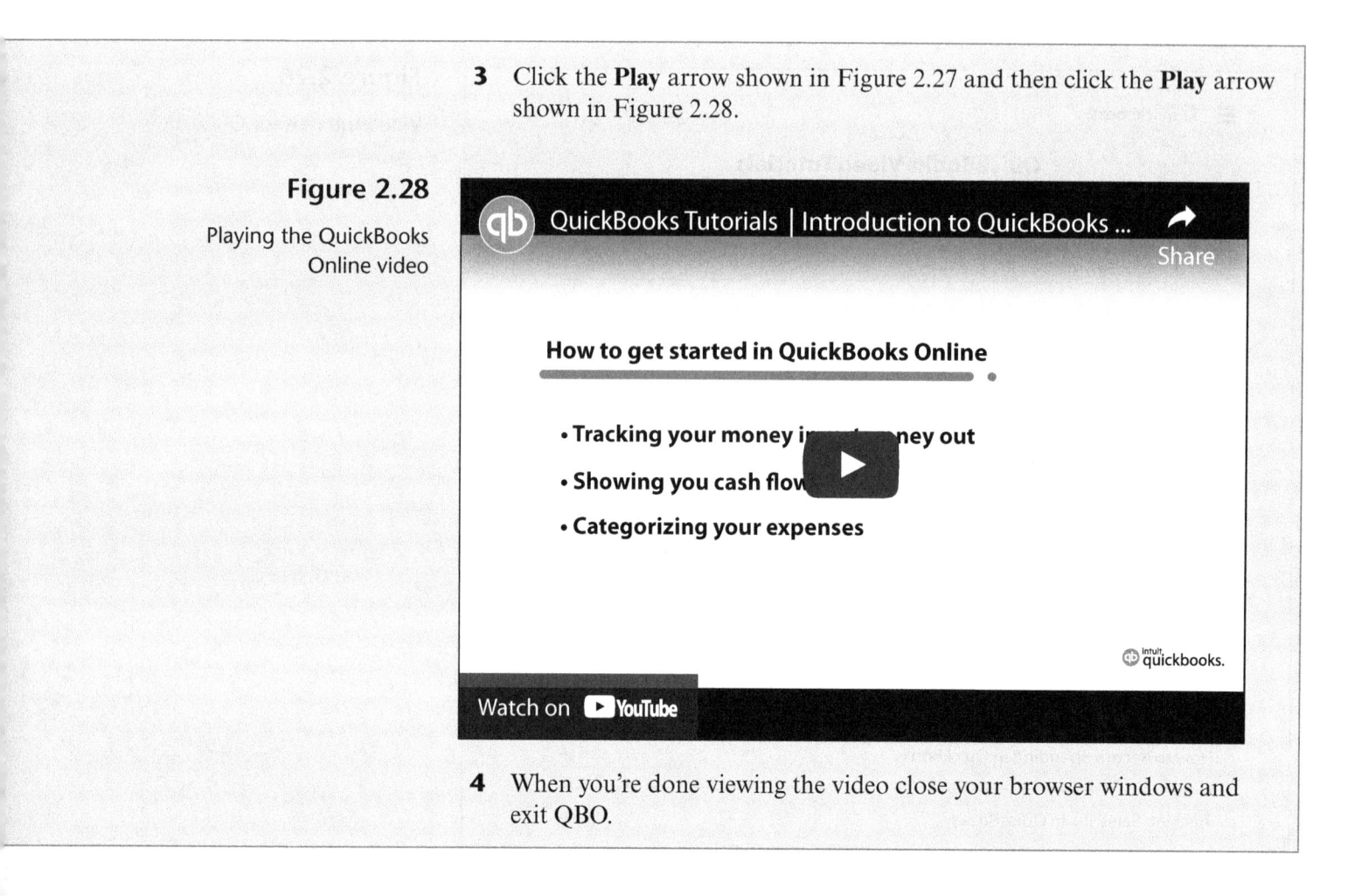

Figure 2.28

Playing the QuickBooks Online video

4 When you're done viewing the video close your browser windows and exit QBO.

End Note

You have now been introduced to QBO, its basic features, and how it is similar to but not the same as QBDT. You logged into your Intuit account and provided basic information about your company and learned how to navigate around the QBO application. After assigning your instructor as your accountant, learning more about the help features in QBO, exploring Intuit's video tutorials in this chapter, and exploring the Sample Company in Chapter 1, you're ready to start entering your company's information into your QBO file in Chapter 3. Chapter 3 will demonstrate how to set up your company using the Wild Water Sports company you created. After completing the instructions for Wild Water Sports found in the body of Chapter 3 you will be assigned a case by your instructor. This could be Case 1, 2, 3, 4, 5, or 6 found in the end of Chapter 3 materials.

practice

Chapter 2 Questions

1. How are QBO and QBDT different in the number of companies they can manage per license?
2. Does QBO work offline, without an Internet connection?
3. Do you need to back up QBO files?
4. How are QBO and QBDT similar?
5. What information do you need to supply to assign your instructor as the company's accountant?

Chapter 2 Matching

a. QBO _____ Click to access help
b. QBDT _____ Click to find past transactions
c. Gear icon _____ Click to access QBO employee information
d. Payroll _____ Online version of QuickBooks
e. Navigation bar _____ Click to add your instructor as your accountant
f. (+ New) icon _____ Provides links to QBO tasks and resources
g. Magnifying glass _____ Windows desktop version of QuickBooks
h. Help (?) icon _____ Click to add any transaction
i. Manage Users _____ Click to manage your subscription, users, and settings
j. Dashboard _____ On the left of the Dashboard, it shows a menu of items

chapter 3

Setting Up a New Company: Establishing a Chart of Accounts, Beginning Balances, Customers, Vendors, and Products/Services

Student Learning Outcomes

Upon completion of this chapter, the student will be able to do the following:

- Log into their account
- Change company settings
- Modify the chart of accounts; establish beginning balances; and create new customers, vendors, products, and services
- Close Opening Balance Equity and create and print a Balance Sheet
- Create, print, and export a Transaction Detail by Account report

Overview

You began this process in Chapter 2 when you created your account and provided basic information about the Wild Water Sports company, including the company name, address, industry, type, and so on.

Now you're going to revisit the Wild Water Sports company you worked on in Chapter 2. Each of the following chapters will work the same way. To begin, you will navigate your browser to Wild Water Sports company. The text will demonstrate how to do certain tasks, such as modify defaults, add a new account, add a new transaction, and so on. These demonstrations will occur in the Wild Water Sports company.

Each section of every chapter will begin with a demonstration using the Wild Water Sports company. That is followed by you completing an end-of-chapter case. In the case, you will be asked to perform tasks similar to those demonstrated in the Wild Water Sports company, but now in your new case. The tasks you accomplish on your Wild Water Sports company and your case are permanent and will be there even after you close your QBO browser window. There is no Save File or Save File As command in QBO. Everything is saved for you.

After you make changes to the Wild Water Sports company in each chapter, it is critical that you verify your work. Do that by comparing the trial balance you create at the end of each chapter with the trial balance figure shown at the end of each chapter in this text.

Company Settings

Your first task will be to update the Wild Water Sports company settings.

To modify Wild Water Sports company settings, do the following:

1 Open your Internet browser.

2 Type **https://app.qbo.intuit.com/app/login** into your browser's address text box. If you are using your own personal computer you may be presented with your email or user id. If so, click **Sign In** and then your password. If you are using any other computer you will be required to provide your email or user id as well as your password. You may have to click **Use a different user ID**. If you have been assigned more than one company, click **Wild Water Sports** from the Choose your company window.

3 From the Wild Water Sports company home page, click the **Gear** icon to manage your settings shown in Figure 3.1.

Figure 3.1 Settings

YOUR COMPANY	LISTS	TOOLS	PROFILE
Account and settings	All lists	Order checks	Subscriptions and billing
Manage users	Products and services	Import data	Feedback
Custom form styles	Recurring transactions	Import desktop data	Privacy
Chart of accounts	Attachments	Export data	Switch company
Additional info	Custom fields	Reconcile	
	Tags	Budgeting	
	Rules	Audit log	
		SmartLook	
		Resolution center	

You're viewing QuickBooks in Accountant view. Find out more   Switch to Business view

4 Click **Account and settings**. The first screen is the Wild Water Sports company information shown in Figure 3.2. This is where you will change your company's name, tax form, industry, address, and so on.

Figure 3.2 Company settings

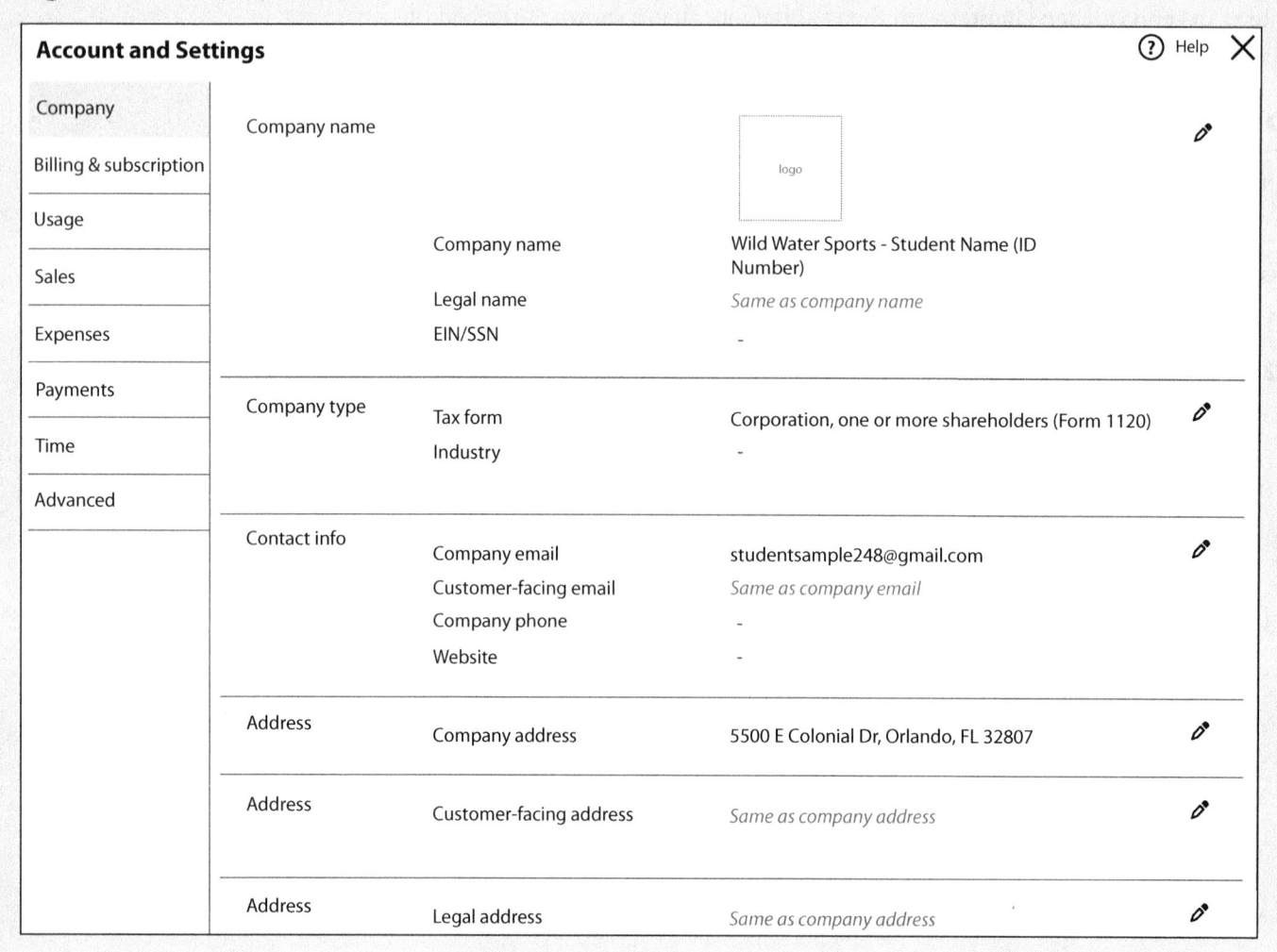

Account and Settings				? Help ✕
Company	Company name		[logo]	✎
Billing & subscription		Company name	Wild Water Sports - Student Name (ID Number)	
Usage		Legal name	*Same as company name*	
Sales		EIN/SSN	-	
Expenses	Company type	Tax form	Corporation, one or more shareholders (Form 1120)	✎
Payments		Industry	-	
Time	Contact info	Company email	studentsample248@gmail.com	✎
Advanced		Customer-facing email	*Same as company email*	
		Company phone	-	
		Website	-	
	Address	Company address	5500 E Colonial Dr, Orlando, FL 32807	✎
	Address	Customer-facing address	*Same as company address*	✎
	Address	Legal address	*Same as company address*	✎

5. Click the **pencil icon** in the Company type section then type **store retailer** into the Industry text box. A drop-down list will appear. Select **All other miscellaneous store retailers** as shown in Figure 3.3. Be sure that Form 1120 is selected as the tax form.

Figure 3.3 Selecting an Industry

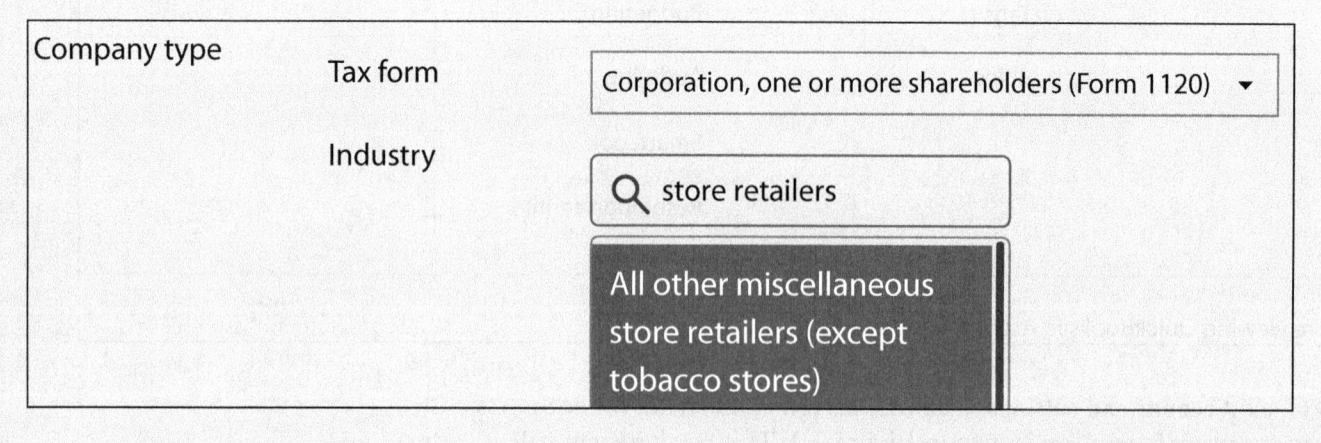

Company type	Tax form	Corporation, one or more shareholders (Form 1120) ▼
	Industry	🔍 store retailers
		All other miscellaneous store retailers (except tobacco stores)

6 Click **Save**.

7 Click the **pencil icon** in the Company name section and type **99-6854102** in the EIN text box and select the **EIN** button as shown in Figure 3.4.

Figure 3.4 Add an EIN

Legal name Used on forms like 1099s.	☑ Same as company name
EIN	● EIN ○ SSN
	99-6854102
	Cancel Save

8 Click **Save**.

9 View the Sales, Expenses, Payments, Time, and Advance tabs noting default selections. Do not change these. Close the Account and Settings window.

Once you have modified the company settings, it is time to modify the chart of accounts.

Modify the Chart of Accounts and Establish Beginning Balances

You will continue your use of the Wild Water Sports company (referred to as WWS in the future) to learn the process of creating, modifying, and deleting accounts and of establishing beginning balances. If you are continuing from above, you will not need to open the file again. If not, follow the steps above to reopen the WWS company. If you leave and return, everything you modified will be saved automatically.

Creating accounts and related beginning balances only occurs when you are utilizing QBO for the first time and your business has been in operation for some time. The transition to QBO from a previous accounting system will indicate business events and balances that occurred prior to the first date of QBO use.

Navigate your browser to the Video Tutorials provided by Intuit (see website address specified in the Preface to this text) and then search on how to set up your chart of accounts.

In this section, you will be adding new checking, inventory, prepaid rent, long-term debt, and common stock accounts to the WWS company. You will also be establishing beginning balances for checking, accounts receivable, prepaid rent, inventory, and accounts payable. Every time you add a beginning balance, an equal and opposite amount is recorded to the Opening Balance Equity account (to keep debits and credits in balance).

QBO lets you establish a beginning amount for all of these accounts using basic journal entries. We will do that for some accounts, such as accounts receivable and accounts payable. For the other accounts, such as checking, inventory, prepaid rent, long-term debt, and common stock, you will set some beginning balances when you set up a new account.

When a new account is added, its account type needs to be specified. Asset account types include the following: bank, accounts receivable, other current assets, fixed assets, and other assets. Liability account types include the following: accounts payable, credit cards, other current liabilities, and long-term liabilities. Equity is its own account type. Income account types include sales of product income and services. Expense account types include cost of goods sold, expenses, and other expense. Every account needs to be assigned to one of these account types. This will dictate where the account appears in all reports, especially the income statement, balance sheet, and statement of cash flows. The detail type will further define where the account appears under its account type. Examples of bank account detail types include cash on hand, checking, money market, and savings.

To begin, let's add a new checking account with a beginning balance of $25,000.00.

To add a new checking account to the chart of accounts and establish a beginning balance, do the following:

1 Click the **Gear** icon and then click **Chart of Accounts**.

2 Click the **New** button in the upper-right corner of the chart of accounts.

3 Fill in the text boxes as shown in Figure 3.5.

4 Click the text **Starting date and opening balance** and then fill in the text boxes as shown in Figure 3.6.

5 Click the **Save** button to view the modified chart of accounts shown in Figure 3.7, which now includes a new checking account with a balance of $25,000.00.

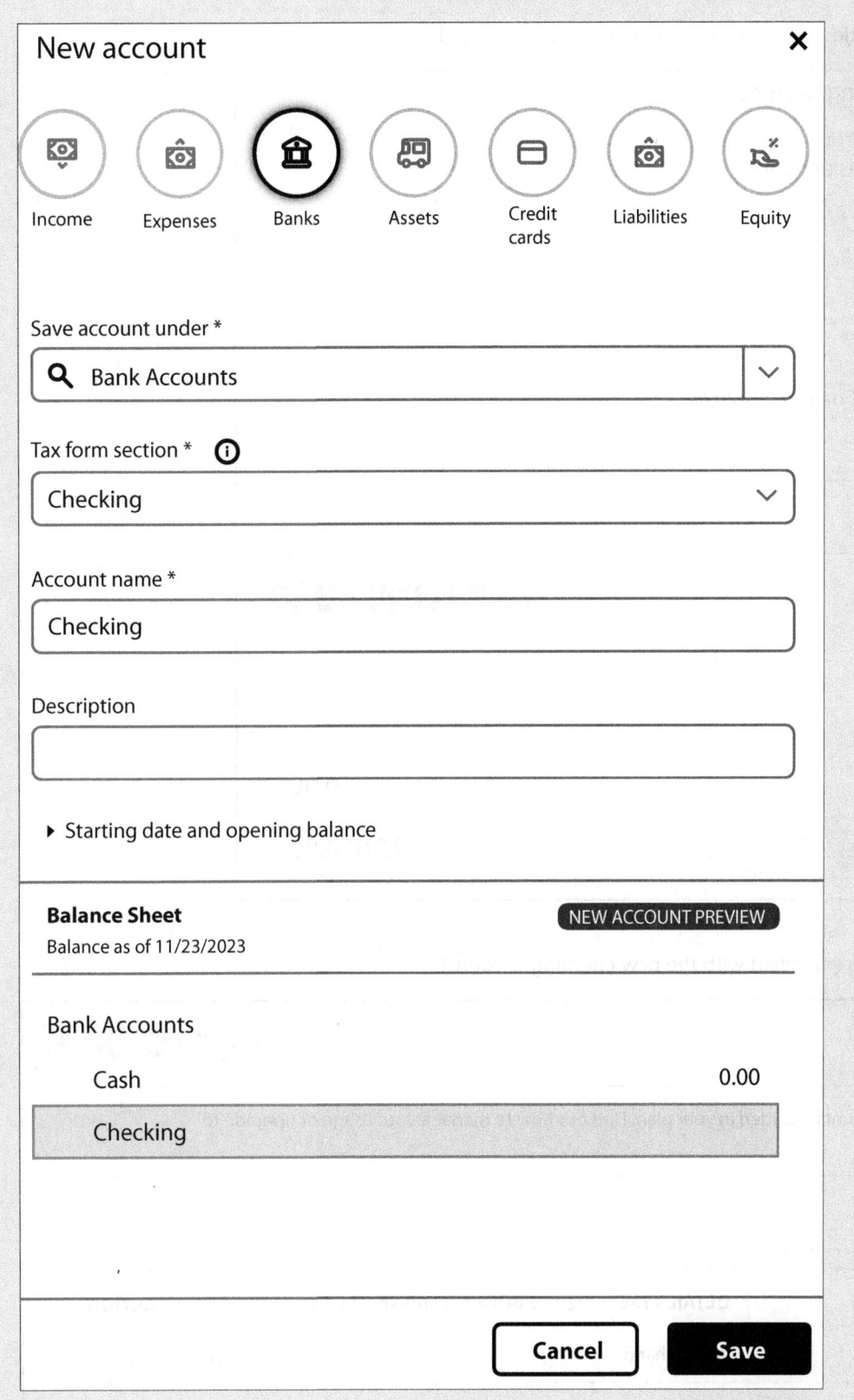

Figure 3.5

Account (adding a new bank account)

Figure 3.6 Account (completing the addition of a new checking account)

▼ Starting date and opening balance

More info on opening balances
Date to start tracking this account in QuickBooks

Other date ▼

Start date

12/31/2026 📅

Account balance at end of day 12/30/2026

25000

Balance Sheet   NEW ACCOUNT PREVIEW
Balance as of 11/23/2023

Bank Accounts

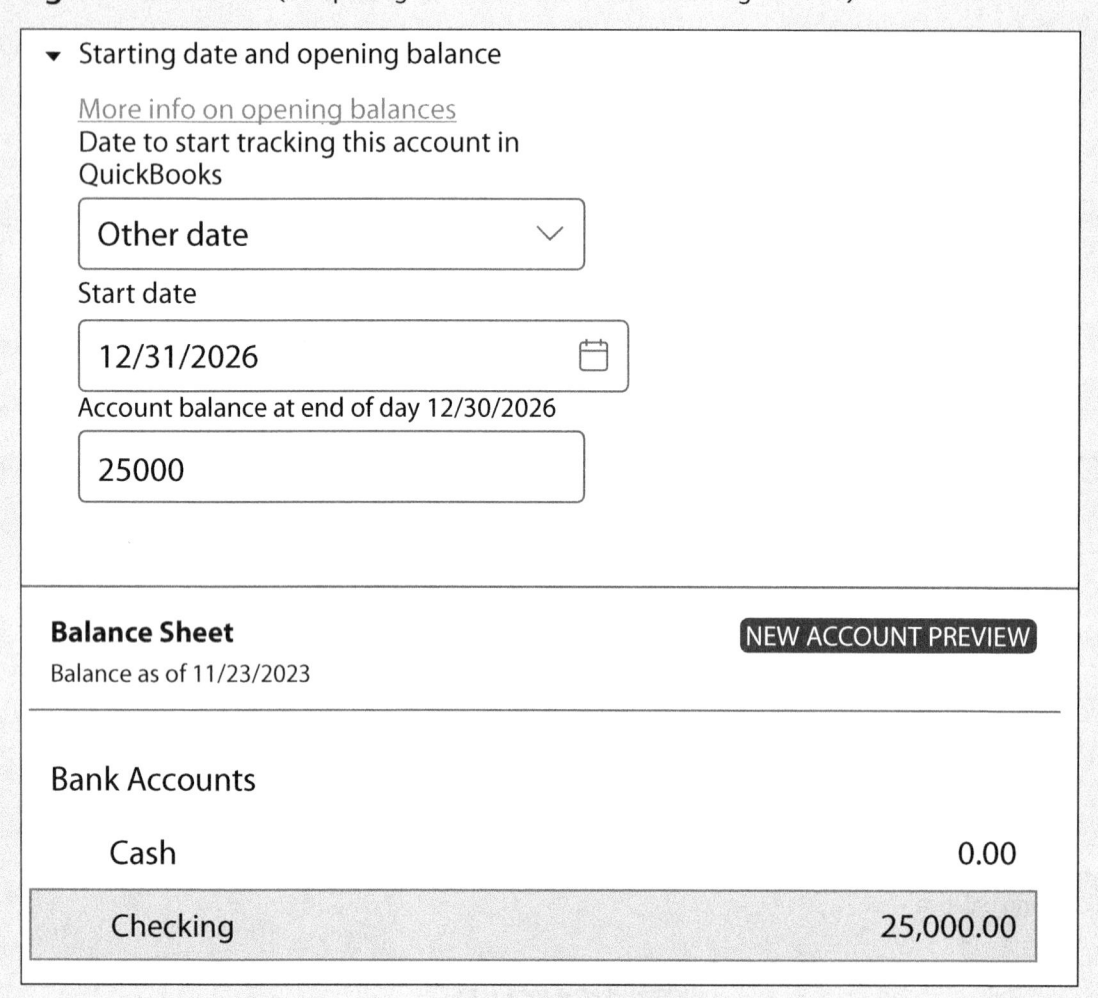

| Cash | 0.00 |
| Checking | 25,000.00 |

Figure 3.7 Chart of Accounts (modified with the new checking account)

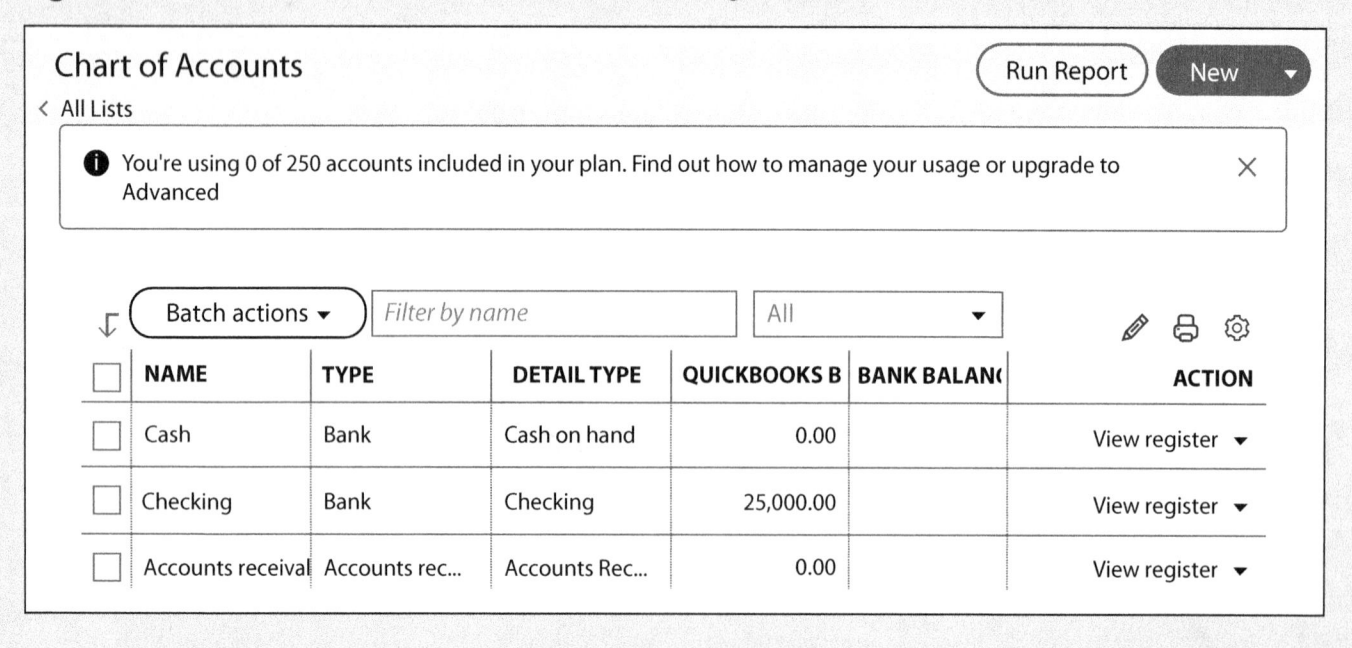

Chart of Accounts   Run Report   New ▼
‹ All Lists

ⓘ You're using 0 of 250 accounts included in your plan. Find out how to manage your usage or upgrade to Advanced ✕

Batch actions ▼   Filter by name   All ▼

NAME	TYPE	DETAIL TYPE	QUICKBOOKS B	BANK BALANC	ACTION
Cash	Bank	Cash on hand	0.00		View register ▼
Checking	Bank	Checking	25,000.00		View register ▼
Accounts receival	Accounts rec...	Accounts Rec...	0.00		View register ▼

So far, we have added $25,000 to the assets of the WWS company as of 12/31/2026. The Opening Balance Equity account has also increased as the result of this adjustment. To continue, let's add a new product. In QBO, products are merchandise a company purchases from a vendor, maintains in inventory, and then sells to customers. Services are efforts made by a company to add value to a customer. In the WWS company, an inventory account exists. If you create a new company, an inventory account may not exist. However, when you add a new product, a new inventory account, called inventory asset, will automatically be created.

Navigate your browser to the Video Tutorials provided by Intuit (see website address specified in the Preface to this text) and then search on how top create an inventory product.

To add a new product and service, do the following:

1. View the chart of accounts and note the Inventory account with a QuickBooks balance of $0.00.
2. Click the **Gear** icon and click **Products and services** from the Lists column.
3. Click **Add an item**.
4. Select **Inventory item** from the Item type information list.
5. Type **Malibu Sunset LX** as the new product in the Name text box.
6. Click the **drop-down arrow** in the Category text box then click **Add New**. Type **Boats** as the Category name, then click **Save**.
7. Type **1** in the Initial quantity on hand text box and **12/31/2026** in the As of date text box.
8. Select **Inventory** as the Inventory asset account.
9. Type **Malibu Sunset LX** in the Description and Purchasing information text boxes.
10. Type **60000** in the Price/rate text box and **48000** in the Purchase cost text box.
11. Select **Sales** as the Income account and **Cost of Goods Sold** as the Expense account.
12. Accept **Taxable - standard rate** from the Sales tax section. Type **Malibu Boats** in the Preferred Vendor text box then click **Add new Malibu Boats**, then click **Save**. Your window should look like Figure 3.8.
13. Click **Create new**.
14. In the Sales Products & Services window click **New**. Click **Service**.
15. Type **Engine Service** as the name of a new service.
16. Check the **I sell this product/service to my customers** check box and then uncheck the **I purchase this service from a vendor** check box.
17. Type **Engine Service** as the Description in the sales forms text box.
18. Type **250** in the Price/rate text box then click **Create New**.
19. Click the **Gear** icon then click **Chart of accounts**.
20. Click **New** then click **Income**.
21. Select **Income** from the Save account under drop-down list text box.

Figure 3.8 Product/Service information window

Add a new product

Basic info

Name*

Malibu Sunset LX

Item type

Inventory item

SKU

Category

Boats

Add an image

Inventory

Initial quantity on hand*

1

As of date*

12/31/2026

What's the as of date?

Reorder point

What's the reorder point?

Inventory asset account*

Inventory

Figure 3.8 (Continued)

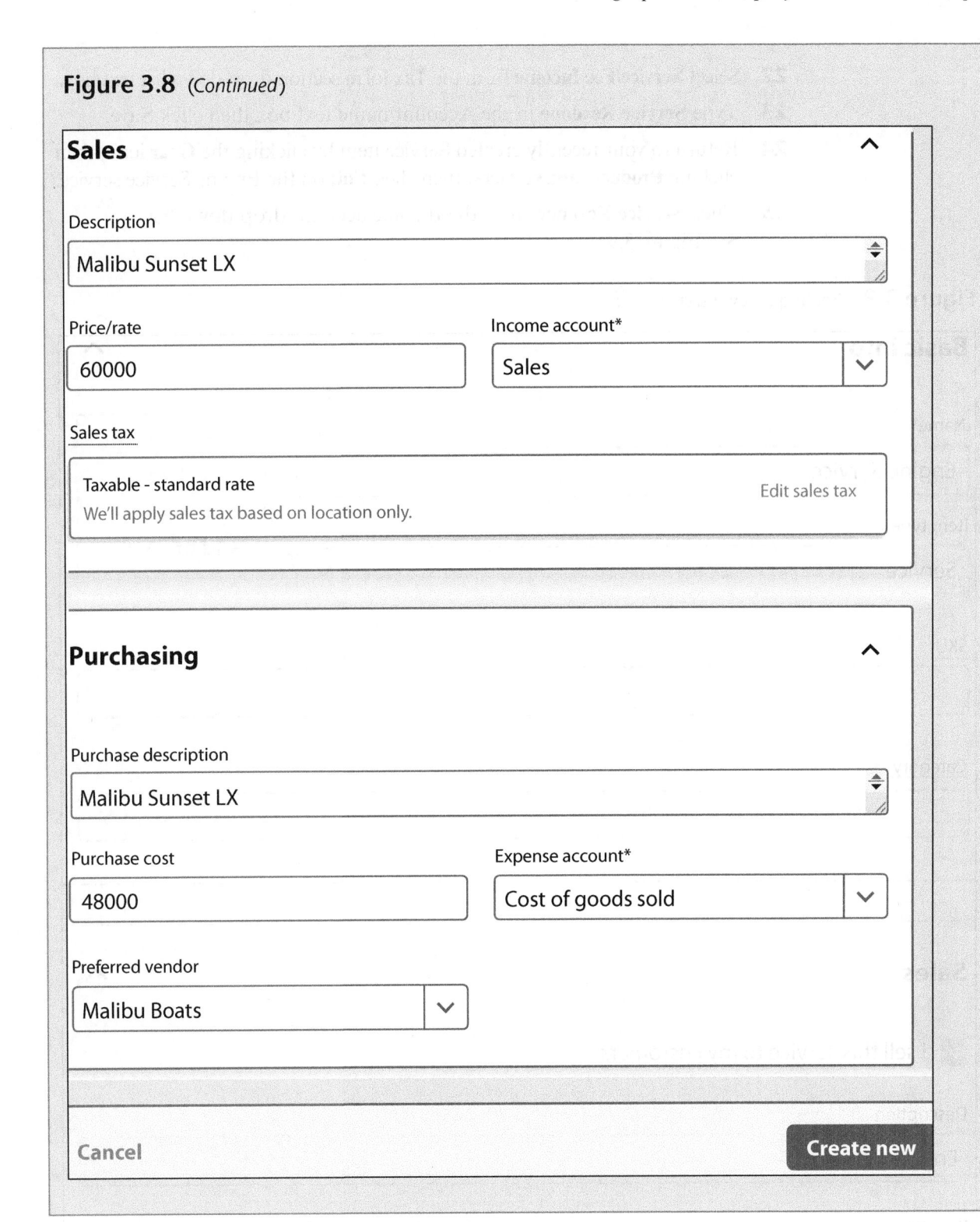

Sales

Description

Malibu Sunset LX

Price/rate: 60000

Income account*: Sales

Sales tax

Taxable - standard rate
We'll apply sales tax based on location only.

Edit sales tax

Purchasing

Purchase description

Malibu Sunset LX

Purchase cost: 48000

Expense account*: Cost of goods sold

Preferred vendor

Malibu Boats

Cancel   Create new

22 Select **Service/Fee Income** from the Tax form section drop-down list text box.

23 Type **Service Revenue** in the Account name text box then click **Save**.

24 Return to your recently created Service item by clicking the **Gear** icon, then clicking **Products and services**, then click **Edit** on the Engine Service service.

25 Click **Service Revenue** from the Income account drop-down list. See Figure 3.9.

Figure 3.9 Creating a new service

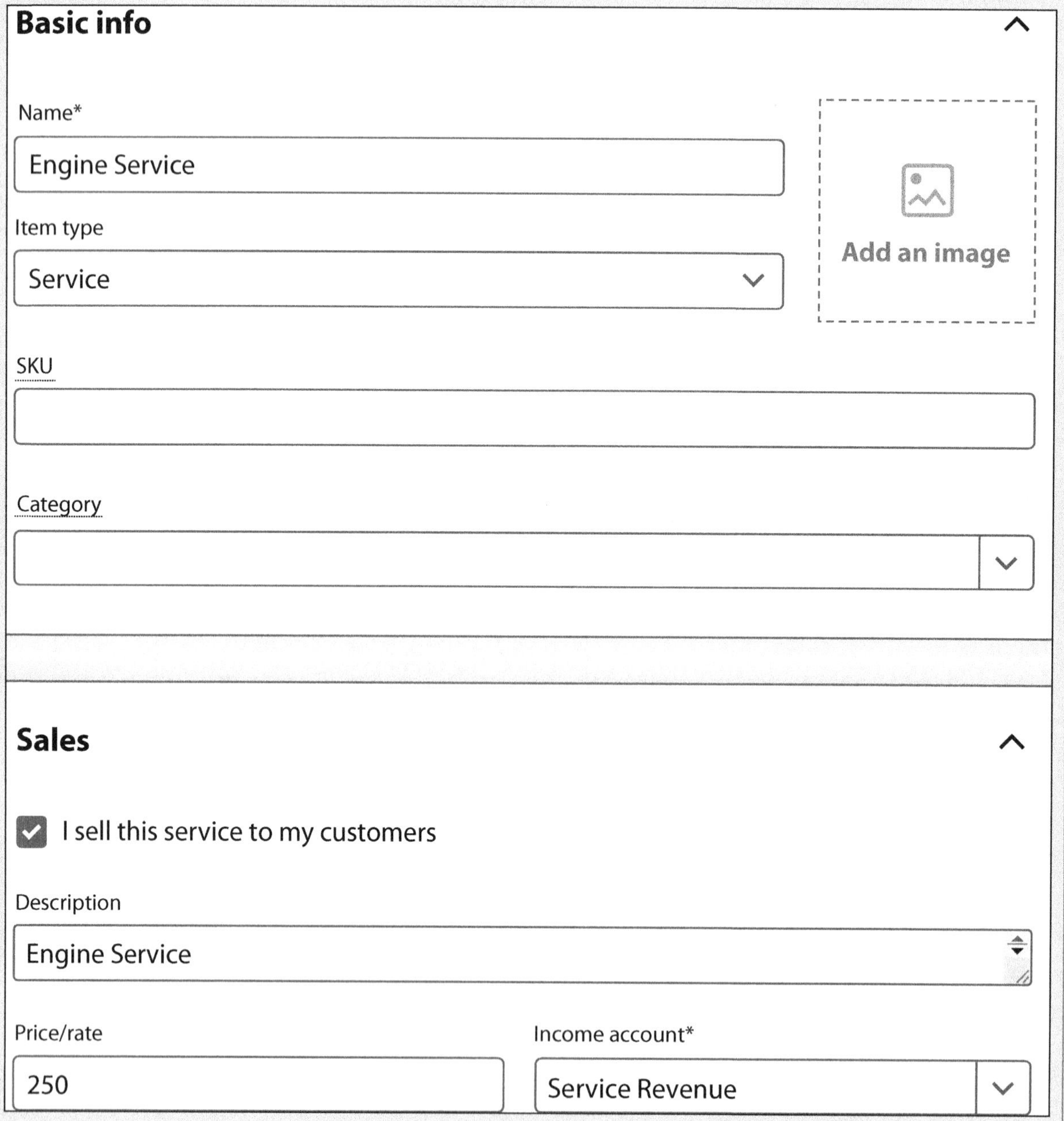

Basic info

Name*

Engine Service

Item type

Service

Add an image

SKU

Category

Sales

☑ I sell this service to my customers

Description

Engine Service

Price/rate

250

Income account*

Service Revenue

26 Click **Edit sales tax**, then select **Nontaxable**.

27 Click **Select** and then click the **Save** button.

28 Scroll down the list of products and services. Note the addition of the new Malibu Sunset LX product, with a quantity of 1, and the new Engine Service added.

29 Click the **Gear** icon and then **Chart of Accounts** and note the new balance in the Inventory account of $48,000.

Following the instructions for adding a new product above, create a new product (Name, Description, and Purchasing information: Malibu Sportster LX with a sales price of $52,000 and a cost of $41,600 on 12/31/26 with an initial quantify on hand of 3, Inventory asset account: Inventory, Income account: Sales, Sales tax: Taxable – standard rate, Expense account: Cost of goods sold, and Preferred Vendor: Malibu Boats).

Following the instructions for adding a new service above, create a new service (Name and Description: Diagnostic Service with a rate of $500, Income account: Service Revenue, Sales tax: Nontaxable).

View the updated Chart of Accounts to see a $25,000 balance in the Checking account, a new Inventory account balance of $172,800, and a new Opening balance equity account of $197,800.

To continue, let's add opening balances to the Prepaid expenses, Long-term business loans, and Common stock accounts.

To add opening balances to Long-term business loans, Prepaid expenses, and Common stock accounts:

1 Continuing in the Chart of Accounts, click **View Register** in the Action column on the Long-term business loans account.

2 Click **Add journal entry**.

3 Type **12/31/2026** in the DATE column.

4 Type **1** in the REF NO. column.

5 Type **Chase Bank** in the PAYEE column then click **Add Chase Bank**.

6 Change Type to **Vendor** and then click **Save**.

7 Select **Opening balance equity** from the ACCOUNT drop-down list.

8 Type **50000** in the INCREASE column and then press the [**Tab**] key to view Figure 3.10.

9 Click **Save**.

Figure 3.10 Creating a beginning balance in the Long-term business loans account

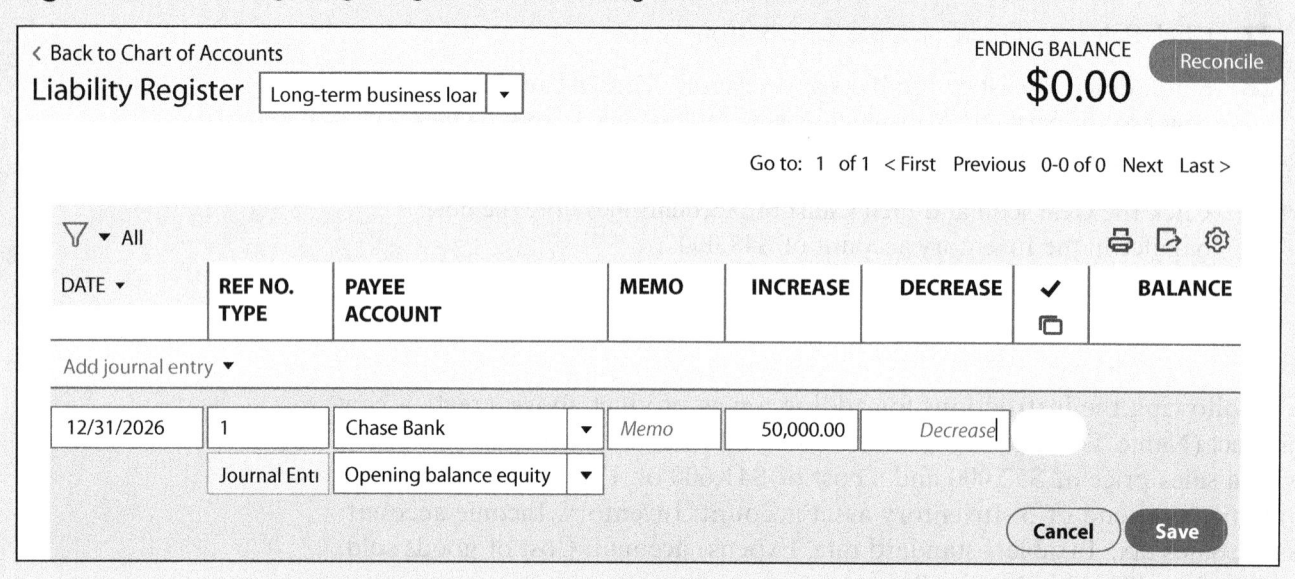

DATE	REF NO. TYPE	PAYEE ACCOUNT	MEMO	INCREASE	DECREASE	✓	BALANCE
12/31/2026	1	Chase Bank	Memo	50,000.00	Decrease		
	Journal Entry	Opening balance equity					

10. Click **Back to Chart of Accounts**, then click **View Register** in the Action column on the Prepaid expenses account.
11. Click **Add deposit** and then select **Deposit** from the drop-down list.
12. Type **12/31/2026** in the DATE column.
13. Type **Allstate Insurance** in the PAYEE column, then click **Add Allstate Insurance**.
14. Change Type to **Vendor** and then click **Save**.
15. Select **Opening balance equity** from the ACCOUNT drop-down list.
16. Type **15000** in the INCREASE column and then press the [**Tab**] key.
17. Click **Save**.
18. Click **Back to Chart of Accounts**, then click **View Register** in the Action column on the Common stock account.
19. Click **Add journal entry**.
20. Type **12/31/2026** in the DATE column.
21. Type **2** in the REF NO. column.
22. Type **Shareholders** in the PAYEE column then click **Add Shareholders**.
23. Change Type to **Vendor** and then click **Save**.
24. Select **Opening balance equity** from the ACCOUNT drop-down list.
25. Type **1000** in the INCREASE column and then press the [**Tab**] key.
26. Click **Save**.

27 Click **Reports** from the Navigation bar.

28 Type **Trial Balance** in the Find a report by name text box and then click **Trial Balance**.

29 Select **Custom** from the Report period drop-down list.

30 Type **1/1/2027** in both the first and second text boxes then click **Run report** to view the Trial Balance shown in Figure 3.11.

Figure 3.11 Trial Balance as of 1/1/2027

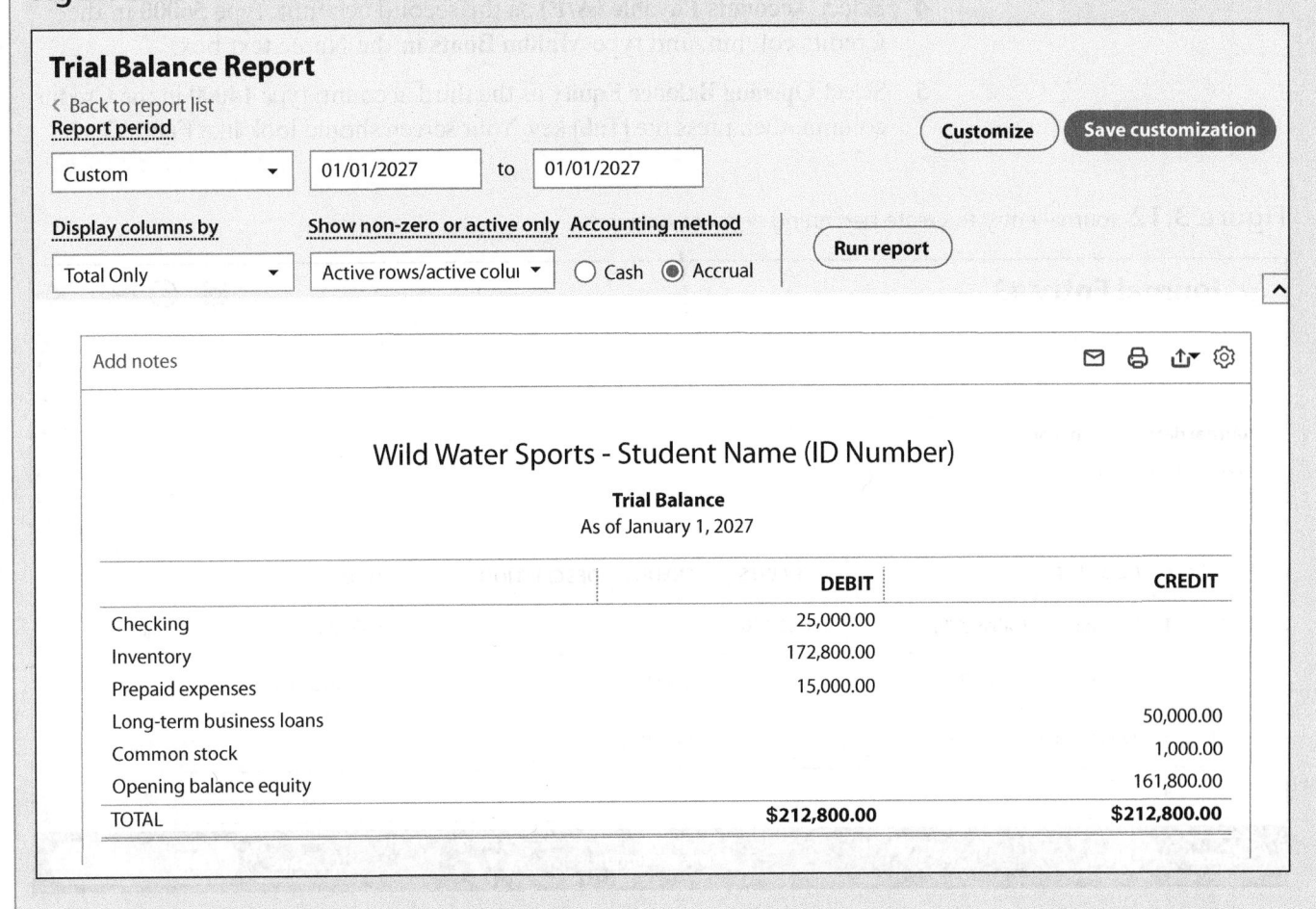

Trial Balance Report

Wild Water Sports - Student Name (ID Number)
Trial Balance
As of January 1, 2027

	DEBIT	CREDIT
Checking	25,000.00	
Inventory	172,800.00	
Prepaid expenses	15,000.00	
Long-term business loans		50,000.00
Common stock		1,000.00
Opening balance equity		161,800.00
TOTAL	$212,800.00	$212,800.00

31 Click **Save customization** then click **Save**.

Now we will set up beginning balances in accounts receivable and accounts payable by using journal entries, and add a new customer and vendor at the same time. Journal entries are commonly used to adjust accounts. A customer is an entity to whom you sell products or provide a service. A vendor is an entity from whom you purchase products or services.

Navigate your browser to the Video Tutorials provided by Intuit (see website address specified in the Preface to this text) and then search on how to use journal entries.

To create accounts receivable and accounts payable beginning balances:

1. Click the **+ New** icon, then click on **Journal Entry** from the Other column.
2. Type **12/31/2026** in the date text box.
3. Select **Accounts Receivable (A/R)** as the first account and type **70000** in the Debits column and type **Refugio** as a new customer in the Name text box and then click **Add new Refugio**. Click **Save** in the new Customer window.
4. Select **Accounts Payable (A/P)** as the second account, type **56000** in the Credits column, and type **Malibu Boats** in the Name text box.
5. Select **Opening Balance Equity** as the third account, type **14000** in the Credits column, then press the **[Tab]** key. Your screen should look like Figure 3.12.

Figure 3.12 Journal entry to create beginning account balances

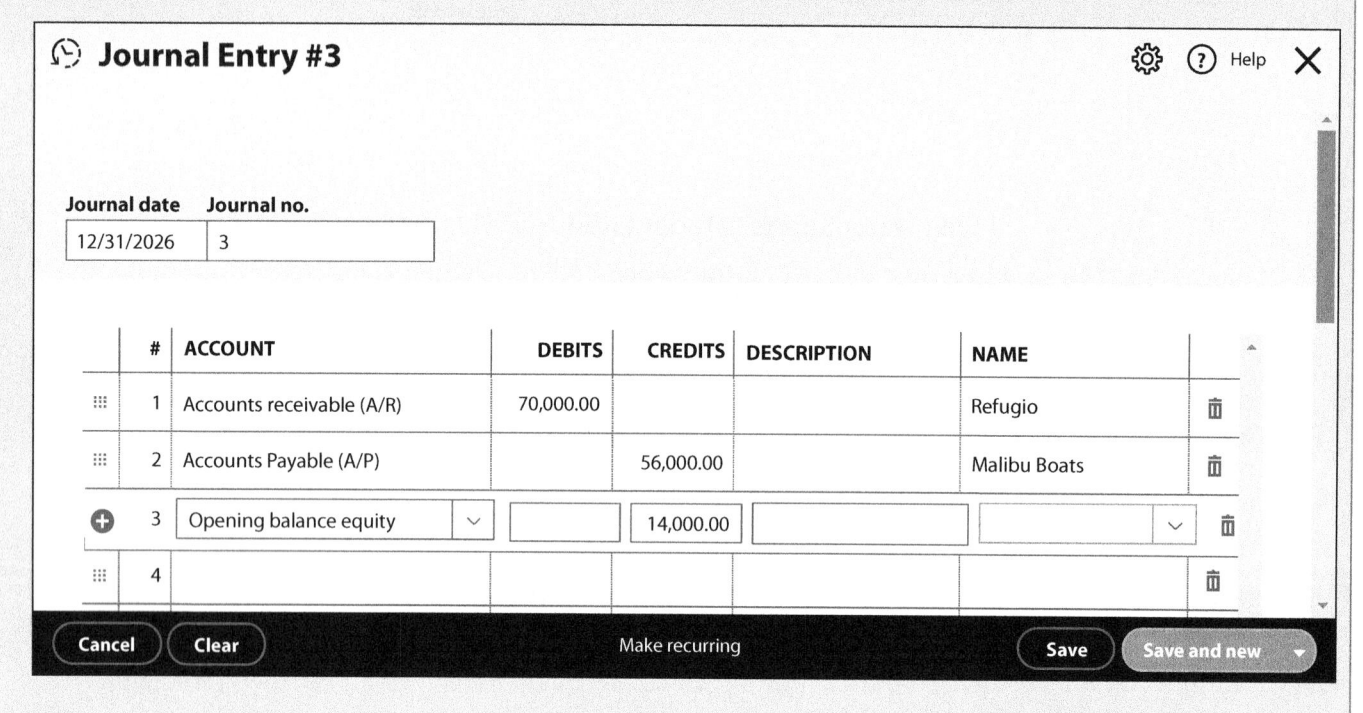

#	ACCOUNT	DEBITS	CREDITS	DESCRIPTION	NAME
1	Accounts receivable (A/R)	70,000.00			Refugio
2	Accounts Payable (A/P)		56,000.00		Malibu Boats
3	Opening balance equity		14,000.00		
4					

Journal date: 12/31/2026 Journal no.: 3

6. Click **Save and close**.
7. Click **Reports**, click the **Custom reports** tab, and then click **Trial Balance** to view Figure 3.13.

Figure 3.13

Updated trial balance report

Wild Water Sports - Student Name (ID Number)		
Trial Balance		
As of January 1, 2027		
	DEBIT	**CREDIT**
Checking	25,000.00	
Accounts receivable (A/R)	70,000.00	
Inventory	172,800.00	
Prepaid expenses	15,000.00	
Accounts Payable (A/P)		56,000.00
Long-term business loans		50,000.00
Common stock		1,000.00
Opening balance equity		175,800.00
TOTAL	**$282,800.00**	**$282,800.00**

So far, we have added a $175,800 (Checking $25,000 + Accounts Receivable $70,000 + Inventory $172,800 + Prepaid expenses $15,000 − Accounts Payable $56,000 − Long-term business loans $50,000 − Common stock $1,000) net increase to the Wild Water Sports company as of 1/1/27. The Opening Balance Equity account has increased as a result of this adjustment.

Finally, let's add some fixed asset accounts. The company had equipment it had purchased and partially depreciated in 2026. Thus, as of 1/1/2027, we need to set up some fixed asset accounts related to equipment. These assets will continue to be depreciated over their estimated useful lives so it will be necessary to create an equipment account and two subaccounts: original cost and accumulated depreciation.

To create the equipment, original cost, and accumulated depreciation accounts:

1. Click the **Gear** icon.
2. Click **Chart of Accounts**.
3. From the Chart of accounts click **New**.
4. Select **Assets** from the top of the New account window.
5. Select **Fixed Assets** from the drop-down list in the Save account under text box.

66 Chapter 3 *Setting Up a New Company*

6. Select **Fixed Asset Other Tools Equipment** from the drop-down list in the Tax form section text box.
7. Type **Equipment** in the Account name text box.
8. Click **Save** to save this account.
9. From the Chart of accounts click **New**.
10. Select **Assets** from the top of the New account window.
11. Select **Equipment** from the drop-down list in the Save account under text box.
12. Select **Fixed Asset Other Tools Equipment** from the drop-down list in the Tax form section text box.
13. Type **Original Cost** in the Account name text box.
14. Click **Starting date and opening balance**.
15. Select **Other Date** from the drop-down list in the Select Date text box.
16. Type **12/31/2026** in the Start date text box. (This date will be different for each case.)
17. Type **40000** in the Account balance at the end of day text box. (This amount will be different for each case.)
18. Click **Save** to save this account.
19. From the Chart of accounts click **New**.
20. Select **Assets** from the top of the New account window.
21. Select **Equipment** from the drop-down list in the Save account under text box.
22. Select **Accumulated Depreciation** from the drop-down list in the Tax form section text box.
23. Type **Accumulated depreciation** in the Account name text box.
24. Click **Starting date and opening balance**.
25. Select **Other Date** from the drop-down list in the Select Date text box.
26. Type **12/31/26** in the Start date text box. (This date will be different for each case.)
27. Type **10000** in the Account balance at the end of day text box. (This amount will be different for each case.) Your window should look like Figure 3.14.
28. Click **Save**.

Setting Up a New Company **Chapter 3** 67

[Income] [Expenses] [Banks] [**Assets**] [Credit cards] [Liabilities]

[Equity]

Save account under *

🔍 Equipment

Tax form section * ⓘ

Accumulated Depreciation ⌄

Account name *

Accumulated depreciation

Description

▼ Starting date and opening balance

More info on opening balances
Date to start tracking this account in QuickBooks

Other date ⌄

Start date

12/31/2026 📅

Account balance at end of day 12/30/2026

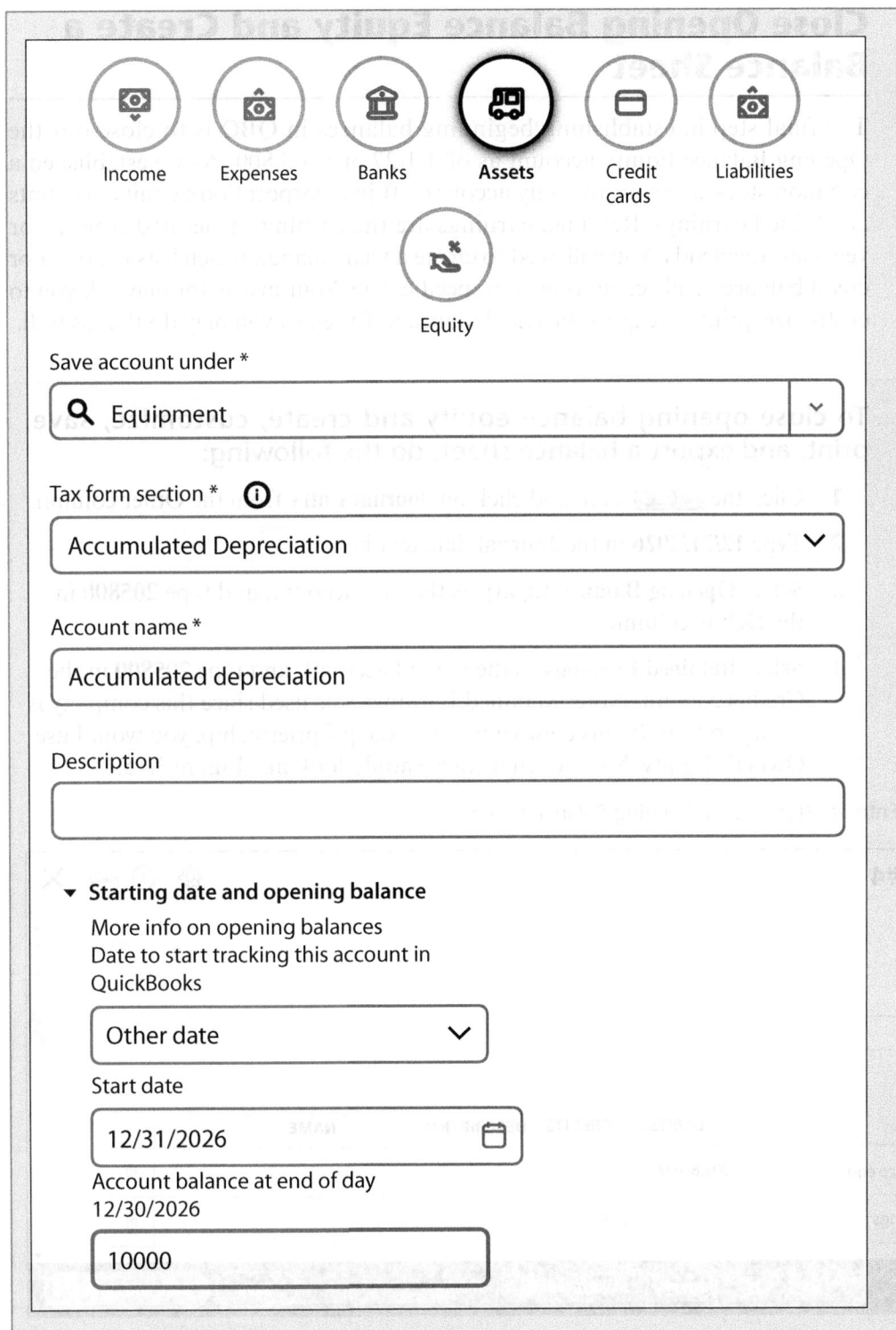

10000

Figure 3.14

Adding a new accumulated depreciation account

12 Click the **Printer** icon at the top of the report, and follow instructions to print your report as either a PDF file or a printed document and then close the Print window.

13 Click the **Save customization** button.

14 Type **Balance Sheet as of 1/1/27** in the Custom report name text box as shown in Figure 3.17.

Figure 3.17

Save report customizations

Custom report name

Balance Sheet as of 1/1/27

Add this report to a group

None ▼

Add new group

Share with

None ▼

Save

Navigate your browser to the Video Tutorials provided by Intuit (see website address specified in the Preface to this text) and then search on how to save customized reports.

15 Click **Save**.

16 Click the **Export** icon shown next to the Printer icon at the top of the report and then select **Export to Excel** from the drop-down list to begin the export to Excel process.

17 Click **Save** after you have navigated to a place on your computer to save this file.

18 Open Excel and then open the file you just saved.

19 After viewing your newly created Excel file, close Excel.

Trial Balance

The work you completed in this chapter influenced the company's trial balance. You decided to create a Trial Balance report after entering all business events described in this chapter and investigate any differences between your report and that shown in Figure 3.18.

To create a trial balance:

1 Click **Reports**, then select the **Custom reports** tab, then select **Trial Balance**. Change the to date of the report to 1/1/2027 to view the Trial Balance as shown in Figure 3.18.

Figure 3.18 Trial Balance

Wild Water Sports - Student Name (ID Number)
Trial Balance
As of January 1, 2027

	DEBIT	CREDIT
Checking	25,000.00	
Accounts receivable (A/R)	70,000.00	
Inventory	172,800.00	
Prepaid expenses	15,000.00	
Equipment:Accumulated depreciation		10,000.00
Equipment:Original Cost	40,000.00	
Accounts Payable (A/P)		56,000.00
Long-term business loans		50,000.00
Common stock		1,000.00
Opening balance equity		0.00
Retained Earnings		205,800.00
TOTAL	$322,800.00	$322,800.00

2 Compare your trial balance report with Figure 3.18.

3 If you note any differences, continue below to create a Transaction Detail by Account report.

Create, Print, and Export a Transaction Detail by Account

Often, you will want to investigate a detailed list of transactions you have recorded for a specific period. In your end-of-chapter cases, a usual explanation for an incorrect report is recording a transaction in the incorrect period. To explore this option, you will create a transaction detail by account report for a specific period. You can create such a report for a large period to see if your transactions were recorded in the proper period and to see where you may have entered a wrong amount or account.

To create, print, and export a transaction detail by account report for the period 1/1/20 to 12/31/30, do the following:

1 Click **Reports** from the navigation bar.

2 Type **Transaction** in the Find a report by name text box.

3 Select **Transaction Detail by Account** and then click **Switch to classic view**.

4 Scroll to the top of the report window and then select **Custom** from the Report period drop-down text box and then press [**Tab**].

5 Type **01/01/2020** in the text box and then press [**Tab**].

6. Type **12/31/2030** in the text box and then press [**Tab**].
7. Click **Run report**. The top of the report is shown in Figure 3.19.

Figure 3.19 Transaction Detail by Account Report (top section)

Wild Water Sports - Student Name (ID Number)

Transaction Detail by Account
January 2020 - December 2030

DATE	TRANSACTION TYPE	NUM	NAME	MEMO/DESCRIPTION	SPLIT	AMOUNT	BALANCE
▼ Checking							
12/31/2026	Deposit			Opening Balance	Opening balance equity	25,000.00	25,000.00
Total for Checking						**$25,000.00**	
▼ Accounts receivable (A/R)							
12/31/2026	Journal Entry	3			-Split-	70,000.00	70,000.00
Total for Accounts receivable (A/R)						**$70,000.00**	
▼ Inventory							
12/31/2026	Inventory Starting Value	START		Malibu Sunset LX - Opening inve...	Opening balance equity	48,000.00	48,000.00
12/31/2026	Inventory Starting Value	START		Malibu Sportster LX - Opening in...	Opening balance equity	124,800.00	172,800.00
Total for Inventory						**$172,800.00**	
▼ Prepaid expenses							
12/31/2026	Deposit		Allstate Insurance		Opening balance equity	15,000.00	15,000.00
Total for Prepaid expenses						**$15,000.00**	
▼ Equipment							
▼ Accumulated Depreciation							
12/31/2026	Journal Entry			Opening Balance	-Split-	−10,000.00	−10,000.00
Total for Accumulated Depreciation						**$−10,000.00**	
▼ Original Cost							
12/31/2026	Journal Entry			Opening Balance	-Split-	40,000.00	40,000.00
Total for Original Cost						**$40,000.00**	
Total for Equipment						**$30,000.00**	

8. Click **Deposit** in the Prepaid expenses section.
9. Close this window, scroll down the report, and investigate other transactions.
10. Scroll back to the top of this report, and click **Save customization**.
11. Leave Transaction Detail by Account as the custom report name and then click **Save**. Export this report like you exported the Balance Sheet earlier in this chapter.
12. Click the **Print** button to set this report up for printing; however, do not print this report as it is too long and unnecessary. Click **Cancel**.
13. Click the **Account** icon (in this case **S** for the owner Sample Student) and then click **Sign Out**.

End Note

In this chapter, using the Wild Water Sports company you have modified company settings, added new accounts to the chart of accounts, and added beginning balances where appropriate. You have added customers, vendors, products, and services and closed the Opening Balance Equity account. You are ready to add operating activities like sales receipts, invoices, and cash receipts.

Chapter 3 Questions

1. How do you access company settings?
2. When is it appropriate to add beginning balances to accounts?
3. What steps need to be followed to add an account to the chart of accounts?
4. When you add a beginning balance to an account, what other account is affected?
5. What information is required when adding a new product to QBO?
6. What additional information is required when you add beginning balance amounts to the accounts receivable account?
7. What additional information is required when you add beginning balance amounts to the accounts payable account?
8. Which additional account is used when you close Opening Balance Equity?
9. How do you access the Balance Sheet report?
10. How can you review a Transactions Report for any account when you are viewing the Balance Sheet?

Chapter 3 Matching

a. Transactions report _____ Entity to whom you sell products/services
b. Trial balance _____ Account used to offset beginning balance adjustments
c. Journal entry _____ Merchandise a company purchases from a vendor
d. Opening Balance Equity _____ Efforts made by a company to add value to a customer
e. Customer _____ A listing of the debit or credit balances as of a specific date
f. Vendor _____ Dictates where an account appears in all reports
g. Product _____ Transactions for an account for a specified period
h. Service _____ Entity from whom you purchase products/services
i. Account type _____ Checking
j. Detailed type example _____ Commonly used to adjust accounts

Chapter 3 Cases

The following cases require you to accept a new invitation from your instructor. Each of the following cases continues throughout the text in a sequential manner. For example, if you are assigned Case 01, you will use the file you modified in this chapter in all of the following chapters. Each of the following cases is similar in concepts assessed but differs in amounts and transactions. See the Preface to this text for a matrix of each student case and its attributes.

To create your company, do the following:

1. Open the email you received from your instructor and click **Accept Invitation**. A new browser window should open a QBO sign up page.

2. Click **Sign In** (as shown in Figure 3.20) to accept your email or user ID and then type your password and click **Continue**.

Figure 3.20

Sign In window (for logging in)

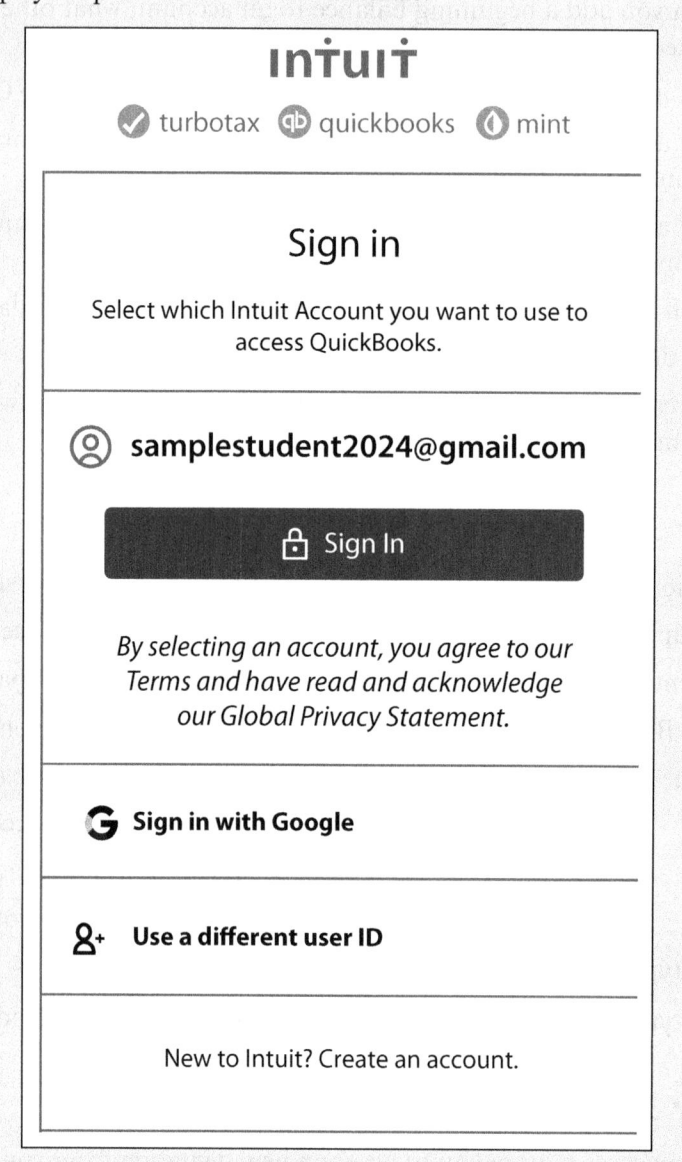

intuit

✓ turbotax qb quickbooks ◌ mint

Sign in

Select which Intuit Account you want to use to access QuickBooks.

👤 samplestudent2024@gmail.com

🔒 Sign In

By selecting an account, you agree to our Terms and have read and acknowledge our Global Privacy Statement.

G Sign in with Google

👤+ Use a different user ID

New to Intuit? Create an account.

3. Once your file is created you should see a welcome screen. Click **Next** to continue.

4. Type **Case # - Student Name** as your business name replacing # with the case number your instructor assigned and Student Name with your name. (Note: in figures provided below Case 1 - Student Name is used.)

5. Follow the company set up process you used for Wild Water Sports in Chapter 2.

6. Specific company settings for the case you are assigned are provided at the end of this chapter.

Case 1

Your company is a distributor of surfboards located in La Jolla, California. The company does not collect sales tax as all of its customers are resellers. Leave Industry text box blank. You began business in 2023 and want to use QBO starting January 1, 2024. Beginning balances as of 12/31/23 have been provided below.

You must make changes to your company. Based on what you learned in the text using the Wild Water Sports company, you are to make the following changes to the case you created in Chapter 2:

1 Modify settings as follows:

   a. Company
      i) Company name—Modify the company name to Case 01 – Student Name (ID Number) replacing Student Name with your name and ID Number with the number your instructor indicated.
      ii) Company type—Modify the Tax form by selecting **Form 1120** from the drop-down list of forms. Leave Industry text box blank and then click **Save**.

   b. Sales—Turn on – Track inventory quantity on hand. (This will automatically show items table on expense and purchase forms.)

   c. Expenses
      i)   Turn on – Track expenses and items by customer.
      ii) Turn on – Make expenses and items billable (no markup, track billable expenses and items as income in a single account, and no sales tax charged).
      iii) Default bill payment terms net 30.
      iv) Turn on – Use purchase orders (no custom fields).

   d. Payments—No changes

   e. Advanced
      i) Time tracking
         (1) Turn on – Add Service field to timesheets.
         (2) Turn on – Make Single-Time Activity Billable to Customer.

2 Create new accounts and related beginning balances as follows:

Account Type	Detail Type	Name	Balance	As of
Bank	Checking	Checking	25,000.00	12/31/23
Fixed Assets*	Furniture & Fixtures	Original cost	40,000.00	12/31/23
Fixed Assets*	Furniture & Fixtures	Depreciation	10,000.00	12/31/23
Long-Term Liabilities	Notes Payable	Notes Payable	60,000.00	12/31/23
Equity	Common Stock	Common Stock	1,000.00	12/31/23

*When entering a new fixed asset, place a check in the **Track depreciation of this asset** check box to reveal Original cost and Depreciation text boxes. Enter amounts from above as positive numbers.

3   Create two new products and one new service item as follows:

   a. Products
      i) Name/Description – Rook 15, initial quantity 12/31/23 – 10, inventory asset account – Inventory Asset (this account will automatically be created in the chart of accounts when you add this product), price – $650, cost – $400, income account – Sales, expense account – Cost of Goods Sold
      ii) Name/Description – The Water Hog, track quantity, initial quantity 12/31/23 – 8, inventory asset account – Inventory Asset, price – $860, cost — $500, income account – Sales, expense account – Cost of Goods Sold

   b. Service—Name/Description – Consulting, rate – $25, income account – Services. Click **+ Add new**, Account Type: Income, Detail Type: Service/Fee Income, Name: Services

   c. Make changes to the following accounts via journal entry 1 as of 12/31/23 with an offset to Opening Balance Equity. Note: You'll have to add these accounts first.

Account	Amount	Name
Accounts Receivable	5,000.00	Blondie's Boards (new customer)
Prepaid Expenses	3,000.00	
Accounts Payable	4,500.00	Channel Islands (new vendor)

4   Close the Opening Balance Equity account to Retained Earnings via journal entry 2 as of 12/31/23.

5   Prepare and print a Trial Balance report as of 12/31/23, save it as a customized report named Trial Balance 12/31/23, and share it with all users. Click **Reports**, then scroll down the page to the For my accountant section, and click **Trial Balance**. Then select **Custom** as the report period and type **1/1/23** and **12/31/23** as the from–to dates. Your report should look like Figure 3.21.

6   If your trial balance differs from what is shown in Figure 3.21, do the following:

   a. Make sure all of your changes were dated 12/31/23.
   b. Click on the debit or credit balance to view a transactions report for each account, and investigate why your answer is different.
   c. Ask your instructor for assistance.
   d. Be sure your company matches the above as you will be adding additional business events in Chapter 4.

7   Export your Trial Balance report to Excel, and save it with the file name Student Name (replace with your name) Ch 03 Case 01 Trial Balance.xlsx.

Figure 3.21

Trial Balance (as of 12/31/23)

Case 1
TRIAL BALANCE
As of December 31, 2023

	DEBIT	CREDIT
Checking	25,000.00	
Accounts Receivable	5,000.00	
Inventory Asset	8,000.00	
Prepaid Expenses	3,000.00	
Furniture & Fixtures:Depreciation		10,000.00
Furniture & Fixtures:Original cost	40,000.00	
Accounts Payable		4,500.00
Notes Payable		60,000.00
Common Stock		1,000.00
Opening Balance Equity		0.00
Retained Earnings		5,500.00
TOTAL	**$81,000.00**	**$81,000.00**

8. Prepare and print a Transaction Detail by Account report for transactions between 1/1/24 and 12/31/24, save it as a customized report named Transaction Detail by Account, and share it with all users. If asked, indicate that your business is accrual based.

9. Use your Transaction Detail by Account report to locate any differences in your Trial Balance report created above.

    a. Make sure that all of your changes were dated 12/31/23.

    b. Click on the line that does not match to view the transaction for that account, and investigate why your answer differs.

    c. Ask your instructor for assistance.

    d. Be sure your company matches the above as you will be adding additional business events in Chapter 4.

10. Export your Transactions Detail by Account report to Excel, and save it with the file name Student Name (replace with your name) Ch 03 Case 01 Transaction Detail by Account.xlsx.

11. Sign out of your company.

Case 2

Your company is a distributor of remote control toys located in La Jolla, California. The company does not collect sales tax as all of its customers are resellers. You began business in 2024 and want to use QBO starting January 1, 2025. Beginning balances as of 12/31/24 have been provided below.

You must make changes to your company. Based on what you learned in the text using the Wild Water Sports company, you are to make the following changes to the case you created in Chapter 2:

1 Modify settings as follows:

a. Company—Company name – Modify the company name to Case 02 – Student Name (ID Number) replacing Student Name with your name and ID Number with the number your instructor indicated.

b. Sales—Turn on – Track quantity on hand. (This will automatically show items table on expense and purchase forms.)

c. Expenses
   i) Turn on – Track expenses and items by customer.
   ii) Turn on – Make expenses and items billable (no markup, track billable expenses and items as income in a single account, no sales tax charged).
   iii) Default bill payment terms net 30.
   iv) Turn on – Use purchase orders (no custom fields).

d. Payments—No changes

e. Advanced
   i) Time tracking
      (1) Turn on – Add Service field to timesheets.
      (2) Turn on – Make Single-Time Activity Billable to Customer.

2 Create new accounts and related beginning balances as follows:

Account Type	Detail Type	Name	Balance	As of
Bank	Checking	Checking	5,000.00	12/31/24
Fixed Assets*	Machinery & Equipment	Original cost	10,000.00	12/31/24
Fixed Assets*	Machinery & Equipment	Depreciation	1,000.00	12/31/24
Long-Term Liabilities	Notes Payable	Notes Payable	12,000.00	12/31/24
Equity	Common Stock	Common Stock	100.00	12/31/24

*When entering a new fixed asset, place a check in the **Track depreciation of this asset** check box to reveal Original cost and Depreciation text boxes. Enter amounts from above as positive numbers.

3 Create two new products and one new service item:

a. Products
   i) Name/Description/Purchasing Information – Broon F830 Ride, initial quantity 12/31/24 – 4, inventory asset account – Inventory Asset. Note: This account will automatically be created in the chart of accounts when you add this product. Price – $1,500, cost – $800, income account – Sales, expense account – Cost of Goods Sold.
   ii) Name/Description/Purchasing Information – Sea Wind Carbon Sailboat, initial quantity 12/31/24 – 3, inventory asset account – Inventory Asset, price – $1,200, cost – $620, income account – Sales, expense account – Cost of Goods Sold.

b. Service—Name/Description – Repairs, rate – $45, income account – Services. Click + **Add new** in the Income account text box, Account Type: Income, Detail Type: Service/Fee Income, Name: Services.

c. Make changes to the following accounts via journal entry 1 as of 12/31/24 with an offset to Opening Balance Equity. Note: You'll have to add these accounts first.

Account	Amount	Name
Accounts Receivable	925.00	Benson's RC (new customer)
Prepaid Expenses	2,400.00	
Accounts Payable	1,900.00	Kyosho (new vendor)

4 Close the Opening Balance Equity account to Retained Earnings via journal entry 2 as of 12/31/24.

5 Prepare and print a Trial Balance report as of 12/31/24 (Click **Reports**, then scroll down the page to the For my accountant section, and click **Trial Balance**. Then select **Custom** as the report period and type **1/1/24** and **12/31/24** as the from–to dates.), save it as a customized report named Trial Balance 12/31/24, and share it with all users. Your report should look like Figure 3.22.

Figure 3.22

Trial Balance (as of 12/31/24)

Case 2
TRIAL BALANCE
As of December 31, 2024

	DEBIT	CREDIT
Checking	5,000.00	
Accounts Receivable	925.00	
Inventory Asset	5,060.00	
Prepaid Expenses	2,400.00	
Machinery & Equipment:Depreciation		1,000.00
Machinery & Equipment:Original cost	10,000.00	
Accounts Payable		1,900.00
Notes Payable		12,000.00
Common Stock		100.00
Opening Balance Equity		0.00
Retained Earnings		8,385.00
TOTAL	**$23,385.00**	**$23,385.00**

6 If your trial balance is different from what is shown in Figure 3.22, do the following:

a. Make sure all of your changes were dated 12/31/24.

b. Click on the debit or credit balance to view a transactions report for each account, and investigate why your answer is different.

c. Ask your instructor for assistance.

d. Be sure your company matches the above as you will be adding additional business events in Chapter 4.

7 Export your Trial Balance report to Excel, and save it with the file name Student Name (replace with your name) Ch 03 Case 02 Trial Balance.xlsx.

8 Prepare and print a Transaction Detail by Account report for all transactions between 1/1/10 and 12/31/28, save it as a customized report named Transaction Detail by Account, and share it with all users. If asked, indicate that your business is accrual based.

9 Use your Transaction Detail by Account report to locate any differences in your Trial Balance report created above.

   a. Make sure all of your changes were dated 12/31/24.

   b. Click on the line that does not match to view the transaction for that account, and investigate why your answer differs.

   c. Ask your instructor for assistance.

   d. Be sure your company matches the above as you will be adding additional business events in Chapter 4.

10 Export your Transactions Detail by Account report to Excel and save it with the file name Student Name (replace with your name) Ch 03 Case 02 Transaction Detail by Account.xlsx.

11 Sign out of your company.

Case 3

Your company sells and services cell phones. They are a sole proprietor located in La Jolla, California. The company does collect sales tax as all of its customers are consumers. (See Appendix 1 for directions on how to add a sales tax to a company file.) They began business in 2025 and want to use QBO starting January 1, 2026. Beginning balances as of 12/31/25 have been provided below.

You must make changes to your company. Based on what you learned in the text using the Wild Water Sports company, you are to make the following changes to the case you created in Chapter 2:

1 Modify settings as follows:

   a. Company—Company name – Modify the company name to Case 03 – Student Name (ID Number) replacing Student Name with your name and ID Number with the number your instructor indicated. Use 3990 La Jolla Shores Drive, La Jolla, CA 92037 as the company's address.

   b. SSN—Add 987-65-4321 as your business social security number as you are a sole proprietor.

   c. Sales—Make sure that Track inventory quantity on hand is on. (This will automatically show items table on expense and purchase forms.)

   d. Expenses
      i) Turn on – Track expenses and items by customer.
      ii) Turn on – Make expenses and items billable (no markup, track billable expenses and items as income in a single account, and charge sales tax).
      iii) Set default bill payment terms to Due on receipt.
      iv) Turn on – Use purchase orders (no custom fields).

e. Payments—No changes
f. Time Timesheet
   i) Turn on – Show service field to timesheets.
   ii) Turn on – Allow time to be billable.

2 Follow steps provided in Appendix 1 to add sales tax paid annually beginning 1/1/26.

3 Create new accounts and related beginning balances (Account Type, Detail Type, Name, Balance as of 12/31/25) as follows:

a. Bank, Checking, Checking, $12,000

b. Fixed Assets, Machinery & Equipment, Original cost, $15,000

   Note: When entering a new fixed asset, place a check in the **Track depreciation of this asset** check box to reveal Original cost and Depreciation text boxes. Enter amounts from above as positive numbers.

   Fixed Assets, Machinery & Equipment, Depreciation, $2,000

c. Long-Term Liabilities, Notes Payable, Notes Payable, $23,000

d. Equity, Owner's Equity, Owner's Equity, 0

4 Create two new products (Name/Description, initial quantity 12/31/25, inventory asset account, price, cost, income account, expense account):

a. Apple iPhone 7, 10, Inventory Asset, $750, $500. Note: This account will automatically be created in the chart of accounts when you add this product. Sales of Product Income, Cost of Goods Sold, taxable.

b. Pixel, 3, Inventory Asset, $650, $400, Sales of Product Income, Cost of Goods Sold, taxable.

5 Create two new service items (Name/Description, rate, income account):

a. Apple Repairs, $45, Services, not taxable. (Click + **Add new** in the Income account text box, Account Type: Income, Detail Type: Service/Fee Income, Name: Services.)

b. Pixel Repairs, $40, Services, not taxable.

6 Make changes to the following accounts via journal entry 1 as of 12/31/25 with an offset to Opening Balance Equity:

Account	Amount	Name
Accounts Receivable (A/R)	4,125.00	GHO Marketing (new customer)
Prepaid Expenses	2,750.00	
Accounts Payable (A/P)	5,000.00	Apple Inc. (new vendor)

7 Close the Opening Balance Equity account (which should have a balance of $10,075) to Owner's Equity via journal entry 2 as of 12/31/25. (Note: Use Owner's Equity as this company is a sole proprietorship. Retained Earnings would have been used if this company had been a corporation.)

8   Prepare and print a Trial Balance report as of 12/31/25, click the **Run report** button, and then save it as a customized report named Trial Balance 12/31/25, and share it with all users. Click **Reports**, then scroll down the page to the For my accountant section, and click **Trial Balance**. Then select **Custom** as the report period and type **1/1/25** and **12/31/25** as the from–to dates. Your report should look like Figure 3.23.

Figure 3.23 Trial Balance

Case 03 - Student Name (ID Number)
Trial Balance
As of December 31, 2025

	DEBIT	CREDIT
Checking	12,000.00	
Accounts receivable (A/R)	4,125.00	
Inventory Asset	6,200.00	
Prepaid expenses	2,750.00	
Machinery & Equipment:Depreciation		2,000.00
Machinery & Equipment:Original cost	15,000.00	
Accounts Payable (A/P)		5,000.00
Notes Payable		23,000.00
Opening balance equity		0.00
Owner's Equity		10,075.00
TOTAL	**$40,075.00**	**$40,075.00**

9   If your trial balance differs from what is shown in Figure 3.23, do the following:

   a. Make sure all of your changes were dated 12/31/25.

   b. Click on the debit or credit balance to view a transactions report for each account, and investigate why your answer is different.

   c. Ask your instructor for assistance.

   d. Be sure your company matches the above as you will be adding additional business events in Chapter 4.

10 Export your Trial Balance report to Excel, and save it with the file name Student Name (replace with your name) Ch 03 Case 03 Trial Balance.xlsx.

11 Prepare and print a Transaction Detail by Account report for all transactions between 1/1/10 and 12/31/30, save it as a customized report named Transaction Detail by Account, and share it with all users. If asked, indicate that your business is accrual based.

12. Use your Transaction Detail by Account report to locate any differences in your Trial Balance report created above.
    a. Make sure all of your changes were dated 12/31/25.
    b. Click on the line that does not match to view the transaction for that account, and investigate why your answer differs.
    c. Ask your instructor for assistance.
    d. Be sure your company matches the above as you will be adding additional business events in Chapter 4.
13. Export your Transactions Detail by Account report to Excel and save it with the file name Student Name (replace with your name) Ch 03 Case 03 Transaction Detail by Account.xlsx.
14. Sign out of your company.

Case 4

Your company is a sports gym serving the Hollywood area in California. They sell month-to-month memberships to individuals and businesses as well as T-shirts, yoga pants, and other sports-related accessories. They began their business in 2026 and want to use QBO starting January 1, 2027. Beginning balances as of 12/31/26 have been provided below.

Based on what you learned in the text using the Wild Water Sports company, you are to make the following changes to the case you created in Chapter 2.

1. Modify settings as follows (click the **Gear** icon and then click **Account and Settings**):
    a. Company
        i) Name – Case 04 – Student Name (ID Number)
        ii) EIN – 98-9875461
        iii) Tax form – Form 1120
        iv) Industry – Fitness and Recreational Sports Centers
        v) Email – Your email address
        vi) Address – 6540 Sunset Blvd., Hollywood, CA 90028
    b. Sales (turn the following on, and all others turn off or leave off)
        i) Preferred invoice terms – Net 30
        ii) Custom transaction numbers
        iii) Show Product/Service column on sales form
        iv) Track quantity and price/rate
        v) Track inventory quantity on hand
        vi) Show aging table at the bottom of the statement
    c. Expenses (turn the following on, and all others turn off or leave off)
        i) Show items table on expense and purchase forms
        ii) Use purchase orders
    d. Payments—No changes
    e. Advanced—No changes

2 Add sales tax that is payable to the California State Board of Equalization. (Follow the steps provided in Appendix 1.)

3 Create new accounts and related beginning balances where appropriate. (Click the **Gear** icon and then click **Chart of Accounts**.)

  a. First account
     i) Account Type – Banks, Save account under **Bank Accounts**
     ii) Tax form section – Checking
     iii) Name – Checking
     iv) Start date 12/31/2026, balance as of 12/31/26 – $27,000

  b. Second account
     i) Account Type – Assets, Save account under Other Current Assets.
     ii) Tax form section – Prepaid Expenses
     iii) Name – Prepaid rent
     iv) Start date 12/31/2026, balance as of 12/31/26 – $12,000

  c. Third, fourth, and fifth accounts
     i) Account Type – Assets, Save account under Fixed Assets
     ii) Tax form section – Fixed Asset Furniture
     iii) Name – Furniture
     iv) Start date 12/31/2026, balance $0
     v) Account Type – Assets, Save account under Furniture
     vi) Tax form section – Fixed Asset Furniture
     vii) Name – Original Cost
     viii) Start date 12/31/2026, balance $65,000
     ix) Account Type – Assets, Save account under Furniture
     x) Tax form section – Accumulated Depreciation
     xi) Name – Accumulated Depreciation
     xii) Start date 12/31/2026, balance – $10,000

  d. Sixth, seventh, and eighth accounts
     i) Account Type – Assets, Save account under Fixed Assets
     ii) Tax form section – Vehicles
     iii) Name – Vehicles
     iv) Start date 12/31/2026, balance $0
     v) Account Type – Assets, Save account under Vehicles
     vi) Tax form section – Vehicles
     vii) Name – Original Cost
     viii) Start date 12/31/2026, balance $115,000
     ix) Account Type – Assets, Save account under Vehicles
     x) Tax form section – Accumulated Depreciation
     xi) Name – Accumulated Depreciation
     xii) Start date 12/31/2026, balance – $6,500

  e. Ninth account
     i) Account Type – Liabilities, Save account under Long Term Liabilities.
     ii) Tax form section – Other Long Term Liabilities
     iii) Name – Long-term debt
     iv) Start date 12/31/2026, balance $82,000

f. Tenth account
   i) Account Type – Equity, Save account under Equity.
   ii) Tax form section – Common Stock
   iii) Name – Common stock
   iv) Start date 12/31/2026, balance $1,000

4 Create two new Inventory products as follows:
   a. First product
      i) Name – T-shirts
      ii) Initial quantity on hand – 250
      iii) As of date – 12/31/26
      iv) Inventory asset account – Inventory Asset
      v) Description – T-shirts
      vi) Sales price/rate – $25
      vii) Income account – Sales of Product Income
      viii) Is taxable – Yes
      ix) Purchasing information – T-shirts
      x) Cost – $12
      xi) Expense account – Cost of Goods Sold
   b. Second product
      i) Name – Yoga pants
      ii) Initial quantity on hand – 125
      iii) As of date – 12/31/26
      iv) Inventory asset account – Inventory Asset
      v) Description – Yoga pants
      vi) Sales price/rate – $45
      vii) Income account – Sales of Product Income
      viii) Is taxable – Yes
      ix) Purchasing information – Yoga pants
      x) Cost – $20
      xi) Expense account – Cost of Goods Sold

5 Create two new service items as follows:
   a. First service
      i) Name and description – Monthly Fee
      ii) Sales information – Yes you do sell this service to customers. "Monthly Fee"
      iii) Sales price/rate – $150
      iv) Income account – Sales
      v) Is taxable – No
      vi) Purchasing information – No you don't purchase this service from a vendor
   b. Second service
      i) Name and description – Training
      ii) Sales information – Yes you do sell this service to customers. "Training"
      iii) Sales price/rate – $75
      iv) Income account – Sales

v) Is taxable – No
vi) Purchasing information – No you don't purchase this service from a vendor

6   Prepare journal entry 1 as of 12/31/26 with an offset to Opening Balance Equity to record the following beginning balances (if your chart of accounts doesn't already have an accounts receivable or accounts payable account you'll need to add them):

   a. Accounts Receivable (A/R) – Debit $8,500 – Disney (new customer)
   b. Accounts Payable (A/P) – Credit $18,000 – Precor (new vendor)

7   Prepare journal entry 2 as of 12/31/26 to close the Opening Balance Equity to Retained Earnings ($115,500).

8   Prepare and print a Trial Balance report with a custom reporting period of 12/31/2026 to 12/31/2026 and then save it as a customized report named Trial Balance 12/31/2026. Your report should look like Figure 3.24.

Figure 3.24 Trial Balance

Trial Balance
As of December 31, 2026

	DEBIT	CREDIT
Checking	27,000.00	
Accounts Receivable (A/R)	8,500.00	
Inventory Asset	5,500.00	
Prepaid rent	12,000.00	
Furniture:Accumulated Depreciation		10,000.00
Furniture:Original Cost	65,000.00	
Vehicles:Accumulated Depreciation		6,500.00
Vehicles:Original Cost	115,000.00	
Accounts Payable (A/P)		18,000.00
Long-term debt		82,000.00
Common Stock		1,000.00
Opening Balance Equity		0.00
Retained Earnings		115,500.00
TOTAL	$233,000.00	$233,000.00

9   If necessary, prepare and print a Transaction Detail by Account report for all transactions between 1/1/20 and 12/31/30, and save it as a customized report named Transaction Detail by Account. If asked, indicate that your business is accrual based.

10 Use your Transaction Detail by Account report to locate any differences in your Trial Balance report created above.

    a   Make sure all your changes were dated 12/31/26.

    b. Click on the line that does not match to view the transaction for that account and investigate why your answer differs.

    c. Ask your instructor for assistance.

    d. Be sure your company matches the above as you will be adding additional business events in Chapter 4.

Case 5

Your company is a software engineering firm in the state of Alabama. They develop training materials and computer workstations for government and commercial enterprises. In addition, they provide program support, training, and technical solutions. They want to use QBO starting January 1, 2028. Beginning balances as of 12/31/27 have been provided below.

Based on what you learned in the text using the Wild Water Sports company, you are to make the following changes to the case you created in Chapter 2.

1 Modify settings as follows (click the **Gear** icon and then click **Account and Settings**):

    a. Company
        i) Name – Case 05 – Student Name (ID Number)
        ii) SSN – 556-95-7847
        iii) Company type – Sole Proprietor
        iv) Tax form – Form 1040
        v) Industry – Software Publishers
        vi) Email – your email address
        vii) Address – 5100 Bradford Drive, Huntsville, AL 35805. If the address is not listed in the drop-down list, enter it manually.

    b. Sales (turn the following on, and all others turn off or leave off)
        i) Preferred invoice terms – Net 30
        ii) Custom transaction numbers
        iii) Show Product/Service column on sales form
        iv) Track quantity and price/rate
        v) Track inventory quantity on hand
        vi) Show aging table at bottom of statement

    c. Expenses (turn the following on, and all others turn off or leave off)
        i) Show items table on expense and purchase forms
        ii) Use purchase orders

    d. Payments—No changes

    e. Advanced—No changes

2 Add sales tax that is quarterly. (Follow the steps provided in Appendix 1.) Since this company is in Alabama, the instructions and Figure A.1 are different than what's listed for California. There are three agencies that receive tax payments: Alabama Department of Revenue; Alabama, Madison County; and Alabama, Huntsville. Select the filing frequency of quarterly in the three screens. Start date is 01/01/28.

3. Create new accounts and related beginning balances where appropriate (click the **Gear** icon and then click **Chart of Accounts**):
   a. First account
      i) Account type – Banks, Save account under – Bank Accounts
      ii) Tax form section – Checking
      iii) Account name – Checking
      iv) Starting date and opening balance – 12/31/27, $30,000
   b. Second, third, and fourth accounts
      i) Account type – Assets, Save account under – Fixed Assets
      ii) Tax form section – Fixed Asset Computers
      iii) Account name – Fixed Asset Computers
      iv) Starting date and opening balance – n/a
      v) Account type – Assets, Save account under – Fixed Asset Computers
      vi) Tax form section – Fixed Asset Computers
      vii) Account name – Original Cost
      viii) Starting date and opening balance – 12/31/27, $250,000
      ix) Account type – Assets, Save account under – Fixed Asset Computers
      x) Tax form section – Accumulated Depreciation
      xi) Account name – Depreciation
      xii) Starting date and opening balance – 12/31/27, $25,000
   c. Fifth, sixth, and seventh accounts
      i) Account type – Assets, Save account under – Fixed Assets
      ii) Tax form section – Fixed Asset Furniture
      iii) Account name – Fixed Asset Furniture
      iv) Starting date and opening balance – n/a
      v) Account type – Assets, Save account under – Fixed Asset Furniture
      vi) Tax form section – Fixed Asset Furniture
      vii) Account name – Original Cost
      viii) Starting date and opening balance – 12/31/27, $80,000
      ix) Account type – Assets, Save account under – Fixed Asset Furniture
      x) Tax form section – Accumulated Depreciation
      xi) Account name – Depreciation
      xii) Starting date and opening balance – 12/31/27, $8,000
   d. Eighth account
      i) Account type – Liabilities, Save account under – Long-Term Liabilities
      ii) Tax form section – Notes Payable
      iii) Account name – Notes Payable
      iv) Starting date and opening balance – 12/31/27, $45,000
   e. Ninth account
      i) Account type – Equity, Save account under – Equity
      ii) Tax form section – Owner's Equity
      iii) Account name – Owner's Equity
      iv) Starting date and opening balance – 12/31/27, $10,000

f. Tenth account
   i) Account type – Income, Save account under – Income
   ii) Tax form section – Service/Fee Income
   iii) Account name – Consulting

4 Create two new inventory products as follows:

a. First product
   i) Name – Training Materials – Volume 1
   ii) Initial quantity on hand – 20
   iii) As of date – 12/31/27
   iv) Inventory asset account – Inventory
   v) Description – Training Materials – Volume 1
   vi) Sales price/rate – $15,000
   vii) Income account – Sales
   viii) Taxable – standard rate
   ix) Purchasing information – Training Materials – Volume 1
   x) Cost – $8,000
   xi) Expense account – Cost of Goods Sold

b. Second product
   i) Name – Training Materials – Volume 2
   ii) Initial quantity on hand – 30
   iii) As of date – 12/31/27
   iv) Inventory asset account – Inventory
   v) Description – Training Materials – Volume 2
   vi) Sales price/rate – $20,000
   vii) Income account – Sales
   viii) Taxable – standard rate
   ix) Purchasing information – Training Materials – Volume 2
   x) Cost – $10,000
   xi) Expense account – Cost of Goods Sold

5 Create two new service items as follows:

a. First service
   i) Name and Description – Program Support
   ii) Sales information – Yes you do sell this service to customers.
   iii) Sales price/rate – $300
   iv) Income account – Consulting
   v) Nontaxable
   vi) Purchasing information – No you don't purchase this service from a vendor

b. Second service
   i) Name and Description – Technical Solutions
   ii) Sales information – Yes you do sell this service to customers.
   iii) Sales price/rate – $400
   iv) Income account – Consulting
   v) Nontaxable
   vi) Purchase information – No you don't purchase this service from a vendor

6. Prepare journal entry 1 as of 12/31/27 with an offset to Opening Balance Equity to record the following beginning balances:
   a. Accounts Receivable (A/R) – Debit $150,000 – NASA (new customer)
   b. Prepaid Expenses – Debit $10,000
   c. Accounts Payable (A/P) Credit $20,000 – Wild Research Inc. (new vendor)
   d. Notes Payable Credit $500,000 – Chase Bank (new vendor)
7. Prepare journal entry 2 as of 12/31/27 to close the Opening Balance Equity to Owner's Equity ($372,000).
8. Prepare and print a Trial Balance report with a custom reporting period of 1/1/27 to 12/31/27 and then save it as a customized report named Trial Balance 12/31/27. Your report should look like Figure 3.25.

Figure 3.25 Trial Balance

Case 05 - Student Name (ID Number)
Trial Balance
As of December 31, 2027

	DEBIT	CREDIT
Checking	30,000.00	
Accounts Receivable (A/R)	150,000.00	
Inventory	460,000.00	
Prepaid expenses	10,000.00	
Fixed Asset Computers:Depreciation		25,000.00
Fixed Asset Computers:Original Cost	250,000.00	
Fixed Asset Furniture:Depreciation		8,000.00
Fixed Asset Furniture:Original Cost	80,000.00	
Accounts Payable (A/P)		20,000.00
Notes Payable		545,000.00
Opening balance equity		0.00
Owner's Equity		382,000.00
TOTAL	$980,000.00	$980,000.00

9. Prepare and print a Transaction Detail by Account report for all transactions between 1/1/20 and 12/31/30, and save it as a customized report named Transaction Detail by Account. If asked, indicate that your business is accrual based.
10. Use your Transaction Detail by Account report to locate any differences in your Trial Balance report created above.
    a. Make sure all your changes were dated 12/31/27.
    b. Click on the line that does not match to view the transaction for that account, and investigate why your answer differs.

c. Ask your instructor for assistance.

d. Be sure your company matches the above as you will be adding additional business events in Chapter 4.

Case 6

Your company is a Recreational Vehicle (RV) dealership in the state of Washington. They sell new RVs and related accessories to individuals and businesses. In addition, they repair and service RVs. They began business in 2021 and want to use QBO starting January 1, 2023. Beginning balances as of 12/31/22 have been provided below.

Based on what you learned in the text using the Wild Water Sports company, you are to make the following changes to the case you created in Chapter 2.

1 Modify settings as follows (click the **Gear** icon and then click **Account and Settings**):

   a. Company
      i) Name – Case 06 – Student Name (ID Number)
      ii) EIN – 99-9811161
      iii) Tax form – Form 1120
      iv) Industry – Automotive Dealers
      v) Email – your email address
      vi) Address – 4309 E Valley Hwy E, Sumner, WA 98390

   b. Sales (turn the following on, all others turn off or leave off)
      i) Preferred invoice terms – Net 30
      ii) Custom transaction numbers
      iii) Show Product/Service column on sales form
      iv) Track quantity and price/rate
      v) Track inventory quantity on hand
      vi) Show aging table at bottom of statement

   c. Expenses (turn the following on, all others turn off or leave off)
      i) Show items table on expense and purchase forms
      ii) Use purchase orders

   d. Payments—No changes

   e. Advanced—No changes

2 Add sales tax that is payable to the Washington State Department of Revenue. (Follow the steps provided in Appendix 1.)

3 Create new accounts and related beginning balances where appropriate (click the **Gear** icon and then click **Chart of Accounts**):

   a. First account
      i) Account Type – Bank
      ii) Detail Type – Checking
      iii) Name – Checking
      iv) Balance as of 12/31/22 – $50,000

   b. Second account
      i) Account Type – Accounts Receivable (A/R)
      ii) Detail Type – Accounts Receivable (A/R)
      iii) Name – Accounts Receivable (A/R)
      iv) Balance as of 12/31/22 – n/a

c. Third account
   i) Account Type – Other Current Assets
   ii) Detail Type – Loans to Officers
   iii) Name – Loans to Officers
   iv) Balance as of 12/31/22 – $15,000
d. Fourth and fifth accounts (Note: When entering a new fixed asset, place a check in the **Track depreciation of this asset** check box to reveal Original cost and Depreciation text boxes. Enter both amounts from above as positive numbers.)
   i) Account Type – Fixed Asset
   ii) Detail Type – Buildings
   iii) Name – Buildings
   iv) Original cost $150,000
   v) Depreciation $15,000
   vi) Balance as of 12/31/22
e. Sixth and seventh accounts (see note above)
   i) Account Type – Fixed Asset
   ii) Detail Type – Machinery & Equipment
   iii) Name – Machinery & Equipment
   iv) Original cost $100,000
   v) Depreciation $10,000
   vi) Balance as of 12/31/22
f. Eighth account
   i) Account Type – Accounts Payable (A/P)
   ii) Detail Type – Accounts Payable (A/P)
   iii) Name – Accounts Payable (A/P)
   iv) Balance as of 12/31/22 – n/a
g. Ninth account
   i) Account Type – Long-Term Liabilities
   ii) Detail Type – Notes Payable
   iii) Name – Notes Payable
   iv) Balance as of 12/31/22 – n/a
h. Tenth account
   i) Account Type – Equity
   ii) Detail Type – Common Stock
   iii) Name – Common Stock
   iv) Balance as of 12/31/22 – n/a
i. Eleventh account
   i) Account Type – Equity
   ii) Detail Type – Paid-In Capital or Surplus
   iii) Name – Paid-In Capital
   iv) Balance as of 12/31/22 – n/a

4 Create two new Inventory products as follows:
   a. First product
      i) Name – 2022 Winnebago Revel 44E
      ii) Initial quantity on hand – 2
      iii) As of date – 12/31/22
      iv) Inventory asset account – Inventory Asset

v) Description – 2022 Winnebago Revel 44E
vi) Sales price/rate – $150,000
vii) Income account – Sales of Product Income
viii) Sales Tax Category – Taxable-Standard rate
ix) Purchasing information – 2022 Winnebago Revel 44E
x) Cost – $120,000
xi) Expense account – Cost of Goods Sold

b. Second product
i) Name – 2022 Winnebago View 24G
ii) Initial quantity on hand – 3
iii) As of date – 12/31/22
iv) Inventory asset account – Inventory Asset
v) Description – 2022 Winnebago View 24G
vi) Sales price/rate – $140,000
vii) Income account – Sales of Product Income
viii) Sales Tax Category – Taxable-Standard rate
ix) Purchasing information – 2022 Winnebago View 24G
x) Cost – $112,000
xi) Expense account – Cost of Goods Sold

5 Create two new service items as follows:

a. First service
i) Name – Lube, Oil, Filter
ii) Description – Yes you do sell this service to customers. "Lube, Oil, Filter"
iii) Sales price/rate – $300
iv) Income account – Sales
v) Sales Tax Category – Nontaxable
vi) Purchasing information – No you don't purchase this service from a vendor

b. Second service
i) Name – Transmission Service
ii) Description – Yes you do sell this service to customers. "Transmission Service"
iii) Sales price/rate – $350
iv) Income account – Sales
v) Sales Tax Category – Nontaxable
vi) Purchasing information – No you don't purchase this service from a vendor

6 Prepare journal entry 1 as of 12/31/22 with an offset to Opening Balance Equity to record the following beginning balances:

a. Accounts Receivable (A/R) – Debit $10,000 – Sam Ski (new customer)

b. Accounts Payable (A/P) – Credit $464,000 – Winnebago (new vendor)

c. Notes Payable Credit $100,000 – Chase Bank (new vendor)

d. Common Stock Credit $1,000

e. Paid-In Capital Credit $250,000

f. Opening Balance Equity Debit $805,000

7. Prepare journal entry 2 as of 12/31/22 to close the Opening Balance Equity to Retained Earnings ($61,000).

8. Prepare and print a Trial Balance report with a custom reporting period of 1/1/22 to 12/31/22 and then save it as a customized report named Trial Balance 12/31/22. Your report should look like Figure 3.26.

Figure 3.26

Trial Balance

Case 06 - Student Name (ID Number)

TRIAL BALANCE
As of December 31, 2022

	DEBIT	CREDIT
Checking	50,000.00	
Accounts Receivable (A/R)	10,000.00	
Inventory Asset	576,000.00	
Loans To Officers	15,000.00	
Buildings:Depreciation		15,000.00
Buildings:Original cost	150,000.00	
Machinery & Equipment:Depreciation		10,000.00
Machinery & Equipment:Original cost	100,000.00	
Accounts Payable (A/P)		464,000.00
Notes Payable		100,000.00
Common Stock		1,000.00
Opening Balance Equity		0.00
Paid-In Capital		250,000.00
Retained Earnings		61,000.00
TOTAL	**$901,000.00**	**$901,000.00**

9. Prepare and print a Transaction Detail by Account report for all transactions between 1/1/10 and 12/31/25 and then save it as a customized report named Transaction Detail by Account. If asked, indicate that your business is accrual based.

10. Use your Transaction Detail by Account report to locate any differences in your Trial Balance report created above.

    a. Make sure all your changes were dated 12/31/22.

    b. Click on the line that does not match to view the transaction for that account and investigate why your answer differs.

    c. Ask your instructor for assistance.

    d. Be sure your company matches the above as you will be adding additional business events in Chapter 4.

Recording Operating Activities: Sales and Cash Receipts

Student Learning Outcomes

Upon completion of this chapter, the student will be able to do the following:

- Add a new service, product, and customer
- Record a sales receipt
- Record an invoice for services rendered on account
- Record an invoice for products sold on account
- Record cash receipts (payments received on account)
- Deposit payments received on account
- Prepare Trial Balance and Transaction Detail by Account reports

Overview

In Chapter 3 you modified company settings, added new accounts to the chart of accounts, and added beginning balances where appropriate. You added customers, vendors, products, and services and closed the Opening Balance Equity account. In this chapter, you will add operating activities like sales receipts, invoices, and cash receipts. Specifically, you will be recording operating activities, such as adding new services, new products, new customers, new sales receipts, new invoices, and new cash receipts to the Wild Water Sports company. At the end of the chapter, you will perform the same tasks completed on the Wild Water Sports company on a case assigned by your instructor.

Services, Products, and Customers

In this section, you will add new services, products, and customers. To add new services and products, you will access the Product and Services section using the Gear icon. To add customers, you will use the Customers menu item in the navigation bar, but first we'll verify your starting numbers are correct.

Chapter 4 Recording Operating Activities: Sales and Cash Receipts

Navigate your browser to the Video Tutorials provided by Intuit (see website address specified in the Preface to this text) and then search on How to Set Up Service Items.

To add new services, products, and customers to the Wild Water Sports company, do the following:

1. Sign into your QBO account, then open the Wild Water Sports company you used in Chapter 3.
2. Click **Reports** then click the **Custom reports** tab, then click **Trial Balance** to open the Trial Balance report. Set the to and from dates to **01/01/2027**. Compare your report to Figure 4.1. If your report doesn't match Figure 4.1, go back to your work in Chapter 3 to fix your errors. Otherwise close your Trial Balance report.

Figure 4.1
Wild Water Sports trial balance as of 1/1/27

Wild Water Sports - Student Name (ID Number)
Trial Balance
As of January 1, 2027

	DEBIT	CREDIT
Checking	25,000.00	
Accounts receivable (A/R)	70,000.00	
Inventory	172,800.00	
Prepaid expenses	15,000.00	
Equipment:Accumulated depreciation		10,000.00
Equipment:Original Cost	40,000.00	
Accounts Payable (A/P)		56,000.00
Long-term business loans		50,000.00
Common stock		1,000.00
Opening balance equity		0.00
Retained Earnings		205,800.00
TOTAL	$322,800.00	$322,800.00

3. Click the **Gear** icon, and click **Products and services**.
4. Click **New** in the upper-right corner of the Products and Services list.
5. Click **Service**.
6. Type **Cleaning** in the Name and Description text boxes.
7. Check the I sell this product/service to my customers check box, and then type **500** in the Price/rate text box.
8. Select Service Revenue as the Income account and then click **Edit sales tax**, then click **Nontaxable,** and then click **Select**. Your window should now look like Figure 4.2.

Recording Operating Activities: Sales and Cash Receipts **Chapter 4** 97

Figure 4.2

Adding a new service

Cleaning

Basic info

Name*: Cleaning

Item type: Service

SKU:

Category:

Sales

☑ I sell this service to my customers

Description: Cleaning

Price/rate: 500

Income account*: Service Revenue

Sales tax: Nontaxable

9. Click the **Create new** button.
10. Click the down arrow in **New** and select **Inventory item.**
11. Type **Tige 25 zx** in the Name text box.
12. Type **0** in the Initial Quantity On Hand text box and type **1/1/2027** in the As Of Date text box.
13. Select **Inventory** as the Inventory asset account.
14. Type **Tige 25 zx** in the Description and Purchasing information text boxes. Select **Boats** as the Category.
15. Type **225000** in the Sales price/rate text box, then type **01/01/2027** in the As of date text box, and then type **180000** in the Cost text box.

VIDEO LINK

Navigate your browser to the Video Tutorials provided by Intuit (see website address specified in the Preface to this text) and then search on How to Create an Inventory Product.

98 Chapter 4   *Recording Operating Activities: Sales and Cash Receipts*

16 Select **Sales** from the Income account drop-down list and **Cost of Goods Sold** from the Expense account drop-down list.

17 Click **Edit sales tax**, then click **Taxable**, and then click **Select**. A partial view of the Product or Service Information window should look like Figure 4.3. Note that the Wild Water Sports company had already set up Sales Taxes. To learn more about setting up Sales Taxes read Appendix 1—Sales Taxes.

Figure 4.3

Adding a new product (partial view)

Navigate your browser to the Video Tutorials provided by Intuit (see website address specified in the Preface to this text) and then search on How to Set Up Sales Tax.

Add a new product
Basic info
Name*
Tige 25 zx
Item type
Inventory item
SKU
Category
Inventory
Initial quantity on hand*   As of date*
0   01/01/2027
Reorder point   What's the reorder point?   Inventory asset account*
Inventory

18 Click the **Create new** button.

19 Click the **Category** title to sort the products and services list by category. Scroll down the revised list of Products and Services to see the service and product you entered as shown in Figure 4.4.

Figure 4.4 Updated list of Products and Services (partial view)

NAME	QTY ON HAND	CATEGORY ↑	SKU	TYPE	PRICE
Tige 25 zx	0 OUT	Boats		Inventory	225000
Malibu Sportster LX	3	Boats		Inventory	52000
Malibu Sunset LX	1	Boats		Inventory	60000
Cleaning				Service	500

20 Click **Sales** from the navigation bar, then click **Customers**, and then click the **New customer** button.

21 Type **James** in the First name text box and **Rogers** in the Last name text box. Type **j.rogers@gmail.com** in the Email text box and then type **805 588 1234** in the Mobile number text box.

22 Type **Performance Rentals** in the Company name, Customer display name, and Name to print on checks text boxes.

23 Type **15 Hwy 22, Orlando, FL 32807 United States** in the appropriate text boxes. Click **Save** to view the data you just entered and then click the **Customer Details** column title. A partial view of the Customer information window is shown in Figure 4.5.

Navigate your browser to the Video Tutorials provided by Intuit (see website address specified in the Preface to this text) and then search on How to Manage Customers.

Figure 4.5 Customer information window (partial view)

Performance Rentals

Company: Performance Rentals
Billing address: 15 Hwy 22, Orlando, FL 32807, United States
Notes: Add notes

SUMMARY
$0.00 Open balance
$0.00 Overdue payment

Transaction List | Statements | Recurring Transactions | **Customer Details** | Late Fees

Contact info
- Customer: Performance Rentals
- Email: j.rogers@gmail.com
- Phone: -
- Mobile: (805) 588-1234

Additional info
- Billing address: 15 Hwy 22, Orlando, FL 32807, United States
- Shipping address: 15 Hwy 22, Orlando, FL 32807, United States
- Terms: -

24. Click the **Edit** button. Scroll down the page to the Payments section and select **Net 30** from the Terms text box, then click **Save**.

25. The Performance Rentals customer window appears as shown in Figure 4.6.

Figure 4.6 Performance Rentals customer window

Performance Rentals

Company	Billing address	SUMMARY
Performance Rentals	15 Hwy 22, Orlando, FL 32807, United States	**$0.00** Open balance
Notes		**$0.00** Overdue payment
Add notes		

Transaction List | Statements | Recurring Transactions | **Customer Details** | Late Fees

Contact info

Customer	Performance Rentals
Email	j.rogers@gmail.com
Phone	-
Mobile	(805) 588-1234

Additional info

Billing address	15 Hwy 22, Orlando, FL 32807, United States
Shipping address	15 Hwy 22, Orlando, FL 32807, United States
Terms	Net 30

26. Click **Dashboards**.

Navigate your browser to the Video Tutorials provided by Intuit (see website address specified in the Preface to this text) and then search on Sales Receipt versus Invoice.

You have now added a new service, a new product, and a new customer. Next up, adding sales receipts to record cash sales and invoices to record credit sales.

Sales Receipts and Invoices

A business uses sales receipts to record sales transactions on a daily basis when payment is received at the same time as a product or service is delivered. Sales invoices are used to record sales transactions when customers are granted credit terms and given some time to pay after a product or service is delivered. In either case, sales are recorded when the product is sold or service is rendered.

Recording Operating Activities: Sales and Cash Receipts **Chapter 4** **101**

To add sales receipts and invoices to the Wild Water Sports company, do the following:

1. Continue from where you left off. If you closed the Wild Water Sports company, follow the steps at the beginning of this chapter to reopen it.

2. Click the **+ New** icon, and select **Sales receipt** as shown in Figure 4.7.

CUSTOMERS	VENDORS	EMPLOYEES	OTHER
Invoice	Expense	Payroll ↑	Bank deposit
Receive payment	Check	Time entry	Transfer
Estimate	Bill	Add employee ↑	Journal entry
Credit memo	Pay bills	Add contractor	Statement
Sales receipt	Purchase order		Inventory qty adjustment
Refund receipt	Vendor credit		Pay down credit card
Delayed credit	Credit card credit		Add product/service
Delayed charge	Print checks		
Add customer	Add vendor		

Figure 4.7

Create window (adding a sales receipt)

VIDEO LINK

Navigate your browser to the Video Tutorials provided by Intuit (see website address specified in the Preface to this text) and then search on How to Record a Sales Receipt.

3. Click **+ Add new** from the Customer drop-down list, then type **Southtown Watersports** as the new customer's company name, then select **Due on receipt** from the Terms text box, and then type **3333 Scott Futrell Dr. Charlotte NC 28208** as their address. Click **Save**.

4. Change the Sales Receipt date to **01/04/2027**.

5. Select **Check** from the Payment methods drop-down list and **6985** as the Reference no.

6. Select **Payments to Deposit** from the Deposit to drop-down text box. The check will be recorded in the Payments to deposit account as deposits for this company are made every other day.

7. On line 1 of the sales receipt, select **Malibu Sportster LX** in the Product/Service column.

8. Type **1** in the QTY (Quantity) column and then press [**Tab**]. The sales receipt should look like Figure 4.8. Note: you may have to click **See the math** in the sales tax section to apply sales tax.

9. Click **See the math** to view Figure 4.9 which shows how sales tax was calculated.

Figure 4.8 Sales Receipt

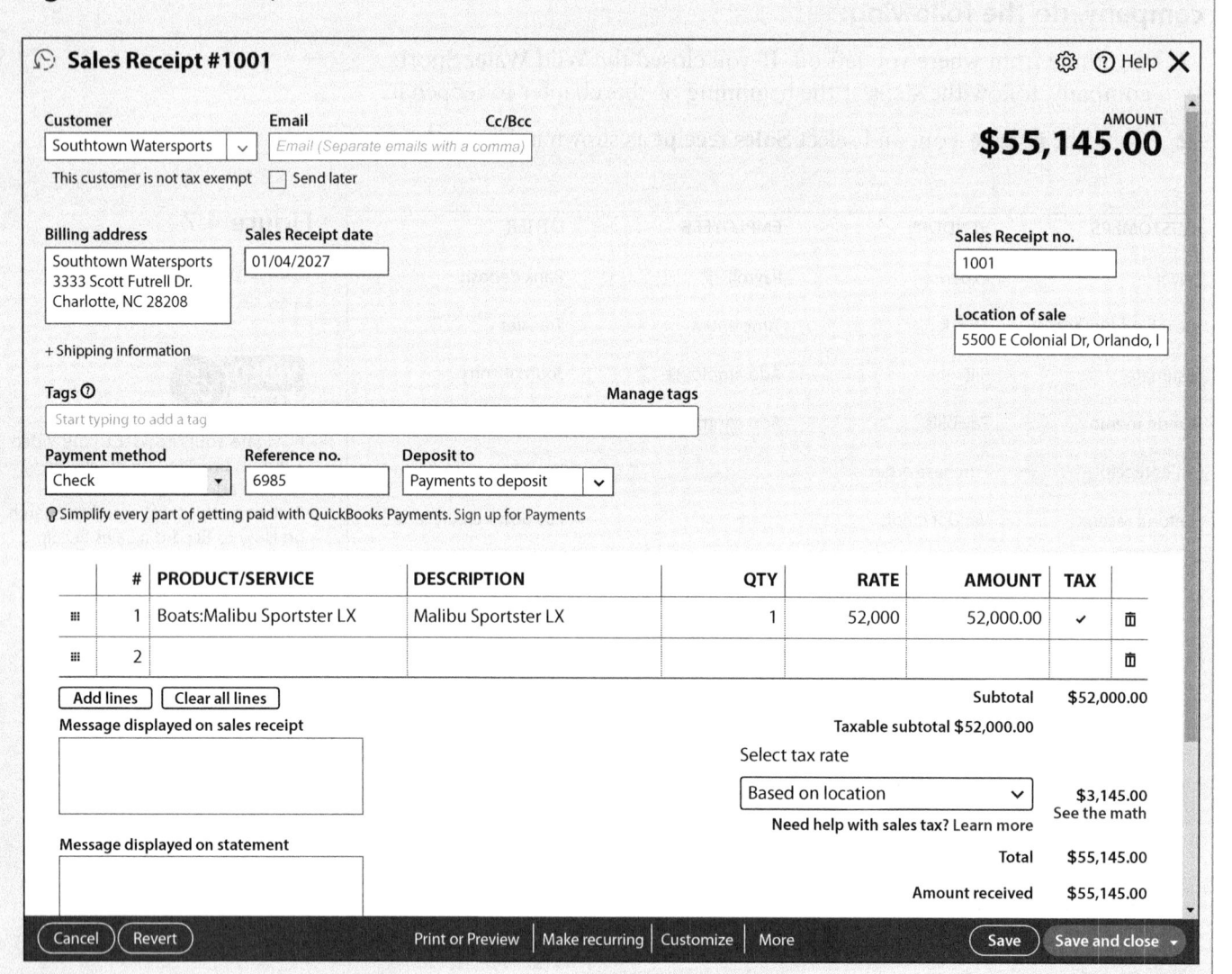

	#	PRODUCT/SERVICE	DESCRIPTION	QTY	RATE	AMOUNT	TAX
	1	Boats:Malibu Sportster LX	Malibu Sportster LX	1	52,000	52,000.00	✓
	2						

Sales Receipt #1001 — Customer: Southtown Watersports — Sales Receipt date: 01/04/2027 — Sales Receipt no.: 1001 — Location of sale: 5500 E Colonial Dr, Orlando, l — Payment method: Check — Reference no.: 6985 — Deposit to: Payments to deposit — Amount: $55,145.00

Subtotal $52,000.00
Taxable subtotal $52,000.00
Select tax rate: Based on location — $3,145.00
Total $55,145.00
Amount received $55,145.00

10. Click **Close** and then click **Save and close** in the Sales Receipt window.

11. Click the **+ New** icon, and select **Invoice**. If a window displays asking if you want to take a tour, click the **Go to invoice** button.

12. Select **Performance Rentals** from the Customer drop-down list in the upper-left corner of the Invoice window.

13. Type **Net 30** in the Terms text box and then type **01/06/2027** in the Invoice date text box. The Invoice no. text box should show 1002 as the invoice number.

14. On line 1 of the invoice, select **Malibu Sportster LX** as the product sold.

15. Type **1** in the QTY column.

16. On line 2 of the invoice, select **Malibu Sunset LX** as the product sold and type **1** in the QTY column.

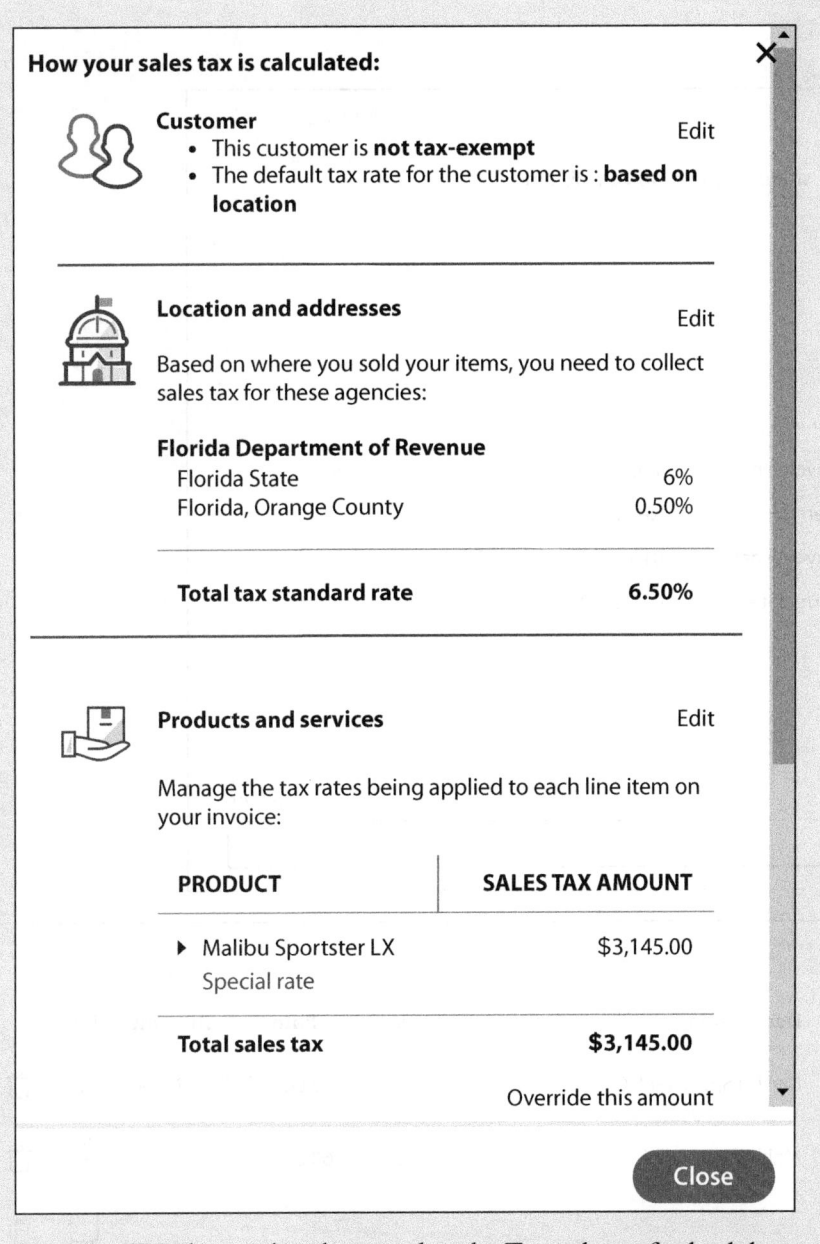

Recording Operating Activities: Sales and Cash Receipts   **Chapter 4**   103

Figure 4.9

Sales tax calculations

How your sales tax is calculated:

Customer Edit
- This customer is **not tax-exempt**
- The default tax rate for the customer is : **based on location**

Location and addresses Edit

Based on where you sold your items, you need to collect sales tax for these agencies:

Florida Department of Revenue
Florida State   6%
Florida, Orange County   0.50%

Total tax standard rate   **6.50%**

Products and services Edit

Manage the tax rates being applied to each line item on your invoice:

PRODUCT	SALES TAX AMOUNT
▸ Malibu Sportster LX Special rate	$3,145.00
Total sales tax	**$3,145.00**

Override this amount

Close

17 Press the [**Tab**] key and make sure that the Tax column for both boats are checked. Note: you may have to click **See the math** to apply sales tax. The invoice should look like Figure 4.10. Click **Save and close** in the Invoice window.

18 To record an invoice for services rendered, click the **+ New** and then click **Invoice** like you did in the previous example.

19 Click **+ Add new** in the Customer drop-down text.

20 Type **Florida Ski School** in the Company name text box and then type **Net 30** as their terms.

21 Type **10900 Chase Road Windermere FL 34786** as their address and then click **Save**.

22 Type **01/10/2027** as the Invoice date.

Figure 4.10 Invoice

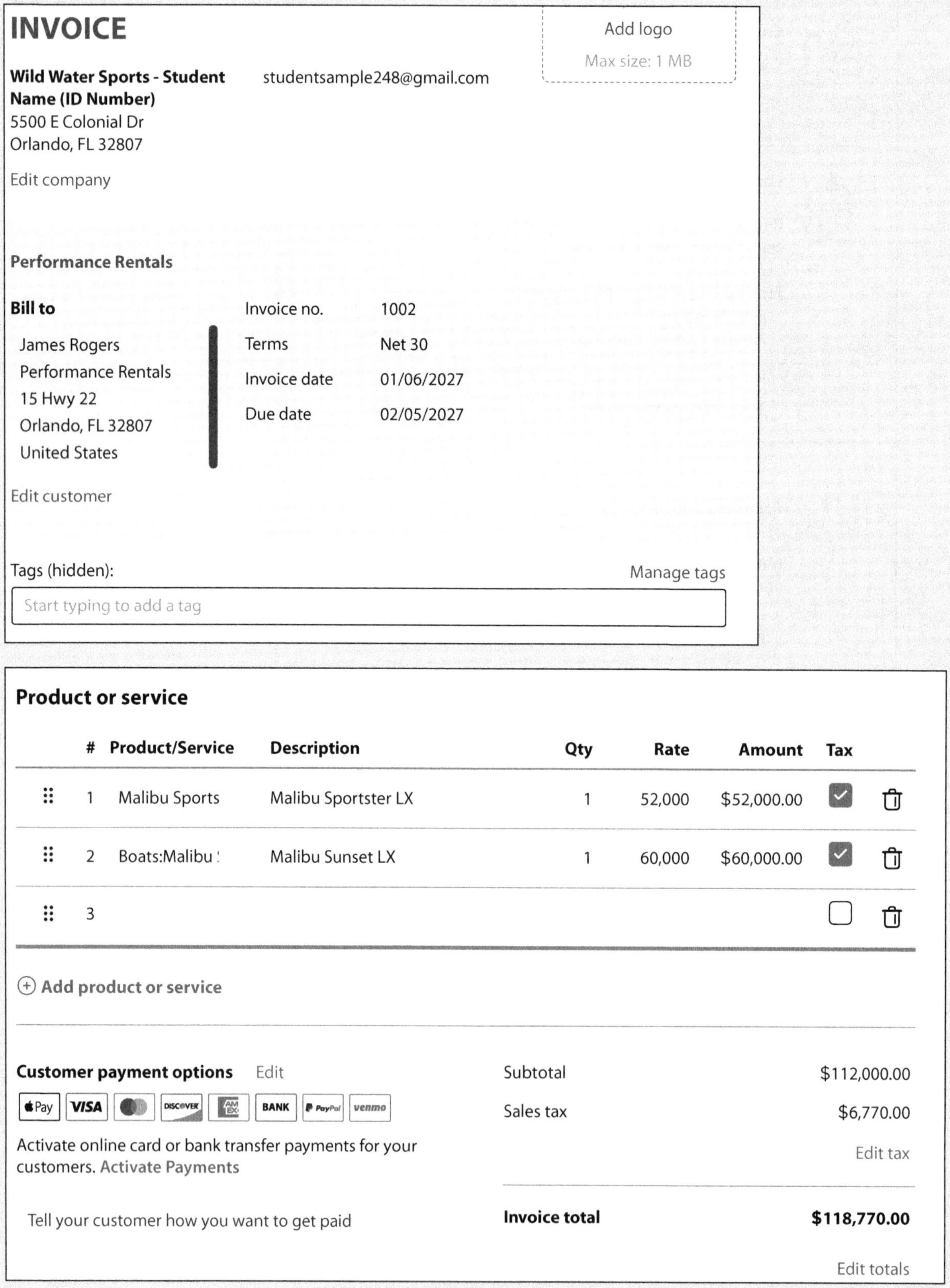

INVOICE

Add logo
Max size: 1 MB

Wild Water Sports - Student Name (ID Number) studentsample248@gmail.com
5500 E Colonial Dr
Orlando, FL 32807

Edit company

Performance Rentals

Bill to

James Rogers	Invoice no. 1002
Performance Rentals	Terms Net 30
15 Hwy 22	Invoice date 01/06/2027
Orlando, FL 32807	Due date 02/05/2027
United States	

Edit customer

Tags (hidden):   Manage tags

Start typing to add a tag

Product or service

#	Product/Service	Description	Qty	Rate	Amount	Tax
1	Malibu Sports	Malibu Sportster LX	1	52,000	$52,000.00	✓
2	Boats:Malibu	Malibu Sunset LX	1	60,000	$60,000.00	✓
3						☐

⊕ Add product or service

Customer payment options Edit

 Pay | VISA | ⬤ | DISCOVER | AMEX | BANK | PayPal | venmo

Activate online card or bank transfer payments for your customers. **Activate Payments**

Tell your customer how you want to get paid

Subtotal	$112,000.00
Sales tax	$6,770.00
	Edit tax
Invoice total	**$118,770.00**
	Edit totals

23 Select **Diagnostic Service** from the Product/Service text box, then type **4** as the quantity, then press **[Tab]** to view invoice 1003 shown in Figure 4.11.

Recording Operating Activities: Sales and Cash Receipts **Chapter 4** 105

Figure 4.11 Invoice for services rendered

Florida Ski School

Bill to
Florida Ski School
10900 Chase Road
Windermere, FL 34786

Invoice no. 1003
Terms Net 30
Invoice date 01/10/2027
Due date 02/09/2027

Edit customer

Tags (hidden): Manage tags

Start typing to add a tag

Product or service

#	Product/Service	Description	Qty	Rate	Amount	Tax
1	Diagnostic Ser	Diagnostic Service	4	500	$2,000.00	
2						

⊕ Add product or service

Customer payment options Edit

ÉPay VISA ●● DISCOVER AMEX BANK PayPal venmo

Activate online card or bank transfer payments for your customers. Activate Payments

Tell your customer how you want to get paid

Subtotal $2,000.00
Sales tax $0.00
Edit tax
Invoice total **$2,000.00**

24 Click **Save and close**.

25 Click **Sales** and then select **All Sales**. Click on the column title **Date** to sort the report by date. A listing of recent transactions is shown in Figure 4.12.

Figure 4.12 All Sales

DATE ▲	TYPE	NO.	CUSTOMER	MEMO	AMOUNT	STATUS
12/31/26	Journal Entry	3	Refugio		$70,000.00	Open
1/4/27	Sales Receipt	1001	Southtown Watersports		$55,145.00	✓ Paid
1/6/27	Invoice	1002	Performance Rentals		$118,770.00	Due on 2/5/27
1/10/27	Invoice	1003	Florida Ski School		$2,000.00	Due on 2/9/27

Cash Receipts

In QBO, the concept of cash receipts is referred to as receiving payments. Thus, to record the receipt of payment from a customer, you can use the Receive Payment item in the Create menu to record the transaction, or you can use Receive Payment from the Action column in a customer's list of transactions. Once a payment is received, it must be deposited into your bank account. This is a separate but important process in QBO.

To record the receipt of a payment from a customer, do the following:

1. Continue from where you left off. If you closed the Wild Water Sports company, follow the steps at the beginning of this chapter to reopen it.
2. Click the [+ New] icon, and select **Receive payment** as shown in Figure 4.13.

Figure 4.13

Receive Payment (recording the receipt of a customer payment)

Navigate your browser to the Video Tutorials provided by Intuit (see website address specified in the Preface to this text) and then search on How to Record the Receipt of Payment on an Invoice.

CUSTOMERS
Invoice
Receive payment
Estimate
Credit memo
Sales receipt
Refund receipt
Delayed credit
Delayed charge
Add customer

3. Select **Refugio** from the Customer drop-down list in the upper-left corner of the Receive Payment window.
4. Type **1/12/2027** as the Payment date.
5. Select **Check** as the Payment method. Select **Payments to deposit** from the Deposit to text box.
6. Place a check in the **Journal Entry #3** check box as shown in Figure 4.14. This was the accounts receivable balance recorded when you set up your company's accounts. Click **Save and close**.
7. Recall that when the two payments above were received they were recorded to an account titled Payments to deposit. Now it's time to deposit one of those payments to our bank and record that deposit into our checking account. Click the [+ New] icon, and select **Bank deposit** from the Other column as shown in Figure 4.15.

Figure 4.14 Receive Payment window

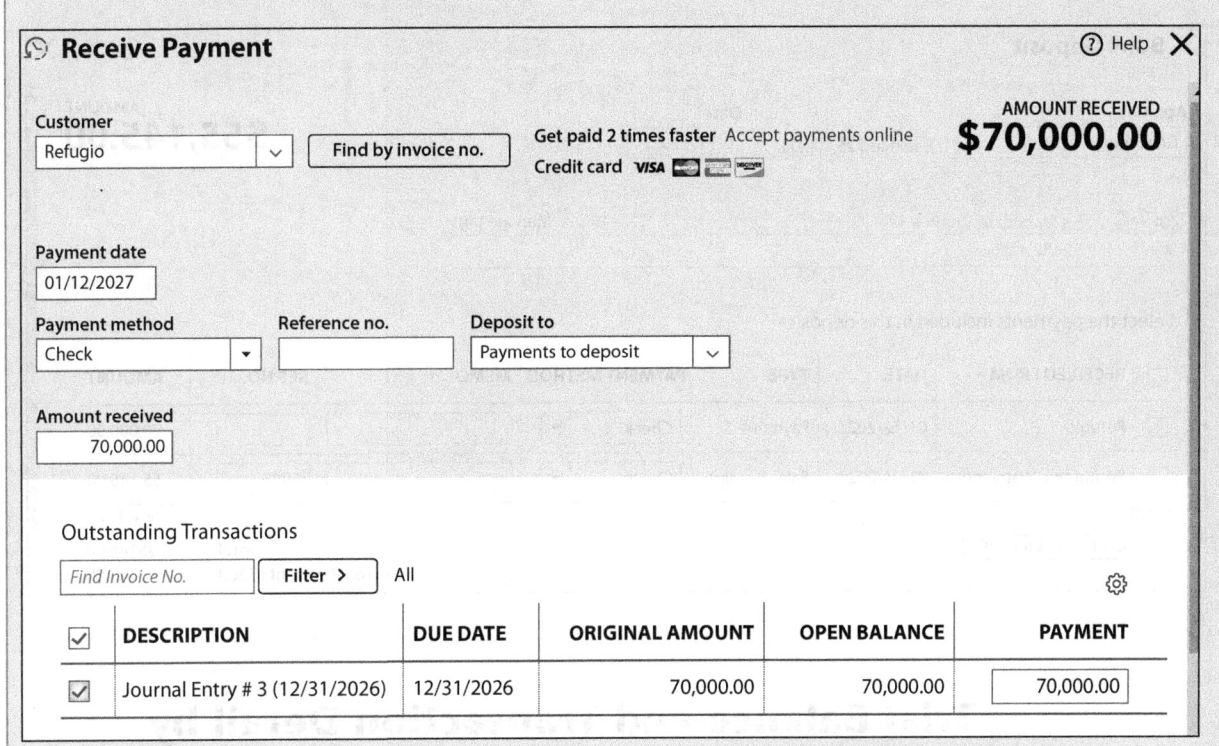

Receive Payment			Help ✕
Customer Refugio ▾	Find by invoice no.	Get paid 2 times faster Accept payments online Credit card VISA 💳 💳 💳	**AMOUNT RECEIVED** **$70,000.00**

Payment date
01/12/2027

Payment method	**Reference no.**	**Deposit to**
Check ▾		Payments to deposit ▾

Amount received
70,000.00

Outstanding Transactions

Find Invoice No.   Filter >   All   ⚙

✓	DESCRIPTION	DUE DATE	ORIGINAL AMOUNT	OPEN BALANCE	PAYMENT
✓	Journal Entry # 3 (12/31/2026)	12/31/2026	70,000.00	70,000.00	70,000.00

OTHER

Bank deposit

Transfer

Journal entry

Statement

Inventory qty adjustment

Pay down credit card

Add product/service

Figure 4.15

Create window (inputting a bank deposit)

VIDEO LINK 🔗

Navigate your browser to the Video Tutorials provided by Intuit (see website address specified in the Preface to this text) and then search on How to Record a Bank Deposit.

8 Select **Checking** as the account you're depositing to then select **1/12/2027** as the date of deposit. Select the payment received from **Southtown Watersports** from the list of existing payments as shown in Figure 4.16.

9 Click **Save and close**.

Figure 4.16 Deposit window

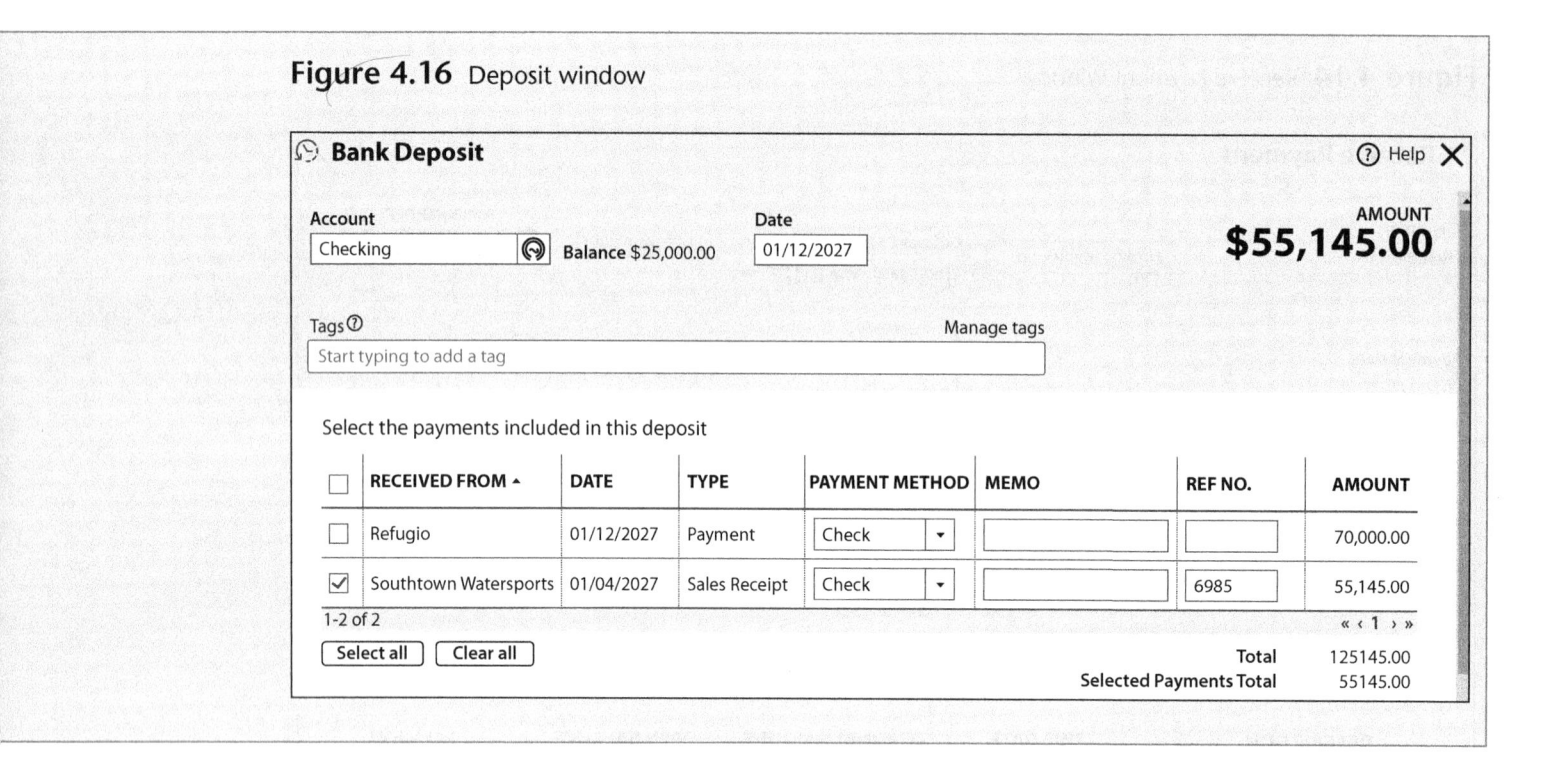

	RECEIVED FROM ▲	DATE	TYPE	PAYMENT METHOD	MEMO	REF NO.	AMOUNT
☐	Refugio	01/12/2027	Payment	Check			70,000.00
☑	Southtown Watersports	01/04/2027	Sales Receipt	Check		6985	55,145.00

Bank Deposit — Account: Checking, Balance $25,000.00, Date 01/12/2027, Amount $55,145.00

Total 125145.00
Selected Payments Total 55145.00

Trial Balance and Transaction Detail by Account

In Wild Water Sports and the cases found at the end of each chapter, you will be asked to create a Trial Balance report as of a certain date. You will compare your Trial Balance report with the one provided in the case to see if you have correctly recorded various business events. If your Trial Balance differs, you will need to fix your errors.

A usual explanation for an incorrect Trial Balance report is recording a transaction in an incorrect period, not recording it at all, or recording it incorrectly. To investigate, you will need to create a transaction detail by account report for a specific period. You can create such a report for all transactions to see if yours were recorded in the proper period and to see where you may have entered a wrong amount or account.

To create, print, and export a trial balance and transaction detail by account report:

1. Continue from your work earlier.
2. Click **Reports** from the navigation bar.
3. Click the **Custom reports** tab.
4. Select **Trial Balance**.
5. Type **01/01/2027** and **01/13/2027** as the from and to dates. You may have to scroll to the top of this report to see the Report period date text boxes.
6. Click **Run report**. The report is shown in Figure 4.17.

Figure 4.17 Trial Balance Report as of 1/13/2027

Wild Water Sports - Student Name (ID Number)
Trial Balance
As of January 13, 2027

	DEBIT	CREDIT
Checking	80,145.00	
Accounts receivable (A/R)	120,770.00	
Inventory	41,600.00	
Payments to deposit	70,000.00	
Prepaid expenses	15,000.00	
Equipment:Accumulated depreciation		10,000.00
Equipment:Original Cost	40,000.00	
Accounts Payable (A/P)		56,000.00
Florida Department of Revenue Payable		9,915.00
Long-term business loans		50,000.00
Common stock		1,000.00
Opening balance equity		0.00
Retained Earnings		205,800.00
Sales		164,000.00
Service Revenue		2,000.00
Cost of goods sold	131,200.00	
TOTAL	$498,715.00	$498,715.00

7   Click **Reports**, then click the **Custom Reports** tab, then click **Transaction Detail by Account**.

8   Click in the **Report Period** text box and select **All Dates** to view the report shown in Figure 4.18.

9   Click **Save customization**, then type **Transaction Detail by Account All Dates** as the report name, then click **Save**.

10 Click the **Print** icon to print this report.

11 Sign out of this company.

Figure 4.18 Transaction Detail by Account Report (partial view)

Wild Water Sports - Student Name (ID Number)
Transaction Detail by Account
All Dates

DATE	TRANSACTION TYPE	NUM	NAME	MEMO/DESCRIPTION	SPLIT	AMOUNT	BALANCE
▼ Checking							
12/31/2026	Deposit			Opening Balance	Opening balance equity	25,000.00	25,000.00
01/12/2027	Deposit		Southtown Watersports		Payments to deposit	55,145.00	80,145.00
Total for Checking						**$80,145.00**	
▼ Accounts receivable (A/R)							
12/31/2026	Journal Entry	3			-Split-	70,000.00	70,000.00
01/06/2027	Invoice	1002	Performance Rentals		-Split-	118,770.00	188,770.00
01/10/2027	Invoice	1003	Florida Ski School		Service Revenue	2,000.00	190,770.00
01/12/2027	Payment		Refugio		Payments to deposit	−70,000.00	120,770.00
Total for Accounts receivable (A/R)						**$120,770.00**	
▼ Inventory							
12/31/2026	Inventory Starting Value	START		Malibu Sportster LX - Opening in...	Opening balance equity	124,800.00	124,800.00
12/31/2026	Inventory Starting Value	START		Malibu Sunset LX - Opening inve...	Opening balance equity	48,000.00	172,800.00
01/01/2027	Inventory Starting Value	START		Tige 25 zx - Opening inventory a...	Opening balance equity	0.00	172,800.00
01/04/2027	Sales Receipt	1001	Southtown Watersports	Malibu Sportster LX	Payments to deposit	−41,600.00	131,200.00
01/06/2027	Invoice	1002	Performance Rentals	Malibu Sportster LX	Accounts receivable (A/R)	−41,600.00	89,600.00
01/06/2027	Invoice	1002	Performance Rentals	Malibu Sunset LX	Accounts receivable (A/R)	−48,000.00	41,600.00
Total for Inventory						**$41,600.00**	
▼ Payments to deposit							
01/04/2027	Sales Receipt	1001	Southtown Watersports		Sales	55,145.00	55,145.00
01/12/2027	Payment		Refugio		Accounts receivable (A/R)	70,000.00	125,145.00
01/12/2027	Deposit		Southtown Watersports		Checking	−55,145.00	70,000.00
Total for Payments to deposit						**$70,000.00**	
▼ Prepaid expenses							
12/31/2026	Deposit		Allstate Insurance		Opening balance equity	15,000.00	15,000.00
Total for Prepaid expenses						**$15,000.00**	

Be sure to verify that your Trial Balance and Transaction Detail by Account reports match those shown above. This report can help in identifying and correcting errors.

End Note

You have now added a customer, product, and service. You have recorded a sales receipt, invoice, payment received from a customer, and deposit to a bank account. These are operating activities. Additional operating activities related to purchases and cash payments follow in Chapter 5.

Chapter 4 Questions

1. What steps need to be followed to add a new product or service?
2. What steps need to be followed to record a new sales receipt?
3. What steps need to be followed to record a new invoice?
4. What steps need to be followed to record a new payment from a customer?
5. What steps need to be followed to record a new deposit to the bank?
6. What are the differences between adding a new product and adding a new service?
7. What is the difference between a sales receipt and a sales invoice?

Chapter 4 Matching

a. Invoice _____ A service in the Wild Water Sports company

b. Sales receipt _____ Providing the bank a payment from a customer

c. Product _____ Used when recording a sale on account

d. Service _____ Used to add invoices, sales receipts, or bank deposits

e. (+ New) icon _____ A customer in the Wild Water Sports company

f. Payment from a customer _____ Quantities of this are not tracked

g. Deposit _____ Used when cash is collected at the time of a sale

h. Cleaning _____ Cash receipts received from a sale

i. Tige 25 zx _____ Quantities of this are tracked

j. Performance Rentals _____ A product that is added in the Wild Water Sports company

Chapter 4 Cases

The following cases require you to open the company you updated in Chapter 3. Each of the following cases continues throughout the text in a sequential manner. For example, if you are assigned Case 01, you will use the file you modified in this chapter in all of the following chapters. Each of the following cases is similar in concepts assessed but differs in amounts and transactions. See the Preface to this text for a matrix of each student case and its attributes.

To reopen your company, do the following:

1. Open your Internet browser.
2. Type **https://qbo.intuit.com** into your browser's address text box.
3. Type your user ID and password into the text boxes as you have done before.

Case 1

Add some operating activities (sales and cash receipts) to your company. Based on what you learned in the text using the Wild Water Sports company, you are to make the following changes to the Case 1 company you modified in Chapter 3:

1. Add a new customer – Name: Sarah Hay, Company: Hey Hays Surf, Display name as: Sarah Hay, Address: 230 Beach Way, La Jolla, CA, 92039.

2. Add a new service – Tune-Up, rate: $85.00, income account: Services.

3. Add a new product – Fred Rubble, initial quantity on hand: 0, as of date: 1/1/24, Inventory asset account: Inventory Asset, price: $950.00, cost: $600.00, income account: Sales, expense account: Cost of Goods Sold.

4. Record a new sales receipt on 1/3/24 – Customer: Blondie's Boards, payment method: Check, reference no.: 893, deposit to: Undeposited Funds (add this new current asset account), product: Rook 15, quantity: 2.

5. Record a new invoice on 1/4/24 – Customer: Sarah Hay, terms: Net 30, service: Tune-Up, quantity: 2, product: The Water Hog, quantity: 1.

6. Record a new cash payment received on 1/5/24 – Customer: Blondie's Boards, payment method: Check, reference no.: 984, deposit to: Undeposited Funds, amount received: $5,000.00. (Be sure to place a check in the Journal Entry #1 check box.)

7. Record a deposit made on 1/8/24 to the checking account – Received from: Blondie's Boards, amount received: $1,300.00, related to: Sales Receipt.

8. Prepare a Trial Balance report with a From date of 1/1/24 and a To date of 1/31/24, save it as a customized report named Trial Balance 1/31/24, and share it with all users. Your report should look like Figure 4.19. If asked, indicate that your business is accrual based.

9. If your trial balance differs from what is shown in Figure 4.19, do the following:
    a. Make sure that all of your changes were dated in January 2024.
    b. Click on the debit or credit balance to view a transactions report for each account, and investigate why your answer differs.
    c. Ask your instructor for assistance.
    d. Be sure your company matches the above as you will be adding additional business events in Chapter 5.

10. Export your Trial Balance report to Excel, and save it with the file name Student Name (replace with your name) Ch 04 Case 01 Trial Balance.xlsx.

11. Open and print the custom report you created in Chapter 3 called Transaction Detail by Account.

Figure 4.19

Trial Balance (as of 1/31/24)

Case 1
TRIAL BALANCE
As of January 31, 2024

	DEBIT	CREDIT
Checking	26,300.00	
Accounts Receivable	1,030.00	
Inventory Asset	6,700.00	
Prepaid Expenses	3,000.00	
Undeposited Funds	5,000.00	
Furniture & Fixtures:Depreciation		10,000.00
Furniture & Fixtures:Original cost	40,000.00	
Accounts Payable		4,500.00
Notes Payable		60,000.00
Common Stock		1,000.00
Opening Balance Equity		0.00
Retained Earnings		5,500.00
Sales		2,160.00
Services		170.00
Cost of Goods Sold	1,300.00	
TOTAL	$83,330.00	$83,330.00

12 Use your Transaction Detail by Account report to locate any differences in your Trial Balance report created above.

    a. Make sure all of your changes were dated in January 2024.

    b. Click on the line that does not match to view the transaction for that account, and investigate why your answer differs.

    c. Ask your instructor for assistance.

    d. Be sure your company matches the above as you will be adding additional business events in Chapter 5.

13 Export your Transactions Detail by Account report to Excel and save it with the file name Student Name (replace with your name) Ch 04 Case 01 Transaction Detail by Account.xlsx.

14 Sign out of your company.

Case 2

Add some operating activities (sales and cash receipts) to your company. Based on what you learned in the text using the Wild Water Sports company, you are to make the following changes to the Case 2 company you modified in Chapter 3:

1 Add a new customer – Hagen's Toys, 3983 Torrey Pines, La Jolla, CA, 92039.

2 Add a new service – Custom Painting, rate: $45.00, income account: Services.

3. Add two new products – GO Aircraft Radio, initial quantity on hand: 0, as of date: 1/1/25, Inventory asset account: Inventory Asset, price: $4,999.00, cost: $2,500.00, income account: Sales, expense account: Cost of Goods Sold and Taylor 22cc, initial quantity on hand: 0, as of date: 1/1/25, Inventory asset account: Inventory Asset, price: $2,999.00, cost: $1,500.00, income account: Sales, expense account: Cost of Goods Sold.

4. Record a new sales receipt on 1/3/25 – Customer: Benson's RC, payment method: Credit Card, reference no.: 16756, deposit to: Undeposited Funds, product: Broon F830 Ride, quantity: 3.

5. Record a new invoice on 1/4/25 – Customer: Hagen's Toys, terms: Net 30, service: Custom Painting, quantity: 5, product: Seawind Carbon Sailboat, quantity: 1.

6. Record a new cash payment received on 1/7/25 – Customer: Benson's RC, payment method: Check, reference no.: 9847, deposit to: Undeposited Funds, amount received: $925.00. (Be sure to place a check in the Journal Entry #1 check box.)

7. Record a deposit made on 1/7/25 to the checking account – Received from: Benson's RC, amount received: $4,500.00, related to: Sales Receipt.

8. Prepare a Trial Balance report with a From date of 1/1/25 and a To date of 1/31/25, save it as a customized report named Trial Balance 1/31/25, and share it with all users. Your report should look like Figure 4.20. If asked, indicate that your business is accrual based.

9. If your trial balance differs from what is shown in Figure 4.20, do the following:

    a. Make sure that all of your changes were dated in January 2025.

    b. Click on the debit or credit balance to view a transactions report for each account, and investigate why your answer differs.

    c. Ask your instructor for assistance.

    d. Be sure your company matches the above as you will be adding additional business events in Chapter 5.

10. Export your Trial Balance report to Excel, and save it with the file name Student Name (replace with your name) Ch 04 Case 02 Trial Balance.xlsx.

11. Open and print the custom report you created in Chapter 3, which is called Transaction Detail by Account.

12. Use your Transaction Detail by Account report to locate any differences in your Trial Balance report created above.

    a. Make sure that all of your changes were dated in January 2025.

    b. Click on the line that does not match to view the transaction for that account, and investigate why your answer differs.

    c. Ask your instructor for assistance.

    d. Be sure your company matches the above as you will be adding additional business events in Chapter 5.

Figure 4.20
Trial Balance (as of 1/31/25)

Case 2
TRIAL BALANCE
As of January 31, 2025

	DEBIT	CREDIT
Checking	9,500.00	
Accounts Receivable	1,425.00	
Inventory Asset	2,040.00	
Prepaid Expenses	2,400.00	
Undeposited Funds	925.00	
Machinery & Equipment:Depreciation		1,000.00
Machinery & Equipment:Original cost	10,000.00	
Accounts Payable		1,900.00
Notes Payable		12,000.00
Common Stock		100.00
Opening Balance Equity		0.00
Retained Earnings		8,385.00
Sales		5,700.00
Services		225.00
Cost of Goods Sold	3,020.00	
TOTAL	**$29,310.00**	**$29,310.00**

13 Export your Transactions Detail by Account report to Excel, and save it with the file name Student Name (replace with your name) Ch 04 Case 02 Transaction Detail by Account.xlsx.

14 Sign out of your company.

Case 3

Now it's time for you to add some operating activities (sales and cash receipts) to your company. Based on what you learned in the text using the Wild Water Sports company, you are to make the following changes to the Case 3 company you modified in Chapter 3:

1 Add a new customer – Surfer Sales, 3983 Torrey Pines, La Jolla, CA, 92039.

2 Add a new service – Phone Consulting, rate: $35.00, income account: Services, not taxable.

3 Add two new products – Apple iPhone 6s, initial quantity on hand: 0, inventory asset account: Inventory Asset, price: $549.00, cost: $349.00, income account: Sales of Product Income, expense account: Cost of Goods Sold, taxable and Apple iPhone 7 Plus, initial quantity on hand: 0, inventory asset account: Inventory Asset, price: $800, cost: $600.00, income account: Sales of Product Income, expense account: Cost of Goods Sold, taxable. Use 12/31/25 for the as of date.

4   Record a new sales receipt on 1/3/26 – customer: Surfer Sales, payment method: Credit Card, reference no.: 16756, deposit to: Payments to deposit product: Apple iPhone 7, quantity: 6, and 3 hours of Phone Consulting. Click **See the math** to update amounts.

5   Record a new invoice on 1/6/26 – customer: GHO Marketing, terms: Net 30, 3 hours of Apple Repairs, product: Apple iPhone 7, quantity: 3. Click **See the math** to update amounts.

6   Record a new cash payment received on 1/7/26 – customer: GHO Marketing, payment method: Check, reference no.: 9847, deposit to: Payments to deposit, amount received: $4,125.00. (Be sure to place a check in the Journal Entry #1 check box.)

7   Record a deposit made on 1/9/26 to the checking account of $9,078.75, which was received from Surfer Sales, amount $4,953.75, and related to Sales Receipt and GHO Marketing, amount $4,125.00, related to Payment.

8   Prepare a Trial Balance report with a From date of 1/1/26 and a To date of 1/31/26 and then save it as a customized report named Trial Balance 1/31/26 and share it with all users. Your report should look like Figure 4.21.

Figure 4.21 Trial Balance as of 1/31/26

Case 03 - Student Name (ID Number)

Trial Balance
As of January 31, 2026

	DEBIT	CREDIT
Checking	21,078.75	
Accounts receivable (A/R)	2,559.38	
Inventory Asset	1,700.00	
Payments to deposit	0.00	
Prepaid expenses	2,750.00	
Machinery & Equipment:Depreciation		2,000.00
Machinery & Equipment:Original cost	15,000.00	
Accounts Payable (A/P)		5,000.00
California Department of Tax and Fee Administration ...		523.13
Notes Payable		23,000.00
Opening balance equity		0.00
Owner's Equity		10,075.00
Sales of Product Income		6,750.00
Services		240.00
Cost of goods sold	4,500.00	
TOTAL	$47,588.13	$47,588.13

9 If your trial balance is different than Figure 4.21, do the following:

    a. Make sure that all of your changes were dated in January 2026.

    b. Click on the debit or credit balance to view a transactions report for each account, and investigate why your answer is different.

    c. Ask your instructor for assistance.

    d. Be sure your company matches the above as you will be adding additional business events in Chapter 5.

10 Export your Trial Balance report to Excel, and save it with the file name Student Name (replace with your name) Ch 04 Case 03 Trial Balance.xlsx.

11 Open and print the custom report you created in Chapter 3, which is called Transaction Detail by Account.

12 Use your Transaction Detail by Account report to locate any differences in your Trial Balance report created above.

    a. Make sure that all of your changes were dated in January 2026.

    b. Click on the line that doesn't match to view the transaction for that account, and investigate why your answer is different.

    c. Ask your instructor for assistance.

    d. Be sure your company matches the above as you will be adding additional business events in Chapter 5.

13 Export your Transactions Detail by Account report to MS Excel and save it with the file name Student Name (replace with your name) Ch 04 Case 03 Transaction Detail by Account.xlsx.

14 Sign out of your company.

Case 4

Now it's time for you to add some operating activities (sales and cash receipts) to your company. Based on what you learned in the text using the Wild Water Sports company, you are to make the following changes to the Case 4 company you modified in Chapter 3:

1 Add two new accounts.

    a. First account

        i) Account type: Assets

        ii) Save account under: Other Current Assets

        iii) Tax form section: Other Current Assets

        iv) Account name: Prepaid insurance

    b. Second account

        i) Account type: Expenses

        ii) Save account under: Other Business Expenses

        iii) Tax form section: Other Business Expenses

        iv) Account name: Laundry services

2 Add three new customers.

   a. Flyer Corporation, 32 Wilshire Blvd., Hollywood, CA 90028, terms: Net 30

   b. ABC Studios, 2300 W Riverside Dr., Burbank, CA 91506, terms: Net 30

   c. Shepard Inc., 10 Hollywood Blvd., Hollywood, CA 90028, terms: Due on receipt

3 Modify an existing customer (use Help to learn how to do this).

   a. Company – Disney

   b. Address – 500 South Buena Vista Street, Burbank, CA 91505, terms: Net 30

4 Add three new vendors.

   a. Bowflex Inc., 3393 Main St., Vancouver, WA 98607, terms: Net 30

   b. NordicTrack Inc., 23 First St., Logan, UT 84321, terms: Net 30

   c. Laundry Service Inc., 432 Sunset Blvd., Hollywood, CA, 90028, terms: Due on receipt

5 Modify an existing vendor (use Help to learn how to do this).

   a. Company – Precor

   b. Address – 20031 142nd Avenue NE, Woodinville, WA 98072, terms: Net 30

6 Create a new service item as follows:

   a. Name/Description – Monthly Fee – Corporate Membership 50 Employees

   b. Description – Yes you do sell this service to customers

   c. Sales price/rate – $6,000

   d. Income account – Sales

   e. Is taxable – No

   f. Purchasing information – No you don't purchase this service from a vendor

7 Modify two existing service items (use Help to learn how to do this).

   a. Old Name/Description – Monthly Fee – New Name/Description – Monthly Fee – Individual

   b. Old Name/Description – Training – New Name/Description – Training – Individual

8 Add two new products.

   a. First product

      i) Name – Bowflex Dumbbells

      ii) Initial quantity on hand – 0

      iii) As of date – 12/31/26

      iv) Inventory asset account – Inventory Asset

v) Description – Bowflex Dumbbells

vi) Sales price/rate – $249

vii) Income account – Sales of Product Income

viii) Is taxable – Yes

ix) Purchasing information – Bowflex Dumbbells

x) Cost – $200

xi) Expense account – Cost of Goods Sold

b. Second product

i) Name – Power Block Elite Dumbbells

ii) Initial quantity on hand – 0

iii) As of date – 12/31/26

iv) Inventory asset account – Inventory Asset

v) Description – Power Block Elite Dumbbells

vi) Sales price/rate – $299

vii) Income account – Sales of Product Income

viii) Is taxable – Yes

ix) Purchasing information – Power Block Elite Dumbbells

x) Cost – $199

xi) Expense account – Cost of Goods Sold

9 Record a new sales receipt to Shepard Inc. on 1/5/27 for 6 months of Monthly Fee – Individual, 10 hours of Training – Individual, 1 T-shirt, and 1 pair of Yoga pants. Total $1,726.65 (including sales tax) received via check number 6571 and deposited to the Payments to deposit account. If Payments to deposit account is not shown in the drop-down list you'll need to add it as a new other current asset. (Alternatively, if an Undeposited Funds account is shown use that account.)

10 Record a new ABC Studios invoice 1002 on 1/6/27 for 1 Monthly Fee – Corporate Membership 50 Employees and 50 T-shirts for a total amount of $7,368.75 (including sales tax).

11 Record a new Flyer Corporation invoice 1003 on 1/6/27 for 1 Monthly Fee – Corporate Membership 50 Employees and 50 hours of Training – Individual and 50 pairs of Yoga pants for a total amount of $12,213.75 (including sales tax).

12 Record a partial cash payment of $6,000.00 received on 1/7/27 from Disney using check 9744 recorded to the Payments to deposit account. (Be sure to place a check in the Journal Entry #1 check box.)

13 Record a bank deposit of $7,726.65 made on 1/8/27 from Disney and Shepard Inc.

14 Prepare and print a Trial Balance report with a custom reporting period of 1/1/27 to 1/8/27 and then save it as a customized report named Trial Balance 1/8/27. Your report should look like Figure 4.22.

Figure 4.22 Trial Balance as of 1/8/27

Trial Balance
As of January 8, 2027

	DEBIT	CREDIT
Checking	34,726.65	
Accounts Receivable (A/R)	22,082.50	
Inventory Asset	3,868.00	
Payments to deposit	0.00	
Prepaid rent	12,000.00	
Furniture:Accumulated Depreciation		10,000.00
Furniture:Original Cost	65,000.00	
Vehicles:Accumulated Depreciation		6,500.00
Vehicles:Original Cost	115,000.00	
Accounts Payable (A/P)		18,000.00
California Department of Tax and Fee Administration Payable		339.15
Long-term debt		82,000.00
Common Stock		1,000.00
Opening Balance Equity		0.00
Retained Earnings		115,500.00
Sales		17,400.00
Sales of Product Income		3,570.00
Cost of Goods Sold	1,632.00	
TOTAL	$254,309.15	$254,309.15

15 If necessary, prepare and print a Transaction Detail by Account report you previously saved.

16 Use your Transaction Detail by Account report to locate any differences in your Trial Balance report created above.

  a. Make sure all your changes were dated in January 2027.

  b. Click on the line that does not match to view the transaction for that account, and investigate why your answer differs.

  c. Ask your instructor for assistance.

  d. Be sure your company matches the above as you will be adding additional business events in Chapter 5.

Case 5

Now it's time for you to add some operating activities (sales and cash receipts) to your company. Based on using what you learned in the text using the Wild Water Sports company, you are to make the following changes to the Case 5 company you modified in Chapter 3:

1. Add a new account.
   a. Account type – Expenses, Save account under – Expenses
   b. Tax form section – Legal & Professional Fees
   c. Account name – Recruiting

2. Add two new customers.
   a. US Department of Defense, 25203 Baneberry, San Antonio, TX, 78260, terms: Net 15
   b. Boeing, 3365 160th Ave SE 3307, Bellevue, WA, 98008, terms: Net 30

3. Modify an existing customer (use help to learn how to do this).
   a. Company – Boeing
   b. Address – 4800 Oak Grove Dr, Pasadena, CA, 91109

4. Add three new vendors.
   a. United Rentals, 376 Dan Tibbs Rd, Huntsville, AL 35806, terms: Net 30
   b. Indeed, 6433 Champion Grandview Way, Austin, TX, 78750, terms: Net 30
   c. HP Computers, 1501 Page Mill Rd, Palo Alto, CA, 94020, terms: Net 30

5. Modify an existing vendor (use Help to learn how to do this).
   a. Company – Chase Bank
   b. Address – 416 West Jefferson, Louisville, KY, 40202, terms: Due on receipt

6. Create a new service item as follows:
   a. Name/Description – Consulting
   b. You sell this product/service to my customers
   c. Price/rate – $350
   d. Income account – Consulting
   e. Nontaxable
   f. Purchasing information – No you don't purchase this service from a vendor

7. Modify two existing service items (use Help to learn how to do this).
   a. Old name/Description – Technical Solutions – New name/Description – Technical Solutions – Commercial
   b. Old name/Description – Program Support – New name/Description – Program Support – Government

8. Add two new inventory products.
   a. First product
      i) Name – Computer Workstation 100
      ii) Initial quantity on hand – 0
      iii) As of date – 12/31/27
      iv) Inventory asset account – Inventory
      v) Description – Computer Workstation 100
      vi) Price/rate – $15,000
      vii) Income account – Sales
      viii) Taxable – standard rate
      ix) Purchasing Information – Computer Workstation 100
      x) Cost – $7,000
      xi) Expense account – Cost of Goods Sold
   b. Second product
      i) Name – Computer Workstation 500
      ii) Initial quantity on hand – 0
      iii) As of date – 12/31/27
      iv) Inventory asset account – Inventory
      v) Description – Computer Workstation 500
      vi) Price/rate – $35,000
      vii) Income account – Sales
      viii) Taxable – standard rate
      ix) Purchasing Information – Computer Workstation 500
      x) Cost – $17,000
      xi) Expense account – Cost of Goods Sold

9. Record a new sales receipt 1001 to a new customer Blue Origin on 1/4/28 for 50 hours of consulting and received payment via check number 1687 and recorded to the Payments to Deposit account.

10. Record a new invoice 1002 on 1/6/28 to the US Department of Defense for 100 hours of Program Support – Government. If asked, select **I'll create invoice for my accounting, but won't send any**. If asked how I want to get paid, select **Check**.

11. Record a new invoice 1003 on 1/7/28 to Boeing for 80 hours of Technical Solutions – Commercial and 1 Training Materials – Volume 1 for a total invoice of $48,350.00 including sales tax.

12. Record a cash payment of $70,000.00 received on 1/10/28 from NASA using check 18842 recorded to the Payments to Deposit account. Select **Journal Entry #1** in Outstanding Transactions section.

13. Record a bank deposit to the Checking account for $87,500.00 made on 1/12/28 from Blue Origin and NASA.

14. Prepare and print a Trial Balance report with a custom reporting period of 1/1/28 to 1/31/28 and then save it as a customized report named Trial Balance 1/31/28. Your report should look like Figure 4.23.

15. Open and print your previously saved report Transaction Detail by Account.

Figure 4.23

Trial Balance

Case 05 - Student Name (ID Number)
Trial Balance
As of January 31, 2028

	DEBIT	CREDIT
Checking	117,500.00	
Accounts Receivable (A/R)	158,350.00	
Inventory	452,000.00	
Payments to deposit	0.00	
Prepaid expenses	10,000.00	
Fixed Asset Computers:Depreciation		25,000.00
Fixed Asset Computers:Original Cost	250,000.00	
Fixed Asset Furniture:Depreciation		8,000.00
Fixed Asset Furniture:Original Cost	80,000.00	
Accounts Payable (A/P)		20,000.00
Alabama Department of Revenue Payable		600.00
Alabama, Huntsville Payable		675.00
Alabama, Madison County Payable		75.00
Notes Payable		545,000.00
Opening balance equity		0.00
Owner's Equity		382,000.00
Consulting		79,500.00
Sales		15,000.00
Cost of goods sold	8,000.00	
TOTAL	$1,075,850.00	$1,075,850.00

16 Use your Transaction Detail by Account report to locate any differences in your Trial Balance report created above.

   a. Make sure all your changes were dated in January 2028.

   b. Click on the line that does not match to view the transaction for that account, and investigate why your answer differs.

   c. Ask your instructor for assistance.

   d. Be sure your company matches the above as you will be adding additional business events in Chapter 5.

Case 6

Now it's time for you to add some operating activities (sales and cash receipts) to your company. Based on using what you learned in the text using the Wild Water Sports company, you are to make the following changes to the Case 6 company you modified in Chapter 3:

1 Add two new accounts.

   a. First account
      i) Account Type – Other Current Assets
      ii) Detail Type/Name – Prepaid Expenses

b. Second account
   i) Account Type – Other Current Assets
   ii) Detail Type – Inventory
   iii) Name – Inventory Parts

2 Change the name of expense account Repairs & Maintenance to Repairs.

3 Add two new customers.

   a. Ebony Williams, 4101 S Sheridan Ave., Tacoma, WA, 98418, terms: Net 30

   b. Deja Smith, 4648 N Defiance St., Tacoma, WA, 98407, terms: Net 30

4 Modify an existing customer.

   a. Company – Sam Ski

   b. Address – 5633 89th Ave SE, Mercer Island, WA, 98040, terms: Net 30

5 Add two new vendors.

   a. Airstream, Inc., 419 West Pike Street, Jackson Center, OH 45334, terms: Net 30

   b. Thor Motor Coach, 701 County Road 15 Elkhart, Indiana 46516, terms: Net 30

6 Modify an existing vendor.

   a. Company – Winnebago (change Company and Display name to Winnebago, Inc.)

   b. Address – 605 West Crystal Lake Road, Forest City, IA, 50436, terms: Net 30

7 Create two new service items as follows:

   a. First service
      i) Name – Basic 6,000-mile service
      ii) Description – Yes you do sell this service to customers
      iii) Sales price/rate – $450
      iv) Income account – Sales
      v) Sales Tax Category – Nontaxable
      vi) Purchasing information – No you don't purchase this service from a vendor

   b. Second service
      i) Name – Roof inspection and repair
      ii) Description – Yes you do sell this service to customers
      iii) Sales price/rate – $500
      iv) Income account – Sales
      v) Sales Tax Category – Nontaxable
      vi) Purchasing information – No you don't purchase this service from a vendor

c. Third service
  i) Name – Sewer system inspection and repair
  ii) Description – Yes you do sell this service to customers
  iii) Sales price/rate – $600
  iv) Income account – Sales
  v) Sales Tax Category – Nontaxable
  vi) Purchasing information – No you don't purchase this service from a vendor

8 Add two new inventory products.

  a. First product
   i) Name – 2023 Thor Motor Coach Palazzo 33.2
   ii) Inventory asset account – Inventory Asset
   iii) Description – 2023 Thor Motor Coach Palazzo 33.2
   iv) Sales price/rate – $180,000
   v) Income account – Sales of Product Income
   vi) Sales Tax Category – Taxable – Standard rate
   vii) Purchasing information – 2023 Thor Motor Coach Palazzo 33.2
   viii) Cost – $144,000
   ix) Expense account – Cost of Goods Sold
   x) Preferred Vendor – Thor Motor Coach
   xi) Initial quantity on hand – 0
   xii) As of date – 12/31/22

  b. Second product
   i) Name – 2023 Airstream Flying Cloud 27FB TWIN
   ii) Inventory asset account – Inventory Asset
   iii) Description – 2023 Airstream Flying Cloud 27FB TWIN
   iv) Sales price/rate – $99,000
   v) Income account – Sales of Product Income
   vi) Sales Tax Category – Taxable – Standard rate
   vii) Purchasing information – 2023 Airstream Flying Cloud 27FB TWIN
   viii) Cost – $80,000
   ix) Expense account – Cost of Goods Sold
   x) Preferred Vendor – Airstream, Inc.
   xi) Initial quantity on hand – 0
   xii) As of date – 12/31/22

9 Record a new sales receipt 1001 on 01/05/23 to a new customer Donald Biden for the sale of a 2022 Winnebago Revel 44E for $150,000 plus sales tax of $13,950 with payment method credit card for a total of $163,950.

10 Record a new invoice 1002 on 01/09/23 to Deja Smith for the sale of a 2022 Winnebago View 24G for $140,000 plus sales tax of $13,020 on account for a total of $153,020.

11 Record a new cash payment received on 1/11/23 – Customer: Sam Ski, payment method: Check, deposit to: Undeposited Funds, amount received: $10,000.

12 Record a deposit made on 1/12/23 to the checking account of $10,000 which was received from: Sam Ski.

13 Prepare and print a Trial Balance report with a custom reporting period of 1/1/23 to 1/31/23 and then save it as a customized report named Trial Balance 1/31/23. Your report should look like Figure 4.24.

Figure 4.24 Trial Balance

Case 06 - Student Name (ID Number)
TRIAL BALANCE
As of January 31, 2023

	DEBIT	CREDIT
Checking	223,950.00	
Accounts Receivable (A/R)	153,020.00	
Inventory Asset	344,000.00	
Loans To Officers	15,000.00	
Undeposited Funds	0.00	
Buildings:Depreciation		15,000.00
Buildings:Original cost	150,000.00	
Machinery & Equipment:Depreciation		10,000.00
Machinery & Equipment:Original cost	100,000.00	
Accounts Payable (A/P)		464,000.00
Washington State Department of Revenue Payable		26,970.00
Notes Payable		100,000.00
Common Stock		1,000.00
Opening Balance Equity		0.00
Paid-In Capital		250,000.00
Retained Earnings		61,000.00
Sales of Product Income		290,000.00
Cost of Goods Sold	232,000.00	
TOTAL	**$1,217,970.00**	**$1,217,970.00**

14 Prepare and print a Transaction Detail by Account report for all dates and then save it as a customized report named Transaction Detail by Account All Dates. If asked, indicate that your business is accrual based.

15 Use your Transaction Detail by Account report to locate any differences in your Trial Balance report created above.

   a. Make sure all your changes were dated in January 2023.

   b. Click on the line that does not match to view the transaction for that account and investigate why your answer differs.

   c. Ask your instructor for assistance.

   d. Be sure your company matches the above as you will be adding additional business events in Chapter 5.

Recording Operating Activities: Purchases and Cash Payments

5

Student Learning Outcomes

Upon completion of this chapter, the student will be able to do the following:

- Add a vendor
- Record a purchase order
- Record a bill for the receipt of products/services on account
- Record the payment of bills
- Record credit card charges
- Record checks
- Prepare a Trial Balance

Overview

In Chapter 4 you added new accounts, new customers, new vendors, new products, and new services to your Wild Water Sports company. In addition, you recorded operating activities like sales receipts, invoices, cash receipts, and bank deposits. In this chapter, you will add additional operating activities to the Wild Water Sports company like purchase orders, bills, payment of bills, credit card charges, and checks. At the end of this chapter, you will perform similar tasks on the case assigned by your instructor.

To verify the accuracy of your Wild Water Sports company:

1. Sign into your QBO account then open the Wild Water Sports company you used in Chapter 4.

2. Click **Reports**, then click the **Custom reports** tab, then click **Trial Balance** to open the Trial Balance report. Set the from and to dates to **1/1/27** and **1/13/27**, respectively. Compare your report to Figure 5.1. If your report doesn't match Figure 5.1 go back to your work in Chapter 4 to fix your errors. Otherwise, close your Trial Balance report.

Figure 5.1

Wild Water Sports Trial Balance as of 1/13/27

Wild Water Sports - Student Name (ID Number)
Trial Balance
As of January 13, 2027

	DEBIT	CREDIT
Checking	80,145.00	
Accounts receivable (A/R)	120,770.00	
Inventory	41,600.00	
Payments to deposit	70,000.00	
Prepaid expenses	15,000.00	
Equipment:Accumulated depreciation		10,000.00
Equipment:Original Cost	40,000.00	
Accounts Payable (A/P)		56,000.00
Florida Department of Revenue Payable		9,915.00
Long-term business loans		50,000.00
Common stock		1,000.00
Opening balance equity		0.00
Retained Earnings		205,800.00
Sales		164,000.00
Service Revenue		2,000.00
Cost of goods sold	131,200.00	
TOTAL	**$498,715.00**	**$498,715.00**

Vendors

Navigate your browser to the Video Tutorials provided by Intuit (see website address specified in the Preface to this text) and then search on How to Manage Vendors.

In this section, you will be adding new vendors. Recall that vendors are your company's suppliers of products and services. To add vendors, you will use the Expenses menu item in the navigation bar.

To add new vendors to the Wild Water Sports company:

1. Click **Expenses**, then click **Vendors** in the navigation bar, and then click the **New vendor** button.
2. Type **Tige** in the Company name text box.
3. Type the address **1801 TX Hwy 36 Abilene, TX 79602** in the appropriate text boxes.
4. Select **Net 30** from the Terms text box to view Figure 5.2.
5. Click **Save**.

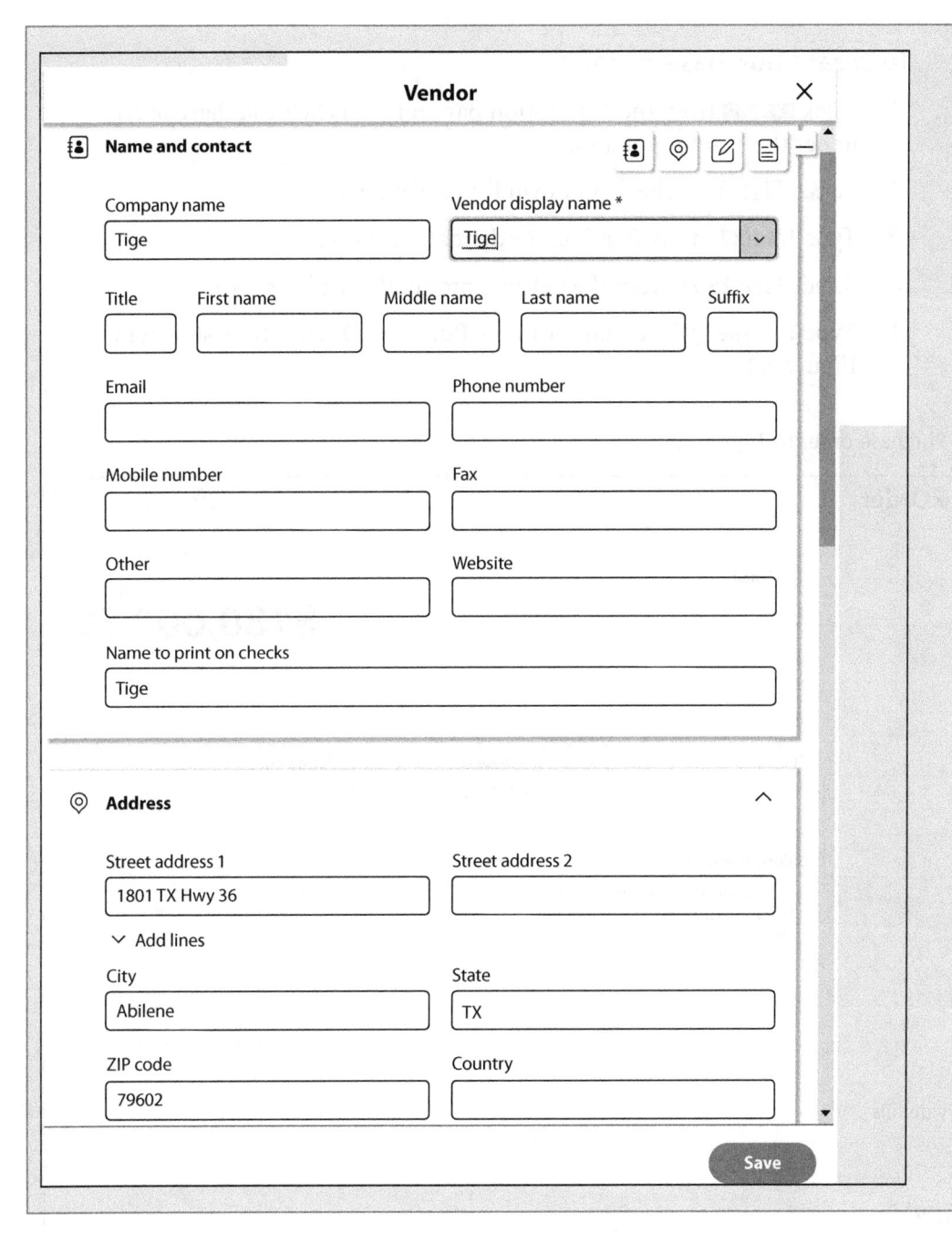

Figure 5.2

Vendor Information window (partial view)

You have now added a new vendor. If you need to edit a vendor's information, just click **Expenses**, then **Vendors**, then click on a vendor, then click **Edit**. Update the vendor information, then click **Save**. Next up is adding purchase orders.

Purchase Orders

A business uses purchase orders to formally order products or services from its vendors. Purchase orders are also used as a reference and control for products received. During the creation of a purchase order, you can create a new product or refer to an existing product. Purchase orders can be used to acquire inventory for future sale or for products ordered for a specific customer.

Navigate your browser to the Video Tutorials provided by Intuit (see website address specified in the Preface to this text) and then search on How to Enter Purchase Orders.

To create purchase orders:

1 Click [+ New] from the Navigation bar and then click **Purchase order** under the Vendor column.

2 Select **Tige** from the drop-down list of Vendors.

3 Type **1/14/27** in the Purchase Order date text box.

4 Select **Tige 25 zx** from the Select a product/service text box.

5 Type **1** in the QTY column to view Purchase Order #1001 shown in Figure 5.3.

Figure 5.3 Purchase order to Tige

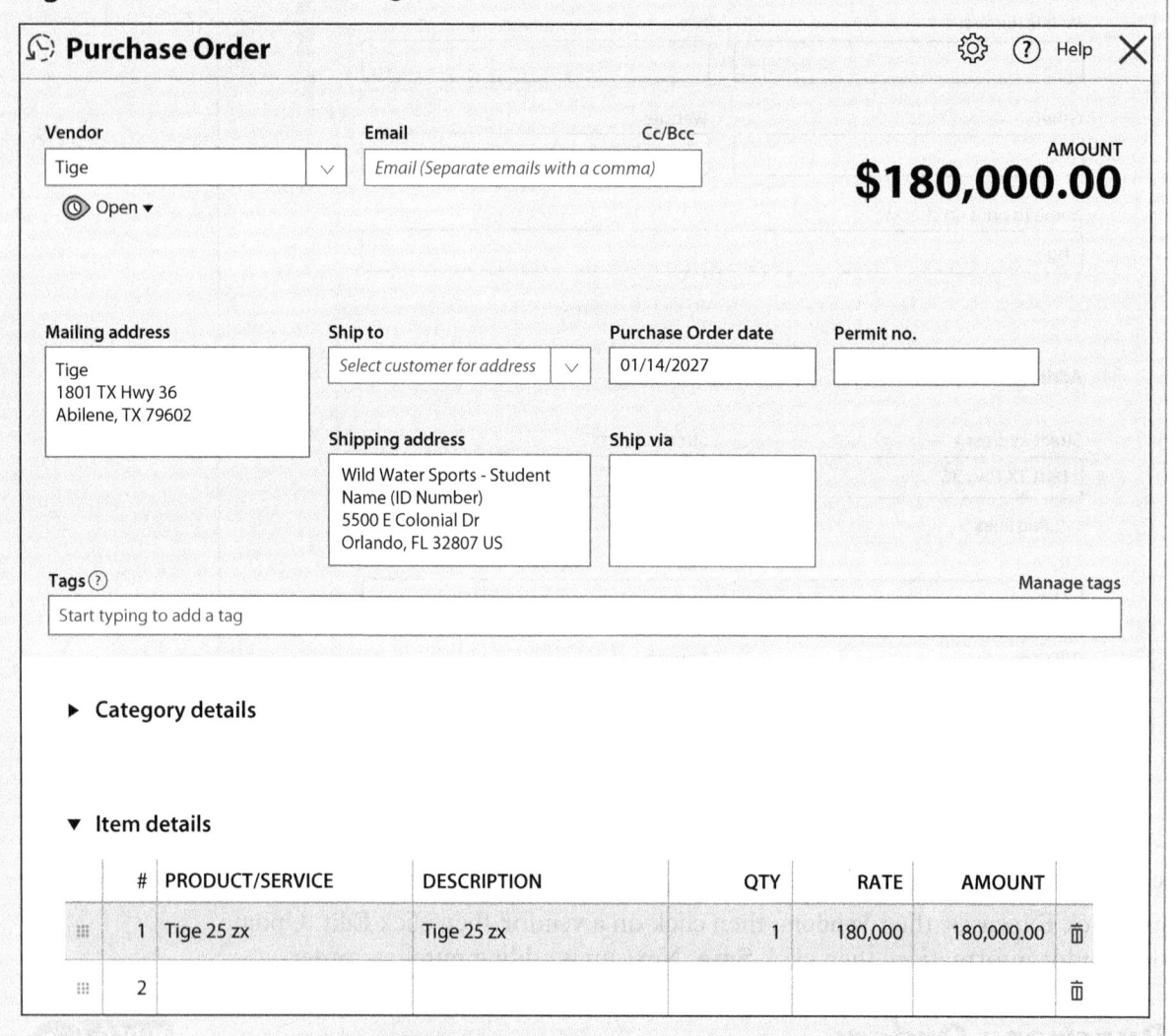

Purchase Order

Vendor	Email	Cc/Bcc	AMOUNT
Tige	Email (Separate emails with a comma)		**$180,000.00**

Open ▼

Mailing address	Ship to	Purchase Order date	Permit no.
Tige 1801 TX Hwy 36 Abilene, TX 79602	Select customer for address	01/14/2027	

	Shipping address	Ship via
	Wild Water Sports - Student Name (ID Number) 5500 E Colonial Dr Orlando, FL 32807 US	

Tags ?   Manage tags

Start typing to add a tag

▶ Category details

▼ Item details

#	PRODUCT/SERVICE	DESCRIPTION	QTY	RATE	AMOUNT
1	Tige 25 zx	Tige 25 zx	1	180,000	180,000.00
2					

6 Click **Save and new**.

7 Click **+ Add new** from the Vendor text box.

8 Type **Centurion Boats** as the Company name.

9 Add the following address information: **2047 Grogan Avenue, Merced, CA 95341** and set terms to **Net 30**.

Recording Operating Activities: Purchases and Cash Payments **Chapter 5** **131**

10 Click **Save**.

11 Type **1/15/27** in the Purchase Order date text box.

12 Type **2023 Vi22** from the Select a product/service text box and then click **+ Add new 2023 Vi22**.

13 Select **Inventory item**.

14 Type **0** as the Initial quantity on hand and **01/05/2027** in the As of date text box.

15 Select **Inventory** as the Inventory asset account.

16 Type **2023 Vi22** in the Description and Purchasing information text boxes.

17 Type **115000** in the Price/rate text box and **90000** in the Purchase cost text box. Select **Sales** as the Income account, Cost of goods sold as the Expense account, and Taxable – standard rate as the Sales tax.

18 Click **Create new**.

19 Type **1** in the QTY column to view Purchase Order #1002 shown in Figure 5.4.

Figure 5.4 Purchase order to Centurion Boats

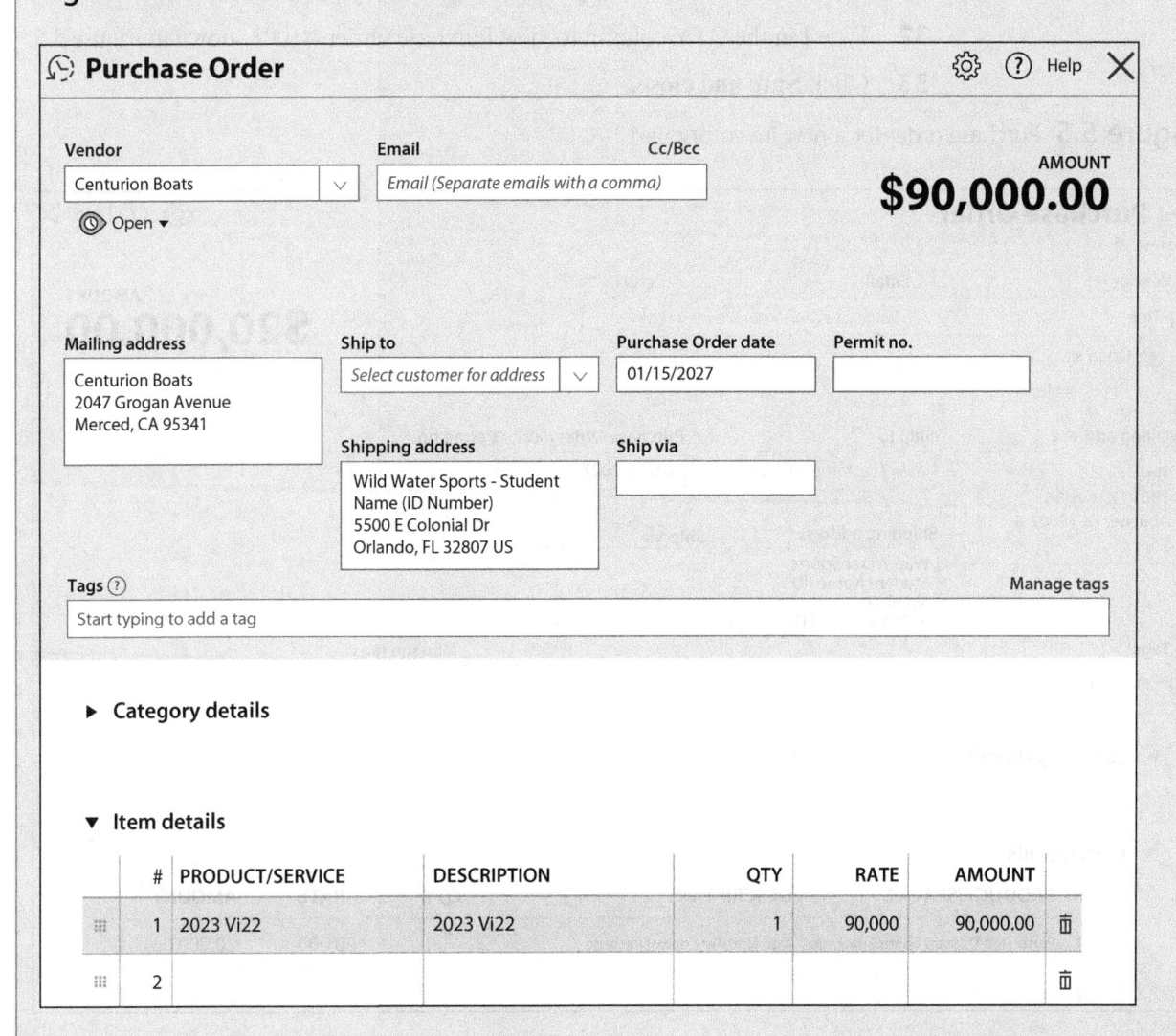

Purchase Order

Vendor: Centurion Boats

AMOUNT **$90,000.00**

Mailing address: Centurion Boats, 2047 Grogan Avenue, Merced, CA 95341

Ship to: Select customer for address

Purchase Order date: 01/15/2027

Shipping address: Wild Water Sports - Student Name (ID Number), 5500 E Colonial Dr, Orlando, FL 32807 US

#	PRODUCT/SERVICE	DESCRIPTION	QTY	RATE	AMOUNT
1	2023 Vi22	2023 Vi22	1	90,000	90,000.00
2					

20. Click **Save and new**.
21. Select **Tige** as the Vendor.
22. Type **1/15/27** in the Purchase Order date text box.
23. Type **Tige Thruster Control Package** in the Product/Service text box and then click **+ Add new Tige Thruster Control Package**.
24. Select **Inventory item**.
25. Type **0** as the Initial quantity on hand and **01/15/2027** in the As of date text box.
26. Select **Inventory** as the Inventory asset account.
27. Type **Tige Thruster Control Package** in the Description and Purchasing information text boxes.
28. Type **25000** in the Price/rate text box and **20000** in the Purchase cost text box.
29. Type **Sales Parts** in the Income account text box, then click **+ Add new Sales Parts**, then click **Save and close** to accept the new income account.
30. Select **Cost of goods sold** as the Expense account.
31. Click **Create new** to accept the new inventory part.
32. Type **1** in the QTY column to view Purchase Order #1003 shown in Figure 5.5.
33. Click **Save and close**.

Figure 5.5 Purchase order for a new inventory part

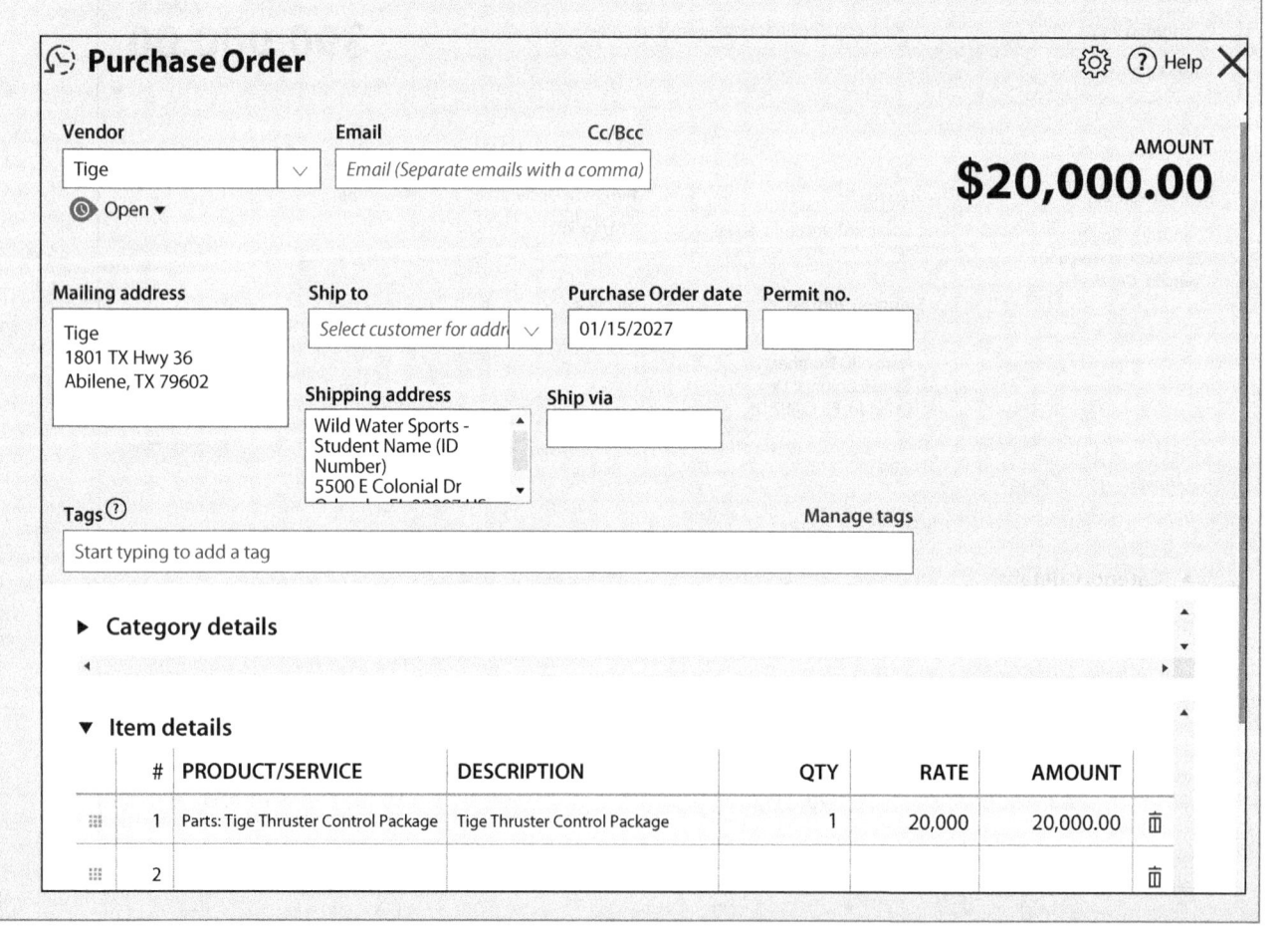

Bills

In the previous chapter, you created invoices to customers for products or services rendered. That invoice served as a bill to that customer, signifying a sales transaction for you and a bill to them. Likewise, when you enter into a business transaction, such as purchasing a product or service from a vendor, you expect them to send you an invoice. In QBO, the invoice you receive from a vendor is called a bill. Bills are recorded in QBO to signify the receipt of a product or service and a related liability, usually accounts payable. The inventory account is affected when the bill represents a product being delivered.

In QBO, the terms of those bills could be one of the following: due on receipt, net 10, net 15, net 30, or net 60. The net reference means the bill is due to be paid within a specified number of days, for example, 10, 15, 30, or 60 days. Other terms, for example, 2/10 net 30, provide for a 2% discount on the invoice if paid within 10 days; otherwise, a payment is required within 30 days. Even though you can set up such terms to appear on invoices to customers and bills from vendors, QBO does not calculate them automatically. To simplify your learning of QBO, discounts have not been implemented in this text.

In this section, you will focus on recording a bill for the receipt of services and products on account, meaning you will have been given terms (usually net 30), so you will not have to pay the bill for 30 days after the bill date. The first bill was for a product received which had been previously ordered using a purchase order. The second bill was for a new product, which had not been previously ordered using a purchase order. Both of these purchases will affect inventory and are, thus, recorded in the Items detail section of a bill. The last two bills are services that were rendered and thus do not affect inventory and are therefore recorded in the Category details section of a bill.

Navigate your browser to the Video Tutorials provided by Intuit (see website address specified in the Preface to this text) and then search on How to Enter Bills.

To record a bill from a vendor for the receipt of products/services on account, do the following:

1 Continue from where you left off.

2 Click the [+ New] icon, and click **Bill** in the Vendors column as shown in Figure 5.6.

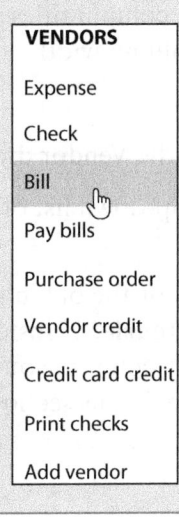

VENDORS
Expense
Check
Bill
Pay bills
Purchase order
Vendor credit
Credit card credit
Print checks
Add vendor

Figure 5.6

+ New window (entering bills)

134 Chapter 5   *Recording Operating Activities: Purchases and Cash Payments*

3. Select **Tige** from the Vendor drop-down list.
4. Accept **Net 30** from the drop-down list of Terms. Type **1/18/27** as the Bill date.
5. Collapse the Category details section of the bill by clicking on the arrow next to Category details.
6. Expand the Item details section of the bill by clicking on the arrow next to Item details.
7. Click **Add** in the Add to Bill section, which identifies an open purchase order #1001 from this vendor located on the right of the bill as shown in Figure 5.7.

Figure 5.7 Bill (adding purchase order information)

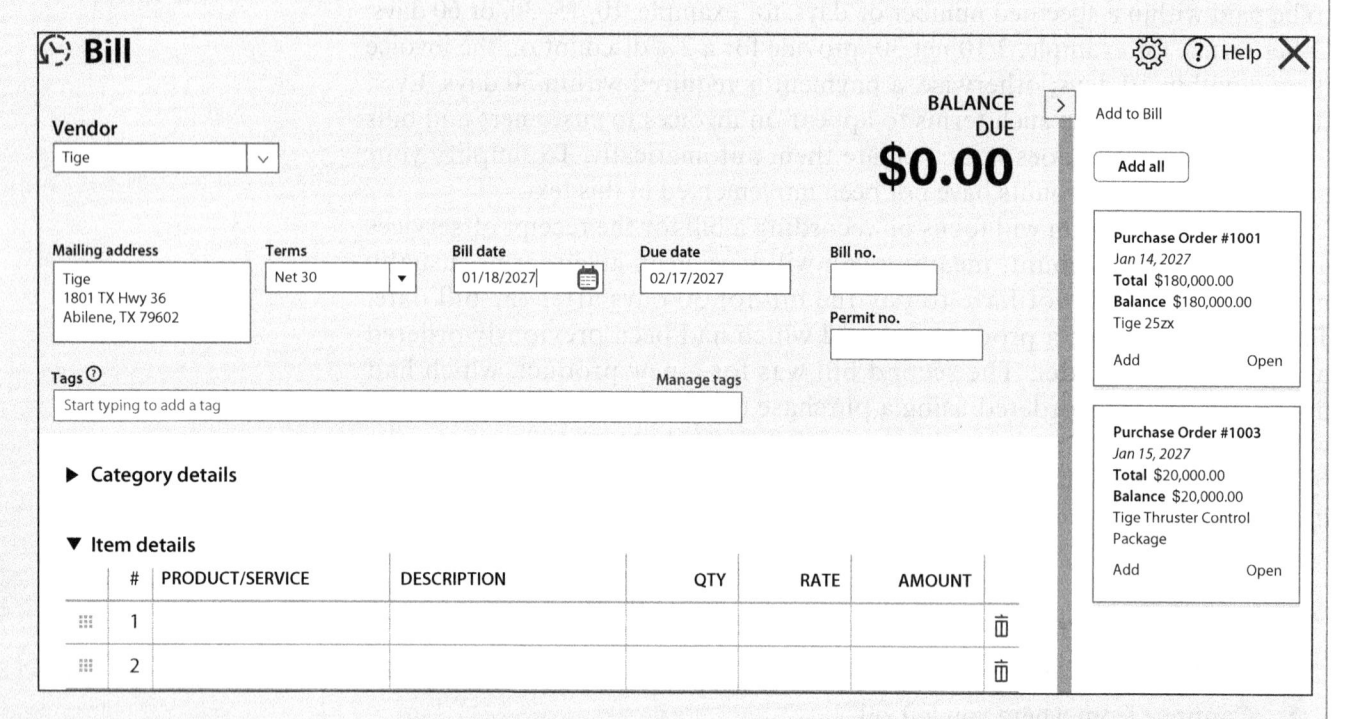

Bill						
Vendor				**BALANCE DUE**		Add to Bill
Tige				**$0.00**		Add all

Mailing address	Terms	Bill date	Due date	Bill no.
Tige 1801 TX Hwy 36 Abilene, TX 79602	Net 30	01/18/2027	02/17/2027	
				Permit no.

Purchase Order #1001
Jan 14, 2027
Total $180,000.00
Balance $180,000.00
Tige 25zx

Add   Open

Tags
Start typing to add a tag   Manage tags

▶ Category details

Purchase Order #1003
Jan 15, 2027
Total $20,000.00
Balance $20,000.00
Tige Thruster Control Package

Add   Open

▼ Item details

#	PRODUCT/SERVICE	DESCRIPTION	QTY	RATE	AMOUNT	
1						🗑
2						🗑

8. The bill now contains information from purchase order #1001 as shown in Figure 5.8. **Trouble?** If information provided in the Product/Service column (or any other column) is cut off or not visible, simply place your cursor between column titles and drag to the left or right to decrease or increase the column width.
9. Click **Save and new**.
10. Select **Malibu Boats** from the Vendor drop-down list.
11. Select **Net 30** from the drop-down list of Terms. Type **1/18/27** as the Bill date.
12. Select **+ Add new** on line 1 of the bill in the Product/Service column of the Item details section. **Trouble?** If instead of seeing a Product/Service column you see a Category column, you are in the Category details section instead of the Item details section (a common mistake).

Recording Operating Activities: Purchases and Cash Payments   Chapter 5   135

Figure 5.8 Bill (after purchase order information is added)

Bill

1 linked Purchase Order

Vendor
Tige

BALANCE DUE
$180,000.00

Mailing address	Terms	Bill date	Due date	Bill no.
Tige 1801 TX Hwy 36 Abilene, TX 79602	Net 30	01/18/2027	02/17/2027	

Permit no.

Tags
Start typing to add a tag   Manage tags

▶ **Category details**

▼ **Item details**

#	PRODUCT/SERVICE	DESCRIPTION	QTY	RATE	AMOUNT	
1	Boats:Tige 25 zx	Tige 25zx	1	180,000	180,000.00	
2						

Add lines   Clear all lines   Total $180,000.00

---

13 Add a new product as you have done before—Item type: **Inventory item**, Name and Description: **Wake Accessory Package**, initial quantity on hand: **0**, As of date: **01/18/2027**, inventory asset account: **Inventory**, Price/rate: **500**, Purchase cost: **350**, income account: **Sales Parts**, expense account: **Cost of Goods Sold**, Sales tax: Taxable – standard rate. Click **Create new** in the Product/Service Information window.

14 Type **5** on line 1 of the bill in the QTY column.

15 Click **Save and new**.

16 Type **Best Buy Geek Squad** from the Vendor drop-down list, then click **+ Add new Best Buy Geek Squad**. Type **Best Buy Geek Squad** as the Vendor display name, then click **Save** to save the new vendor.

17 Select **Net 30** from the drop-down list of Terms. Type **1/19/27** as the Bill date.

18 Expand the Category details section of the bill by clicking on the arrow next to Category details.

19 Collapse the Item details section of the bill by clicking on the arrow next to Item details.

20 Select **Rent:Equipment rental** on line 1 of the bill in the Category column.

21 Type **6000** on line 1 of the bill in the Amount column and then press [**Tab**]. Your window should look like Figure 5.9.

Figure 5.9 Bill (for services)

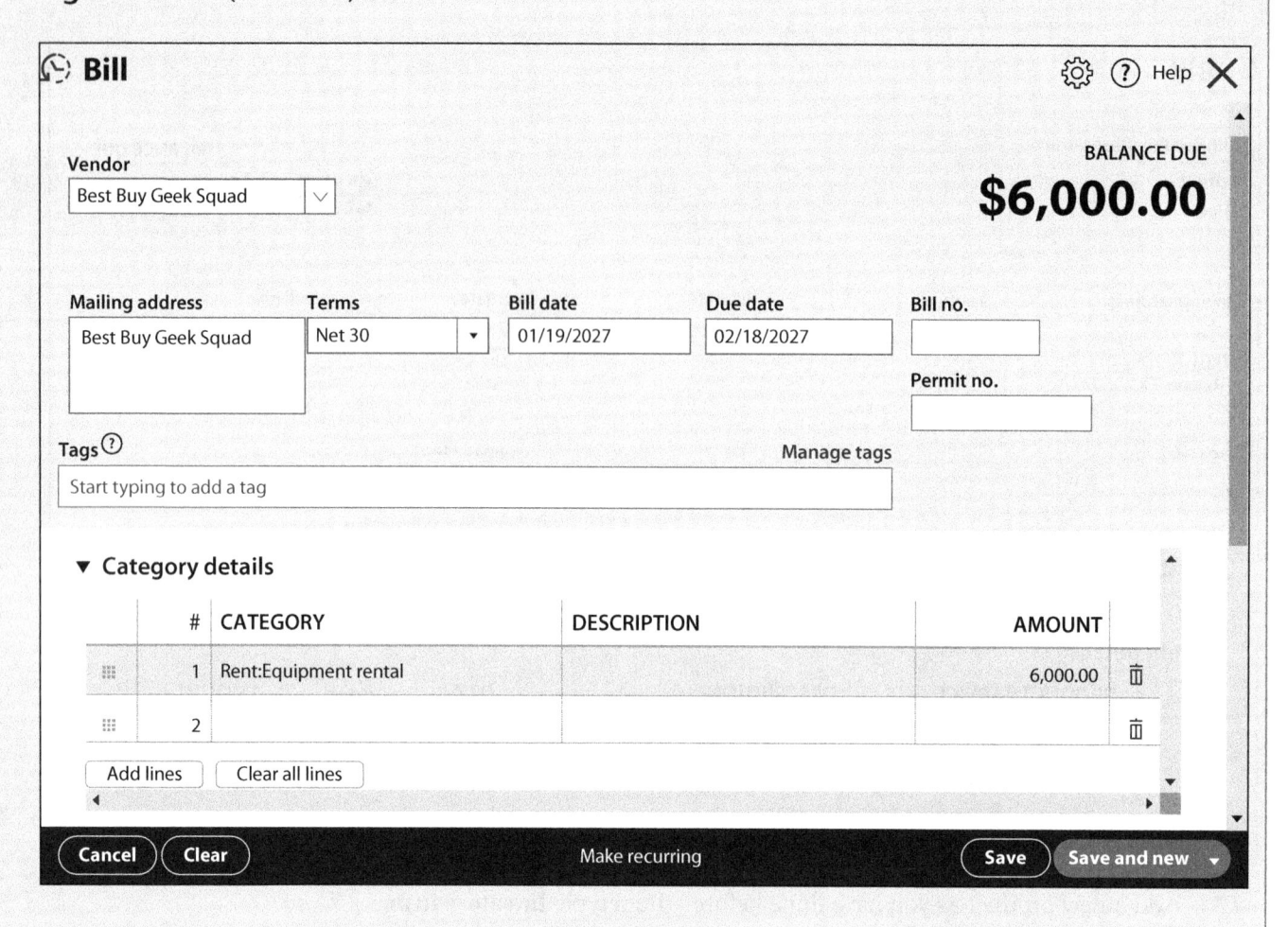

Bill						⚙ ? Help ✕

Vendor
Best Buy Geek Squad

BALANCE DUE
$6,000.00

Mailing address	Terms	Bill date	Due date	Bill no.
Best Buy Geek Squad	Net 30	01/19/2027	02/18/2027	

Permit no.

Tags ? Manage tags
Start typing to add a tag

▼ **Category details**

#	CATEGORY	DESCRIPTION	AMOUNT	
1	Rent:Equipment rental		6,000.00	🗑
2				🗑

Add lines   Clear all lines

Cancel   Clear   Make recurring   Save   Save and new ▼

22 Click **Save and new**.

23 Select **Allstate Insurance** from the Choose a vendor drop-down list.

24 Select **Net 30** from the drop-down list of Terms.

25 Type **1/19/27** as the Bill date.

26 Select **Prepaid expenses** on line 1 of the bill in the Category column.

27 Type **2500** on line 1 of the bill in the Amount column and then press **[Tab]**. Your window should look like Figure 5.10.

28 Click **Save and close**.

Figure 5.10 Bill for Prepaid Expenses (recording)

[Screenshot of Bill entry form: Vendor: Allstate Insurance; Mailing address: Allstate Insurance; Terms: Net 30; Bill date: 01/19/2027; Due date: 02/18/2027; Balance Due: $2,500.00; Category details — 1 Prepaid expenses, 2,500.00]

All bills entered increased an asset or an expense account. Inventory purchases were all recorded in the Item details section and increased the quantity of those products (as long as they were originally set up as "tracked" products). Equipment rental was recorded as an expense and the prepaid insurance was recorded as an asset (Prepaid Expenses). All bills increased the accounts payable liability account.

Payment of Bills, Use of a Credit Card, Payments for Items other than Bills

In this section, you will focus on recording the payment of a bill for the receipt of services and/or products on account, recording credit card charges, or recording the payment by check for other items.

VIDEO LINK

Navigate your browser to the Video Tutorials provided by Intuit (see website address specified in the Preface to this text) and then search on How to Record Bill Payments.

To pay bills, do the following:

1. Continue from where you left off.
2. Click the [+ New] icon, and click **Pay bills** in the Vendors column as shown in Figure 5.11.

Figure 5.11 + New window (paying bills)

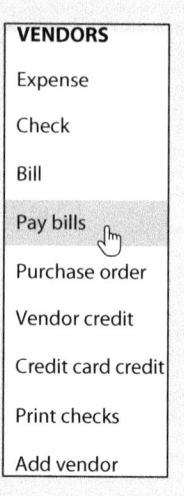

VENDORS
Expense
Check
Bill
Pay bills
Purchase order
Vendor credit
Credit card credit
Print checks
Add vendor

3. A listing of possible bills that can be paid appears. In the Pay Bills window, select **Checking** as the Payment account and then type **01/18/2027** in the Payment date text box and then type **1001** as the Starting check no. and then press **[Tab]**. Your screen should look like Figure 5.12.

Figure 5.12 Bills to pay

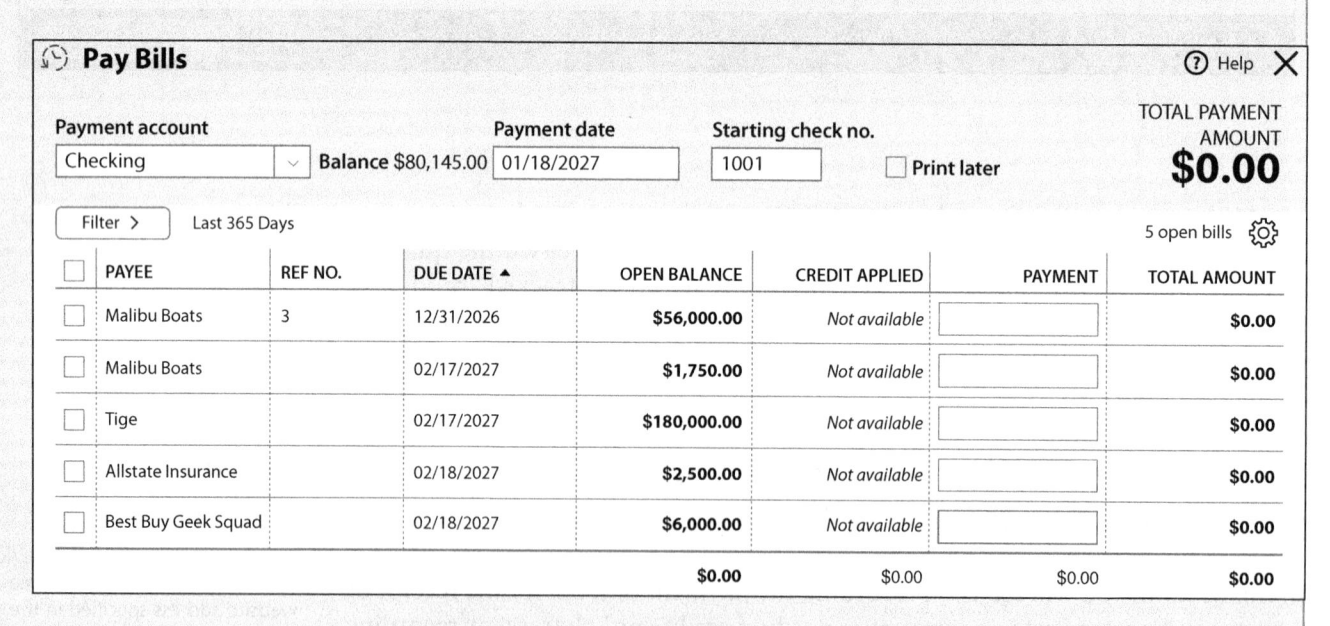

Pay Bills

Payment account: Checking   Balance $80,145.00
Payment date: 01/18/2027
Starting check no.: 1001   ☐ Print later
TOTAL PAYMENT AMOUNT: **$0.00**

Filter > Last 365 Days   5 open bills

	PAYEE	REF NO.	DUE DATE ▲	OPEN BALANCE	CREDIT APPLIED	PAYMENT	TOTAL AMOUNT
☐	Malibu Boats	3	12/31/2026	$56,000.00	Not available		$0.00
☐	Malibu Boats		02/17/2027	$1,750.00	Not available		$0.00
☐	Tige		02/17/2027	$180,000.00	Not available		$0.00
☐	Allstate Insurance		02/18/2027	$2,500.00	Not available		$0.00
☐	Best Buy Geek Squad		02/18/2027	$6,000.00	Not available		$0.00
				$0.00	$0.00	$0.00	$0.00

4. Click the **Due Date** column to sort bills by due date and then click in the check box of the **Malibu Boats 12/31/2026** bill to show bills to be paid as shown in Figure 5.13.
5. Click **Save and close**.

Recording Operating Activities: Purchases and Cash Payments **Chapter 5** 139

Figure 5.13 Bills to pay (selecting)

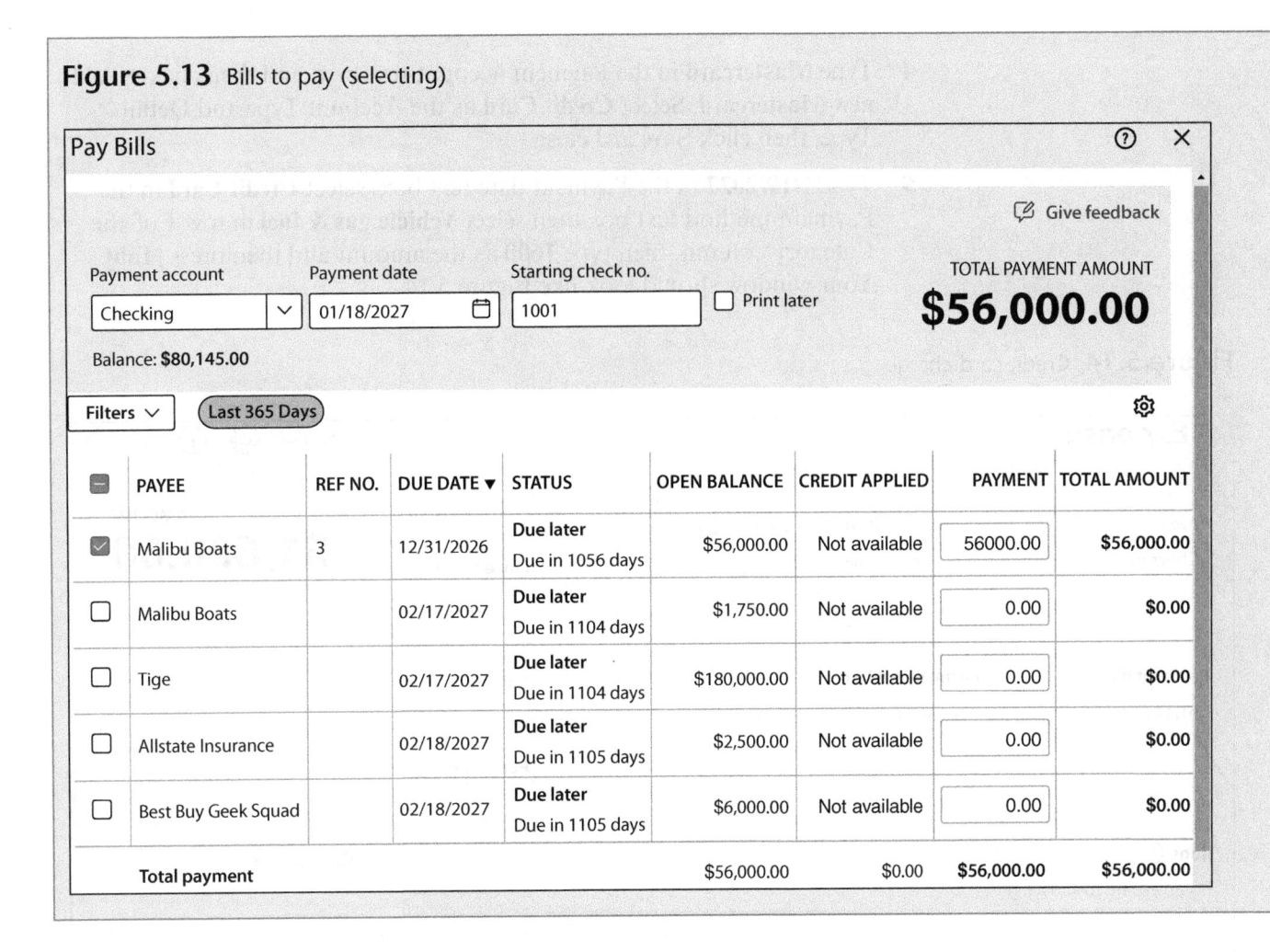

	PAYEE	REF NO.	DUE DATE ▼	STATUS	OPEN BALANCE	CREDIT APPLIED	PAYMENT	TOTAL AMOUNT
☑	Malibu Boats	3	12/31/2026	Due later / Due in 1056 days	$56,000.00	Not available	56000.00	$56,000.00
☐	Malibu Boats		02/17/2027	Due later / Due in 1104 days	$1,750.00	Not available	0.00	$0.00
☐	Tige		02/17/2027	Due later / Due in 1104 days	$180,000.00	Not available	0.00	$0.00
☐	Allstate Insurance		02/18/2027	Due later / Due in 1105 days	$2,500.00	Not available	0.00	$0.00
☐	Best Buy Geek Squad		02/18/2027	Due later / Due in 1105 days	$6,000.00	Not available	0.00	$0.00
	Total payment				$56,000.00	$0.00	$56,000.00	$56,000.00

Payment account: Checking Balance: $80,145.00
Payment date: 01/18/2027
Starting check no.: 1001
TOTAL PAYMENT AMOUNT: **$56,000.00**

Trouble: Intuit has added a new column to this screen titled Status which calculates the number of days before this bill is due. However, it uses your computer's current date which is different than the dates being used for this case. Thus, you should ignore this information.

You have now paid a bill for products/services received for which you received a bill. However, often you will pay for a product/service or another expense for which you have not received a bill. Often, these are vendors who give you no terms and require you to pay immediately. These terms are called *due on receipt*. For example, a credit card charge for fuel or a check for supplies. To record these transactions, you will use either the Expense task or the Check task after clicking the (+ New) icon. For ease of use, you will be directed to use the Expense task for all credit card transactions and the Check task for all checking account payments even though the Expense task can be used for either credit card charges or check payments.

To record a credit card or check payment, do the following:

1. Click the (+ New) icon.
2. Click **Expense** under the Vendors column.
3. Type **Chevron**, in the Payee text box, and then select **+ Add new Chevron**, Type **Chevron** in the Vendor display name text box, then click **Save**.

4   Type **Mastercard** in the Payment account text box, and then click **+ Add new Mastercard**. Select **Credit Card** as the Account Type and Detail Type, then click **Save and close**.

5   Type **1/19/2027** in the Payment date text box, select **Credit Card** in the Payment method text box then select **Vehicle gas & fuel** in row 1 of the Category column, then type **1600** as the amount and then press **[Tab]**. Your window should look like Figure 5.14.

Figure 5.14 Credit card charge

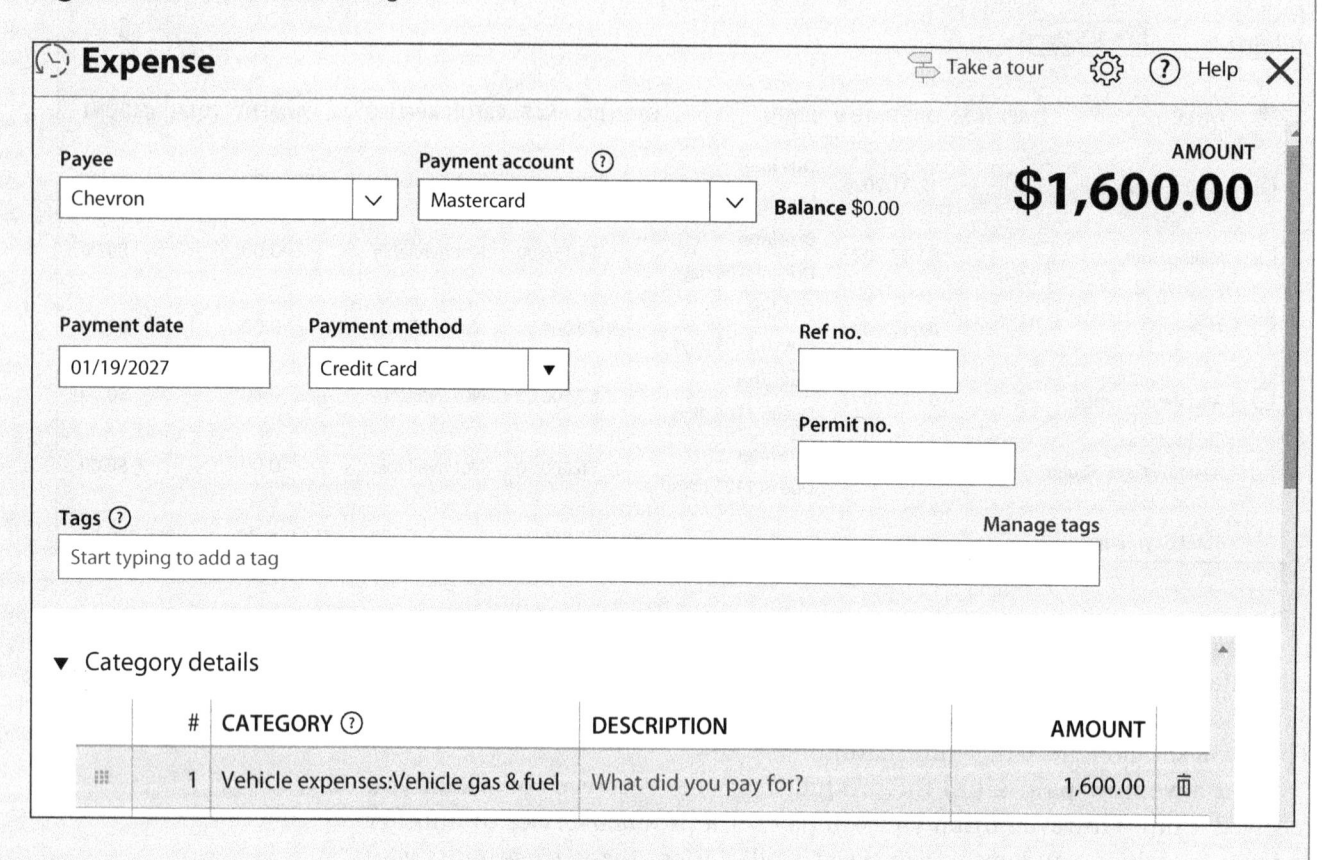

Payee	Payment account		AMOUNT
Chevron	Mastercard	Balance $0.00	**$1,600.00**

Payment date	Payment method	Ref no.
01/19/2027	Credit Card	

Permit no.

Tags   Manage tags
Start typing to add a tag

▼ Category details

#	CATEGORY	DESCRIPTION	AMOUNT
1	Vehicle expenses:Vehicle gas & fuel	What did you pay for?	1,600.00

6   Click **Save and close**.

7   Click the **+ New** icon.

8   Click **Check** under the Vendors column.

9   Type **Verizon** in the Payee text box, then click **+ Add new Verizon**. Click **Save**.

10 Select **Checking** from the drop-down list in the Bank Account text box.

11 Accept **1002** as the Check no. and **1/19/2027** as the Payment date.

12 Select **Phone service** in row 1 of the Category column, and type **1800** as the amount, and then press **[Tab]** as shown in Figure 5.15.

13 Click **Save and close**.

Figure 5.15 Check 1002 payment to Verizon

⟳ **Check #1002**		⚙ ? Help ✕

Payee	Bank Account		AMOUNT
Verizon ⌄	Checking ⌄ Balance $24,145.00		**$1,800.00**

Mailing address: Verizon
Payment date: 01/19/2027

Check no.: 1002
☐ Print later
Permit no.:

Tags ?   Manage tags
Start typing to add a tag

▼ Category details

#	CATEGORY	DESCRIPTION	AMOUNT	
1	Utilities:Phone service	What did you pay for?	1,800.00	🗑

Trial Balance

The work you completed in this chapter had an effect on the company's trial balance. You decided to create a Trial Balance report and investigate the checking, inventory asset, and accounts payable accounts. In the process, you realized that purchase orders do not affect a company's accounts until products are received or services are rendered.

To create a trial balance and investigate some account activity, do the following:

1. Click **Reports**, then select the **Custom reports** tab, then select **Trial Balance**. Change the to date of the report to **1/19/2027** to view the Trial Balance as shown in Figure 5.16.

2. Click the Checking account balance of **22,345.00** and then click the **Switch to classic view** button to produce a Transaction Report for the Checking Account. See Figure 5.17. Note that some of the reports can be viewed in either modern or classic view.

3. Click the **Printer** icon to print this report.

4. Click **Back to report summary**.

Figure 5.16 Trial Balance (upper portion)

Trial Balance Report
< Back to report list
Report period

| Custom ▼ | 01/01/2027 | to | 01/19/2027 |

Customize | Save customization

Add notes

Wild Water Sports - Student Name (ID Number)
Trial Balance
As of January 19, 2027

	DEBIT	CREDIT
Checking	22,345.00	
Accounts receivable (A/R)	120,770.00	
Inventory	223,350.00	
Payments to deposit	70,000.00	
Prepaid expenses	17,500.00	
Equipment:Accumulated depre...		10,000.00
Equipment:Original Cost	40,000.00	
Accounts Payable (A/P)		190,250.00
Mastercard		1,600.00
Florida Department of Revenue ...		9,915.00
Long-term business loans		50,000.00
Common stock		1,000.00
Opening balance equity		0.00
Retained Earnings		205,800.00
Sales		164,000.00
Service Revenue		2,000.00
Cost of goods sold	131,200.00	
Rent:Equipment rental	6,000.00	
Utilities:Phone service	1,800.00	
Vehicle expenses:Vehicle gas & ...	1,600.00	
TOTAL	**$634,565.00**	**$634,565.00**

Figure 5.17 Transaction Report (for the Checking account)

Transaction Report
January 1-19, 2027

DATE	TRANSACTION TYPE	NUM	NAME	MEMO/DESCRIPTION	ACCOUNT	SPLIT	AMOUNT	BALANCE
▼ Checking								
Beginning Balance								25,000.00
01/12/2027	Deposit		Southtown Watersports		Checking	Payments to deposit	55,145.00	80,145.00
01/18/2027	Bill Payment (Check)	1001	Malibu Boats		Checking	Accounts Payable (A/P)	−56,000.00	24,145.00
01/19/2027	Check	1002	Verizon		Checking	Utilities:Phone service	−1,800.00	22,345.00
Total for Checking							**$ −2,655.00**	
TOTAL							**$ −2,655.00**	

5. Click the Inventory account balance of **223,350.00** and then click the **Switch to classic view** button to produce a Transaction Report for the Inventory account. The two bills for product purchases you recorded earlier in this chapter are shown in Figure 5.18.

Figure 5.18 Transaction Report (for the Inventory account)

	Wild Water Sports - Student Name (ID Number)							
	Transaction Report							
	January 1-19, 2027							
DATE	TRANSACTION TYPE	NUM	NAME	MEMO/DESCRIPTION	ACCOUNT	SPLIT	AMOUNT	BALANCE
▼ Inventory								
Beginning Balance								172,800.00
01/01/2027	Inventory Starting Value	START		Tige 25 zx - Opening inventory a...	Inventory	Opening balance equity	0.00	172,800.00
01/04/2027	Sales Receipt	1001	Southtown Watersports	Malibu Sportster LX	Inventory	Payments to deposit	–41,600.00	131,200.00
01/05/2027	Inventory Starting Value	START		2023 Vi22 - Opening inventory a...	Inventory	Opening balance equity	0.00	131,200.00
01/06/2027	Invoice	1002	Performance Rentals	Malibu Sportster LX	Inventory	Accounts receivable (A/R)	–41,600.00	89,600.00
01/06/2027	Invoice	1002	Performance Rentals	Malibu Sunset LX	Inventory	Accounts receivable (A/R)	–48,000.00	41,600.00
01/15/2027	Inventory Starting Value	START		Tige Thruster Control Package - ...	Inventory	Opening balance equity	0.00	41,600.00
01/18/2027	Bill		Malibu Boats	Wake Accessory Package	Inventory	Accounts Payable (A/P)	1,750.00	43,350.00
01/18/2027	Bill		Tige	Tige 25 zx	Inventory	Accounts Payable (A/P)	180,000.00	223,350.00
01/18/2027	Inventory Starting Value	START		Wake Accessory Package - Open...	Inventory	Opening balance equity	0.00	223,350.00
Total for Inventory							**$50,550.00**	
TOTAL							**$50,550.00**	

6 Click the **Printer** icon to print this report.

7 Click **Back to report summary**.

8 Click the Accounts Payable (A/P) account balance of **190,250.00** and then click the **Switch to classic view** button to produce a Transaction Report for the Accounts Payable (A/P) account. The bills for product and service purchases and the bill payments you recorded earlier in this chapter are shown in Figure 5.19.

Figure 5.19 Transaction Report (for the Accounts Payable account)

	Wild Water Sports - Student Name (ID Number)							
	Transaction Report							
	January 1-19, 2027							
DATE	TRANSACTION TYPE	NUM	NAME	MEMO/DESCRIPTION	ACCOUNT	SPLIT	AMOUNT	BALANCE
▼ Accounts Payable (A/P)								
Beginning Balance								56,000.00
01/18/2027	Bill		Malibu Boats		Accounts Payable (A/P)	Inventory	1,750.00	57,750.00
01/18/2027	Bill		Tige		Accounts Payable (A/P)	Inventory	180,000.00	237,750.00
01/18/2027	Bill Payment (Check)	1001	Malibu Boats		Accounts Payable (A/P)	Checking	–56,000.00	181,750.00
01/19/2027	Bill		Best Buy Geek Squad		Accounts Payable (A/P)	Rent:Equipment rental	6,000.00	187,750.00
01/19/2027	Bill		Allstate Insurance		Accounts Payable (A/P)	Prepaid expenses	2,500.00	190,250.00
Total for Accounts Payable (A/P)							**$134,250.00**	
TOTAL							**$134,250.00**	

9 Click the **Printer** icon to print this report.

10 Click **Back to report summary**.

11 Sign out of QBO.

Be sure to verify that your Trial Balance report matches the one shown above. Create a Detailed Transaction by Account report like you did in Chapter 4 to help locate any discrepancies.

End Note

In this chapter, you added a vendor, a product, purchase orders, bills, payment of bills, a credit card purchase, and a check payment. You also produced a trial balance and drilled down through that trial balance to see the effect the bills and payment of bills affected accounts. In the next chapter, you will work with investing and financing activities.

practice

Chapter 5 Questions

1. Why does a business use purchase orders?
2. Describe the steps to create a new product from within a purchase order.
3. What happens when you create a new purchase order to a vendor from whom you recently placed a different purchase order?
4. What accounts are affected when a bill from a vendor supplying you products is recorded?
5. What appears when you click **Pay bills** after clicking the (+ New) icon?
6. Describe the process for increasing or decreasing the width of a column in the listing of bills to pay.
7. What are the steps to record a credit card charge?
8. What are the steps to record a check written to pay something other than bills?
9. What are the steps to view a transaction report for the checking account from a trial balance?
10. What are the steps to view a transaction report for the inventory account from a trial balance?

Chapter 5 Matching

a. Purchase order _____ Purchases that affect inventory are recorded here
b. Due on receipt _____ An invoice sent by a vendor to a customer
c. Bill _____ Purchases that don't affect inventory are recorded here
d. Net 30 _____ Task used to record checks in the checking account
e. Item detail section _____ Suppliers of products and services
f. Category detail section _____ A formal means to order products from vendors
g. Pay Bills _____ Pay a bill within 30 days after the bill date
h. Check _____ Task used to record credit card charges
i. Expense _____ Terms that provide no credit
j. Vendor _____ Paying vendors who have billed you

Chapter 5 Cases

The following cases require you to open the company you updated in Chapter 4. Each of the following cases continues throughout the text in a sequential manner. For example, if you are assigned Case 01, you will use the file you modified in this chapter in all of the following chapters. Each of the following cases is similar in concepts assessed but differs in amounts and transactions. See the Preface to this text for a matrix of each student case and its attributes.

To reopen your company, do the following:

1. Open your Internet browser.
2. Type **https://qbo.intuit.com** into your browser's address text box.
3. Type your user ID and password into the text boxes as you have done before.

Case 1

Add some operating activities (purchases, credit card charges, and cash payments) to your company.

Based on what you learned in the text using the Wild Water Sports company, you are to make the following changes to the Case 1 company you modified in Chapter 4:

1. Add a new vendor – Stewart Surfboards, 2102 S El Camino Real, San Clemente, CA 92672, terms: net 30.

2. Add a new vendor – Village Travel, 100 S El Camino Real, San Clemente, CA 92672, terms: due on receipt.

3. Add a new vendor – Office Depot, 101 Main St., San Diego, CA 92600, terms: due on receipt.

4. Add a new account – account type: Credit Card, detail type: Credit Card, name: VISA.

5. Add a new account – account type: Other Current Assets, detail type: Other Current Assets, name: Supplies Asset.

6. Add a new tracked product – Name/description: California Nose Rider, initial quantity on hand: 0, As of date: 01/02/24, inventory asset account: Inventory Asset, price: 3,200.00, cost: 1,700.00, income account: Sales, expense account: Cost of Goods Sold.

7. Add a new tracked product – Name/description: 808, initial quantity on hand: 0, As of date: 01/02/24, inventory asset account: Inventory Asset, price: 2,700.00, cost: 1,500.00, income account: Sales, expense account: Cost of Goods Sold.

8. Record a new purchase order for products on 1/2/24 – Vendor: Channel Islands, product 1: Fred Rubble, QTY: 5, product 2: Rook 15, QTY: 4, product 3: The Water Hog, QTY: 1.

9. Record a new purchase order for products on 1/3/24 – Vendor: Stewart Surfboards, product 1: 808, QTY: 2, product 2: California Nose Rider, QTY: 1.

10. Record a new bill based on a purchase order #1001 on 1/5/24 – Vendor: Channel Islands, terms: Net 15. All items ordered were received.

11. Record a new bill without a purchase order on 1/8/24 – New vendor: San Diego Gas & Electric, terms: Net 15, category: Utilities, amount: 145.00.

Recording Operating Activities: Purchases and Cash Payments **Chapter 5** 147

12 Record a new bill without a purchase order on 1/9/24 – New vendor: Prime Properties, terms: Net 15, category 1: Rent or Lease, amount: 2,500.00, category 2: Prepaid Expenses, amount: 5,000.00.

13 Pay all bills due to Channel Islands on 1/19/24 using the checking account and starting with Check no. 1001.

14 Record a credit card charge on 1/10/24 – vendor: Village Travel, using credit card: VISA, category: Travel, amount: 1,800.00.

15 Record check on 1/11/24 – no.: 1002, vendor: Office Depot, amount: 375.00, account: Supplies Asset.

16 Open your previously customized report named Trial Balance 1/31/24. If a cash or accrual message appears, just close the message. Your report should look like Figure 5.20.

Case 1
TRIAL BALANCE
As of January 31, 2024

	DEBIT	CREDIT
Checking	16,325.00	
Accounts Receivable	1,030.00	
Inventory Asset	11,800.00	
Prepaid Expenses	8,000.00	
Supplies Asset	375.00	
Undeposited Funds	5,000.00	
Furniture & Fixtures:Depreciation		10,000.00
Furniture & Fixtures:Original cost	40,000.00	
Accounts Payable		7,645.00
VISA		1,800.00
Notes Payable		60,000.00
Common Stock		1,000.00
Opening Balance Equity		0.00
Retained Earnings		5,500.00
Sales		2,160.00
Services		170.00
Cost of Goods Sold	1,300.00	
Rent or Lease	2,500.00	
Travel	1,800.00	
Utilities	145.00	
TOTAL	**$88,275.00**	**$88,275.00**

Figure 5.20

Trial Balance (as of 1/31/24)

17 Create and print a Transaction Report for the Checking account as you did earlier in the chapter.

18 Create and print a Transaction Report for the Inventory Asset account as you did earlier in the chapter.

19 Create and print a Transaction Report for the Accounts Payable (A/P) account as you did earlier in the chapter.

20 If your trial balance differs from what is shown in Figure 5.20, do the following:

   a. Make sure all of your changes were dated in January 2024.

   b. View the Transaction Reports you just created to locate any errors.

   c. Ask your instructor for assistance.

   d. Be sure your company matches the above as you will be adding additional business events in Chapter 6.

21 Export your Trial Balance report to Excel, and save it with the file name Student Name (replace with your name) Ch 05 Case 01 Trial Balance.xlsx.

22 Open and print the custom report you created in the last chapter called Transaction Detail by Account.

23 Export your Transactions Detail by Account report to Excel, and save it with the file name Student Name (replace with your name) Ch 05 Case 01 Transaction Detail by Account.xlsx.

24 Sign out of your company.

Case 2

Add some operating activities (purchases, credit card charges, and cash payments) to your company.

Based on what you learned in the text using the Wild Water Sports company, you are to make the following changes to the Case 2 company you modified in Chapter 4:

1 Add a new vendor – E-flite, 700 Annapolis Ln N Suite #175, Plymouth, MN, 55447, terms: net 15.

2 Add a new vendor – Village Steak House, 100 S El Camino Real, San Clemente, CA 92672, terms: due on receipt.

3 Add a new vendor – Staples, 101 Main St., San Diego, CA 92600, terms: due on receipt.

4 Add a new account – account type: Credit Card, detail type: Credit Card, name: AMEX.

5 Add a new account – account type: Other Current Assets, detail type: Other Current Assets, name: Supplies Asset.

6 Add a new product – name/description: Sport Cub S, initial quantity on hand: 0, As of date: 01/02/25, inventory asset account: Inventory Asset, price: 600.00, cost: 479.00, income account: Sales, expense account: Cost of Goods Sold.

7 Add a new product – name/description: Mystique RES, initial quantity on hand: 0, As of date: 01/02/25, inventory asset account: Inventory Asset, price: 450.00, cost: 325.00, income account: Sales, expense account: Cost of Goods Sold.

8 Record a new purchase order for products on 1/2/25 – vendor: E-flite, product 1: Sport Cub S, QTY: 5, product 2: Mystique RES, QTY: 3.

9 Record a new purchase order for products on 1/3/25 – vendor: Kyosho, product 1: Broon F830 Ride, QTY: 4, product 2: GO Aircraft Radio, QTY: 2, product 3: Seawind Carbon Sailboat, QTY: 1.

10 Record a new bill based on a purchase order #1001 on 1/7/25 – vendor: E-flite, terms: Net 15. All items ordered were received.

11 Record a new bill without a purchase order on 1/8/25 – new vendor: San Diego News-Press, terms: Net 15, category: Advertising, amount: 500.00. Note: If your chart of accounts contains Advertising and Marketing, then change the account to read Advertising only.

12 Record a new bill without a purchase order on 1/10/25 – new vendor: Gomez Insurance, terms: Net 15, category 1: Insurance, amount: 400.00, category 2: Prepaid Expenses, amount: 4,400.00.

13 Pay bill due to Kyosho on 1/18/25 using the checking account and starting with Check no. 1001.

14 Record a credit card charge on 1/11/25 – vendor: Village Steak House, using credit card: AMEX, category: Meals and Entertainment, amount: 240.00.

15 Record check on 1/14/25 – no.: 1002, vendor: Staples, amount: 450.00, account: Supplies Asset.

16 Open your previously customized report named Trial Balance 1/31/25. Your report should look like Figure 5.21.

Case 2
TRIAL BALANCE
As of January 31, 2025

	DEBIT	CREDIT
Checking	7,150.00	
Accounts Receivable	1,425.00	
Inventory Asset	5,410.00	
Prepaid Expenses	6,800.00	
Supplies Asset	450.00	
Undeposited Funds	925.00	
Machinery & Equipment:Depreciation		1,000.00
Machinery & Equipment:Original cost	10,000.00	
Accounts Payable		8,670.00
AMEX		240.00
Notes Payable		12,000.00
Common Stock		100.00
Opening Balance Equity		0.00
Retained Earnings		8,385.00
Sales		5,700.00
Services		225.00
Cost of Goods Sold	3,020.00	
Advertising	500.00	
Insurance	400.00	
Meals and Entertainment	240.00	
TOTAL	**$36,320.00**	**$36,320.00**

Figure 5.21

Trial Balance (as of 1/31/25)

17 Create and print a Transaction Report for the Checking account as you did earlier in the chapter.

18 Create and print a Transaction Report for the Inventory Asset account as you did earlier in the chapter.

19 Create and print a Transaction Report for the Accounts Payable (A/P) account as you did earlier in the chapter.

20 If your trial balance differs from what is shown in Figure 5.21, do the following:

   a. Make sure that all of your changes were dated in January 2025.
   b. View the Transaction Reports you created to locate any errors.
   c. Ask your instructor for assistance.
   d. Be sure your company matches the above as you will be adding additional business events in Chapter 6.

21 Export your Trial Balance report to Excel, and save it with the file name Student Name (replace with your name) Ch 05 Case 02 Trial Balance.xlsx.

22 Open and print the custom report you created in the last chapter called Transaction Detail by Account.

23 Export your Transactions Detail by Account report to Excel, and save it with the file name Student Name (replace with your name) Ch 05 Case 02 Transaction Detail by Account.xlsx.

24 Sign out of your company.

Case 3

Now it's time for you to add some operating activities (purchases, credit card charges, and cash payments) to your company.

Based on what you learned in the text using the Wild Water Sports company, you are to make the following changes to the Case 3 company you modified in Chapter 4:

1 Add a new vendor – Google, Inc., 1600 Amphitheatre Parkway, Mountain View, CA 94043, terms: Net 15.

2 Add a new vendor – Samsung, Inc., 105 Challenger Rd., Ridgefield Park, NJ 07660, terms: Net 15.

3 Add a new vendor – Staples, Inc., 101 Main St., San Diego, CA 92600, terms: Net 30.

4 Modify Apple Inc. (existing Vendor) – Name should be Apple Computer, Inc., address: 1 Infinite Loop Cupertino, CA 95014, terms: Net 15.

5 Add a new account – account type: Credit Card, detail type: Credit Card, name: AMEX.

6 Add a new account – account type: Other Current Assets, detail type: Other Current Assets, name: Supplies Asset.

7 Add a new product – Name/Description & Purchasing information: Samsung Galaxy 8, initial quantity on hand: 0, inventory asset account: Inventory Asset, Sales price: 450.00, cost: 350.00, income account: Sales of Product Income, expense account: Cost of Goods Sold. (Use 01/06/2026 as the "as of date.") Sales tax: Taxable – standard rate.

8 Add a new product – Name/Description & Purchasing information: Samsung Note, initial quantity on hand: 0, inventory asset account: Inventory Asset, Sales price: 850.00, cost: 650.00, income account: Sales of Product Income, expense account: Cost of Goods Sold. (Use 01/06/2026 as the "as of date.") Sales tax: Taxable – standard rate.

9 Record a new purchase order (1001) for products on 1/6/26 – vendor: Google, Inc., Pixel, QTY: 10.

10 Record a new purchase order (1002) for products on 1/7/26 – vendor: Samsung, Inc., product 1: Samsung Galaxy 8, QTY: 5, product 2: Samsung Note, QTY: 8.

11 Record a new bill based on a purchase order #1001 dated 1/6/26 – vendor: Google, Inc., terms: Net 15. All items ordered were received on 1/10/26 (the bill date).

12 Record a new bill without a purchase order on 1/8/26 – new vendor: News-Press, terms: Net 15, category: Advertising & Marketing, amount: 1,300.00.

13 Record a new bill without a purchase order on 1/10/26 – new vendor: Hathaway Insurance, terms: Net 15, category 1: Insurance, amount: 300.00, category 2: Prepaid expenses, amount: 3,300.00.

14 Pay bill due to Apple Computer, Inc. on 1/18/26 using the checking account and starting with Check no. 321.

15 Record a credit card charge on 1/11/26 – new vendor: Village Steak House, using credit card: AMEX, category: Meals, amount: 123.00.

16 Record check on 1/14/26 – no.: 322, vendor: Staples, amount: 327.00, category: Supplies Asset.

17 Open and print your previously customized report named Trial Balance 1/31/26. Your report should look like Figure 5.22.

Figure 5.22 Trial Balance as of 1/31/26

Case 03 - Student Name (ID Number)
Trial Balance
As of January 31, 2026

	DEBIT	CREDIT
Checking	15,751.75	
Accounts receivable (A/R)	2,559.38	
Inventory Asset	5,700.00	
Payments to deposit	0.00	
Prepaid expenses	6,050.00	
Supplies Asset	327.00	
Machinery & Equipment:Depreciation		2,000.00
Machinery & Equipment:Original cost	15,000.00	
Accounts Payable (A/P)		8,900.00
AMEX		123.00
California Department of Tax and Fee Administration ...		523.13
Notes Payable		23,000.00
Opening balance equity		0.00
Owner's Equity		10,075.00
Sales of Product Income		6,750.00
Services		240.00
Cost of goods sold	4,500.00	
Advertising & marketing	1,300.00	
Insurance	300.00	
Meals	123.00	
TOTAL	**$51,611.13**	**$51,611.13**

18 Create and print a Transaction Report for the Checking account like you did in the chapter.

19 Create and print a Transaction Report for the Accounts Receivable (A/R) account.

20 Create and print a Transaction Report for the Inventory Asset account like you did in the chapter.

21 Create and print a Transaction Report for the Accounts Payable (A/P) account like you did in the chapter.

22 If your trial balance is different than Figure 5.22, do the following:

　a. Make sure that all of your changes were dated in January 2026.

　b. View the Transaction Reports you just created to locate any errors.

c. Ask your instructor for assistance.

d. Be sure your company matches the above as you will be adding additional business events in Chapter 6.

23 Export your Trial Balance report to Excel, and save it with the file name Student Name (replace with your name) Ch 05 Case 03 Trial Balance.xlsx.

24 Open and print the custom report you created in the last chapter called Transaction Detail by Account.

25 Export your Transactions Detail by Account report to Excel, and save it with the file name Student Name (replace with your name) Ch 05 Case 03 Transaction Detail by Account.xlsx.

26 Sign out of your company.

Case 4

Now it's time for you to add some operating activities (purchases and cash payments) to your company.

Based on what you learned in the text using the Wild Water Sports company, you are to make the following changes to the Case 4 company you modified in Chapter 4:

1 Add a new vendor – GEICO Insurance, 335 Park Ave., Los Angeles, CA 90034, terms: Net 15.

2 Add a new account – Account Type: Assets, Save account under: Other Current Assets, Tax form section: Other Current Assets, Account name: Supplies Asset.

3 Add a new account – Account Type: Credit Cards, Save account under: Credit Card, Tax form section: Credit Card, name: VISA.

4 Add a new service – Name/Description information: Towel Service, Sales price/rate: 20.00, income account: Sales, Is taxable: No.

5 Record sales receipt 1004 to a new customer: Enterprise Inc., on 1/4/27 for 5 Monthly Fee – Corporate Membership 50 Employees and 50 Towel Service. Check no. 9847 was received and immediately deposited to the company's checking account in the amount of $31,000.

6 Record a new purchase order (1001) for products on 1/7/27 – vendor: Bowflex, product: Bowflex Dumbbells, QTY: 25.

7 Record a new purchase order (1002) for products on 1/8/27 – vendor: Precor, product: Power Block Elite Dumbbells, QTY: 15.

8 Record a new bill based on a purchase order #1001 dated 1/7/27 – vendor: Bowflex, terms: Net 15. All items ordered were received on 1/15/27 (the bill date).

9 Record a new bill without a purchase order on 1/16/27 – new vendor: Supreme Marketing, terms: Net 15, category: Advertising & marketing, amount: $1,800.00.

10 Record a new bill without a purchase order on 1/18/27 – vendor: Laundry Service, terms: Net 15, category: Supplies Asset, amount: $1,400.00.

11 Pay bills due to Precor and Laundry Service on 1/18/27 using the checking account and starting with Check no. 25498.

12 Record credit card charge on 1/20/27 – vendor: GEICO Insurance, using credit card: VISA, category: Insurance, amount: $2,400.00.

13 Record check on 1/21/27 – Check no.: 25500, vendor: NordicTrack, amount: $750.00, category: Repairs & Maintenance.

14 Prepare and print the Trial Balance 1/31/27 report you saved previously. Your report should look like Figure 5.23.

15 Create and print a Transaction Report for the Checking account.

16 Create and print a Transaction Report for the Accounts Receivable (A/R) account.

17 Create and print a Transaction Report for the Inventory Asset account.

Figure 5.23 Trial Balance as of 1/31/27

Trial Balance
As of January 31, 2027

	DEBIT	CREDIT
Checking	45,576.65	
Accounts Receivable (A/R)	22,082.50	
Inventory Asset	8,868.00	
Payments to deposit	0.00	
Prepaid rent	12,000.00	
Supplies Asset	1,400.00	
Furniture:Accumulated Depreciation		10,000.00
Furniture:Original Cost	65,000.00	
Vehicles:Accumulated Depreciation		6,500.00
Vehicles:Original Cost	115,000.00	
Accounts Payable (A/P)		6,800.00
VISA		2,400.00
California Department of Tax and Fee Administration Payable		339.15
Long-term debt		82,000.00
Common Stock		1,000.00
Opening Balance Equity		0.00
Retained Earnings		115,500.00
Sales		48,400.00
Sales of Product Income		3,570.00
Cost of Goods Sold	1,632.00	
Advertising & Marketing	1,800.00	
Insurance	2,400.00	
Repairs & Maintenance	750.00	
TOTAL	$276,509.15	$276,509.15

18 Create and print a Transaction Report for the Accounts Payable (A/P) account.

19 Investigate differences between your trial balance and the trial balance shown above.

20 If necessary, prepare and print the Transaction Detail by Account report you saved previously to investigate identified differences.

   a. Make sure all your changes were dated in January 2027.

   b. Click on the line that does not match to view the transaction for that account, and investigate why your answer differs.

   c. Ask your instructor for assistance.

   d. Be sure your company matches the above as you will be adding additional business events in Chapter 6.

Case 5

Now it's time for you to add some operating activities (purchases and cash payments) to your company.

Based on using what you learned in the text using the Wild Water Sports company, you are to make the following changes to the Case 5 company you modified in Chapter 4:

1 Add a new vendor – State Farm Insurance, 9542 Argyle Forest Blvd #12, Jacksonville, FL, 32222, terms: Net 30.

2 Add a new account – Account Type: Assets, Save account under: Other Current Assets, Tax form section: Other Current Assets, Account name: Supplies Asset.

3 Add a new account – Account Type: Credit cards, Save account under: Credit Cards, Tax form section: Credit Card, Account name: AMEX.

4 Add a new service – Name and description: Training, Price/rate: 100.00, income account: Training, a new account (Save account under: Income, Tax form section: Service/Fee Income, Account name: Training), nontaxable.

5 Record sales receipt 1004 to Blue Origin on 1/13/28 for 35 hours of Training and 10 Training Materials Volume 1. Check no. 105866 was received and immediately deposited to the company's checking account in the amount of $167,000 (including sales tax).

6 Record a new purchase order on 1/14/28 – vendor: HP Computers, product: Computer Workstation 100, QTY: 50.

7 Record a new purchase order on 1/17/28 – vendor: Wild Research, Inc., product 1: Training Materials – Volume 1, QTY: 10, product 2: Training Materials – Volume 2, QTY: 10.

8 Record a new bill based on a purchase order dated 1/14/28 – vendor: HP Computers, terms: Net 30. All items ordered were received on 1/18/28 (the bill date).

9. Record a new bill without a purchase order on 1/19/28 – new vendor: Acme Equipment, terms: Net 15, category: Equipment rental, amount: $7,500.

10. Record a new bill without a purchase order on 1/20/28 – vendor: State Farm Insurance, terms: Net 30, category: Prepaid Expenses, amount: $12,000.

11. Pay bills to Wild Research, Inc., and Acme Equipment on 1/19/28 using the checking account and starting with Check no. 3005.

12. Record credit card charge on 1/20/28 – vendor: Indeed, using credit card: AMEX, category: Recruiting, amount: $6,300.

13. Record check on 1/21/28 – Check no.: 3007, new vendor: Rocket Marketing, amount: $3,000, category: Advertising & marketing.

Figure 5.24 Trial Balance as of 1/31/28

Case 05 - Student Name (ID Number)
Trial Balance
As of January 31, 2028

	DEBIT	CREDIT
Checking	254,000.00	
Accounts Receivable (A/R)	158,350.00	
Inventory	722,000.00	
Payments to deposit	0.00	
Prepaid expenses	22,000.00	
Fixed Asset Computers:Depreciation		25,000.00
Fixed Asset Computers:Original Cost	250,000.00	
Fixed Asset Furniture:Depreciation		8,000.00
Fixed Asset Furniture:Original Cost	80,000.00	
Accounts Payable (A/P)		362,000.00
AMEX		6,300.00
Alabama Department of Revenue Payable		6,600.00
Alabama, Huntsville Payable		7,425.00
Alabama, Madison County Payable		825.00
Notes Payable		545,000.00
Opening balance equity		0.00
Owner's Equity		382,000.00
Consulting		79,500.00
Sales		165,000.00
Training		3,500.00
Cost of goods sold	88,000.00	
Advertising & Marketing	3,000.00	
Equipment rental	7,500.00	
Recruiting	6,300.00	
TOTAL	**$1,591,150.00**	**$1,591,150.00**

14 Prepare and print the Trial Balance 1/31/28 report you saved previously. Your report should look like Figure 5.24.

15 Create and print a Transaction Report for the Checking account.

16 Create and print a Transaction Report for the Accounts Receivable (A/R) account.

17 Create and print a Transaction Report for the Inventory account.

18 Create and print a Transaction Report for the Accounts Payable (A/P) account.

19 Investigate differences between your trial balance and the trial balance shown above.

20 If necessary, prepare and print the Transaction Detail by Account report you saved previously to investigate identified differences.

  a. Make sure all your changes were dated in January 2028.

  b. Click on the line that does not match to view the transaction for that account and investigate why your answer differs.

  c. Ask your instructor for assistance.

  d. Be sure your company matches the above as you will be adding additional business events in Chapter 6.

Case 6

Now it's time for you to add some operating activities (purchases and cash payments) to your company.

Based on using what you learned in the text using the Wild Water Sports company, you are to make the following changes to the Case 6 company you modified in Chapter 4:

1 Add a new vendor – State Farm Insurance, 2764 1st Ave S, Suite 110, Seattle, WA 98134, terms: Net 15.

2 Add a new vendor – National Covers, 2270 Cosmos Court #100, Carlsbad, CA, 92011, terms: Net 15.

3 Add a new account – Account Type: Other Current Assets, Detail Type: Investments – Other, name: Investments.

4 Add a new account – Account Type: Credit Card, Detail Type: Credit Card, name: AMEX.

5 Add a new product.

  a. Name – 2023 Airstream Globetrotter 30RB

  b. Inventory asset account – Inventory Asset

  c. Description – 2023 Airstream Globetrotter 30RB

  d. Sales price/rate – $125,000

  e. Income account – Sales of Product Income

  f. Sales tax category – Taxable – standard rate

  g. Purchasing information – 2023 Globetrotter 30RB

  h. Cost – $100,000

i. Expense account – Cost of Goods Sold
j. Preferred Vendor – Airstream, Inc.
k. Initial quantity on hand – 0
l. As of date – 12/31/22

6 Add a new product.
a. Name – RV Cover
b. Inventory asset account – Inventory Parts
c. Description – RV Cover
d. Sales price/rate – $600
e. Income account – Sales of Product Income
f. Sales tax category – Taxable – standard rate
g. Purchasing information – RV Cover
h. Cost – $480
i. Expense account – Cost of Goods Sold
j. Preferred Vendor – National Covers
k. Initial quantity on hand – 0
l. As of date – 12/31/22

7 Add a new product.
a. Name – Trailer Cover
b. Inventory asset account – Inventory Parts
c. Description – Trailer Cover
d. Sales price/rate – $500
e. Income account – Sales of Product Income
f. Sales tax category – Taxable – standard rate
g. Purchasing information – Trailer Cover
h. Cost – $400
i. Expense account – Cost of Goods Sold
j. Preferred Vendor – National Covers
k. Initial quantity on hand – 0
l. As of date – 12/31/22

8 Record a new purchase order (1001) for two trailers on 1/7/23 – vendor: Airstream, Inc., product 1: 2023 Airstream Flying Cloud 27FB TWIN, QTY:1, product 2: 2023 Airstream Globetrotter 30RB, QTY: 1.

9 Record a new purchase order (1002) for inventory parts on 1/8/23 – vendor: National Covers, product 1: RV Cover, QTY: 5, product 2: Trailer Cover, QTY: 4.

10 Record a new bill based on a purchase order #1001 dated 1/13/23 – vendor: Airstream, Inc., terms: Net 30. All items ordered were received on 1/13/23 (the bill date).

11 Record a new bill without a purchase order on 1/16/23 – new vendor: Pacific Marketing, terms: Net 15, account: Advertising & Marketing, amount: $8,000.

12 Record a new bill without a purchase order on 1/17/23 – vendor: State Farm Insurance, terms: Net 15, account: Prepaid Expenses, amount: $18,000.

13 Paid $150,000 on bill due to Winnebago, Inc. on 1/18/23 using the checking account and starting Check no. 589.

14 Record expense on 1/19/23 – new vendor: Elite Events, using credit card: AMEX, account: Advertising & Marketing, amount: $6,000.

15 Record check on 1/19/23, Check no.: 590, new vendor: Jay's Detail, amount: $1,800, account: Contractors.

16 Record a new bill based on a purchase order #1002 dated 1/8/23 – vendor: National Covers, terms: Net 30. All items ordered were received on 1/20/23 (the bill date).

Figure 5.25 Trial Balance as of 1/31/23

Case 06 - Student Name (ID Number)
TRIAL BALANCE
As of January 31, 2023

	DEBIT	CREDIT
Checking	72,150.00	
Accounts Receivable (A/R)	153,020.00	
Inventory Asset	524,000.00	
Inventory Parts	4,000.00	
Loans To Officers	15,000.00	
Prepaid Expenses	18,000.00	
Undeposited Funds	0.00	
Buildings:Depreciation		15,000.00
Buildings:Original cost	150,000.00	
Machinery & Equipment:Depreciation		10,000.00
Machinery & Equipment:Original cost	100,000.00	
Accounts Payable (A/P)		524,000.00
AMEX		6,000.00
Washington State Department of Revenue Payable		26,970.00
Notes Payable		100,000.00
Common Stock		1,000.00
Opening Balance Equity		0.00
Paid-In Capital		250,000.00
Retained Earnings		61,000.00
Sales of Product Income		290,000.00
Cost of Goods Sold	232,000.00	
Advertising & Marketing	14,000.00	
Contractors	1,800.00	
TOTAL	$1,283,970.00	$1,283,970.00

17 Prepare and print the Trial Balance 1/31/23 report you saved previously. Your report should look like Figure 5.25.

18 Investigate differences between your trial balance and the trial balance shown above.

19 If necessary, prepare and print the Transaction Detail by Account report for all dates you saved previously to investigate identified differences.

  a. Make sure all your changes were dated in January 2023.

  b. Click on the line that does not match to view the transaction for that account, and investigate why your answer differs.

  c. Ask your instructor for assistance.

  d. Be sure your company matches the above as you will be adding additional business events in Chapter 6.

Recording Investing and Financing Activities

chapter 6

Student Learning Outcomes

Upon completion of this chapter, the student will be able to do the following:

- Record the acquisition of a fixed asset
- Record the acquisition of a long-term investment
- Record the sale of common stock
- Record the payment of a dividend
- Record a long-term borrowing (long-term debt)
- Record payment on long-term borrowing (long-term debt)
- Record the acquisition of a fixed asset by taking on new debt

Overview

In Chapter 5 you added new vendors, purchase orders, bills, credit card charges, and checks to your Wild Water Sports company and then paid some bills. In this chapter, you will add some investing and financing like the acquisition of a fixed asset and a long-term investment, as well as the sale of stock payment of dividends, acquiring and paying long-term debt. At the end of this chapter, you will perform similar tasks on the case assigned by your instructor.

To verify the accuracy of your Wild Water Sports company:

1. Sign into your QBO account, then open the Wild Water Sports company you used in Chapter 5.

2. Click **Reports**, then click the **Custom reports** tab, then click **Trial Balance** to open the Trial Balance report. Set the from and to dates to **1/1/27** and **1/31/27**, respectively. Compare your report to Figure 6.1. If your report doesn't match Figure 6.1, go back to your work in Chapter 5 to fix your errors. Otherwise, close your Trial Balance report.

Figure 6.1 Wild Water Sports trial balance as of 1/31/27

Wild Water Sports - Student Name (ID Number)
Trial Balance
As of January 31, 2027

	DEBIT	CREDIT
Checking	22,345.00	
Accounts receivable (A/R)	120,770.00	
Inventory	223,350.00	
Payments to deposit	70,000.00	
Prepaid expenses	17,500.00	
Equipment:Accumulated depreciation		10,000.00
Equipment:Original Cost	40,000.00	
Accounts Payable (A/P)		190,250.00
Mastercard		1,600.00
Florida Department of Revenue Payable		9,915.00
Long-term business loans		50,000.00
Common stock		1,000.00
Opening balance equity		0.00
Retained Earnings		205,800.00
Sales		164,000.00
Service Revenue		2,000.00
Cost of goods sold	131,200.00	
Rent:Equipment rental	6,000.00	
Utilities:Phone service	1,800.00	
Vehicle expenses:Vehicle gas & fuel	1,600.00	
TOTAL	$634,565.00	$634,565.00

Fixed Assets

In this section, you will be recording the acquisition of fixed assets. Fixed assets are long-term tangible property that a firm owns and uses in the production of its income, and are not expected to be consumed or converted into cash any sooner than at least one year's time. Normally, a fixed asset's cost is depreciated over time as a means of allocating its cost over its useful life. The depreciation is recorded to a depreciation expense account and added to an accumulated depreciation (contra-asset) account. That process will be explained in the chapter on adjusting entries.

To add an asset, you will use the Check task accessed by clicking the (+ New) icon. Alternatively, you could purchase new fixed assets with using a credit card or take on new debt. The Wild Water Sports company has a fixed asset account for equipment, which you'll use to record the purchase of a computer. If you were to purchase some other type of fixed asset, furniture for example, you would need to create two additional subaccounts to the Furniture & Fixtures account: Original Cost and Accumulated Depreciation.

To record the purchase of a new computer and network equipment, do the following:

1. Continue from above.
2. Make sure the navigation bar is open.
3. Click the (+ New) icon and then click **Check**.
4. Select **+ Add new** from the drop-down list in the Choose a payee text box.
5. Type **Best Buy** in the Company name text box, select **Vendor** as the Contact type, and click **Save**.
6. Type **1/20/27** as the Payment date and **1003** as the Check no.
7. Select **Original cost** under Equipment in the Category column of line 1.
8. Type **8000** in the Amount column of line 1 and then press **[Tab]**.
   Your screen should look like Figure 6.2.
9. Click **Save and new**.
10. Select **+ Add new** in the Payee text box and then type **Office Max** as the vendor, then click **Save**, then type **1/20/27** as the Payment date.
11. Select **+ Add new** from the drop-down list in the Category column of line 1.

Figure 6.2 Purchase of computer

#	CATEGORY	DESCRIPTION	AMOUNT
1	Equipment:Original Cost	What did you pay for?	8,000.00

Check #1003 — Payee: Best Buy — Bank Account: Checking — Balance $22,345.00 — AMOUNT $8,000.00

Mailing address: Best Buy — Payment date: 01/20/2027 — Check no.: 1003

12. Select **Fixed Assets** from the drop-down list in the Account Type text box.
13. Select **Fixed Asset Furniture** from the drop-down list in the Detail type text box.
14. Type **Furniture** in the Name text box, then place a check in the Track depreciation of this asset check box, and then click **Save and close**.
15. Type **Furniture:Original cost** in the Category column of line 1.
16. Type **10000** in the Amount column of line 1 and then press [**Tab**] to see Figure 6.3.

Figure 6.3 Purchase of furniture

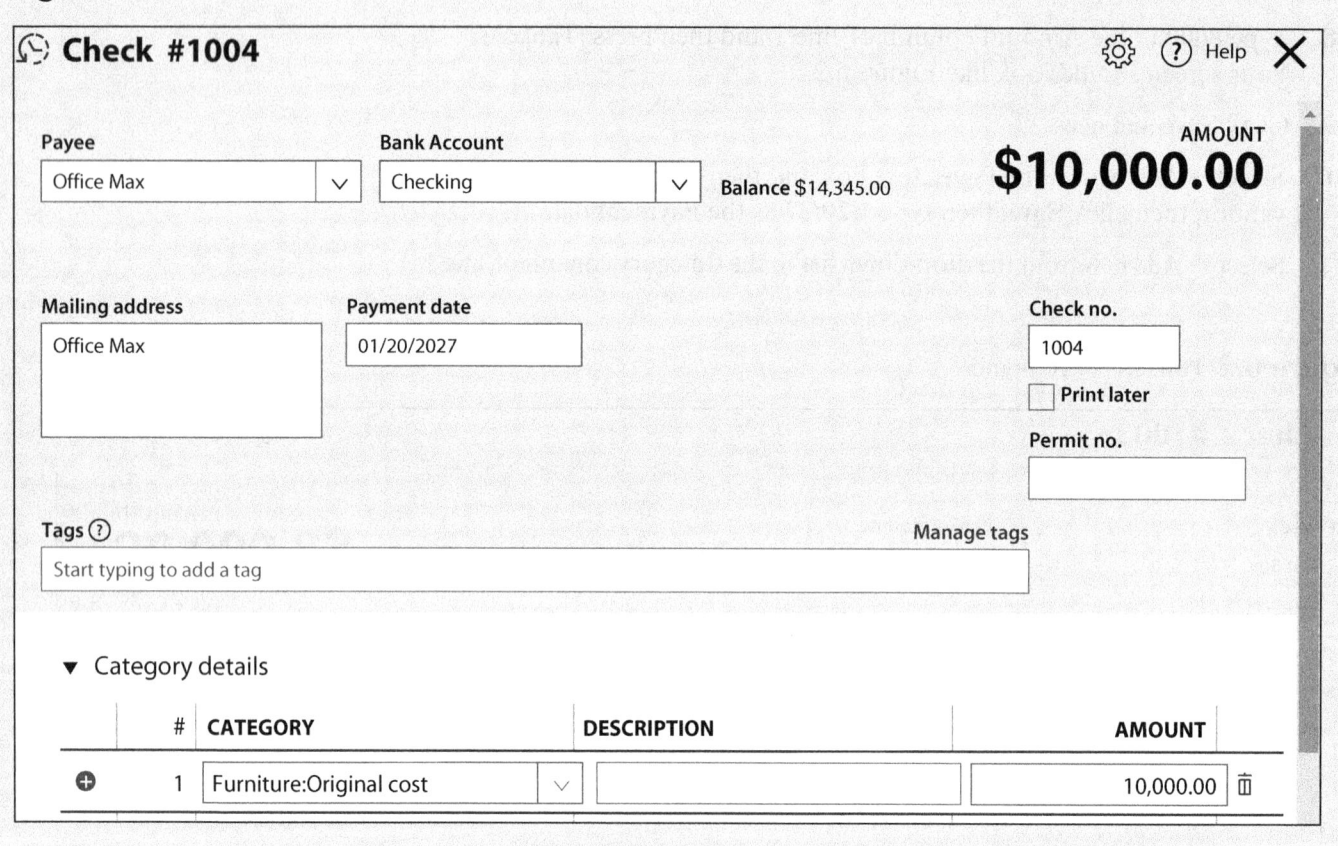

Check #1004			
Payee: Office Max	Bank Account: Checking	Balance $14,345.00	AMOUNT $10,000.00
Mailing address: Office Max	Payment date: 01/20/2027		Check no.: 1004

#	CATEGORY	DESCRIPTION	AMOUNT
1	Furniture:Original cost		10,000.00

17. Click **Save and close**.

You have recorded the purchase of two new fixed assets.

Long-Term Investments

The acquisition of a long-term investment is another type of investing activity. In general, a long-term investment is the purchase of a financial instrument (bond, common stock, and preferred stock) that matures in more than one year.

To record the purchase of a long-term investment, do the following:

1. Continue from where you left off.
2. Click the **+ New** icon, and select **Check**.
3. Select **+ Add new** from the drop-down list in the Choose a payee text box.
4. Type **Scottrade** in the Company name text box, select **Vendor** as the Type, and click **Save**.
5. Type **1/21/27** as the payment date and **1005** as the check no.
6. Select **+ Add new** from the drop-down list in the Category column of line 1.
7. Select **Other Assets** from the drop-down list in the Account Type text box.
8. Select **Other Long-term Assets** from the drop-down list in the Detail Type text box.
9. Type **Investments** in the Name text box, and click **Save and close**.
10. Type **3000** in the Amount column of line 1 and then press [**Tab**] to see Figure 6.4. Note that your check number may be different than shown below.

Figure 6.4 Purchase of a long-term investment

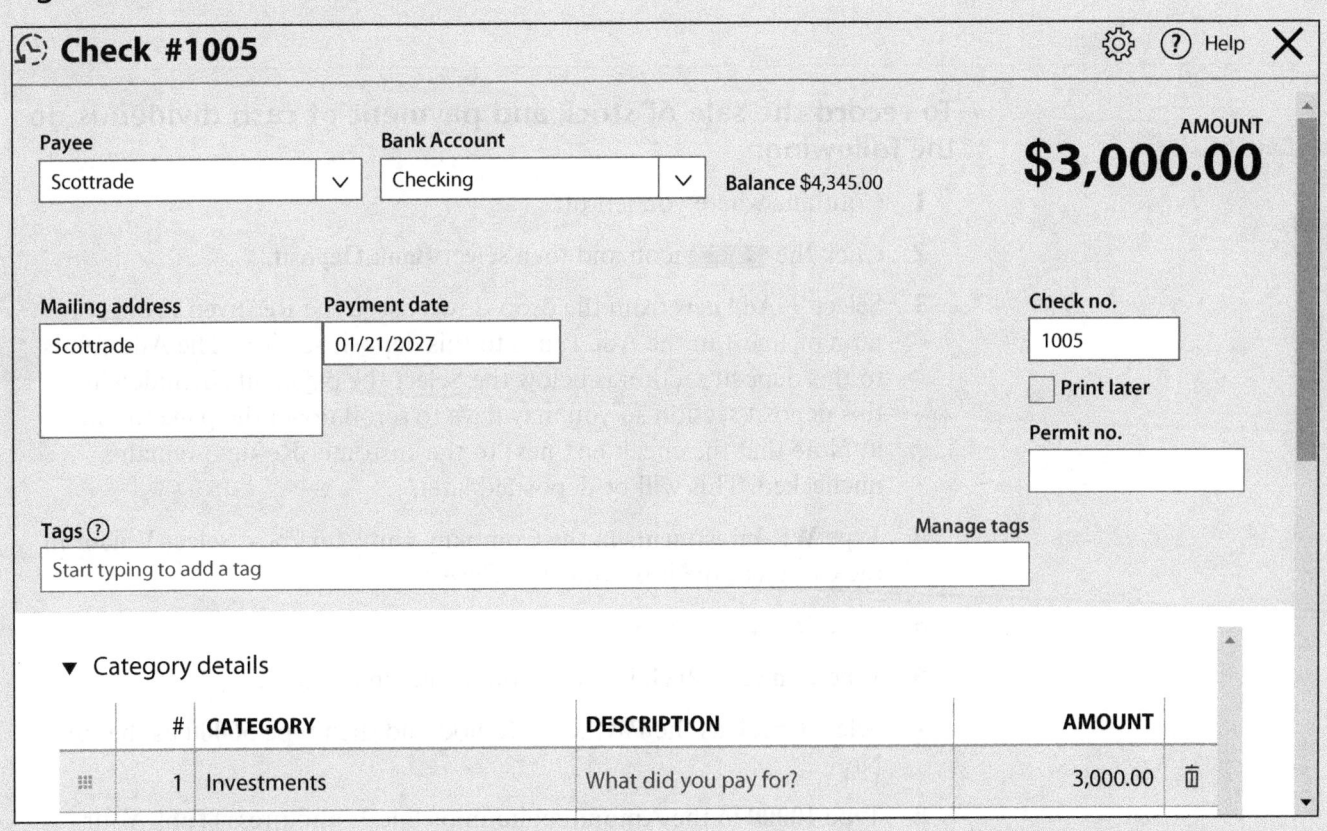

Check #1005

Payee	Bank Account		AMOUNT
Scottrade	Checking	Balance $4,345.00	**$3,000.00**

Mailing address: Scottrade
Payment date: 01/21/2027
Check no.: 1005
☐ Print later
Permit no.:

Tags — Manage tags
Start typing to add a tag

▼ Category details

#	CATEGORY	DESCRIPTION	AMOUNT
1	Investments	What did you pay for?	3,000.00

11. Click **Save and close**.

You have recorded the purchase of a long-term investment.

Equity Transactions (Common Stock, Dividends, Owner Investments, and Owner Withdrawals)

In a corporation, the sale of common stock and the payment of cash dividends to shareholders are two common financing activities. Common stock is a stockholders' equity account. Dividends are a distribution of earnings to shareholders and are accounted for as a reduction in retained earnings. Both of these are cash activities in that the sale of stock results in a cash receipt (you will account for it as a bank deposit), whereas the payment of a cash dividend results in a cash payment. One previous payment from a customer (Refugio) appears when you attempt to record a bank deposit from the issuance of stock. These payments have been received but not recorded. Ignore those for now. To simplify this transaction, we will assume that the common stock is no-par common stock, and thus, no additional paid-in capital exists. Also, we'll assume that the dividend declaration, record, and payment dates are all the same.

In a sole proprietorship, there is no common stock or dividends. Instead, there are owner investments and owner withdrawals. Owner investments are recorded by entering a bank deposit to the Owner's Equity account. Owner withdrawals are recorded by entering a check to the Owner's Equity account. Since the Wild Water Sports company is a corporation, an example of sole proprietorship transactions is not provided.

To record the sale of stock and payment of cash dividends do the following:

1   Continue where you left off.

2   Click the `+ New` icon and then select **Bank Deposit**.

3   Select **+ Add new** from the drop-down list in the Received From column of line 1 in the Add funds to this deposit section. The Add funds to this deposit section is below the Select the payments included in this deposit section so you may have to scroll down the page to find it. Note that the check box next to the customer Refugio remains unchecked. This will be deposited later.

4   Type **WB Investments** in the Company name text box, select **Vendor** in the Contact type box, and click **Save**.

5   Type **1/21/27** in Date text box.

6   Type **Common stock** in the Account column of line 1.

7   Select **Check** as the Payment Method and then type **56000** as the Ref No.

8   Type **10000** in the Amount column of line 1, and press [**Tab**]. Your screen should look like Figure 6.5.

Figure 6.5 Recording the deposit of funds from the sale of common stock

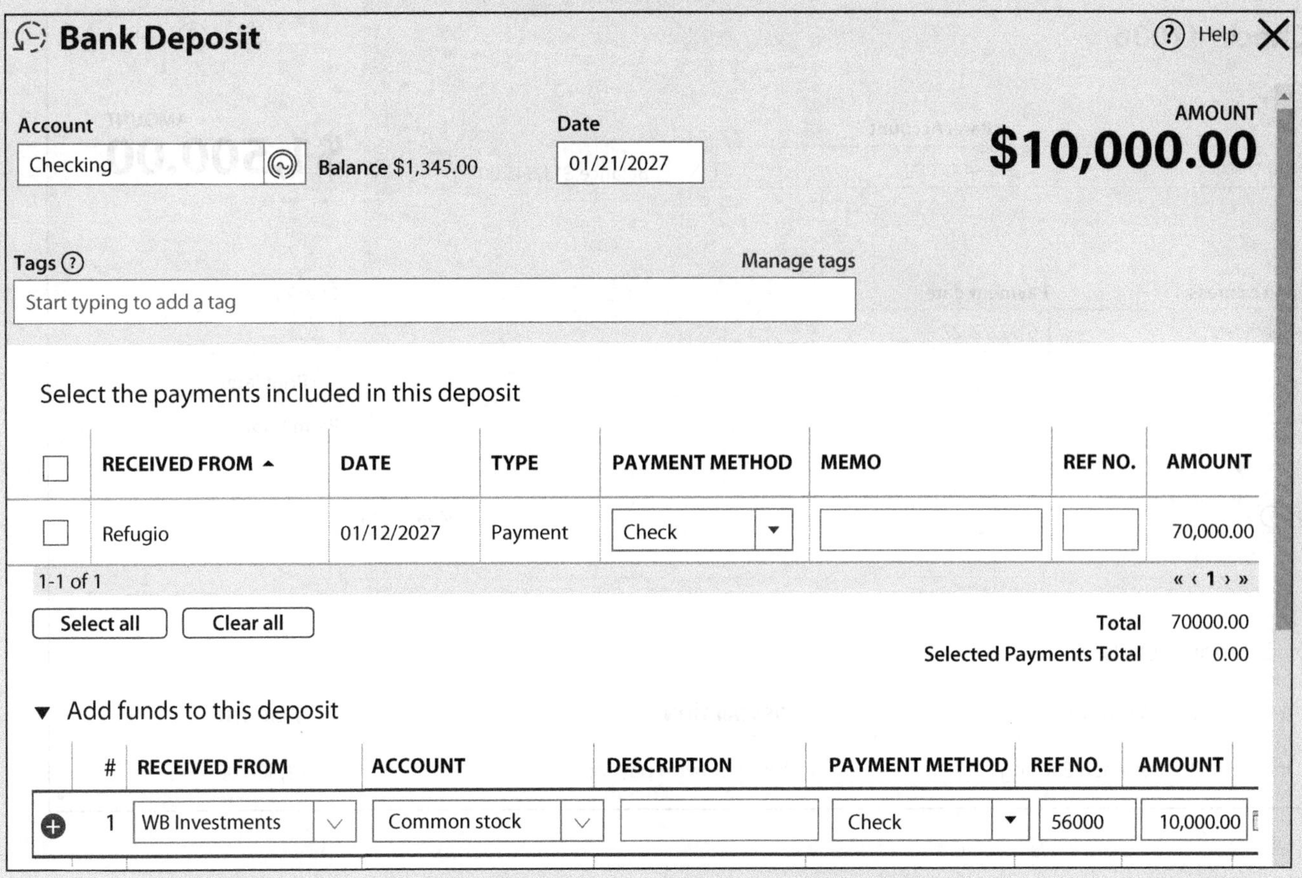

Bank Deposit

Account: Checking — Balance $1,345.00
Date: 01/21/2027
AMOUNT: $10,000.00

Tags — Manage tags
Start typing to add a tag

Select the payments included in this deposit

	RECEIVED FROM ▲	DATE	TYPE	PAYMENT METHOD	MEMO	REF NO.	AMOUNT
☐	Refugio	01/12/2027	Payment	Check			70,000.00

1-1 of 1 « ‹ 1 › »

[Select all] [Clear all]   Total 70000.00
Selected Payments Total 0.00

▼ Add funds to this deposit

#	RECEIVED FROM	ACCOUNT	DESCRIPTION	PAYMENT METHOD	REF NO.	AMOUNT
⊕ 1	WB Investments	Common stock		Check	56000	10,000.00

9. Click **Save and close**.
10. Click the **+ New** icon, and select **Check**.
11. Type **Shareholders** in the Payee text box.
12. Type **1/22/2027** in the Payment date text box and then type **1006** in the Check no. text box.
13. Select **Retained Earnings** from the drop-down list in the Category column of line 1.
14. Type **1500** in the Amount column of line 1, and press **[Tab]**. Your screen should look like Figure 6.6.
15. Click **Save and close**.

Figure 6.6 Payment of dividends

Check #1006		Help

Payee	Bank Account		AMOUNT
Shareholders	Checking	Balance $11,345.00	**$1,500.00**

Mailing address	Payment date		Check no.
Shareholders	01/22/2027		1006
			☐ Print later
			Permit no.

Tags — Manage tags
Start typing to add a tag

▼ Category details

#	CATEGORY	DESCRIPTION	AMOUNT
1	Retained Earnings	What did you pay for?	1,500.00

Long-Term Debt

The borrowing of funds on a long-term basis and the repayment of debt are two additional financing activities. Both of these are cash activities in that the borrowing of funds results in a cash receipt (you will account for it as a bank deposit), whereas the payment of the debt results in a cash payment. There is one previous payment from a customer that appears when you attempt to record a bank deposit from the borrowing of funds. These payments have been received but not recorded. You'll ignore those for now. This company decided to refinance their existing long-term business loan with Chase Bank. Thus, you will have to record the receipt of cash from the new loan and pay off the old long-term debt with interest.

To record the receipt of funds from borrowing and the payment of long-term debt in the Wild Water Sports company do the following:

1 Continue from where you left off.

2 Click the ⬚+New⬚ icon and then select **Bank Deposit**.

3. Select **Chase Bank** from the drop-down list in the Received From column of line 1 in the Add funds to this deposit section.
4. Select **Checking** from the Account text box.
5. Type **1/23/27** in the Date text box.
6. Select **Long-term business loans** from the drop-down list in the Account column of line 1.
7. Select **Check** from the drop-down list in the Payment Method column of line 1.
8. Type **150000** in the Amount column of line 1, and press [**Tab**]. Your screen should look like Figure 6.7.
9. Click **Save and close**.
10. Click the [+ New] icon, and select **Check**.
11. Select **Chase Bank** from the drop-down list in the Payee text box.

Figure 6.7 Recording the deposit of funds from refinancing

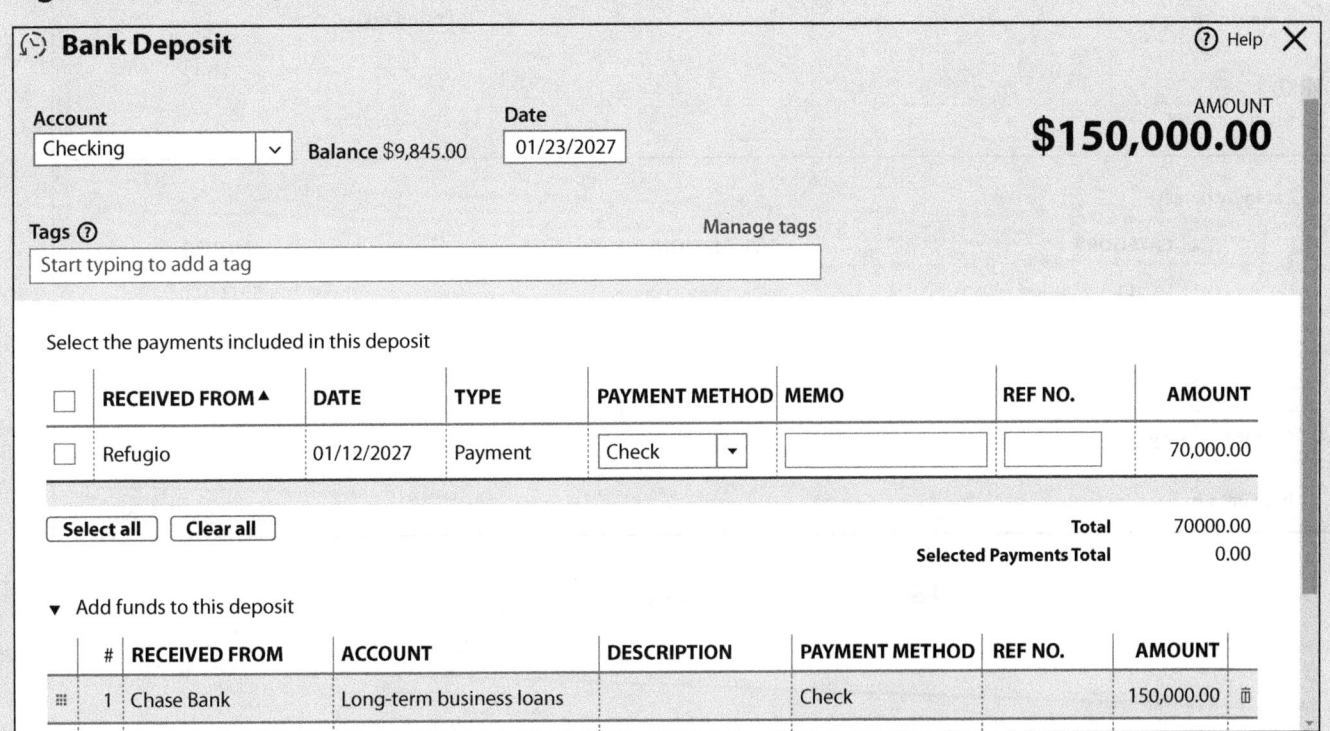

Bank Deposit							Help ✕
Account Checking	Balance $9,845.00	**Date** 01/23/2027					**AMOUNT** $150,000.00

Tags
Start typing to add a tag   Manage tags

Select the payments included in this deposit

	RECEIVED FROM ▲	DATE	TYPE	PAYMENT METHOD	MEMO	REF NO.	AMOUNT
☐	Refugio	01/12/2027	Payment	Check			70,000.00

[Select all] [Clear all]   Total 70000.00
                                       Selected Payments Total 0.00

▼ Add funds to this deposit

#	RECEIVED FROM	ACCOUNT	DESCRIPTION	PAYMENT METHOD	REF NO.	AMOUNT
1	Chase Bank	Long-term business loans		Check		150,000.00

12. Select **Checking** from the Bank Account text box.
13. Type **1/23/27** in the Payment date text box and **1007** in the Check no. text box.
14. Select **Long-term business loans** from the drop-down list in the Category column of line 1.

15. Type **50000** in the Amount column of line 1 and then press [**Tab**]. Note this is the amount shown on the trial balance before the refinancing.

16. Select **Interest paid** from the drop-down list in the Account column of line 2.

17. Type **2500** in the Amount column of line 2, and press [**Tab**]. Your screen should look like Figure 6.8.

Figure 6.8 Repayment of long-term debt with interest

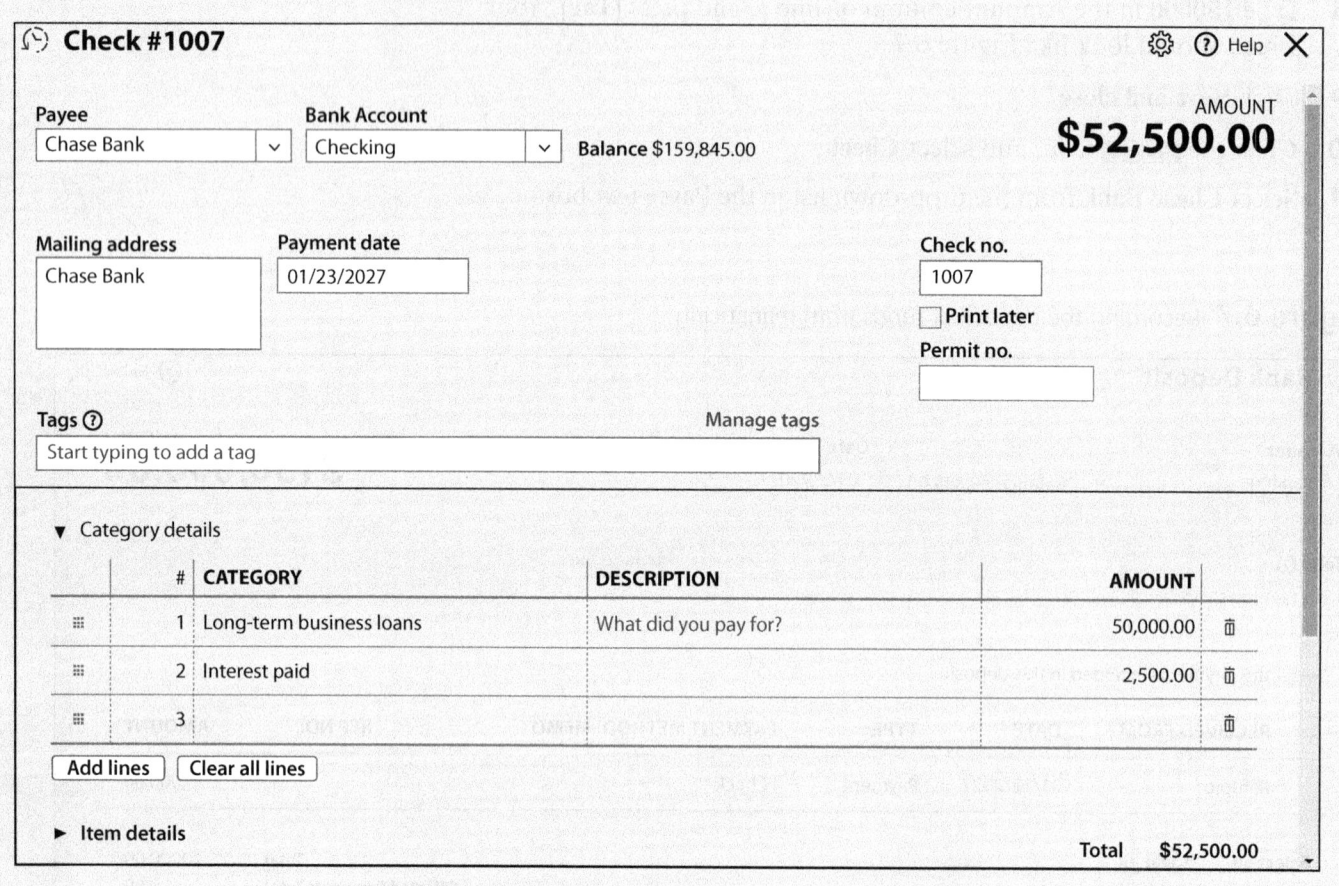

#	CATEGORY	DESCRIPTION	AMOUNT
1	Long-term business loans	What did you pay for?	50,000.00
2	Interest paid		2,500.00
3			

Check #1007 — Payee: Chase Bank — Bank Account: Checking — Balance $159,845.00 — AMOUNT $52,500.00 — Mailing address: Chase Bank — Payment date: 01/23/2027 — Check no. 1007 — Total $52,500.00

18. Click **Save and close**.

Acquisition of a Fixed Asset in Exchange for Long-Term Debt

You completed the process for recording an investing activity (purchase of a fixed asset) and a financing activity (borrowing on a long-term basis). Both of these transactions were recorded by affecting the checking account (cash).

Recording Investing and Financing Activities **Chapter 6** 171

Occasionally, a company acquires a fixed asset by issuing long-term debt, for example, purchasing equipment in exchange for a long-term business loan. This cannot be recorded using the checking account since no funds were exchanged. Instead, you will use the journal entry process to record the fixed asset acquisition and the long-term debt borrowing.

To record the purchase of a fixed asset by issuing debt, do the following:

1. Continue from where you left off.
2. Click the **+ New** icon, and select **Journal Entry**.
3. Type **1/25/27** as the Journal date and **5** as the Journal number.
4. Select **Equipment:Original Cost** from the drop-down list in the Account column of line 1.
5. Type **5000** in the Debits column of line 1.
6. Select **Long-term business loans** from the drop-down list in the Account column of line 2.
7. Accept **5000** in the Credits column of line 2, and press **[Tab]** to view the journal entry as shown in Figure 6.9.

Figure 6.9 Journal Entry to record purchase of fixed asset in exchange for long-term debt

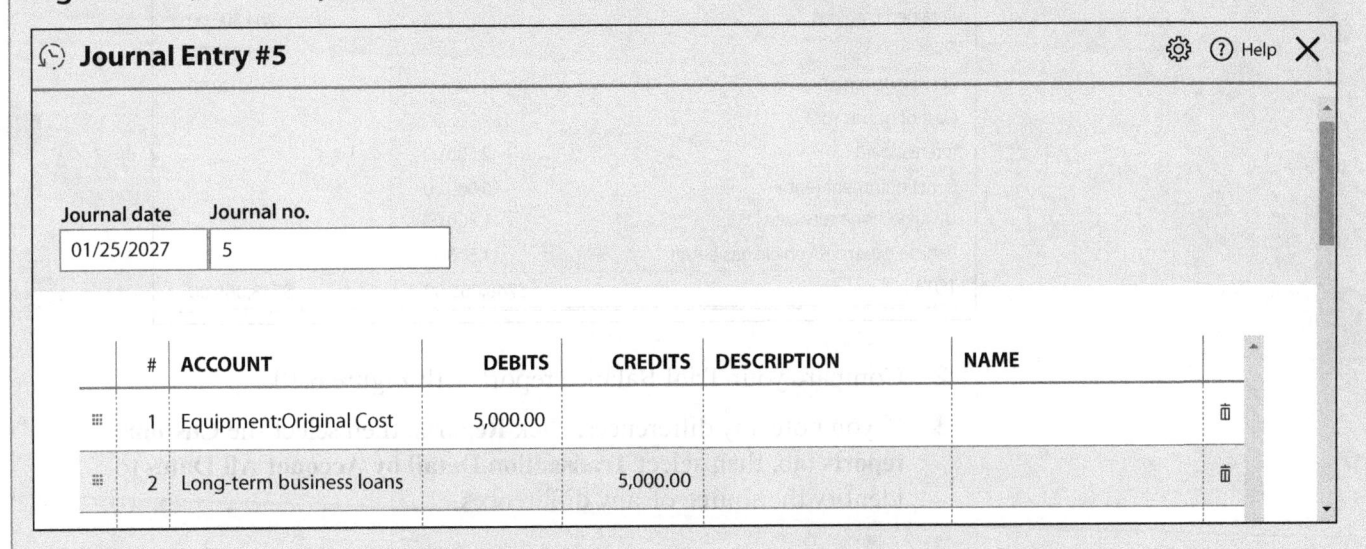

#	ACCOUNT	DEBITS	CREDITS	DESCRIPTION	NAME
1	Equipment:Original Cost	5,000.00			
2	Long-term business loans		5,000.00		

Journal Entry #5
Journal date: 01/25/2027
Journal no.: 5

8. Click **Save and close**.

The work you completed in this chapter influenced the company's trial balance. As in previous chapters, you decided to create a Trial Balance report after entering all business events described in this chapter and investigate any differences between your report and that shown in Figure 6.10.

To create a trial balance:

1. Click **Reports**, then select the **Custom reports** tab, then select **Trial Balance**. Change the to date of the report to **1/31/2027** and then click **Run Report** to view the Trial Balance as shown in Figure 6.10.

Figure 6.10 Trial Balance

Wild Water Sports - Student Name (ID Number)
Trial Balance
As of January 31, 2027

	DEBIT	CREDIT
Checking	107,345.00	
Accounts receivable (A/R)	120,770.00	
Inventory	223,350.00	
Payments to deposit	70,000.00	
Prepaid expenses	17,500.00	
Equipment:Accumulated depreciation		10,000.00
Equipment:Original Cost	53,000.00	
Furniture:Original cost	10,000.00	
Investments	3,000.00	
Accounts Payable (A/P)		190,250.00
Mastercard		1,600.00
Florida Department of Revenue Paya...		9,915.00
Long-term business loans		155,000.00
Common stock		11,000.00
Opening balance equity		0.00
Retained Earnings		204,300.00
Sales		164,000.00
Service Revenue		2,000.00
Cost of goods sold	131,200.00	
Interest paid	2,500.00	
Rent:Equipment rental	6,000.00	
Utilities:Phone service	1,800.00	
Vehicle expenses:Vehicle gas & fuel	1,600.00	
TOTAL	$748,065.00	$748,065.00

2. Compare your Trial Balance report with Figure 6.10.

3. If you note any differences, click **Reports**, then select the **Custom reports** tab, then select **Transaction Detail by Account All Dates** to identify the source of any differences.

End Note

In this chapter, you recorded investing activities: the acquisition of fixed assets and of long-term investments, the sale of common stocks, the payment of a dividend, the borrowing and payment of long-term debt, and the acquisition of fixed assets by taking on new debt. In the next chapter, you will work with payroll.

Chapter 6 Questions

1. What are the steps to record the acquisition of a fixed asset using a check?
2. What are the steps to record the acquisition of a fixed asset for a note payable?
3. What are the steps to record the sale of common stock?
4. What are the steps to record the payment of dividends?
5. What are the steps to record borrowing on a note payable?

Chapter 6 Matching

a. Operating activity
b. Investing activity
c. Financing activity
d. Fixed assets
e. Long-term investment
f. Common stock
g. Dividends
h. Long-term debt
i. Bank deposit
j. Journal entry

_____ Long-term tangible property that a firm owns
_____ Distribution of earnings to shareholders
_____ A stockholders' equity account
_____ Used to record purchase of a fixed asset for a note
_____ A five-year note payable
_____ Sales receipt
_____ A financial instrument that matures in more than one year
_____ Used to record amounts received from a note payable
_____ Sale of common stock
_____ Purchase of common stock

Chapter 6 Cases

The following cases require you to open the company you updated in Chapter 5. Each of the following cases is continued throughout the text in a sequential manner. For example, if you are assigned Case 01, you will use the file you modified in this chapter in all following chapters. Each of the following cases is similar in concepts assessed but differs in amounts and transactions.

To reopen your company, do the following:

1. Open your Internet browser.
2. Type **https://qbo.intuit.com** into your browser's address text box.
3. Type your user ID and password into the text boxes as you have done before.

Case 1

Now add some investing and financing activities to your company.

Based on what you learned in the text using the Wild Water Sports company, you are to make the following changes to the Case 1 company you modified in Chapter 5:

1. Create a new fixed asset account with an account type: Fixed Asset, detail type: Machinery & Equipment, name: Equipment. Track depreciation of this asset.

2. Create a new asset account with an account type: Other Assets, detail type: Other Long-Term Assets, name: Investments.

3. Record the purchase of a new computer on 1/10/24 from Office Depot, check: 1003, amount: $1,375, category: Equipment:Original Cost.

4. Record a long-term investment on 1/11/24 to Etrade (a new vendor), check: 1004, amount: $4,000, category: Investments.

5. Record the sale of common stock on 1/12/24 to Shareholders (a new vendor), deposit amount: $20,000, account: Common Stock payment method: Check.

6. Record the payment of dividends to Shareholders on 1/15/24, check: 1005, in the amount of $500.

7. Record the deposit of funds from a new note payable signed on 1/16/24 with Bank of CA (a new vendor) in the amount of $65,000 payment method: Check.

8. Record the payment to Rabo Bank (a new vendor) to retire an existing note payable on 1/16/24 of $60,000 with interest of $600 using check 1006.

9. Record the purchase of an additional computer on 1/17/24 from Office Depot in exchange for a note payable of $1,800, account: Equipment:Original Cost.

10. Change the name of account Interest Paid to Interest Expense, then open your previously customized report named Trial Balance 1/31/24. Your report should look like Figure 6.11.

11. Create and print a Transaction Report for the Checking account.

12. Create and print a Transaction Report for the Equipment:Original Cost account.

13. Create and print a Transaction Report for the Notes Payable account.

14. Create and print a Transaction Report for the Common Stock account.

Figure 6.11

Trial Balance as of 1/31/24

Case 1
TRIAL BALANCE
As of January 31, 2024

	DEBIT	CREDIT
Checking	34,850.00	
Accounts Receivable	1,030.00	
Inventory Asset	11,800.00	
Prepaid Expenses	8,000.00	
Supplies Asset	375.00	
Undeposited Funds	5,000.00	
Equipment:Original Cost	3,175.00	
Furniture & Fixtures:Depreciation		10,000.00
Furniture & Fixtures:Original cost	40,000.00	
Investments	4,000.00	
Accounts Payable		7,645.00
VISA		1,800.00
Notes Payable		66,800.00
Common Stock		21,000.00
Opening Balance Equity		0.00
Retained Earnings		5,000.00
Sales		2,160.00
Services		170.00
Cost of Goods Sold	1,300.00	
Interest Expense	600.00	
Rent or Lease	2,500.00	
Travel	1,800.00	
Utilities	145.00	
TOTAL	$114,575.00	$114,575.00

15 If your trial balance differs from Figure 6.11, do the following:

    a. Make sure that all of your changes were dated in January 2024.

    b. View the Transaction Reports you just created to locate any errors.

    c. Ask your instructor for assistance.

    d. Be sure your company matches the above as you will be adding additional business events in Chapter 7.

16 Export your Trial Balance report to Excel, and save it with the file name Student Name (replace with your name) Ch 06 Case 01 Trial Balance.xlsx.

17 Sign out of your company.

Case 2

Now add some investing and financing activities to your company.

Based on what you learned in the text using the Wild Water Sports company, you are to make the following changes to the Case 2 company you modified in Chapter 5:

1. Create a new fixed asset account with an account type: Fixed Asset, detail type: Furniture & Fixtures, name: Furniture. Track depreciation of this asset.

2. Create a new asset account with an account type: Other Assets, detail type: Other Long-Term Assets, name: Investments.

3. Record the purchase of new furniture on 1/11/25 from Staples, check: 1003, amount: $2,250, category: Furniture:Original Cost.

4. Record a long-term investment on 1/11/25 to Raymond James (a new vendor), check: 1004, amount: $3,200, category: Investments.

5. Record the sale of common stock on 1/14/25 to Shareholders (a new vendor), deposit amount: $25,000, account: Common Stock, payment method: Check.

6. Record the payment of dividends to Shareholders on 1/15/25, check: 1005, amount: $800, category: Retained Earnings.

7. Record the deposit of funds from a new note payable signed on 1/16/25 with Bank of TJ (a new vendor) in the amount of $25,000, payment method: Check.

8. Record the payment to Community Bank (a new vendor) to retire an existing note payable on 1/16/25 of $12,000 with interest of $300 using check 1006.

9. Record the purchase of additional furniture from Staples on 1/17/25 in exchange for a note payable of $2,625, account: Furniture:Original Cost.

10. Change the name of account Interest Paid to Interest Expense, then open your previously customized report named Trial Balance 1/31/25. Your report should look like Figure 6.12.

11. Create and print a Transaction Report for the Checking account.

12. Create and print a Transaction Report for the Furniture:Original Cost account.

13. Create and print a Transaction Report for the Notes Payable account.

14. Create and print a Transaction Report for the Common Stock account.

15. If your trial balance differs from Figure 6.12, do the following:

    a. Make sure that all of your changes were dated in January 2025.

    b. View the Transaction Reports you created to locate any errors.

    c. Ask your instructor for assistance.

    d. Be sure your company matches the above as you will be adding additional business events in Chapter 7.

Figure 6.12

Trial Balance as of 1/31/25

Case 2
TRIAL BALANCE
As of January 31, 2025

	DEBIT	CREDIT
Checking	38,600.00	
Accounts Receivable	1,425.00	
Inventory Asset	5,410.00	
Prepaid Expenses	6,800.00	
Supplies Asset	450.00	
Undeposited Funds	925.00	
Furniture:Original Cost	4,875.00	
Machinery & Equipment:Depreciation		1,000.00
Machinery & Equipment:Original cost	10,000.00	
Investments	3,200.00	
Accounts Payable		8,670.00
AMEX		240.00
Notes Payable		27,625.00
Common Stock		25,100.00
Opening Balance Equity		0.00
Retained Earnings		7,585.00
Sales		5,700.00
Services		225.00
Cost of Goods Sold	3,020.00	
Advertising	500.00	
Insurance	400.00	
Interest Expense	300.00	
Meals and Entertainment	240.00	
TOTAL	**$76,145.00**	**$76,145.00**

16 Export your Trial Balance report to Excel, and save it with the file name Student Name (replace with your name) Ch 06 Case 02 Trial Balance.xlsx.

17 Open and print the custom report you created in the last chapter called Transaction Detail by Account.

18 Export your Transactions Detail by Account report to Excel, and save it with the file name Student Name (replace with your name) Ch 06 Case 02 Transaction Detail by Account.xlsx.

19 Sign out of your company.

Case 3

Now it's time for you to add some investing and financing activities to your company.

Based on what you learned in the text using the Wild Water Sports company, you are to make the following changes to the Case 3 company you modified in Chapter 5:

1. Open your chart of accounts. Create a new fixed asset account with an account type: Fixed Asset, detail type: Fixed Asset Computers, name: Computers. Track depreciation of this asset.

2. Create a new asset account with a category type: Other Assets, detail type: Other Long-Term Assets, name: Investments.

3. Open your chart of accounts and confirm that it contains an equity account with an account type: Equity, detail type: Owner's Equity, and name: Owner's Equity.

4. Record the purchase of a new computer on 1/12/26 from Staples, Inc., check: 323, amount: $3,000, category: Computers: Original Cost.

5. Record a long-term investment on 1/13/26 to E-Trade (a new vendor), check: 324, amount: $5,700, category: Investments.

6. Record an owner's contribution on 1/14/26 to Owners (a new vendor) after receiving a check that was immediately deposited in the amount: $40,000 to account: Owner's Equity.

7. Record the deposit of funds from a new note payable signed on 1/16/26 with Chase Bank (a new vendor) in the amount of $32,000.

8. Record the payment to Rabobank (a new vendor) to retire an existing note payable on 1/17/26 of $23,000 with interest of $300 using check 325 for a total of $23,300.

9. Record the purchase of machinery and equipment from Leeds, Inc. (a new vendor) on 1/17/26 in exchange for a note payable of $31,800.

10. Open and print your previously customized report named Trial Balance 1/31/26. Your report should look like Figure 6.13.

11. Create and print a Transaction Report for the Checking account.

12. Create and print a Transaction Report for the Computers:Original Cost account.

13. Create and print a Transaction Report for the Notes Payable account.

14. Create and print a Transaction Report for the Owner's Equity account.

15. If your trial balance is different than Figure 6.13, do the following:

    a. Make sure that all of your changes were dated in January 2026.

    b. View the Transaction Reports you just created to locate any errors.

    c. Ask your instructor for assistance.

    d. Be sure your company matches the above as you will be adding additional business events in Chapter 7.

Figure 6.13 Trial Balance as of 1/31/26

Case 03 - Student Name (ID Number)
Trial Balance
As of January 31, 2026

	DEBIT	CREDIT
Checking	55,751.75	
Accounts receivable (A/R)	2,559.38	
Inventory Asset	5,700.00	
Payments to deposit	0.00	
Prepaid expenses	6,050.00	
Supplies Asset	327.00	
Computers:Original cost	3,000.00	
Machinery & Equipment:Depreciation		2,000.00
Machinery & Equipment:Original cost	46,800.00	
Investments	5,700.00	
Accounts Payable (A/P)		8,900.00
AMEX		123.00
California Department of Tax and Fee Administratio...		523.13
Notes Payable		63,800.00
Opening balance equity		0.00
Owner's Equity		50,075.00
Sales of Product Income		6,750.00
Services		240.00
Cost of goods sold	4,500.00	
Advertising & marketing	1,300.00	
Insurance	300.00	
Interest paid	300.00	
Meals	123.00	
TOTAL	**$132,411.13**	**$132,411.13**

16. Export your Trial Balance report to Excel, and save it with the file name Student Name (replace with your name) Ch 06 Case 03 Trial Balance.xlsx.

17. Open and print the custom report you created in the last chapter called Transaction Detail by Account.

18. Export your Transactions Detail by Account report to Excel, and save it with the file name Student Name (replace with your name) Ch 06 Case 03 Transaction Detail by Account.xlsx.

19. Sign out of your company.

Case 4

Now it's time for you to add some investing and financing activities to your company.

Based on what you learned in the text using the Wild Water Sports company, you are to make the following changes to the Case 4 company you modified in Chapter 5:

1. Record the signing of a new long-term business loan (a new Long-Term Liabilities type account) on 1/01/27 with Coast Bank (a new vendor) in the amount of $18,000. A check was received from Coast Bank and immediately deposited.

2. Record the purchase of Furniture on 1/23/27 from ABC Holdings (a new vendor), check: 25501, amount: $35,000.

3. Record the purchase of a long-term investment on 1/25/27 from Barber Investments, Inc. (a new vendor), check: 25502, amount: $8,000. Record to a new Other Assets account type, Other Long-term Assets detail type account named Long-term investments.

4. Record the sale of common stock on 1/26/27 to Shareholders (a new vendor) receiving a $10,000 check that was immediately deposited.

5. Record the purchase of furniture from Pacific Furniture (a new vendor) on 1/27/27 in exchange for a Long-term business loan of $6,000 using journal no. 3.

6. Record the payment of principle ($694) and interest ($120) to Coast Bank on the $18,000 long-term business loan on 1/31/27 with check 25503. Note: principle payment reduces the long-term business loans account.

7. Record the payment of $1,000 in dividends to Shareholders on 1/31/27, check: 25504.

8. Use journal entry 4 to reclassify $82,000 in Long-term debt (Debit) to Long-term business loans (Credit) on 1/31/27.

9. Prepare and print the Trial Balance 1/31/27 report you saved previously. Your report should look like Figure 6.14.

10. Investigate differences between your trial balance and the trial balance shown above.

11. If necessary, prepare and print the Transaction Detail by Account report you saved previously to investigate identified differences.

    a. Make sure all your changes were dated in January 2027.

    b. Click on the line that does not match to view the transaction for that account, and investigate why your answer differs.

    c. Ask your instructor for assistance.

    d. Be sure your company matches the above as you will be adding additional business events in Chapter 7.

Figure 6.14 Trial Balance as of 1/31/27

Trial Balance
As of January 31, 2027

	DEBIT	CREDIT
Checking	28,762.65	
Accounts Receivable (A/R)	22,082.50	
Inventory Asset	8,868.00	
Payments to deposit	0.00	
Prepaid rent	12,000.00	
Supplies Asset	1,400.00	
Furniture:Accumulated Depreciation		10,000.00
Furniture:Original Cost	106,000.00	
Vehicles:Accumulated Depreciation		6,500.00
Vehicles:Original Cost	115,000.00	
Long-term investments	8,000.00	
Accounts Payable (A/P)		6,800.00
VISA		2,400.00
California Department of Tax and Fee Administration Payable		339.15
Long-term business loans		105,306.00
Long-term debt		0.00
Common Stock		11,000.00
Opening Balance Equity		0.00
Retained Earnings		114,500.00
Sales		48,400.00
Sales of Product Income		3,570.00
Cost of Goods Sold	1,632.00	
Advertising & Marketing	1,800.00	
Insurance	2,400.00	
Interest Paid	120.00	
Repairs & Maintenance	750.00	
TOTAL	**$308,815.15**	**$308,815.15**

Case 5

Now it's time for you to add some investing and financing activities to your company.

Based on what you learned in the text using the Wild Water Sports company, you are to make the following changes to the Case 5 company you modified in Chapter 5:

1 Create three new fixed asset accounts

    a. Account type – Assets, Save account under – Fixed Assets

    b. Tax form section – Fixed Asset Copiers

c. Account name – Fixed Asset Copiers

d. Account type – Assets, Save account under – Fixed Assets Copiers

e. Tax form section – Fixed Asset Copiers

f. Account name – Original Cost

g. Account type – Assets, Save account under – Fixed Assets Copiers

h. Tax form section – Accumulated Depreciation

i. Account name – Depreciation

2 Create a new asset account: Save account under – Other Assets, Tax form section – Other Long-term Assets, Account name – Investments.

3 Create an expense account: Save account under – Expenses, Tax form section – Interest Paid, Account name – Interest Expense.

4 Record the signing of a new 6%, 36-month note payable to the Notes Payable account on 1/01/28 with Gold Coast Bank (a new vendor) in the amount of $25,000. A check was received from Gold Coast Bank and immediately deposited.

5 Record the purchase of a new copier on 1/03/28 from Coastal Copy (a new vendor), check: 3008, amount: $25,000.

6 Record the purchase of a long-term investment on 1/25/28 from Fleet Investments, Inc. (a new vendor), check: 3009, amount: $50,000.

7 Record an additional investment as a deposit on 1/26/28 from Owners (a new vendor) receiving an $80,000 check that was immediately deposited as an increase in Owner's Equity.

8 Record the purchase of computers (fixed asset) from Acme Equipment on 1/3/28 in exchange for a note payable to Acme Equipment of $30,000.

9 Record the payment of $20,907 (principal $18,182 and interest $2,725) to Chase Bank on a note payable on 1/31/28 with check 3010.

10 Record the payment of $761 (principal $636 and interest $125) to Gold Coast Bank on a note payable on 1/31/28 with check 3011.

11 Record the payment of $913 (principal $763 and interest $150) to Acme Equipment on a note payable on 1/31/28 with check 3012.

12 Record the payment of $5,000 in withdrawals (use Owner's Equity category) to Owners on 1/31/28, check: 3013.

13 Record a new invoice 1005 on 1/31/28 to a new customer Northrup (Net 15 terms) for 30 Computer Workstation 100 items for a total invoice of $490,500 including sales tax.

14 Prepare and print the Trial Balance 1/31/28 report you saved previously. Your report should look like Figure 6.15.

15 Investigate differences between your trial balance and the trial balance shown above.

Case 05 - Student Name (ID Number)
Trial Balance
As of January 31, 2028

	DEBIT	CREDIT
Checking	256,419.00	
Accounts Receivable (A/R)	648,850.00	
Inventory	512,000.00	
Payments to deposit	0.00	
Prepaid expenses	22,000.00	
Fixed Asset Computers:Depreciation		25,000.00
Fixed Asset Computers:Original Cost	280,000.00	
Fixed Asset Copiers:Original Cost	25,000.00	
Fixed Asset Furniture:Depreciation		8,000.00
Fixed Asset Furniture:Original Cost	80,000.00	
Investments	50,000.00	
Accounts Payable (A/P)		362,000.00
AMEX		6,300.00
Alabama Department of Revenue Payable		24,600.00
Alabama, Huntsville Payable		27,675.00
Alabama, Madison County Payable		3,075.00
Notes Payable		580,419.00
Opening balance equity		0.00
Owner's Equity		457,000.00
Consulting		79,500.00
Sales		615,000.00
Training		3,500.00
Cost of goods sold	298,000.00	
Advertising & marketing	3,000.00	
Equipment rental	7,500.00	
Interest Expense	3,000.00	
Recruiting	6,300.00	
TOTAL	$2,192,069.00	$2,192,069.00

Figure 6.15

Trial Balance as of 1/31/28

16 If necessary, prepare and print the Transaction Detail by Account report you saved previously to investigate identified differences.

   a. Make sure all your changes were dated in January 2028.

   b. Click on the line that does not match to view the transaction for that account, and investigate why your answer differs.

   c. Ask your instructor for assistance.

   d. Be sure your company matches the above as you will be adding additional business events in Chapter 7.

Case 6

Now it's time for you to add some investing and financing activities to your company.

Based on what you learned in the text using the Wild Water Sports company, you are to make the following changes to the Case 6 company you modified in Chapter 5:

1 Create a new fixed asset account with an account type: Fixed Asset, detail type: Fixed Asset Computers, name: Computers. Track depreciation of this asset.

2 Change the name of the Interest Paid category to Interest Expense using the Chart of Accounts edit feature.

3 Record the signing of a new 4%, 36-month note payable on 1/01/23 with Seattle Bank (a new vendor) in the amount of $20,000. This was an addition to the existing $100,000 note payable that existed on 12/31/22. A check was received from Seattle Bank and immediately deposited.

4 Record the purchase of a new computer on 1/23/23 from Best Buy (a new vendor), check: 591, amount: $8,000.

5 Record the purchase of a long-term investment on 1/25/23 from McConnel Investments, Inc. (a new vendor), check: 592, amount: $12,000.

6 Record the sale of common stock on 1/26/23 to Shareholders (a new vendor) receiving a $10,000 check that was immediately deposited ($100 common stock $9,900 Paid-In Capital).

7 Record the purchase of machinery & equipment from GM (a new vendor) on 1/27/23 in exchange for a note payable of $12,000.

8 Record the payment of $3,542.88 (principle $3,142.88 and interest $400.00) to Seattle Bank on the $120,000 note payable on 1/31/23 with check 593.

9 Record the payment of $500 in dividends to Shareholders on 1/31/23, check: 594 (remember to use Retained Earnings to record dividends).

10 Prepare and print the Trial Balance 1/31/23 report you saved previously. Your report should look like Figure 6.16.

Figure 6.16 Trial Balance as of 1/31/23

Case 06 - Student Name (ID Number)
TRIAL BALANCE
As of January 31, 2023

	DEBIT	CREDIT
Checking	78,107.12	
Accounts Receivable (A/R)	153,020.00	
Inventory Asset	524,000.00	
Inventory Parts	4,000.00	
Investments	12,000.00	
Loans To Officers	15,000.00	
Prepaid Expenses	18,000.00	
Undeposited Funds	0.00	
Buildings:Depreciation		15,000.00
Buildings:Original cost	150,000.00	
Computers	8,000.00	
Machinery & Equipment	12,000.00	
Machinery & Equipment:Depreciation		10,000.00
Machinery & Equipment:Original cost	100,000.00	
Accounts Payable (A/P)		524,000.00
AMEX		6,000.00
Washington State Department of Revenue Payable		26,970.00
Notes Payable		128,857.12
Common Stock		1,100.00
Opening Balance Equity		0.00
Paid-In Capital		259,900.00
Retained Earnings		60,500.00
Sales of Product Income		290,000.00
Cost of Goods Sold	232,000.00	
Advertising & Marketing	14,000.00	
Contractors	1,800.00	
Interest Expense	400.00	
TOTAL	**$1,322,327.12**	**$1,322,327.12**

11. Investigate differences between your trial balance and the trial balance shown above.

12. Prepare and print the Transaction Detail by Account report for all dates you saved previously to investigate identified differences.

    a. Make sure all your changes were dated in January 2023.

    b. Click on the line that does not match to view the transaction for that account, and investigate why your answer differs.

    c. Ask your instructor for assistance.

    d. Be sure your company matches the above as you will be adding additional business events in Chapter 7.

chapter 7

Recording Payroll

Student Learning Outcomes

Upon completion of this chapter, the student will be able to do the following:

- Add a new employee
- Add payroll-related general ledger accounts
- Pay employees and record payroll expenses and liabilities

Overview

In Chapter 6, you added some investing and financing activities like the acquisition of a fixed asset and a long-term investment as well as the sale of stock, payment of dividends, and acquiring and paying long-term debt to your Wild Water Sports company. In this chapter, you will add payroll activities like adding employees, adding payroll-related accounts, and recording payroll expenses and liabilities to your Wild Water Sports company. At the end of this chapter, you will perform similar tasks on the case assigned by your instructor.

To verify the accuracy of your Wild Water Sports company:

1. Sign into your QBO account, then open the Wild Water Sports company you used in Chapter 6.

2. Click **Reports**, then click the **Custom reports** tab, then double-click **Trial Balance** to open the Trial Balance report. Set the from and to dates to **1/1/27** and **1/31/27**, respectively. Compare your report to Figure 7.1. If your report doesn't match Figure 7.1, go back to your work in Chapter 6 to fix your errors. Otherwise, close your Trial Balance report.

Figure 7.1 Wild Water Sports trial balance as of 1/31/27

Wild Water Sports - Student Name (ID Number)
Trial Balance
As of January 31, 2027

	DEBIT	CREDIT
Checking	107,345.00	
Accounts receivable (A/R)	120,770.00	
Inventory	223,350.00	
Payments to deposit	70,000.00	
Prepaid expenses	17,500.00	
Equipment:Accumulated depreciation		10,000.00
Equipment:Original Cost	53,000.00	
Furniture:Original cost	10,000.00	
Investments	3,000.00	
Accounts Payable (A/P)		190,250.00
Mastercard		1,600.00
Florida Department of Revenue Paya…		9,915.00
Long-term business loans		155,000.00
Common stock		11,000.00
Opening balance equity		0.00
Retained Earnings		204,300.00
Sales		164,000.00
Service Revenue		2,000.00
Cost of goods sold	131,200.00	
Interest paid	2,500.00	
Rent:Equipment rental	6,000.00	
Utilities:Phone service	1,800.00	
Vehicle expenses:Vehicle gas & fuel	1,600.00	
TOTAL	$748,065.00	$748,065.00

Employees

In this section, you will be adding a new employee to QBO.

To add a new employee to the Wild Water Sports company, do the following:

1. Continue from above.
2. Make sure the navigation bar is open.
3. Click **Payroll** and then click **Employees** from the navigation bar.

Recording Payroll **Chapter 7** 189

4 Click the **Add employee** text.

5 Click **No thanks** when asked if you want to live chat.

6 Type **Donna Chandler** as the employee's name and provide the following address information: **12 Ridgeway Lane, Orlando, FL, 32807**. Your screen should look like Figure 7.2.

Figure 7.2 Employee Information (adding a new employee)

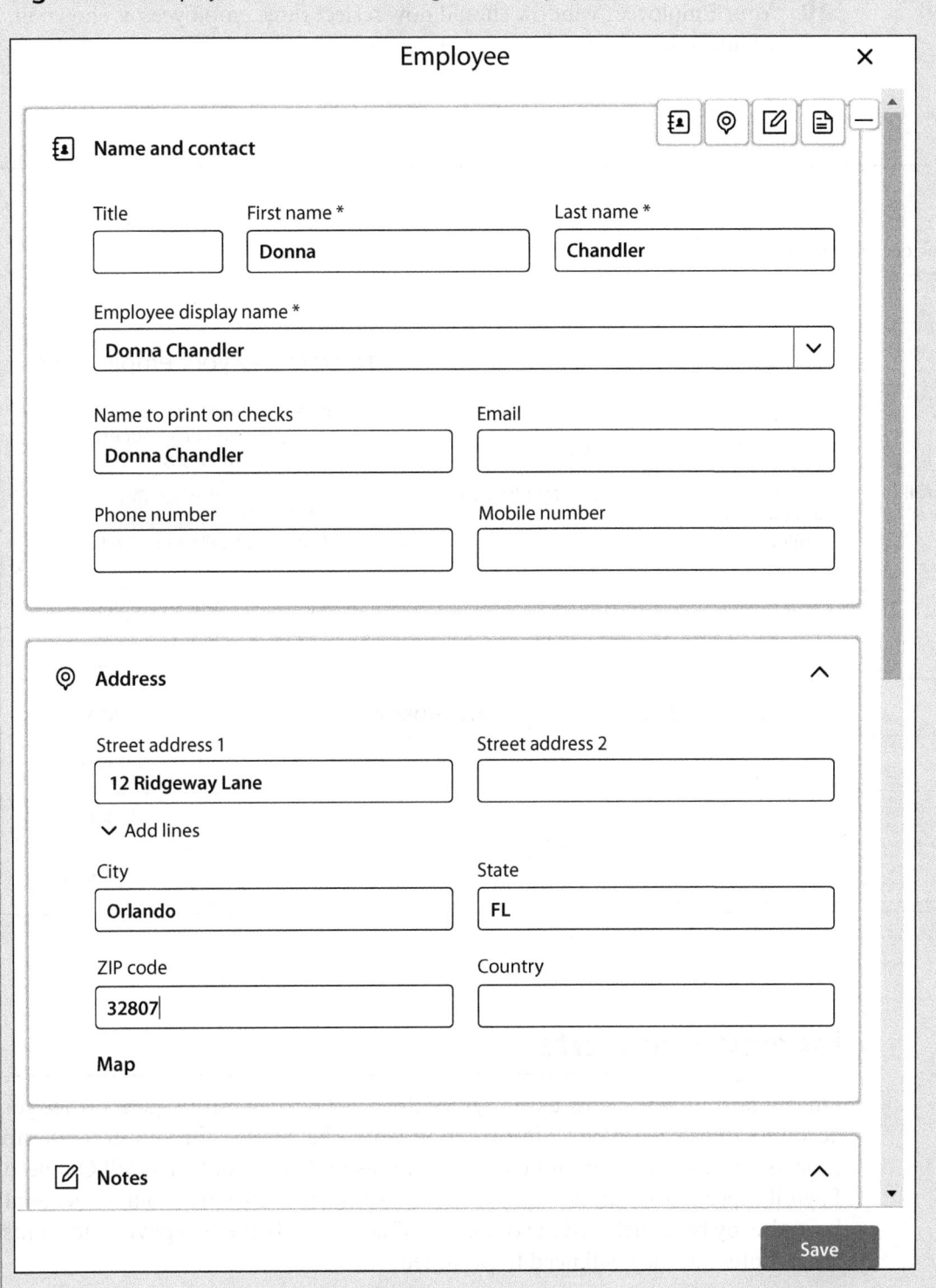

Employee	

Name and contact

Title	First name *	Last name *
	Donna	Chandler

Employee display name *
Donna Chandler

Name to print on checks	Email
Donna Chandler	

Phone number	Mobile number

Address

Street address 1	Street address 2
12 Ridgeway Lane	

∨ Add lines

City	State
Orlando	FL

ZIP code	Country
32807	

Map

Notes

Save

190 Chapter 7 *Recording Payroll*

    7 Click **Save**.

    8 Click **Add an employee**, then click the **Not right now** button when asked to Turn payroll on. Add **Karen Vordale, 1554 Rose Ave. #4, Orlando, FL, 32804** as a second employee. Then click **Save**.

    9 Click **Add an employee**, then add **Ryder Zacovic, 12 Spaceport Court, Orlando, FL, 32804** as a third employee. Then click **Save**.

    10 Your Employees window should now reflect three employees as shown in Figure 7.3.

Figure 7.3 Employees

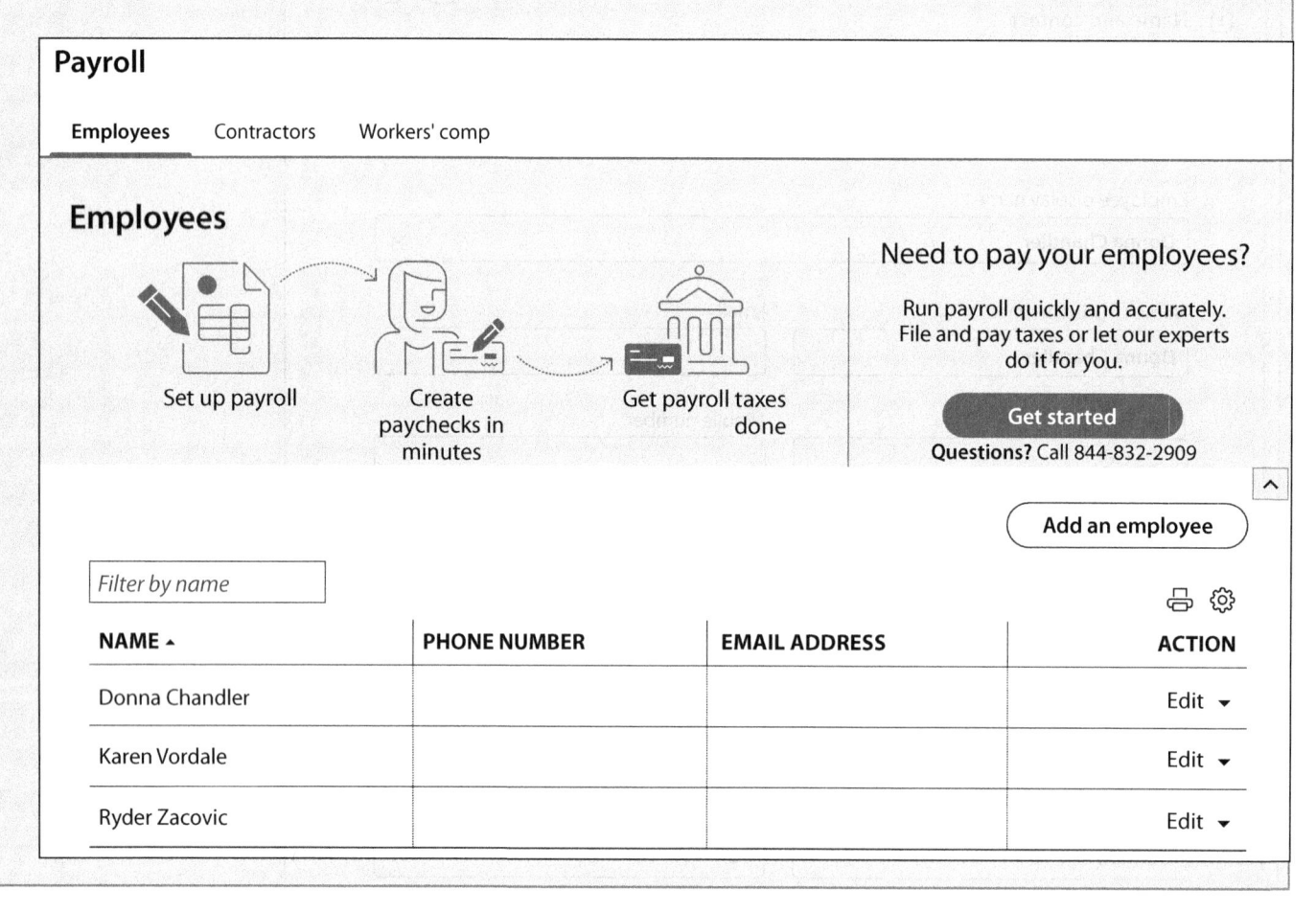

NAME ▲	PHONE NUMBER	EMAIL ADDRESS	ACTION
Donna Chandler			Edit ▾
Karen Vordale			Edit ▾
Ryder Zacovic			Edit ▾

Payroll Accounts

Once again, if you were using QuickBooks Payroll Online, general ledger accounts to capture payroll information would be created for you in the setup process. In this case, even though you're not using QuickBooks Payroll Online, a Payroll expense account and a Payroll tax to pay other current liabilities account have already been included in your chart of accounts. If the two payroll accounts are not present, they will need to be added.

An employer agrees to pay its employees a salary per month or an hourly rate. In either case, for the agreed upon salary or hourly rate times hours worked, amounts are recorded to the Payroll (expense) account. Depending on the state, employees are often required to have an estimated amount of federal and state income taxes withheld from their paychecks by their employers. In addition, employers must withhold Social Security (6.2%) and Medicare (1.45%) taxes. Amounts withheld from employees will be recorded in the Payroll Tax Payable (liability) account until remitted to the U.S. Treasury and state government entities. Employers must match those amounts for Social Security (6.2%) and Medicare (1.45%) taxes. These matching costs will be recorded as additional Payroll expense.

Pay Employees

The payment of employees requires gathering information from each employee that helps determine withholding amounts and payroll expenses. The federal and state governments provide formulas and/or tables to help employers calculate these amounts. In this text, you will be provided these amounts. Additional taxes, such as training, unemployment, and so on, are ignored for this illustration. Since payroll is a recurring event, it will help to make these checks recur, which can be edited for each payroll for changes in hours worked where applicable. In this example, payroll is paid semimonthly. Note: Rounding differences may occur in the withdrawal amounts.

See Figure 7.4 for a payroll for your Wild Water Sports company.

Figure 7.4 Semimonthly payroll information

Pay/Tax/Withholding	Donna	Karen	Ryder	Total
Hours if applicable	n/a	80	60	
Annual salary or hourly rate	$ 60,000	$ 18.00	$ 18.00	
Gross pay	2,500.00	1,440.00	1,080.00	5,020.00
Federal withholding	342.50	197.28	147.96	687.74
Social security employee (6.2%)	155.00	89.28	66.96	311.24
Medicare employee (1.45%)	36.25	20.88	15.66	72.79
Employee withholding	533.75	307.44	230.58	1,071.77
Social security employer (6.2%)	155.00	89.28	66.96	311.24
Medicare company employer (1.45%)	36.25	20.88	15.66	72.79
Employer payroll tax expense	191.25	110.16	82.62	384.03
Net Check amount	1,966.25	1,132.56	849.42	3,948.23

To record the payment of employees in the Wild Water Sports company, do the following:

1. Continue from where you left off.
2. Click the [+ New] icon, and select **Check**.
3. Select **Donna Chandler** from the drop-down list in the **Payee** text box. (Note: Employees are located at the bottom of the list.)
4. Type **1/15/2027** as the payment date and **1008** as the Check no.
5. Select **Payroll expenses** from the drop-down list in the Category column of line 1.
6. Type **2500** in the Amount column of line 1, and press **[Tab]** twice.
7. Select **Payroll wages and tax to pay** from the drop-down list in the Category column of line 2.
8. Type **−533.75** in the Amount column of line 1, and press **[Tab]** twice. (Be sure to enter this amount as a negative number.)
9. Select **Payroll expenses** from the drop-down list in the Category column of line 3.
10. Type **191.25** in the Amount column of line 3, and press **[Tab]** twice.
11. Select **Payroll wages and tax to pay** from the drop-down list in the Category column of line 4.
12. Type **−191.25** in the Amount column of line 4, and press **[Tab]** once. (Be sure to enter this amount as a negative number.) Your screen should look like Figure 7.5.
13. Click **Make recurring** located at the bottom of the screen.
14. Select **Unscheduled** from the drop-down list in the Type text box.
15. Click **Save template**.
16. Click the **Gear** icon.
17. Select **Recurring Transactions** located in the List column.
18. Click **Use** located in the Action column of the Donna Chandler row. The check window will appear again completed like that shown in Figure 7.5.
19. Make sure the date is correct and then click **Save and new**.

Figure 7.5 Check #1008 (paycheck for Donna Chandler)

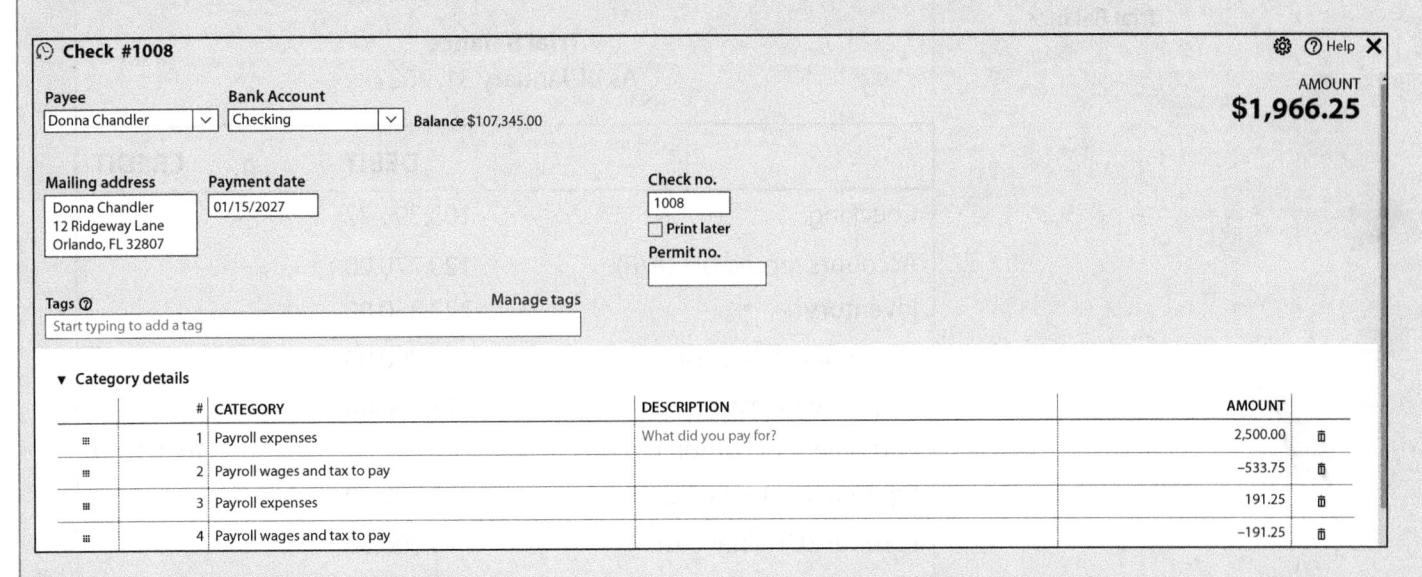

	Check #1008						⚙ ⓘ Help ✕
Payee		**Bank Account**					**AMOUNT**
Donna Chandler	⌄	Checking	⌄	Balance $107,345.00			**$1,966.25**

Mailing address
Donna Chandler
12 Ridgeway Lane
Orlando, FL 32807

Payment date
01/15/2027

Check no.
1008
☐ Print later
Permit no.

Tags ⓘ   Manage tags
Start typing to add a tag

▼ Category details

#	CATEGORY	DESCRIPTION	AMOUNT	
1	Payroll expenses	What did you pay for?	2,500.00	🗑
2	Payroll wages and tax to pay		−533.75	🗑
3	Payroll expenses		191.25	🗑
4	Payroll wages and tax to pay		−191.25	🗑

20 Enter payroll information found in Figure 7.4 for Karen and Ryder in the same way as you entered payroll information for Donna above. Be sure to make each of these unscheduled recurring events.

21 After entering the last check to record payroll above, click **Save and close**.

22 Click **Reports** from the navigation bar.

23 Click the **Custom reports** tab, then click **Trial Balance** to open the Trial Balance report. Set the from and to dates to **1/1/27** and **1/31/27**, respectively, then click **Run Report** to view the report, which is shown in Figure 7.6.

24 Click the **103,396.77** amount on the Checking line to view a transaction report for the checking account as shown in Figure 7.7.

25 Click the **Switch to classic view** button and then match your screen with Figure 7.7.

26 Click **Ryder Zacovic** to view the payroll check as shown in Figure 7.8.

27 Match your screen to Figure 7.8, and close the check window.

28 Click **Back to report summary** to return to the Trial Balance report.

You have recorded payroll for one semimonthly period. You can practice with another payroll using the recurring transactions you have set up.

Figure 7.6

Trial Balance

Wild Water Sports - Student Name (ID Number)
Trial Balance
As of January 31, 2027

	DEBIT	CREDIT
Checking	103,396.77	
Accounts receivable (A/R)	120,770.00	
Inventory	223,350.00	
Payments to deposit	70,000.00	
Prepaid expenses	17,500.00	
Equipment:Accumulated de…		10,000.00
Equipment:Original Cost	53,000.00	
Furniture:Original cost	10,000.00	
Investments	3,000.00	
Accounts Payable (A/P)		190,250.00
Mastercard		1,600.00
Florida Department of Reve…		9,915.00
Payroll wages and tax to pay		1,455.80
Long-term business loans		155,000.00
Common stock		11,000.00
Opening balance equity		0.00
Retained Earnings		204,300.00
Sales		164,000.00
Service Revenue		2,000.00
Cost of goods sold	131,200.00	
Interest paid	2,500.00	
Payroll expenses	5,404.03	
Rent:Equipment rental	6,000.00	
Utilities:Phone service	1,800.00	
Vehicle expenses:Vehicle ga…	1,600.00	
TOTAL	$749,520.80	$749,520.80

Figure 7.7 Transaction Report (checking account)

Wild Water Sports - Student Name (ID Number)
Transaction Report
January 2027

DATE	TRANSACTION TYPE	NUM	NAME	MEMO/DESCRIPTION	ACCOUNT	SPLIT	AMOUNT	BALANCE
▾ Checking								
Beginning Balance								25,000.00
01/12/2027	Deposit		Southtown Watersports		Checking	Payments to deposit	55,145.00	80,145.00
01/15/2027	Check	1008	Donna Chandler		Checking	-Split-	−1,966.25	78,178.75
01/15/2027	Check	1009	Karen Vordale		Checking	-Split-	−1,132.56	77,046.19
01/15/2027	Check	1010	Ryder Zacovic		Checking	-Split-	−849.42	76,196.77
01/18/2027	Bill Payment (Check)	1001	Malibu Boats		Checking	Accounts Payable (A/P)	−56,000.00	20,196.77
01/19/2027	Check	1002	Verizon		Checking	Utilities:Phone service	−1,800.00	18,396.77
01/20/2027	Check	1004	Office Max		Checking	Furniture:Original cost	−10,000.00	8,396.77
01/20/2027	Check	1003	Best Buy		Checking	Equipment:Original Cost	−8,000.00	396.77
01/21/2027	Check	1005	Scottrade		Checking	Investments	−3,000.00	−2,603.23
01/21/2027	Deposit		WB Investments		Checking	Common stock	10,000.00	7,396.77
01/22/2027	Check	1006	Shareholders		Checking	Retained Earnings	−1,500.00	5,896.77
01/23/2027	Check	1007	Chase Bank		Checking	-Split-	−52,500.00	−46,603.23
01/23/2027	Deposit		Chase Bank		Checking	Long-term business loans	150,000.00	103,396.77
Total for Checking							**$78,396.77**	
TOTAL							**$78,396.77**	

Figure 7.8 Check #1010 (Ryder Zacovic payroll check)

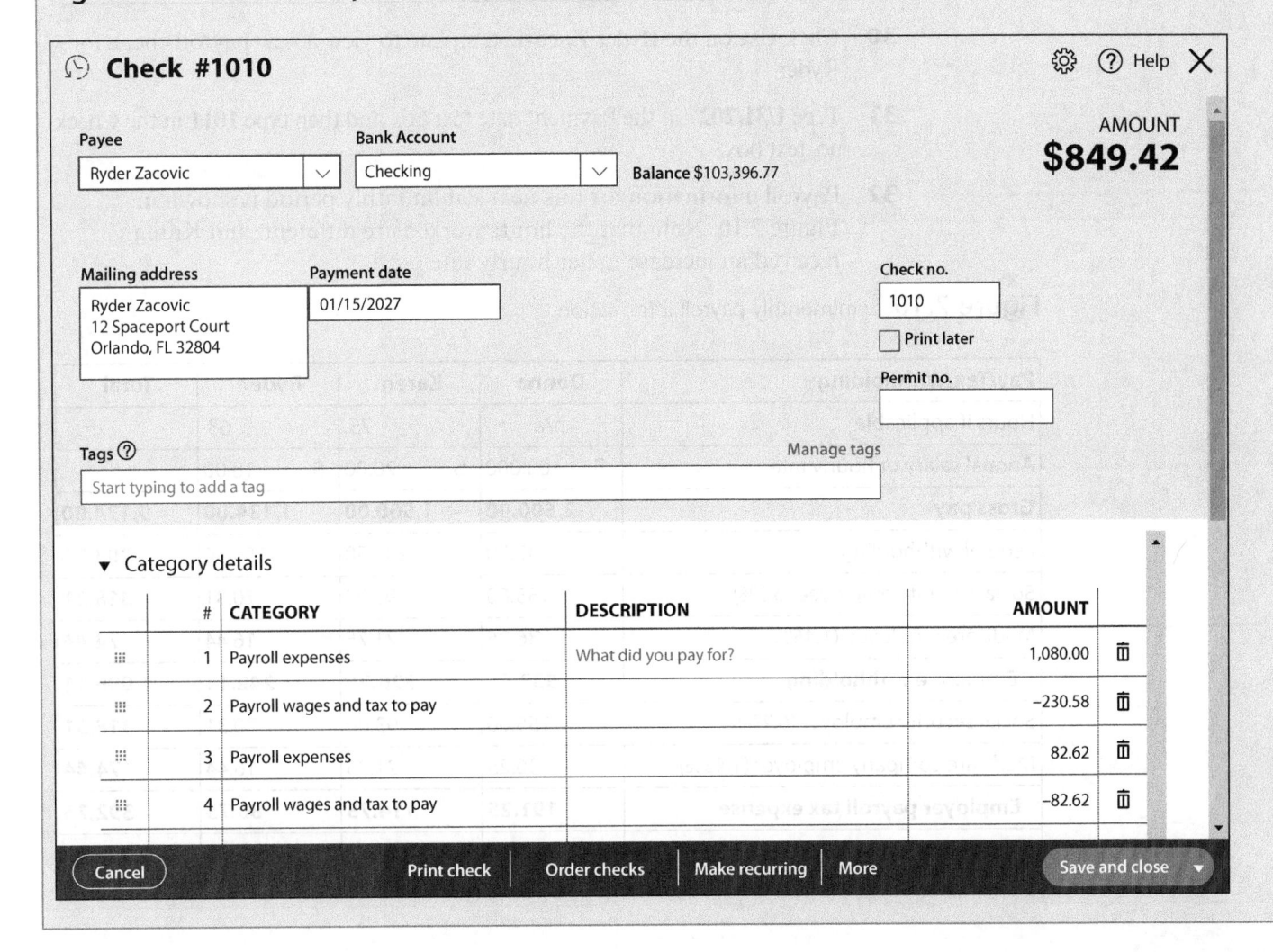

Check #1010

Payee: Ryder Zacovic
Bank Account: Checking   Balance $103,396.77

AMOUNT
$849.42

Mailing address
Ryder Zacovic
12 Spaceport Court
Orlando, FL 32804

Payment date: 01/15/2027

Check no.: 1010
☐ Print later
Permit no.

Tags Manage tags
Start typing to add a tag

▾ Category details

#	CATEGORY	DESCRIPTION	AMOUNT	
1	Payroll expenses	What did you pay for?	1,080.00	🗑
2	Payroll wages and tax to pay		−230.58	🗑
3	Payroll expenses		82.62	🗑
4	Payroll wages and tax to pay		−82.62	🗑

Cancel | Print check | Order checks | Make recurring | More | Save and close

29 Click the **Gear** icon, and click **Recurring Transactions** located in the Lists column to view a list of recurring transactions as shown in Figure 7.9. (If your list does not contain the three employees you recorded, you will need to return to these transactions, and click the **Make recurring** button.)

Figure 7.9 Recurring Transactions

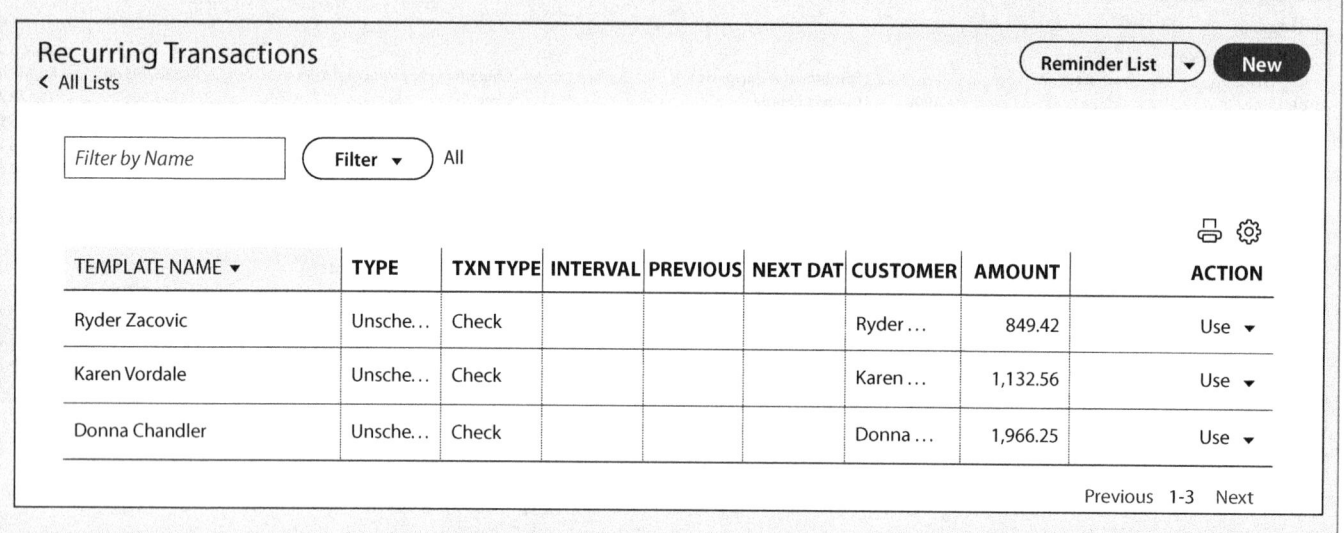

Recurring Transactions
< All Lists

TEMPLATE NAME	TYPE	TXN TYPE	INTERVAL	PREVIOUS	NEXT DAT	CUSTOMER	AMOUNT	ACTION
Ryder Zacovic	Unsche...	Check				Ryder...	849.42	Use ▼
Karen Vordale	Unsche...	Check				Karen...	1,132.56	Use ▼
Donna Chandler	Unsche...	Check				Donna...	1,966.25	Use ▼

Previous 1-3 Next

30 Click **Use** on the **Ryder Zacovic** template to view a new payroll check for Ryder.

31 Type **1/31/2027** in the Payment date text box and then type **1011** in the Check no. text box.

32 Payroll information for this next semimonthly period is shown in Figure 7.10. Note that the hours worked are different, and Karen received an increase in her hourly rate.

Figure 7.10 Semimonthly payroll information

Pay/Tax/Withholding	Donna	Karen	Ryder	Total
Hours if applicable	n/a	75	63	
Annual salary or hourly rate	$60,000	$20.00	$18.00	
Gross pay	**2,500.00**	**1,500.00**	**1,134.00**	**5,134.00**
Federal withholding	342.50	205.50	155.36	**703.36**
Social security employee (6.2%)	155.00	93.00	70.31	**318.31**
Medicare employee (1.45%)	36.25	21.75	16.44	**74.44**
Employee withholding	**533.75**	**320.25**	**242.11**	**1,096.11**
Social security employer (6.2%)	155.00	93.00	70.31	**318.31**
Medicare company employer (1.45%)	36.25	21.75	16.44	**74.44**
Employer payroll tax expense	**191.25**	**114.75**	**86.75**	**392.75**
Net Check amount	1,966.25	1,179.75	891.89	**4,037.89**

33 Type **1134** in the Amount column on line 1.

34 Type **−242.11** in the Amount column on line 2.

35 Type **86.75** in the Amount column on line 3.

36 Type **−86.75** in the Amount column on line 4. Your screen should now look like Figure 7.11.

Figure 7.11 Check #1011 (Ryder Zacovic payroll check)

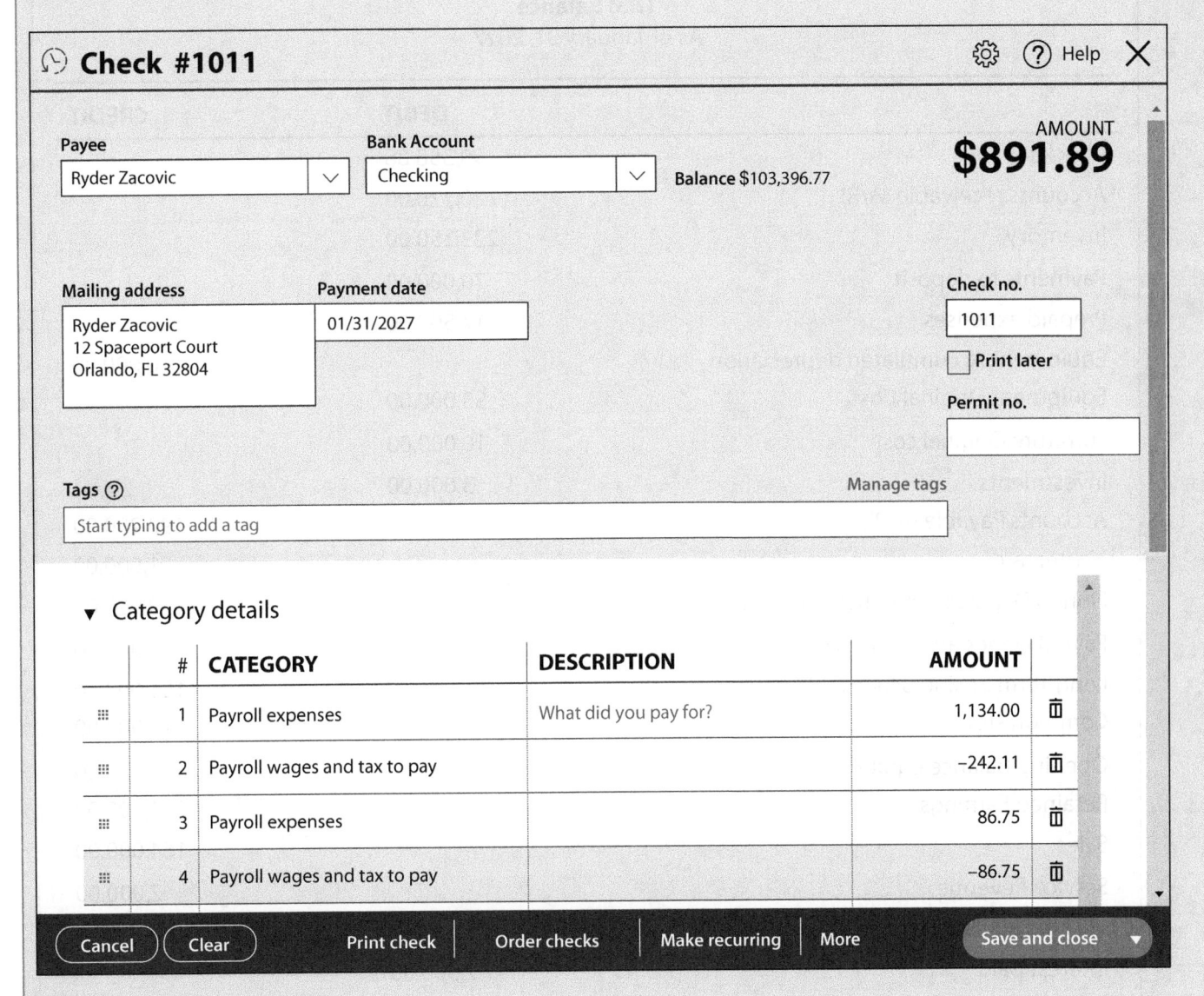

Check #1011   ⚙ ? Help ✕

Payee	Bank Account		AMOUNT
Ryder Zacovic	Checking	Balance $103,396.77	**$891.89**

Mailing address
Ryder Zacovic
12 Spaceport Court
Orlando, FL 32804

Payment date
01/31/2027

Check no.
1011

☐ Print later

Permit no.

Tags   Manage tags
Start typing to add a tag

▼ Category details

#	CATEGORY	DESCRIPTION	AMOUNT	
1	Payroll expenses	What did you pay for?	1,134.00	🗑
2	Payroll wages and tax to pay		−242.11	🗑
3	Payroll expenses		86.75	🗑
4	Payroll wages and tax to pay		−86.75	🗑

Cancel | Clear | Print check | Order checks | Make recurring | More | **Save and close** ▼

---

37 Click **Save and close**.

38 Use the same process (clicking **Use** from the Recurring Transactions list) for Karen and Donna to record their paychecks based on the new information shown in Figure 7.10. (Since Donna is salaried, her information remains the same each pay period, so nothing needs to be changed from the recurring transaction information provided.)

39. Click **Reports**, then click the **Custom reports** tab, then double-click **Trial Balance** to open the Trial Balance report. Confirm that the from and to dates are **1/1/27** and **1/31/27**, respectively, then click **Run Report** to view the report shown in Figure 7.12.

Figure 7.12 Trial Balance

Wild Water Sports - Student Name (ID Number)
Trial Balance
As of January 31, 2027

	DEBIT	CREDIT
Checking	99,358.88	
Accounts receivable (A/R)	120,770.00	
Inventory	223,350.00	
Payments to deposit	70,000.00	
Prepaid expenses	17,500.00	
Equipment:Accumulated depreciation		10,000.00
Equipment:Original Cost	53,000.00	
Furniture:Original cost	10,000.00	
Investments	3,000.00	
Accounts Payable (A/P)		190,250.00
Mastercard		1,600.00
Florida Department of Revenue Payable		9,915.00
Payroll wages and tax to pay		2,944.66
Long-term business loans		155,000.00
Common stock		11,000.00
Opening balance equity		0.00
Retained Earnings		204,300.00
Sales		164,000.00
Service Revenue		2,000.00
Cost of goods sold	131,200.00	
Interest paid	2,500.00	
Payroll expenses	10,930.78	
Rent:Equipment rental	6,000.00	
Utilities:Phone service	1,800.00	
Vehicle expenses:Vehicle gas & fuel	1,600.00	
TOTAL	**$751,009.66**	**$751,009.66**

40 Click the **99,358.88** amount on the Checking line to view a transaction report for the checking account as shown in Figure 7.13.

Figure 7.13 Transaction Report (checking account)

Wild Water Sports - Student Name (ID Number)
Transaction Report
January 2027

DATE	TRANSACTION TYPE	NUM	NAME	MEMO/ DESCRIPTION	ACCOUNT	SPLIT	AMOUNT	BALANCE
▼ Checking								
Beginning Balance								25,000.00
01/12/2027	Deposit		Southtown Watersports		Checking	Payments to deposit	55,145.00	80,145.00
01/15/2027	Check	1008	Donna Chandler		Checking	-Split-	−1,966.25	78,178.75
01/15/2027	Check	1009	Karen Vordale		Checking	-Split-	−1,132.56	77,046.19
01/15/2027	Check	1010	Ryder Zacovic		Checking	-Split-	−849.42	76,196.77
01/18/2027	Bill Payment (Check)	1001	Malibu Boats		Checking	Accounts Payable (A/P)	−56,000.00	20,196.77
01/19/2027	Check	1002	Verizon		Checking	Utilities:Phone service	−1,800.00	18,396.77
01/20/2027	Check	1004	Office Max		Checking	Furniture:Original cost	−10,000.00	8,396.77
01/20/2027	Check	1003	Best Buy		Checking	Equipment:Original Cost	−8,000.00	396.77
01/21/2027	Check	1005	Scottrade		Checking	Investments	−3,000.00	−2,603.23
01/21/2027	Deposit		WB Investments		Checking	Common stock	10,000.00	7,396.77
01/22/2027	Check	1006	Shareholders		Checking	Retained Earnings	−1,500.00	5,896.77
01/23/2027	Check	1007	Chase Bank		Checking	-Split-	−52,500.00	−46,603.23
01/23/2027	Deposit		Chase Bank		Checking	Long-term business loans	150,000.00	103,396.77
01/31/2027	Check	1013	Donna Chandler		Checking	-Split-	−1,966.25	101,430.52
01/31/2027	Check	1012	Karen Vordale		Checking	-Split-	−1,179.75	100,250.77
01/31/2027	Check	1011	Ryder Zacovic		Checking	-Split-	−891.89	99,358.88
Total for Checking							**$74,358.88**	
TOTAL							**$74,358.88**	

41 Click the **Switch to classic view** button and then compare your screen with Figure 7.13, then compare your trial balance with Figure 7.12. Take note of any differences.

42 Click any payroll-related transaction if you want to drill down to the payroll check you recorded to see if you can fix any differences noted.

43 Fix any errors you discover.

You have recorded two semimonthly payrolls for the Wild Water Sports company.

End Note

In this chapter, you added new employees, and paid employees. In the next chapter, you will work with budgets and bank reconciliations.

practice

Chapter 7 Questions

1. What are the steps to create a new employee?
2. What are the steps to create a new account?
3. What are the two minimum accounts needed to account for payroll?
4. What types of costs are included in the Payroll (expense) account?
5. What types of costs are included in the Payroll Tax Payable (liability) account?

Chapter 7 Matching

a. 6.2%
b. 1.45%
c. Payroll
d. Payroll tax payable
e. QBO Payroll
f. Gross pay
g. Recurring transactions
h. Transaction report
i. Unscheduled
j. Record as negative amounts

_____ Account used to record the liability for Federal income tax withheld
_____ An add-on feature to QBO
_____ Rate used to calculate an employee's Medicare tax
_____ Hours worked times hourly rate
_____ Use to more efficiently record periodic payroll
_____ Payroll tax payable
_____ Accessed by clicking an amount on the trial balance
_____ One type of recurring event
_____ Account used to record all payroll expenses
_____ Rate used to calculate an employee's Social Security tax

Chapter 7 Cases

The following cases require you to open the company you updated in Chapter 6. Each of the following cases continues throughout the text in a sequential manner. For example, if you are assigned Case 01, you will use the file you modified in this chapter in all following chapters. Each of the following cases is similar in concepts assessed but differs in amounts and transactions.

> **To reopen your company, do the following:**
> 1. Open your Internet browser.
> 2. Type **https://qbo.intuit.com** into your browser's address text box.
> 3. Type your user ID and password into the text boxes as you have done before.

Case 1

Now add some payroll activities to your company. Do not install QBO Payroll. Based on what you learned in the text using the Wild Water Sports company, you are to make the following changes to the Case 1 company you modified in Chapter 6:

1. Add two new accounts like you did in the chapter: Payroll (expense) and Payroll Tax Payable (liability) if they are not already present.
2. Add a new employee: Ben Franklin, 32 Ocean View Lane, La Jolla, CA, 92037, employee ID number: 556-12-3467.
3. Add a second employee: Betsy Ross, 2323 1st Street, La Jolla, CA, 92037, employee ID number: 458-87-1974.
4. Payroll is paid twice a month on the 17th and the last day of each month.
5. Record payroll (as you did in the chapter) for 1/17/24 based on the information shown in Figure 7.14. After recording each employee's check, be sure to designate it as a recurring transaction.

Figure 7.14
Payroll information for 1/17/24

Pay/Tax/Withholding	Ben	Betsy	Total
Hours if applicable	n/a	73	
Annual salary or hourly rate	$ 95,000	$ 21.50	
Gross pay	**3,958.33**	**1,569.50**	**5,527.83**
Federal withholding	542.29	215.02	757.31
Social security employee (6.2%)	245.42	97.31	342.73
Medicare employee (1.45%)	57.40	22.76	80.16
Employee withholding	**845.11**	**335.09**	**1,180.20**
Social security employer (6.2%)	245.42	97.31	342.73
Medicare company employer (1.45%)	57.40	22.76	80.16
Employer payroll tax expense	**302.82**	**120.07**	**422.89**
Net Check amount	3,113.22	1,234.41	4,347.63

6. Use the recurring transactions template you created above to help you record payroll (as you did in the chapter) for 1/31/24 based on the information shown in Figure 7.15.
7. Open your previously customized report named Trial Balance 1/31/24. Your report should look like Figure 7.16.

Figure 7.15

Payroll information for 1/31/24

Pay/Tax/Withholding	Ben	Betsy	Total
Hours if applicable	n/a	68	
Annual salary or hourly rate	$ 95,000	$ 21.50	
Gross pay	**3,958.33**	**1,462.00**	**5,420.33**
Federal withholding	542.29	200.29	**742.58**
Social security employee (6.2%)	245.42	90.64	**336.06**
Medicare employee (1.45%)	57.40	21.20	**78.60**
Employee withholding	**845.11**	**312.13**	**1,157.24**
Social security employer (6.2%)	245.42	90.64	**336.06**
Medicare company employer (1.45%)	57.40	21.20	**78.60**
Employer payroll tax expense	**302.82**	**111.84**	**414.66**
Net Check amount	3,113.22	1,149.87	**4,263.09**

Figure 7.16

Trial Balance as of 1/31/24

	DEBIT	CREDIT
Checking	26,239.28	
Accounts Receivable	1,030.00	
Inventory Asset	11,800.00	
Prepaid Expenses	8,000.00	
Supplies Asset	375.00	
Undeposited Funds	5,000.00	
Equipment:Original Cost	3,175.00	
Furniture & Fixtures:Depreciation		10,000.00
Furniture & Fixtures:Original cost	40,000.00	
Investments	4,000.00	
Accounts Payable		7,645.00
Visa		1,800.00
Payroll Tax Payable		3,174.99
Notes Payable		66,800.00
Common Stock		21,000.00
Opening Balance Equity		0.00
Retained Earnings		5,000.00
Sales		2,160.00
Services		170.00
Cost of Goods Sold	1,300.00	
Interest Expense	600.00	
Payroll	11,785.71	
Rent or Lease	2,500.00	
Travel	1,800.00	
Utilities	145.00	
TOTAL	$117,749.99	$117,749.99

8   Create and print a Transaction Report for the Checking account.

9   Create and print a Transaction Report for the Payroll Tax Payable account.

10 If your trial balance differs from the one in Figure 7.16, do the following:

    a. Make sure all of your changes were dated in January 2024.

    b. View the Transaction Reports you created to locate any errors.

    c. Ask your instructor for assistance.

    d. Be sure your company matches the above as you will be adding additional business events in Chapter 8.

11 Export your Trial Balance report to Excel, and save it with the file name Student Name (replace with your name) Ch 07 Case 01 Trial Balance.xlsx.

12 Open and print the custom report you created in the last chapter called Transaction Detail by Account.

13 Export your Transactions Detail by Account report to Excel, and save it with the file name Student Name (replace with your name) Ch 07 Case 01 Transaction Detail by Account.xlsx.

14 Sign out of your company.

Case 2

Now add some payroll activities to your company. Do not install QBO Payroll. Based on what you learned in the text using the Wild Water Sports company, you are to make the following changes to the Case 2 company you modified in Chapter 6:

1   Add two new accounts like you did in the chapter: Payroll (expense) and Payroll Tax Payable (liability) if they are not already present.

2   Add a new employee: Frank Benjamin, 32 Ocean View Lane, La Jolla, CA, 92037, employee ID number: 556-12-3467.

3   Add a second employee: Sara Juarez, 2323 1st Street, La Jolla, CA, 92037, employee ID number: 458-87-1974.

4   Payroll is paid twice a month on the 16th and the last day of each month.

5   Record payroll (like you did in the chapter) for 1/16/25 based on the information shown in Figure 7.17. After recording each employee's check, be sure to designate it as a recurring transaction.

Figure 7.17
Payroll information for 1/16/25

Pay/Tax/Withholding	Frank	Sara	Total
Hours if applicable	n/a	71	
Annual salary or hourly rate	$ 72,000	$ 18.75	
Gross pay	**3,000.00**	**1,331.25**	**4,331.25**
Federal withholding	411.00	182.38	593.38
Social security employee (6.2%)	186.00	82.54	268.54
Medicare employee (1.45%)	43.50	19.30	62.80
Employee withholding	**640.50**	**284.22**	**924.72**
Social security employer (6.2%)	186.00	82.54	268.54
Medicare company employer (1.45%)	43.50	19.30	62.80
Employer payroll tax expense	**229.50**	**101.84**	**331.34**
Net Check amount	2,359.50	1,047.03	**3,406.53**

6 Use the recurring transactions template you created above to help you record payroll (as you did in the chapter) for 1/31/25 based on the information shown in Figure 7.18.

Figure 7.18
Payroll information for 1/31/25

Pay/Tax/Withholding	Frank	Sara	Total
Hours if applicable	n/a	66	
Annual salary or hourly rate	$ 72,000	$ 18.75	
Gross pay	**3,000.00**	**1,237.50**	**4,237.50**
Federal withholding	411.00	169.54	580.54
Social security employee (6.2%)	186.00	76.73	262.73
Medicare employee (1.45%)	43.50	17.94	61.44
Employee withholding	**640.50**	**264.21**	**904.71**
Social security employer (6.2%)	186.00	76.73	262.73
Medicare company employer (1.45%)	43.50	17.94	61.44
Employer payroll tax expense	**229.50**	**94.67**	**324.17**
Net Check amount	2,359.50	973.29	**3,332.79**

7 Open your previously customized report named Trial Balance 1/31/25. Your report should look like Figure 7.19.

Figure 7.19

Trial Balance as of 1/31/25

Case 2
TRIAL BALANCE
As of January 31, 2025

	DEBIT	CREDIT
Checking	31,860.68	
Accounts Receivable	1,425.00	
Inventory Asset	5,410.00	
Prepaid Expenses	6,800.00	
Supplies Asset	450.00	
Undeposited Funds	925.00	
Furniture:Original Cost	4,875.00	
Machinery & Equipment:Depreciation		1,000.00
Machinery & Equipment:Original cost	10,000.00	
Investments	3,200.00	
Accounts Payable		8,670.00
AMEX		240.00
Payroll Tax Payable		2,484.94
Notes Payable		27,625.00
Common Stock		25,100.00
Opening Balance Equity		0.00
Retained Earnings		7,585.00
Sales		5,700.00
Services		225.00
Cost of Goods Sold	3,020.00	
Advertising	500.00	
Insurance	400.00	
Interest Expense	300.00	
Meals and Entertainment	240.00	
Payroll	9,224.26	
TOTAL	$78,629.94	$78,629.94

8 Create and print a Transaction Report for the Checking account.

9 Create and print a Transaction Report for the Payroll Tax Payable account.

10 If your trial balance differs from the one in Figure 7.19, do the following:

   a. Make sure all of your changes were dated in January 2025.

   b. View the Transaction Reports you created to locate any errors.

   c. Ask your instructor for assistance.

   d. Be sure your company matches the above as you will be adding additional business events in Chapter 8.

11 Export your Trial Balance report to Excel, and save it with the file name Student Name (replace with your name) Ch 07 Case 02 Trial Balance.xlsx.

12 Open and print the custom report you created in the last chapter called Transaction Detail by Account.

13 Export your Transactions Detail by Account report to Excel, and save it with the file name Student Name (replace with your name) Ch 07 Case 02 Transaction Detail by Account.xlsx.

14 Sign out of your company.

Case 3

Now add some payroll activities to your company. Do not install QBO Payroll. Based on what you learned in the text using the Wild Water Sports company, you are to make the following changes to the Case 3 company you modified in Chapter 6:

1 If necessary, add two new accounts like you did in the chapter: Payroll (expense) and Payroll Tax Payable (liability).

2 Add a new employee: Kira Jennings, 32 Ocean View Lane, La Jolla, CA, 92037, employee ID number: 556-33-3467.

3 Add a second employee: Jedi Vu, 2323 1st Street, La Jolla, CA, 92037, employee ID number: 458-22-1974.

4 Payroll is paid twice a month on the 16th and the last day of each month.

5 Record payroll (like you did in the chapter) for 1/16/26 based on the information shown in Figure 7.20 using checks 326 and 327. Be sure to designate both as a recurring transaction.

Figure 7.20

Payroll information for 1/16/26

Pay/Tax/Withholding	Kira	Jedi	Total
Hours if applicable	n/a	70	
Annual salary or hourly rate	$ 48,000	$ 17.00	
Gross pay	**2,000.00**	**1,190.00**	**3,190.00**
Federal withholding	274.00	163.03	**437.03**
Social security employee (6.2%)	124.00	73.78	**197.78**
Medicare employee (1.45%)	29.00	17.26	**46.26**
Employee withholding	**427.00**	**254.07**	**681.07**
Social security employer (6.2%)	124.00	73.78	**197.78**
Medicare company employer (1.45%)	29.00	17.26	**46.26**
Employer payroll tax expense	**153.00**	**91.04**	**244.04**
Net Check amount	1,573.00	935.93	**2,508.93**

6 Use the recurring transactions template you created above to help you record payroll (like you did in the chapter) for 1/31/26 based on the information shown in Figure 7.21 using checks 328 and 329.

Figure 7.21

Payroll information for 1/31/26

Pay/Tax/Withholding	Kira	Jedi	Total
Hours if applicable	n/a	75	
Annual salary or hourly rate	$ 48,000	$ 17.00	
Gross pay	**2,000.00**	**1,275.00**	**3,275.00**
Federal withholding	274.00	174.68	**448.68**
Social security employee (6.2%)	124.00	79.05	**203.05**
Medicare employee (1.45%)	29.00	18.49	**47.49**
Employee withholding	**427.00**	**272.22**	**699.22**
Social security employer (6.2%)	124.00	79.05	**203.05**
Medicare company employer (1.45%)	29.00	18.49	**47.49**
Employer payroll tax expense	**153.00**	**97.54**	**250.54**
Net Check amount	1,573.00	1,002.78	**2,575.78**

7 Open your previously customized report named Trial Balance 1/31/26. Your report should look like Figure 7.22.

8 Create and print a Transaction Report for the Checking account.

9 Create and print a Transaction Report for the Payroll Tax Payable account.

10 If your trial balance is different than Figure 7.22, do the following:
   a. Make sure that all of your changes were dated in January 2026.
   b. View the Transaction Reports you just created to locate any errors.
   c. Ask your instructor for assistance.
   d. Be sure your company matches the above as you will be adding additional business events in Chapter 8.

11 Export your Trial Balance report to Excel, and save it with the file name Student Name (replace with your name) Ch 07 Case 03 Trial Balance.xlsx.

12 Open and print the customized report you created in the last chapter called Transaction Detail by Account.

13 Export your Transactions Detail by Account report to Excel, and save it with the file name Student Name (replace with your name) Ch 07 Case 03 Transaction Detail by Account.xlsx.

14 Sign out of your company.

Figure 7.22

Trial Balance as of 1/31/26

Case 03 - Student Name (ID Number)
Trial Balance
As of January 31, 2026

	DEBIT	CREDIT
Checking	50,667.04	
Accounts receivable (A/R)	2,559.38	
Inventory Asset	5,700.00	
Payments to deposit	0.00	
Prepaid expenses	6,050.00	
Supplies Asset	327.00	
Computers:Original cost	3,000.00	
Machinery & Equipment:Depreciation		2,000.00
Machinery & Equipment:Original cost	46,800.00	
Investments	5,700.00	
Accounts Payable (A/P)		8,900.00
AMEX		123.00
California Department of Tax and Fe...		523.13
Payroll Tax Payable		1,874.87
Notes Payable		63,800.00
Opening balance equity		0.00
Owner's Equity		50,075.00
Sales of Product Income		6,750.00
Services		240.00
Cost of goods sold	4,500.00	
Advertising & marketing	1,300.00	
Insurance	300.00	
Interest paid	300.00	
Meals	123.00	
Payroll	6,959.58	
TOTAL	$134,286.00	$134,286.00

Case 4

Now add some payroll activities to your company. Do not install QBO Payroll. Based on what you learned in the text using the Wild Water Sports company, you are to make the following changes to the Case 4 company you modified in Chapter 6:

1. Add two new accounts: Payroll expense and Payroll tax to pay (liability) if they are not already present.
2. Add a new employee: Graham O'Leary.
3. Add additional employees: Allegra Munoz and Beckett Yamamomo.
4. Payroll is paid twice a month on the 15th and the last day of each month.

5 Record payroll (like you did in the chapter) for 1/15/27 based on the information shown in Figure 7.23. After recording each employee's check, be sure to designate it as an unscheduled recurring transaction.

Figure 7.23 Payroll information for 1/15/27

Pay/Tax/Withholding	Graham	Allegra	Beckett	Total
Hours if applicable	n/a	75	83	
Annual salary or hourly rate	$ 75,000	$ 25.00	$ 22.00	
Gross pay	**3,125.00**	**1,875.00**	**1,826.00**	**6,826.00**
Federal withholding	428.13	256.88	250.16	**935.16**
Social security employee (6.2%)	193.75	116.25	113.21	**423.21**
Medicare employee (1.45%)	45.31	27.19	26.48	**98.98**
Employee withholding	**667.19**	**400.32**	**389.85**	**1,457.35**
Social security employer (6.2%)	193.75	116.25	113.21	**423.21**
Medicare company employer (1.45%)	45.34	27.19	26.48	**99.01**
Employer payroll tax expense	**239.09**	**143.44**	**139.69**	**522.22**
Net Check amount	2,457.81	1,474.68	1,436.15	**5,368.64**

6 Use the recurring transactions template you created above to help you record payroll (as you did in the chapter) for 1/31/27 based on the information shown in Figure 7.24.

Figure 7.24 Payroll information for 1/31/27

Pay/Tax/Withholding	Graham	Allegra	Beckett	Total
Hours if applicable	n/a	70	88	
Annual salary or hourly rate	$ 75,000	$ 25.00	$ 22.00	
Gross pay	**3,125.00**	**1,750.00**	**1,936.00**	**6,811.00**
Federal withholding	428.13	239.75	265.23	**933.11**
Social security employee (6.2%)	193.75	108.50	120.03	**422.28**
Medicare employee (1.45%)	45.31	25.38	28.07	**98.76**
Employee withholding	**667.19**	**373.63**	**413.33**	**1,454.15**
Social security employer (6.2%)	193.75	108.50	120.03	**422.28**
Medicare company employer (1.45%)	45.34	25.38	28.07	**98.79**
Employer payroll tax expense	**239.09**	**133.88**	**148.10**	**521.07**
Net Check amount	2,457.81	1,376.37	1,522.67	**5,356.85**

7 Prepare and print the Trial Balance 1/31/27 report you saved previously. Your report should look like Figure 7.25.

Figure 7.25 Trial Balance as of 1/31/27

Trial Balance
As of January 31, 2027

	DEBIT	CREDIT
Checking	18,037.16	
Accounts Receivable (A/R)	22,082.50	
Inventory Asset	8,868.00	
Payments to deposit	0.00	
Prepaid rent	12,000.00	
Supplies Asset	1,400.00	
Furniture:Accumulated Depreciation		10,000.00
Furniture:Original Cost	106,000.00	
Vehicles:Accumulated Depreciation		6,500.00
Vehicles:Original Cost	115,000.00	
Long-term investments	8,000.00	
Accounts Payable (A/P)		6,800.00
VISA		2,400.00
California Department of Tax and Fee Administration Payable		339.15
Payroll wages and tax to pay		3,954.80
Long-term business loans		105,306.00
Long-term debt		0.00
Common Stock		11,000.00
Opening Balance Equity		0.00
Retained Earnings		114,500.00
Sales		48,400.00
Sales of Product Income		3,570.00
Cost of Goods Sold	1,632.00	
Advertising & Marketing	1,800.00	
Insurance	2,400.00	
Interest Paid	120.00	
Payroll expenses	14,680.29	
Repairs & Maintenance	750.00	
TOTAL	**$312,769.95**	**$312,769.95**

8   Investigate differences between your trial balance and the trial balance shown above.

9   If necessary, prepare and print the Transaction Detail by Account report you saved previously to investigate identified differences.

   a. Make sure all your changes were dated in January 2027.

   b. Click on the line that does not match to view the transaction for that account, and investigate why your answer differs.

   c. Ask your instructor for assistance.

   d. Be sure your company matches the above as you will be adding additional business events in Chapter 8.

Case 5

Now add some payroll activities to your company. Do not install QBO Payroll. Based on what you learned in the text using the Wild Water Sports company, you are to make the following changes to the Case 5 company you modified in Chapter 6:

1   Add two new payroll accounts if they are not already present. Account type: Expenses, Save account under: Expenses, Tax form section: Payroll Expenses, Account name: Payroll expenses. Account type: Liabilities, Save account under: Other current Liabilities, Tax form section: Payroll Tax Payable, Account name: Payroll wages and tax to pay.

2   Add a new employee: Jamal Hope.

3   Add a second employee: Rebecca Fairly.

4   Add a third employee: Sarah Lockwood.

5   Payroll is paid twice a month on the 15th and the last day of each month.

6   Record payroll (like you did in the chapter) for 1/15/28 based on the information shown in Figure 7.26. After recording each employee's check, be sure to designate it as a recurring transaction.

7   Use the recurring transactions template you created above to help you record payroll (as you did in the chapter) for 1/31/28 based on the information shown in Figure 7.27. You may enter payroll for employees in any order; just keep in mind that your check numbers may not match the Transactions Detail by Account report.

8   Prepare and print the Trial Balance 1/31/28 report you saved previously. Your report should look like Figure 7.28.

9   Investigate differences between your trial balance and the trial balance shown above.

Figure 7.26 Payroll information for 1/15/28

Pay/Tax/Withholding	Jamal	Rebecca	Sarah	Total
Hours if applicable	n/a	n/a	80	
Annual salary or hourly rate	$ 125,000	$ 100,000	$ 40.00	
Gross pay	**5,208.33**	**4,166.67**	**3,200.00**	**12,575.00**
Federal withholding	713.54	570.83	438.40	**1,722.78**
Social security employee (6.2%)	322.92	258.33	198.40	**779.65**
Medicare employee (1.45%)	75.52	60.42	46.40	**182.34**
Employee withholding	**1,111.98**	**889.58**	**683.20**	**2,684.76**
Social security employer (6.2%)	322.92	258.33	198.40	**779.65**
Medicare company employer (1.45%)	75.55	60.45	46.40	**182.40**
Employer payroll tax expense	**398.47**	**318.78**	**244.80**	**962.05**
Net Check amount	4,096.35	3,277.09	2,516.80	**9,890.24**

Figure 7.27 Payroll information for 1/31/28

Pay/Tax/Withholding	Jamal	Rebecca	Sarah	Total
Hours if applicable	n/a	n/a	75	
Annual salary or hourly rate	$ 125,000	$ 100,000	$ 40.00	
Gross pay	**5,208.33**	**4,166.67**	**3,000.00**	**12,375.00**
Federal withholding	713.54	570.83	411.00	**1,695.38**
Social security employee (6.2%)	322.92	258.33	186.00	**767.25**
Medicare employee (1.45%)	75.52	60.42	43.50	**179.44**
Employee withholding	**1,111.98**	**889.58**	**640.50**	**2,642.06**
Social security employer (6.2%)	322.92	258.33	186.00	**767.25**
Medicare company employer (1.45%)	75.55	60.45	43.50	**179.50**
Employer payroll tax expense	**398.47**	**318.78**	**229.50**	**946.75**
Net Check amount	4,096.35	3,277.09	2,359.50	**9,732.94**

Figure 7.28 Trial Balance as of 1/31/28

Case 05 - Student Name (ID Number)
Trial Balance
As of January 31, 2028

	DEBIT	CREDIT
Checking	236,795.82	
Accounts Receivable (A/R)	648,850.00	
Inventory	512,000.00	
Payments to deposit	0.00	
Prepaid expenses	22,000.00	
Fixed Asset Computers:Depreciation		25,000.00
Fixed Asset Computers:Original Cost	280,000.00	
Fixed Asset Copiers:Original Cost	25,000.00	
Fixed Asset Furniture:Depreciation		8,000.00
Fixed Asset Furniture:Original Cost	80,000.00	
Investments	50,000.00	
Accounts Payable (A/P)		362,000.00
AMEX		6,300.00
Alabama Department of Revenue Payable		24,600.00
Alabama, Huntsville Payable		27,675.00
Alabama, Madison County Payable		3,075.00
Payroll wages and tax to pay		7,235.62
Notes Payable		580,419.00
Opening balance equity		0.00
Owner's Equity		457,000.00
Consulting		79,500.00
Sales		615,000.00
Training		3,500.00
Cost of goods sold	298,000.00	
Advertising & marketing	3,000.00	
Equipment rental	7,500.00	
Interest Expense	3,000.00	
Payroll expenses	26,858.80	
Recruiting	6,300.00	
TOTAL	$2,199,304.62	$2,199,304.62

10 If necessary, prepare and print the Transaction Detail by Account report you saved previously to investigate identified differences.

   a. Make sure all your changes were dated in January 2028.

   b. Click on the line that does not match to view the transaction for that account, and investigate why your answer differs.

   c. Ask your instructor for assistance.

   d. Be sure your company matches the above as you will be adding additional business events in Chapter 8.

Case 6

Now add some payroll activities to your company. Do not install QBO Payroll. Based on what you learned in the text using the Wild Water Sports company, you are to make the following changes to the Case 6 company you modified in Chapter 6:

1. Add two new accounts like you did in the chapter: Payroll (expense) and Payroll Tax Payable (liability) if they are not already present.

2. Add new employees:

    a. Oliver Peters, 4737 Forest Ave SE, Mercer Island, WA, 98040, employee ID number: 1347.

    b. Rhett Brady, 1706 9th Ave SE, Puyallup, WA, 98372, employee ID number: 1348.

    c. Emelia Carlstrom, 518 Guptil Ave, Sumer, WA, 98390, employee ID number: 1349.

3. Payroll is paid twice a month on the 15th and the last day of each month.

4. Record payroll (like you did in the chapter) for 1/15/23 based on the information shown in Figure 7.29 using checks 595, 596, and 597. After recording each employee's check, be sure to designate it as a recurring transaction.

Figure 7.29

Payroll information for 1/15/23

Pay/Tax/Withholding	Oliver	Rhett	Emelia
Hours if applicable	n/a	n/a	80
Annual salary or hourly rate	$ 85,000	$ 60,000	$ 35.00
Gross pay	**3,541.67**	**2,500.00**	**2,800.00**
Federal withholding	485.22	342.50	383.60
Social security employee (6.2%)	219.58	155.00	173.60
Medicare employee (1.45%)	51.35	36.25	40.60
Employee withholding	**756.15**	**533.75**	**597.80**
Social security employer (6.2%)	219.59	155.00	173.60
Medicare company employer (1.45%)	51.38	36.28	40.60
Employer payroll tax expense	**270.97**	**191.28**	**214.20**
Net Check amount	2,785.52	1,966.25	2,202.20

Pay/Tax/Withholding	Oliver	Rhett	Emelia
Hours if applicable	n/a	n/a	75
Annual salary or hourly rate	$ 85,000	$ 60,000	$ 35.00
Gross pay	**3,541.67**	**2,500.00**	**2,625.00**
Federal withholding	485.22	342.50	359.63
Social security employee (6.2%)	219.58	155.00	162.75
Medicare employee (1.45%)	51.35	36.25	38.06
Employee withholding	**756.15**	**533.75**	**560.44**
Social security employer (6.2%)	219.59	155.00	162.75
Medicare company employer (1.45%)	51.38	36.28	38.06
Employer payroll tax expense	**270.97**	**191.28**	**200.81**
Net Check amount	2,785.52	1,966.25	2,064.56

Figure 7.30

Payroll information for 1/31/23

5. Use the recurring transactions templates you created above to help you record payroll (as you did in the chapter) for 1/31/23 based on the information shown in Figure 7.30 using checks 598, 599, and 600.

6. Prepare and print the Trial Balance 1/31/23 report you saved previously. Your report should look like Figure 7.31.

7. Investigate differences between your trial balance and the trial balance shown above.

8. If necessary, prepare and print the Transaction Detail by Account report you saved previously to investigate identified differences.

   a. Make sure all your changes were dated in January 2023.

   b. Click on the line that does not match to view the transaction for that account and investigate why your answer differs.

   c. Ask your instructor for assistance.

   d. Be sure your company matches the above as you will be adding additional business events in Chapter 8.

Figure 7.31 Trial Balance as of 1/31/23

Case 06 - Student Name (ID Number)
TRIAL BALANCE
As of January 31, 2023

	DEBIT	CREDIT
Checking	64,336.82	
Accounts Receivable (A/R)	153,020.00	
Inventory Asset	524,000.00	
Inventory Parts	4,000.00	
Investments	12,000.00	
Loans To Officers	15,000.00	
Prepaid Expenses	18,000.00	
Undeposited Funds	0.00	
Buildings:Depreciation		15,000.00
Buildings:Original cost	150,000.00	
Computers	8,000.00	
Machinery & Equipment	12,000.00	
Machinery & Equipment:Depreciation		10,000.00
Machinery & Equipment:Original cost	100,000.00	
Accounts Payable (A/P)		524,000.00
AMEX		6,000.00
Payroll Tax Payable		5,077.55
Washington State Department of Revenue Payable		26,970.00
Notes Payable		128,857.12
Common Stock		1,100.00
Opening Balance Equity		0.00
Paid-In Capital		259,900.00
Retained Earnings		60,500.00
Sales of Product Income		290,000.00
Cost of Goods Sold	232,000.00	
Advertising & Marketing	14,000.00	
Contractors	1,800.00	
Interest Expense	400.00	
Payroll	18,847.85	
TOTAL	**$1,327,404.67**	**$1,327,404.67**

Establishing Budgets and Preparing Bank Reconciliations

chapter 8

Student Learning Outcomes

Upon completion of this chapter, the student will be able to do the following:

- Add budget amounts to create a budget
- Create Profit and Loss budget reports
- Reconcile a checking account and print a reconciliation report

Overview

In Chapter 7, you added payroll activities like adding employees, adding payroll-related accounts, and recording payroll expenses and liabilities to your Wild Water Sports company. In this chapter, you will add a budget, add a Profit and Loss budget report, and add a bank reconciliation to your Wild Water Sports company. At the end of this chapter, you will perform the similar tasks on the case assigned by your instructor.

To verify the accuracy of your Wild Water Sports company:

1. Sign into your QBO account then open the Wild Water Sports company you used in Chapter 7.

2. Click **Reports**, then click the **Custom reports** tab, then double-click **Trial Balance** to open the Trial Balance report. Set the from and to dates to **1/1/27** and **1/31/27**, respectively. Compare your report to Figure 8.1. If your report doesn't match Figure 8.1, go back to your work in Chapter 7 to fix your errors. Otherwise, close your Trial Balance report.

Figure 8.1 Wild Water Sports trial balance as of 1/31/27

Wild Water Sports - Student Name (ID Number)
Trial Balance
As of January 31, 2027

	DEBIT	CREDIT
Checking	99,358.88	
Accounts receivable (A/R)	120,770.00	
Inventory	223,350.00	
Payments to deposit	70,000.00	
Prepaid expenses	17,500.00	
Equipment:Accumulated depreciation		10,000.00
Equipment:Original Cost	53,000.00	
Furniture:Original cost	10,000.00	
Investments	3,000.00	
Accounts Payable (A/P)		190,250.00
Mastercard		1,600.00
Florida Department of Revenue Payable		9,915.00
Payroll wages and tax to pay		2,944.66
Long-term business loans		155,000.00
Common stock		11,000.00
Opening balance equity		0.00
Retained Earnings		204,300.00
Sales		164,000.00
Service Revenue		2,000.00
Cost of goods sold	131,200.00	
Interest paid	2,500.00	
Payroll expenses	10,930.78	
Rent:Equipment rental	6,000.00	
Utilities:Phone service	1,800.00	
Vehicle expenses:Vehicle gas & fuel	1,600.00	
TOTAL	$751,009.66	$751,009.66

Budget Creation

In this section, you will be establishing a Profit and Loss budget in QBO, which tracks amounts in income and expense accounts. QBO will interview you to determine budget amounts. You will be creating your budget from scratch since you have no historical amounts in QBO.

Establishing Budgets and Preparing Bank Reconciliations **Chapter 8** 219

To create a Profit and Loss budget for the Wild Water Sports company, do the following:

1. Continue from above.
2. Make sure the navigation bar is open.
3. Click the **Gear** icon, and select **Budgeting** as shown in Figure 8.2.

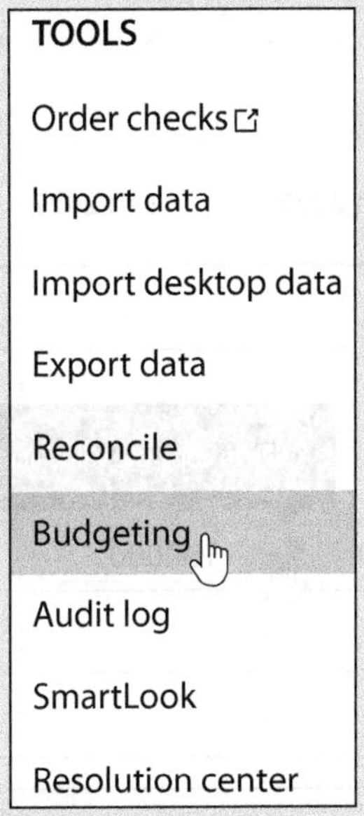

```
TOOLS
Order checks ↗
Import data
Import desktop data
Export data
Reconcile
Budgeting
Audit log
SmartLook
Resolution center
```

Figure 8.2

Budgeting window (accessing the budgeting process)

4. Click **Create budget**.
5. Select **FY2027 (Jan2027-Dec2027)** from the Period drop-down list, select **Profit and Loss** as the Budget type, and select **Consolidated budget** as the Budget format.
6. Click **Next**.
7. Click the pencil icon to the right of Budget_FY27_P&L and change the budget name to **Budget 1**.
8. Make sure that the **Compare reference data** option is not selected.
9. Click in the Jan 2027 **Sales** account.
10. Type **180000** in the Jan text box, and then click the **Copy across** button to copy the Sales budget amount for the entire year as shown in Figure 8.3.

Figure 8.3 Budget worksheet

Budget 1 ✏️

Period

FY 2027 (Jan 2027 - Dec 2027)   Compare reference data ⊙

☐ ∧ Accounts	Budget totals	Jan 2027	Feb 2027	Mar 2027	Apr 2027
☐ ∧ Income					
☐ Billable Expense Income					
☐ Discounts given					
☐ Sales	2160000	180000	180000	180000	180000
☐ Sales of Product Income					
☐ Sales Parts					

Click to copy the value across on the row

11   Type **5000** in the Jan Service Revenue text box. Copy across the Service Revenue amount for the entire year and then click **Save**.

12   Click the **Yearly** button to view by year.

13   Click the **Gear** icon in the budget window, place a check in the **Hide empty rows** check box, and then place a check in the **Compact** check box under Display density. Click the **Apply** button. Your newly entered amounts are shown in Figure 8.4.

14   Click the **Monthly** button to change the view to Month, and then click the **Gear** icon and uncheck the **Hide empty rows** check box. Click the **Apply** button.

15   Scroll down the budget worksheet and type additional January amounts for cost of goods sold: **135000**, advertising & marketing **10000**, interest paid **2500**, payroll expenses **11000**, equipment rental **5000**, Supplies **3000**, Internet & TV services **4000**, phone service **2000**, and vehicle gas & fuel **1000**. Copy across each amount entered for the entire year. Click the **Gear** icon in the budget window then select **Year** to view by year. Place a check in the **Hide empty rows** check box.

16   Click **Save and close**.

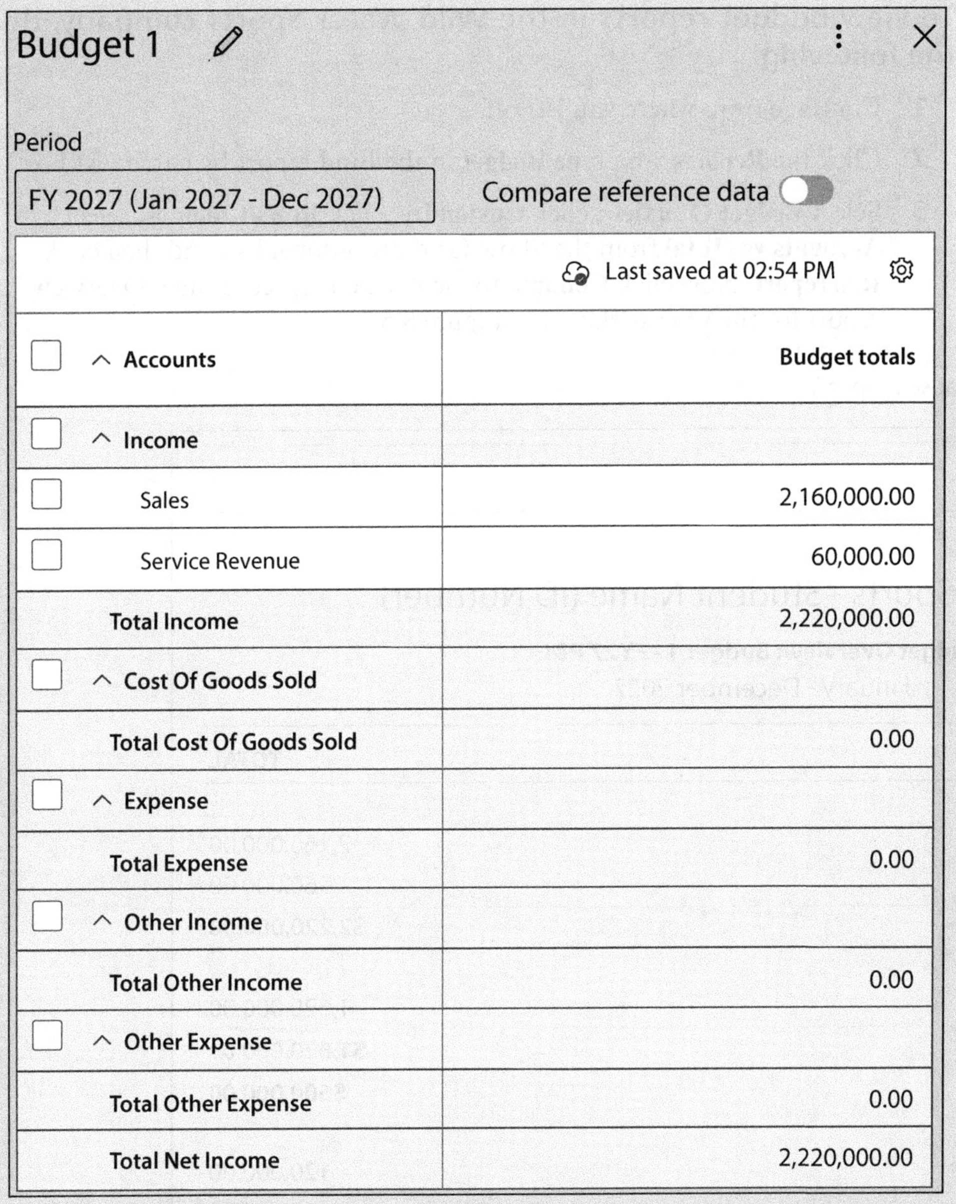

Establishing Budgets and Preparing Bank Reconciliations **Chapter 8** 221

Budget 1

Period

FY 2027 (Jan 2027 - Dec 2027)   Compare reference data

Last saved at 02:54 PM

Accounts	Budget totals
Income	
Sales	2,160,000.00
Service Revenue	60,000.00
Total Income	2,220,000.00
Cost Of Goods Sold	
Total Cost Of Goods Sold	0.00
Expense	
Total Expense	0.00
Other Income	
Total Other Income	0.00
Other Expense	
Total Other Expense	0.00
Total Net Income	2,220,000.00

Figure 8.4
Budget worksheet for annual Income (partial view)

You have entered budgeted amounts and stored them in QBO. Now, you will view budget reports.

Budget Reports

QBO has two basic budget-related reports: Budget Overview and Budget vs. Actual. The overview report only lists budget data. The Budget vs. Actual lists budget data compared to actual transactions inputted into QBO.

To view budget reports in the Wild Water Sports company, do the following:

1. Continue from where you left off.
2. Click the **Reports**, and type **Budget** in the Find report by name text box.
3. Select **Budget Overview**, click **Customize**, click **Rows/Columns**, select **Accounts vs. Total** from the Show Grid drop-down list, and then click **Run report**. Now click **Collapse** to view the collapsed Budget Overview report for the year as shown in Figure 8.5.

Figure 8.5 Budget Overview (collapsed report)

Expand   Sort▼   Add notes

Wild Water Sports - Student Name (ID Number)
Budget Overview: Budget 1 - FY27 P&L
January - December 2027

	TOTAL
▾ Income	
Sales	2,160,000.00
Service Revenue	60,000.00
Total Income	**$2,220,000.00**
▾ Cost of Goods Sold	
Cost of goods sold	1,620,000.00
Total Cost of Goods Sold	**$1,620,000.00**
GROSS PROFIT	$600,000.00
▾ Expenses	
Advertising & marketing	120,000.00
Interest paid	30,000.00
Payroll expenses	132,000.00
Rent	60,000.00
Supplies	36,000.00
Utilities	72,000.00
Total Expenses	**$450,000.00**
NET OPERATING INCOME	$150,000.00
▾ Other Expenses	
Vehicle expenses	12,000.00
Total Other Expenses	**$12,000.00**
NET OTHER INCOME	$ –12,000.00
NET INCOME	$138,000.00

Establishing Budgets and Preparing Bank Reconciliations **Chapter 8** 223

4 Click **Customize** to modify the Budget Overview report.

5 Check the **Without cents** check box as shown in Figure 8.6.

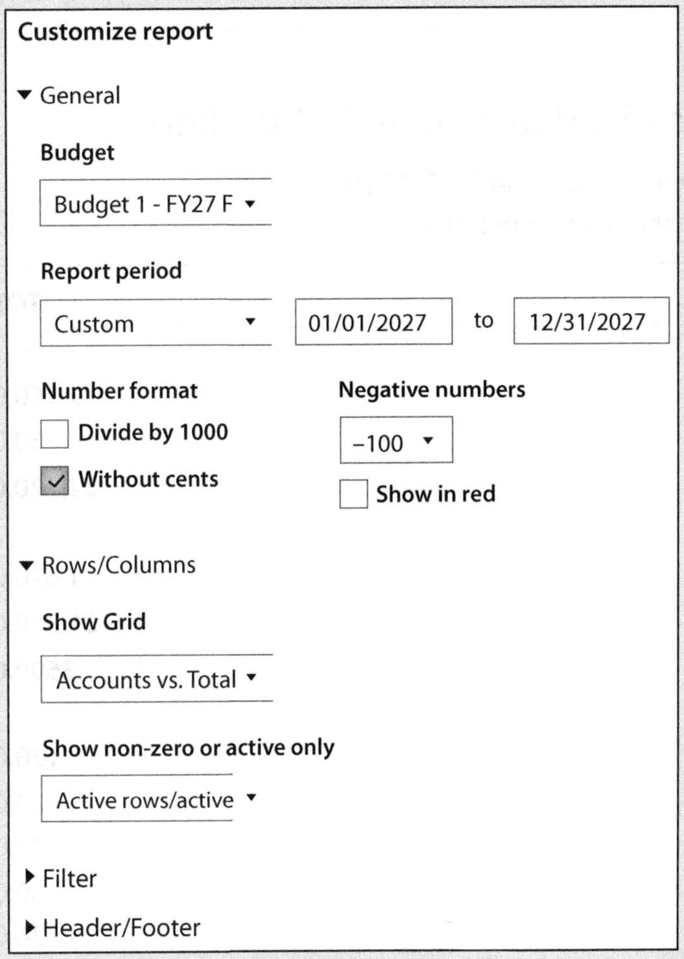

Figure 8.6

Customizing Budget Overview

6 Click **Run report** to view the customized Budget Overview report as shown in Figure 8.7.

7 Click **Save customization**, type **Budget Overview** in the Custom report name text box, and then click **Save**.

8 Click **Reports**, once again type **Budget** into the Find report by name text box, and then select **Budget vs. Actuals** from the list of recommended reports.

9 Click **Collapse**.

10 Click **Customize** to modify the Budget vs. Actuals report.

11 Change the From: and To: dates to **1/1/27** and **1/31/27**, respectively.

12 Click **Rows/Columns**, select **Accounts vs. Total** in the drop-down list in the Show Grid text box, and then check the **Without cents** check box as shown in Figure 8.8.

Figure 8.7 Budget Overview (customized report)

Expand Sort ▾ Add notes

Wild Water Sports - Student Name (ID Number)
Budget Overview: Budget 1 - FY27 P&L
January - December 2027

	TOTAL
▾ Income	
Sales	2,160,000
Service Revenue	60,000
Total Income	**$2,220,000**
▾ Cost of Goods Sold	
Cost of goods sold	1,620,000
Total Cost of Goods Sold	**$1,620,000**
GROSS PROFIT	$600,000
Expenses	
Advertising & marketing	120,000
Interest paid	30,000
Payroll expenses	132,000
Rent	60,000
Supplies	36,000
Utilities	72,000
Total Expenses	**$450,000**
NET OPERATING INCOME	$150,000
▾ Other Expenses	
Vehicle expenses	12,000
Total Other Expenses	**$12,000**
NET OTHER INCOME	$ −12,000
NET INCOME	$138,000

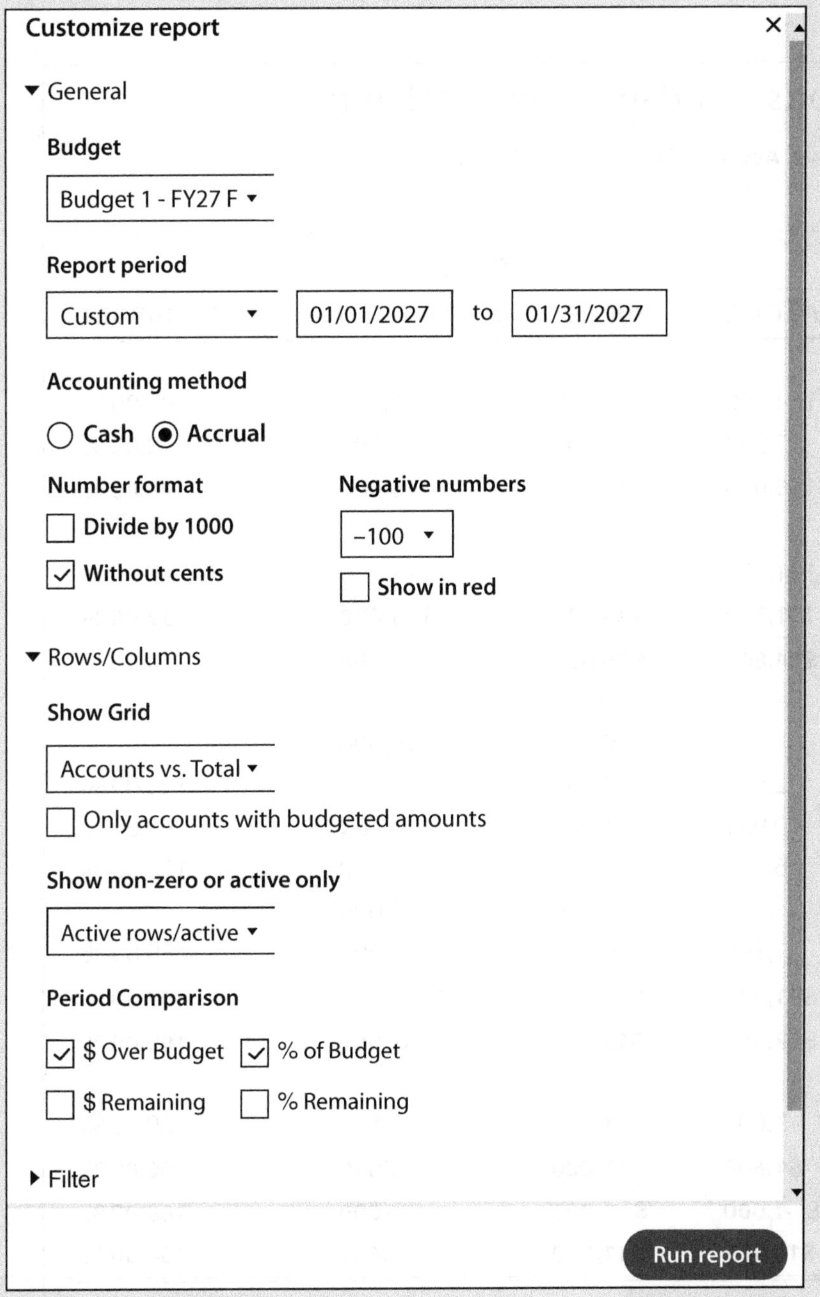

Establishing Budgets and Preparing Bank Reconciliations **Chapter 8** **225**

Figure 8.8

Customizing Budget vs. Actuals

Customize report

▼ **General**

Budget

Budget 1 - FY27 F ▼

Report period

Custom ▼ | 01/01/2027 | to | 01/31/2027

Accounting method

○ Cash ● Accrual

Number format
☐ Divide by 1000
☑ Without cents

Negative numbers
–100 ▼
☐ Show in red

▼ **Rows/Columns**

Show Grid

Accounts vs. Total ▼

☐ Only accounts with budgeted amounts

Show non-zero or active only

Active rows/active ▼

Period Comparison

☑ $ Over Budget ☑ % of Budget
☐ $ Remaining   ☐ % Remaining

▶ Filter

Run report

13 Click **Run report**. A partial view of the customized Budget vs. Actuals report is shown in Figure 8.9. Note: Your actual and budget amounts should match this figure.

14 Click **Save customization**, type **Budget vs. Actuals** in the Custom report name text box, and then click **Save**.

Figure 8.9 Budget vs. Actual report

Wild Water Sports - Student Name (ID Number)
Budget vs. Actuals: Budget 1 - FY27 P&L
January 2027

	TOTAL			
	ACTUAL	BUDGET	OVER BUDGET	% OF BUDGET
▼ Income				
Sales	164,000	180,000	−16,000	91.00 %
Service Revenue	2,000	5,000	−3,000	40.00 %
Total Income	**$166,000**	**$185,000**	**$ −19,000**	**90.00 %**
▼ Cost of Goods Sold				
Cost of goods sold	131,200	135,000	−3,800	97.00 %
Total Cost of Goods Sold	**$131,200**	**$135,000**	**$ −3,800**	**97.00 %**
GROSS PROFIT	$34,800	$50,000	$ −15,200	70.00 %
▼ Expenses				
Advertising & marketing		10,000	−10,000	
Interest paid	2,500	2,500	0	100.00 %
Payroll expenses	10,931	11,000	−69	99.00 %
Rent	6,000	5,000	1,000	120.00 %
Supplies		3,000	−3,000	
Utilities	1,800	6,000	−4,200	30.00 %
Total Expenses	**$21,231**	**$37,500**	**$ −16,269**	**57.00 %**
NET OPERATING INCOME	$13,569	$12,500	$1,069	109.00 %
▼ Other Expenses				
Vehicle expenses	1,600	1,000	600	160.00 %
Total Other Expenses	**$1,600**	**$1,000**	**$600**	**160.00 %**
NET OTHER INCOME	$ −1,600	$ −1,000	$ −600	160.00 %
NET INCOME	$11,969	$11,500	$469	104.00 %

Bank Reconciliation

Good internal control requires frequent reconciliations between bank records and a company's records of cash receipts and payments, completed by someone other than the accountant or bookkeeper who is responsible for maintaining accounting records. The process involves comparing items that appear in the checking account with those items appearing on the bank statement. Deposits that appear in the checking account but do not appear on the bank statement are referred to as deposits in transit. Checks that appear in the checking account but do not appear on the bank statement are referred to as outstanding checks. They usually appear as checks on the next bank statement.

In QBO, if you discover a deposit recorded by the bank but not recorded in the checking account (determined to be an error in the checking account), you should correct the checking account by recording the deposit. Likewise, if you discover a check recorded by the bank but not recorded in the checking account (determined to be an error in the checking account), you should correct the checking account by recording the check. In the following example, neither was identified.

To create reconciliation for the Wild Water Sports company, do the following:

1. Continue from above.
2. Make sure the navigation bar is open.
3. Click the **Gear** icon, and select **Reconcile** as shown in Figure 8.10.

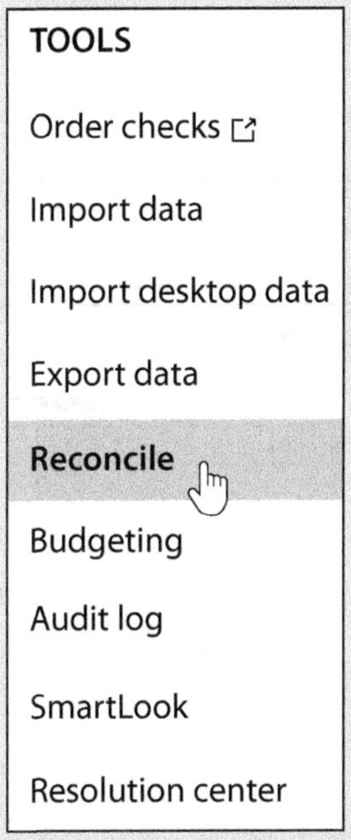

Figure 8.10

Reconciliation process (access)

4. Click **Get Started**, click **Let's get reconciled**, and then make sure the **Checking** account is selected in the Reconcile window as shown in Figure 8.11.
5. Type **1/31/2027** as the Ending date and type **103396.77** as the Ending balance.
6. Click **Start reconciling**.
7. The Reconcile—Checking form shown in Figure 8.12 should appear. Note: The column widths in this figure have been adjusted.

Figure 8.11

Reconcile window

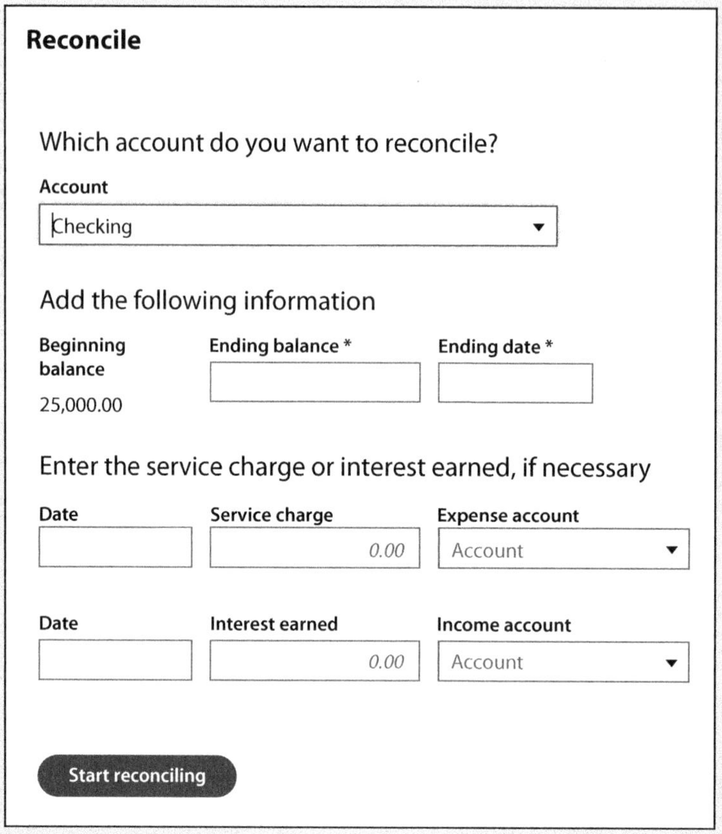

Reconcile

Which account do you want to reconcile?

Account

| Checking ▼ |

Add the following information

Beginning balance
25,000.00

Ending balance *

Ending date *

Enter the service charge or interest earned, if necessary

Date | Service charge 0.00 | Expense account Account ▼

Date | Interest earned 0.00 | Income account Account ▼

Start reconciling

Figure 8.12 Partial view of the Reconcile—Checking form

DATE	TYPE	REF NO.	ACCOUNT	PAYEE	PAYMENT (USD)	DEPOSIT (USD)
01/12/2027	Deposit		Payments to deposit	Southtown Watersports		55,145.00
01/15/2027	Check	1008	- Split -	Donna Chandler	1,966.25	
01/15/2027	Check	1009	- Split -	Karen Vordale	1,132.56	
01/15/2027	Check	1010	- Split -	Ryder Zacovic	849.42	
01/18/2027	Bill Payment	1001	Accounts Payable (A/P)	Malibu Boats	56,000.00	
01/19/2027	Check	1002	Utilities:Phone service	Verizon	1,800.00	
01/20/2027	Check	1003	Equipment:Original Cost	Best Buy	8,000.00	
01/20/2027	Check	1004	Furniture:Original cost	Office Max	10,000.00	
01/21/2027	Deposit		Common stock	WB Investments		10,000.00
01/21/2027	Check	1005	Investments	Scottrade	3,000.00	
01/22/2027	Check	1006	Retained Earnings	Shareholders	1,500.00	
01/23/2027	Deposit		Long-term business lo...	Chase Bank		150,000.00
01/23/2027	Check	1007	- Split -	Chase Bank	52,500.00	
01/31/2027	Check	1011	- Split -	Ryder Zacovic	891.89	
01/31/2027	Check	1012	- Split -	Karen Vordale	1,179.75	
01/31/2027	Check	1013	- Split -	Donna Chandler	1,966.25	

8. After a review of the company's most recent bank statement and a comparison with the company's checking account, you discover appear on the bank statement. Click the **Payments** tab. Place a check next to all checks and payments *except* for checks 1011, 1012, and 1013, none of which had cleared the bank.

9 After a review of the company's most recent bank statement and a comparison with the company's checking account, you discover that all deposits and other credits recorded in the checking account appear on the bank statement. Click the **Deposits** tab. Place a check next to all deposits and other credits.

10 Click the **All** tab. Your account is reconciled as shown by the 0 difference between the Statement Ending Balance and the Cleared Balance as shown in Figure 8.13.

Figure 8.13 Reconcile—Checking form (reconciled account)

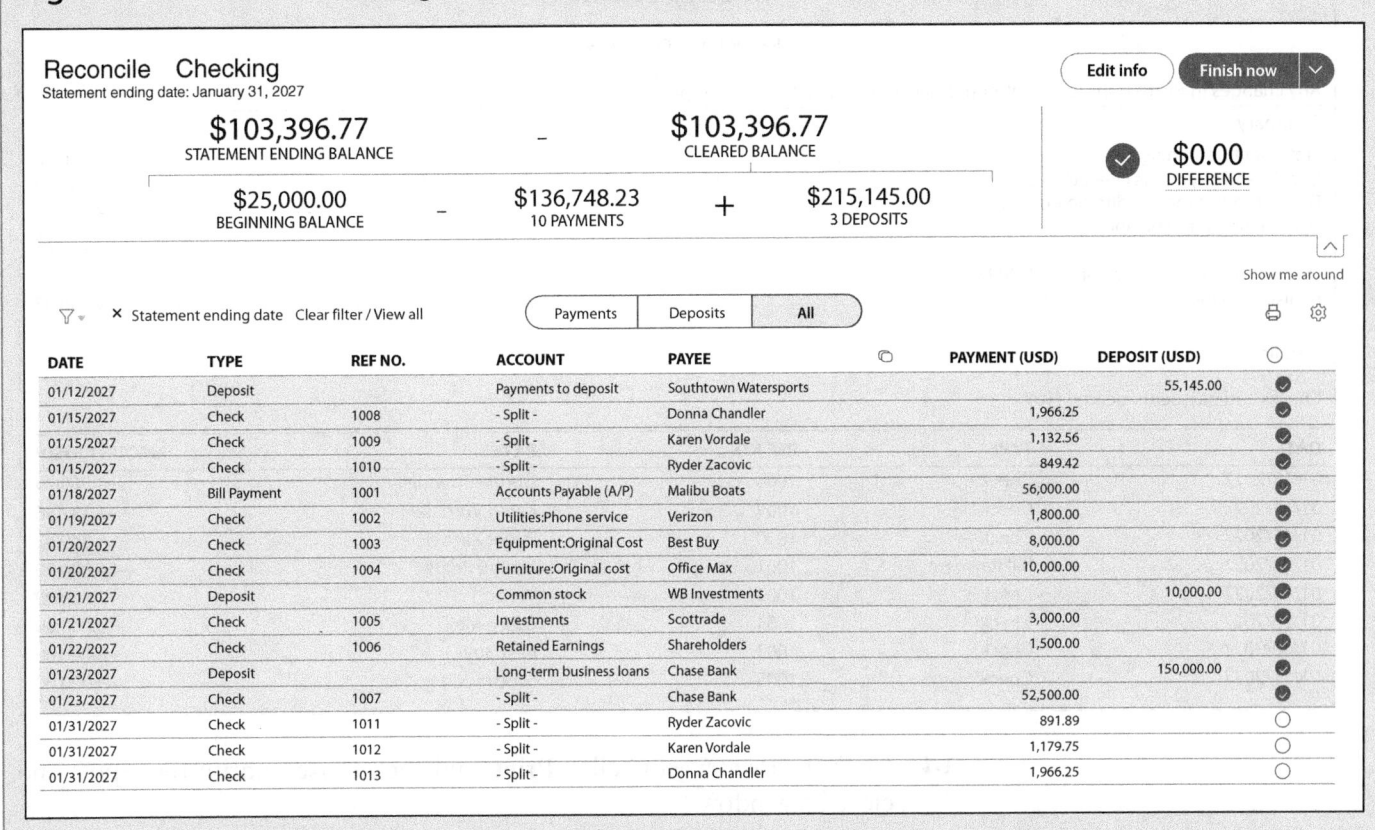

DATE	TYPE	REF NO.	ACCOUNT	PAYEE	PAYMENT (USD)	DEPOSIT (USD)
01/12/2027	Deposit		Payments to deposit	Southtown Watersports		55,145.00
01/15/2027	Check	1008	- Split -	Donna Chandler	1,966.25	
01/15/2027	Check	1009	- Split -	Karen Vordale	1,132.56	
01/15/2027	Check	1010	- Split -	Ryder Zacovic	849.42	
01/18/2027	Bill Payment	1001	Accounts Payable (A/P)	Malibu Boats	56,000.00	
01/19/2027	Check	1002	Utilities:Phone service	Verizon	1,800.00	
01/20/2027	Check	1003	Equipment:Original Cost	Best Buy	8,000.00	
01/20/2027	Check	1004	Furniture:Original cost	Office Max	10,000.00	
01/21/2027	Deposit		Common stock	WB Investments		10,000.00
01/21/2027	Check	1005	Investments	Scottrade	3,000.00	
01/22/2027	Check	1006	Retained Earnings	Shareholders	1,500.00	
01/23/2027	Deposit		Long-term business loans	Chase Bank		150,000.00
01/23/2027	Check	1007	- Split -	Chase Bank	52,500.00	
01/31/2027	Check	1011	- Split -	Ryder Zacovic	891.89	
01/31/2027	Check	1012	- Split -	Karen Vordale	1,179.75	
01/31/2027	Check	1013	- Split -	Donna Chandler	1,966.25	

Statement ending date: January 31, 2027
Statement Ending Balance: $103,396.77
Cleared Balance: $103,396.77
Beginning Balance: $25,000.00
10 Payments: $136,748.23
3 Deposits: $215,145.00
Difference: $0.00

11 Once you have reconciled the checking account and the $0 difference is displayed, click **Finish now** and then click **Done**.

12 Click the text **History by account**. A summary of all reconciliation reports completed should appear as shown in Figure 8.14.

Figure 8.14 Reconcile (reconciliation summary)

History by account

Account: Checking
Report period: Since 365 Days Ago

STATEMENT ENDING D...	RECONCILED ON	ENDING BALANCE	CHANGES	AUTO ADJUSTMENT	STATEMENTS	ACTION
2027						
01/31/ 2027	12/07/2023	103,396.77	0.00		Attach	View report

13. Click **View report** to view the reconciliation report. Place a check in the **Hide additional information** check box. The upper summary portion of that report is shown in Figure 8.15.

Figure 8.15 Summary Reconciliation Report

Wild Water Sports - Student Name (ID Number)
Checking, Period Ending 01/31/2027

RECONCILIATION REPORT

Reconciled on: 12/07/2023

Reconciled by: Glenn Owen

Any changes made to transactions after this date aren't included in this report.

Summary	USD
Statement beginning balance	25,000.00
Checks and payments cleared (10)	−136,748.23
Deposits and other credits cleared (3)	215,145.00
Statement ending balance	103,396.77
Uncleared transactions as of 01/31/2027	−4,037.89
Register balance as of 01/31/2027	99,358.88

Details

Checks and payments cleared (10)

DATE	TYPE	REF NO.	PAYEE	AMOUNT (USD)
01/15/2027	Check	1008	Donna Chandler	−1,966.25
01/15/2027	Check	1009	Karen Vordale	−1,132.56
01/15/2027	Check	1010	Ryder Zacovic	−849.42
01/18/2027	Bill Payment	1001	Malibu Boats	−56,000.00
01/19/2027	Check	1002	Verizon	−1,800.00
01/20/2027	Check	1004	Office Max	−10,000.00
01/20/2027	Check	1003	Best Buy	−8,000.00
01/21/2027	Check	1005	Scottrade	−3,000.00

14. Click the **Printer** icon, click **Print**, and click **Close** to print the report and close its window.

End Note

In this chapter, you created a Profit and Loss budget for 12 months, prepared a Budget Overview report and Budget vs. Actual report, and reconciled your checking account. In the next chapter, you will work with adjusting journal entries.

practice

Chapter 8 Questions

1. What are the steps to create a Profit and Loss budget?
2. What value do budgets provide a business?
3. Why should a business reconcile a checking account?
4. Who should prepare a bank reconciliation?
5. Explain the difference between the Budget Overview report and the Budget vs. Actual report.
6. What button is used to replicate amounts across several months in the budget worksheet?
7. How do you know if you have correctly reconciled an account?
8. What are the steps to change a Budget Overview report from covering a year to covering just one month?
9. What should you do if you discover a deposit was recorded by the bank but not recorded in the checking account (determined to be an error in the checking account)?
10. What are the initial steps to begin a bank reconciliation?

Chapter 8 Matching

a. Budget Overview report   _____   Condenses a report
b. Budget vs. Actual report   _____   Do not appear on the bank statement
c. Deposits in transit   _____   Used to change report dates
d. Outstanding checks   _____   Includes only budget amounts
e. Collapse   _____   Usually appear as checks on the next bank statement
f. Customize   _____   Includes both budget and actual amounts

Chapter 8 Cases

The following cases require you to open the company you updated in Chapter 7. Each of the following cases continues throughout the text in a sequential manner. For example, if you are assigned Case 01, you will use the file you modified in this chapter in all following chapters. Each of the following cases is similar in concepts assessed but differs in amounts and transactions.

> **To reopen your company, do the following:**
> 1. Open your Internet browser.
> 2. Type **https://qbo.intuit.com** into your browser's address text box.
> 3. Type your user ID and password into the text boxes as you have done before.

Case 1

Now it is time to create a budget and reconcile a bank account. Based on what you learned in the text using the Wild Water Sports company, you are to make the following changes to the Case 1 company you modified in Chapter 7:

1 Add an invoice on 1/30/24 to customer: Blondie's Boards, terms: Net 30, for 4 Fred Rubbles, 7 Water Hogs, and 8 Rook 15 surfboards.

2 Add an invoice on 1/31/24 to a new customer: Surf Rider Foundation, terms: Net 30, for 100 hours of consulting.

3 Create a new budget titled "Budget 1." Be sure to select FY 2024 (Jan 2024–Dec 2024) from the Fiscal Year drop-down list in the new budget window. Enter the following budgeted amounts: sales: 40,000, services: 3,000, cost of goods sold: 23,500, interest expense: 600, payroll: 12,000, rent or lease: 2,500, travel: 500, and utilities: 200. Amounts provided should be input for each month of 2024.

4 Create and customize, save customization as Budget Overview Budget 1, print, and export to Excel a Budget Overview report for the month of January 2024. Your report should look like Figure 8.16.

Figure 8.16

Budget Overview (January 2024)

Case 1
BUDGET OVERVIEW: BUDGET 1 - FY24 P&L
January 2024

	TOTAL
Income	
Sales	40,000.00
Services	3,000.00
Total Income	**$43,000.00**
Cost of Goods Sold	
Cost of Goods Sold	23,500.00
Total Cost of Goods Sold	**$23,500.00**
Gross Profit	**$19,500.00**
Expenses	
Interest Expense	600.00
Payroll	12,000.00
Rent or Lease	2,500.00
Travel	500.00
Utilities	200.00
Total Expenses	**$15,800.00**
Net Operating Income	**$3,700.00**
Net Income	**$3,700.00**

5. Create and customize, save customization as Budget vs. Actual Budget 1, print, and export to Excel a Budget vs. Actuals report for the month of January 2024. Your report should look like Figure 8.17.

Figure 8.17 Budget vs. Actuals (January 2024)

Case 1
BUDGET VS. ACTUALS: BUDGET 1 - FY24 P&L
January 2024

	ACTUAL	BUDGET	OVER BUDGET	% OF BUDGET
Income				
Sales	17,180.00	40,000.00	−22,820.00	42.95 %
Services	2,670.00	3,000.00	−330.00	89.00 %
Total Income	$19,850.00	$43,000.00	$ −23,150.00	**46.16 %**
Cost of Goods Sold				
Cost of Goods Sold	10,400.00	23,500.00	−13,100.00	44.26 %
Total Cost of Goods Sold	$10,400.00	$23,500.00	$ −13,100.00	**44.26 %**
Gross Profit	$9,450.00	$19,500.00	$ −10,050.00	**48.46 %**
Expenses				
Interest Expense	600.00	600.00	0.00	100.00 %
Payroll	11,785.71	12,000.00	−214.29	98.21 %
Rent or Lease	2,500.00	2,500.00	0.00	100.00 %
Travel	1,800.00	500.00	1,300.00	360.00 %
Utilities	145.00	200.00	−55.00	72.50 %
Total Expenses	$16,830.71	$15,800.00	$1,030.71	**106.52 %**
Net Operating Income	$−7,380.71	$3,700.00	$ −11,080.71	**−199.48 %**
Net Income	$−7,380.71	$3,700.00	$ −11,080.71	**−199.48 %**

6. Open and print the custom report you created in the last chapter called Transaction Detail by Account.

7. Export your Transaction Detail by Account report to Excel, and save it with the file name Student Name (replace with your name) Ch 08 Case 01 Transaction Detail by Account.xlsx.

8 Reconcile your company's checking account. No service charges were incurred or interest earned. The ending bank statement balance on 1/31/24 was $29,202.37.

9 After a review of the company's most recent bank statement and a comparison with the company's checking account, you discover some checks and payments recorded in the checking account that did not appear on the bank statement. Place a check next to all checks and payments *except* for check 1009 to Ben Franklin for 3,113.22 and check 1010 to Betsy Ross for 1,149.87, neither of which had cleared the bank.

10 After a review of the company's most recent bank statement and a comparison with the company's checking account, you discover some deposits and other credits recorded in the checking account that did not appear on the bank statement. Place a check next to all deposits and other credits *except* for a deposit on 1/8/24 from Blondie's Boards for 1,300, which had not cleared the bank.

11 Print the resulting Reconciliation Report. Select **All dates** from the Report Period drop-down text box, then click **2024**, and then click **View Report** on the statement ending date 01/31/24 line.

12 Sign out of your company.

Case 2

Now it is time to create a budget and reconcile a bank account. Based on what you learned in the text using the Wild Water Sports company, you are to make the following changes to the Case 2 company you modified in Chapter 7:

1 Add an invoice on 1/30/25 to customer: Hagen's Toys, terms: Net 30, for 100 hours of custom painting.

2 Add an invoice on 1/31/25 to a new customer: Zack's RC, terms: Net 30, for 2 Sea Wind Carbon Sailboats and 2 Mystique RES.

3 Create a new budget titled "Budget 1." Be sure to select FY 2025 (Jan 2025–Dec 2025) from the Fiscal Year drop-down list in the new budget window. Enter the following budgeted amounts: sales: 10,000, services: 4,000, cost of goods sold: 5,000, advertising: 500, insurance: 425, interest expense: 300, meals and entertainment: 250, and payroll: 9,000. Amounts provided should be input for each month of 2025.

4 Create and customize, save customization as Budget Overview Budget 1, print, and export to Excel a Budget Overview report for the month of January 2025. Your report should look like Figure 8.18.

Figure 8.18

Budget Overview (January 2025)

Case 2
BUDGET OVERVIEW: BUDGET 1 - FY25 P&L
January 2025

	TOTAL
Income	
Sales	10,000.00
Services	4,000.00
Total Income	**$14,000.00**
Cost of Goods Sold	
Cost of Goods Sold	5,000.00
Total Cost of Goods Sold	**$5,000.00**
Gross Profit	**$9,000.00**
Expenses	
Advertising	500.00
Insurance	425.00
Interest Expense	300.00
Meals and Entertainment	250.00
Payroll	9,000.00
Total Expenses	**$10,475.00**
Net Operating Income	**$ −1,475.00**
Net Income	**$ −1,475.00**

5. Create and customize, save customization as Budget vs. Actuals Budget 1, print, and export to Excel a Budget vs. Actuals report for the month of January 2025. Your report should look like Figure 8.19.

6. Open and print the custom report you created in the last chapter called Transaction Detail by Account.

7. Export your Transaction Detail by Account report to Excel, and save it with the file name Student Name (replace with your name) Ch 08 Case 02 Transaction Detail by Account.xlsx.

8. Reconcile your company's checking account. No service charges were incurred or interest earned. The ending bank statement balance on 1/31/25 was $30,693.47.

Figure 8.19 Budget vs. Actuals (January 2025)

Case 2
BUDGET VS. ACTUALS: BUDGET 1 - FY25 P&L
January 2025

	TOTAL			
	ACTUAL	BUDGET	OVER BUDGET	% OF BUDGET
Income				
Sales	9,000.00	10,000.00	−1,000.00	90.00 %
Services	4,725.00	4,000.00	725.00	118.13 %
Total Income	**$13,725.00**	**$14,000.00**	**$ −275.00**	**98.04 %**
Cost of Goods Sold				
Cost of Goods Sold	4,910.00	5,000.00	−90.00	98.20 %
Total Cost of Goods Sold	**$4,910.00**	**$5,000.00**	**$ −90.00**	**98.20 %**
Gross Profit	**$8,815.00**	**$9,000.00**	**$ −185.00**	**97.94 %**
Expenses				
Advertising	500.00	500.00	0.00	100.00 %
Insurance	400.00	425.00	−25.00	94.12 %
Interest Expense	300.00	300.00	0.00	100.00 %
Meals and Entertainment	240.00	250.00	−10.00	96.00 %
Payroll	9,224.26	9,000.00	224.26	102.49 %
Total Expenses	**$10,664.26**	**$10,475.00**	**$189.26**	**101.81 %**
Net Operating Income	**$ −1,849.26**	**$ −1,475.00**	**$ −374.26**	**125.37 %**
Net Income	**$ −1,849.26**	**$ −1,475.00**	**$ −374.26**	**125.37 %**

9 After a review of the company's most recent bank statement and a comparison with the company's checking account, you discover some checks and payments recorded in the checking account that did not appear on the bank statement. Place a check next to all checks and payments *except* for check 1009 to Frank Benjamin for 2,359.50 and check 1010 to Sara Juarez for 973.29, neither of which had cleared the bank.

10 After a review of the company's most recent bank statement and a comparison with the company's checking account, you discover a deposit and other credit recorded in the checking account that did not appear on the bank statement. Place a check next to all deposits and other credits *except* for a deposit on 1/7/25 from Benson's RC for 4,500, which had not cleared the bank.

11 Print the resulting Reconciliation Report. Select **All dates** from the Report Period drop-down text box, then click **2025**, and then click **View Report** on the statement ending date 01/31/25 line.

12 Sign out of your company.

Case 3

Now it is time to create a budget and reconcile a bank account. Based on what you learned in the text using the Wild Water Sports company, you are to make the following changes to the Case 3 company you modified in Chapter 7:

1 Add the following bill and product received from Samsung, Inc. on 1/30/26, terms: Net 15, received 5 Samsung Galaxy 8 and 8 Samsung Note phones.

2 Add an invoice on 1/30/26 to a new taxable customer: Diamond Girl, Inc., terms: Net 30, for 4 Samsung Galaxy 8 and 5 Samsung Note phones and 6 hours of Phone Consulting. Click **See the math** to update sales tax amounts.

3 Add a payment received from GHO Marketing on 1/31/26 for $2,559.38, which was deposited the same day into the checking account.

4 Create a new budget titled "Budget 1." Be sure to select FY 2026 (Jan 2026–Dec 2026) from the Fiscal Year drop-down list in the new budget window. Enter the following budgeted amounts: sales of product income: 20,000, services: 1,000, cost of goods sold: 10,000, advertising & marketing: 1,000, insurance: 500, interest paid: 350, meals: 250, and payroll: 7,000. Amounts provided should be input for each month of 2026.

5 Create a Budget Overview report for January 2026. Customize your report to show accounts vs. totals. Save customization as Budget Overview. Your report should look like Figure 8.20.

6 Create a Budget vs. Actuals report for the month of January 2026. Customize and save your report to show accounts vs. totals without cents. Your report should look like Figure 8.21.

Figure 8.20 Budget Overview (January 2026)

Case 03 - Student Name (ID Number)	
Budget Overview: Budget 1 - FY26 P&L	
January 2026	
	TOTAL
▼ Income	
Sales of Product Income	20,000.00
Services	1,000.00
Total Income	**$21,000.00**
▼ Cost of Goods Sold	
Cost of goods sold	10,000.00
Total Cost of Goods Sold	**$10,000.00**
GROSS PROFIT	**$11,000.00**
▼ Expenses	
Advertising & marketing	1,000.00
Insurance	500.00
Interest paid	350.00
Meals	250.00
Payroll	7,000.00
Total Expenses	**$9,100.00**
NET OPERATING INCOME	**$1,900.00**
NET INCOME	**$1,900.00**

7. Reconcile your company's checking account. No service charges were incurred or interest earned. The ending bank statement balance on 1/31/26 was $51,669.82.

8. After a review of the company's most recent statement and a comparison with the company's checking account, you note that one check and one deposit that were recorded in the checking account did not appear on the bank statement. Place a check next to all checks and payments *except* for check 329 to Jedi Vu for 1,002.78 and the deposit from GHO Marketing for 2,559.38, which had not cleared the bank.

9. Print the resulting Reconciliation Report after hiding additional information.

10. Sign out of your company.

Figure 8.21 Budget vs. Actuals for January 2026

Case 03 - Student Name (ID Number)
Budget vs. Actuals: Budget 1 - FY26 P&L
January 2026

	ACTUAL	BUDGET	OVER BUDGET	% OF BUDGET
▼ Income				
Sales of Product Income	12,800	20,000	−7,200	64.00 %
Services	450	1,000	−550	45.00 %
Total Income	**$13,250**	**$21,000**	**$ −7,750**	**63.00 %**
▼ Cost of Goods Sold				
Cost of goods sold	9,150	10,000	−850	92.00 %
Total Cost of Goods Sold	**$9,150**	**$10,000**	**$ −850**	**92.00 %**
GROSS PROFIT	$4,100	$11,000	$ −6,900	37.00 %
▼ Expenses				
Advertising & marketing	1,300	1,000	300	130.00 %
Insurance	300	500	−200	60.00 %
Interest paid	300	350	−50	86.00 %
Meals	123	250	−127	49.00 %
Payroll	6,960	7,000	−40	99.00 %
Total Expenses	**$8,983**	**$9,100**	**$ −117**	**99.00 %**
NET OPERATING INCOME	$ −4,883	$1,900	$ −6,783	−257.00 %
NET INCOME	$ −4,883	$1,900	$ −6,783	−257.00 %

Case 4

Now it is time to create a budget and reconcile a bank account. Based on what you learned in the text using the Wild Water Sports company, you are to make the following changes to the Case 4 company you modified in Chapter 7:

1. Create a new budget titled "Budget 1." Be sure to select FY 2027 (Jan 2027–Dec 2027) from the Fiscal Year drop-down list in the new budget window. Enter the following budgeted amounts for 2027: sales: 50,000, sales of product income: 4,000, cost of goods sold: 1,500, advertising & marketing: 2,400, insurance: 2,000, interest paid: 300, payroll expense: 15,000, and repairs & maintenance: $500. Amounts provided should be input for each month of 2027.

2. Create, customize (save customization as Budget Overview), and print a Budget Overview report for the month of January 2027 without cents showing accounts vs. totals. Your report should look like Figure 8.22.

Figure 8.22 Budget Overview for January 2027

Case 04 - Student Name (ID Number)

Budget Overview: Budget 1 - FY27 P&L

January 2027

	TOTAL
▾ Income	
Sales	50,000
Sales of Product Income	4,000
Total Income	**$54,000**
▾ Cost of Goods Sold	
Cost of goods sold	1,500
Total Cost of Goods Sold	**$1,500**
GROSS PROFIT	$52,500
▾ Expenses	
Advertising & marketing	2,400
Insurance	2,000
Interest paid	300
Payroll expenses	15,000
Repairs & maintenance	500
Total Expenses	**$20,200**
NET OPERATING INCOME	$32,300
NET INCOME	$32,300

3. Create, customize (save customization as Budget vs. Actuals), and print a Budget vs. Actuals report for the month of January 2027 without cents showing accounts vs. totals. Your report should look like Figure 8.23.

4. Reconcile your company's checking account. No service charges were incurred or interest earned. The ending bank statement balance on 1/31/27 was $10,936.20.

5. After a review of the company's most recent statement and a comparison with the company's checking account, you note that a $10,000 deposit on 1/26/27 and checks 25509 and 25510 (for $1,376.37 and $1,522.67, respectively) had not cleared the bank.

6. Print the resulting Reconciliation Report (hide additional information).

7. Sign out of your company.

Figure 8.23 Budget vs. Actuals for January 2027

Case 04 - Student Name (ID Number)
Budget vs. Actuals: Budget 1 - FY27 P&L
January 2027

	TOTAL			
	ACTUAL	**BUDGET**	**OVER BUDGET**	**% OF BUDGET**
▼ Income				
Sales	48,400	50,000	−1,600	97.00 %
Sales of Product Income	3,570	4,000	−430	89.00 %
Total Income	**$51,970**	**$54,000**	**$ −2,030**	**96.00 %**
▼ Cost of Goods Sold				
Cost of goods sold	1,632	1,500	132	109.00 %
Total Cost of Goods Sold	**$1,632**	**$1,500**	**$132**	**109.00 %**
GROSS PROFIT	$50,338	$52,500	$ −2,162	96.00 %
▼ Expenses				
Advertising & marketing	1,800	2,400	−600	75.00 %
Insurance	2,400	2,000	400	120.00 %
Interest paid	120	300	−180	40.00 %
Payroll expenses	14,680	15,000	−320	98.00 %
Repairs & maintenance	750	500	250	150.00 %
Total Expenses	**$19,750**	**$20,200**	**$ −450**	**98.00 %**
NET OPERATING INCOME	$30,588	$32,300	$ −1,712	95.00 %
NET INCOME	$30,588	$32,300	$ −1,712	95.00 %

Case 5

Now it is time to create a budget and reconcile a bank account. Based on what you learned in the text using the Wild Water Sports company, you are to make the following changes to the Case 5 company you modified in Chapter 7:

1. Create a new budget titled "Budget 1." Be sure to select FY 2028 (Jan 2028–Dec 2028) from the Fiscal Year drop-down list in the new budget window. Enter the following budgeted amounts for January 2028: consulting: 75,000, sales: 500,000, training: 4,000, cost of goods sold: 250,000, advertising & marketing: 3,500, equipment rental: 8,000, insurance: 6,000, interest expense: 4,000, payroll: 30,000, recruiting: 4,000, and repairs & maintenance: $2,500. Amounts provided should be copied for each month of 2028.

2. Create, customize (save customization as Budget Overview), and print a Budget Overview report for the month of January 2028 without cents showing accounts vs. totals. Your report should look like Figure 8.24.

3. Create, customize (save customization as Budget vs. Actuals), and print a Budget vs. Actuals report for the month of January 2028 without cents showing accounts vs. totals. Your report should look like Figure 8.25.

4. Reconcile your company's checking account. No service charges were incurred or interest earned. The ending bank statement balance on 1/31/28 was $194,109.76.

Figure 8.24 Budget Overview for January 2028

Case 05 - Student Name (ID Number)
Budget Overview: Budget 1 - FY28 P&L
January 2028

	TOTAL
▼ Income	
Consulting	75,000
Sales	500,000
Training	4,000
Total Income	**$579,000**
▼ Cost of Goods Sold	
Cost of goods sold	250,000
Total Cost of Goods Sold	**$250,000**
GROSS PROFIT	$329,000
▼ Expenses	
Advertising & marketing	3,500
Equipment rental	8,000
Insurance	6,000
Interest Expense	4,000
Payroll expenses	30,000
Recruiting	4,000
Repairs & maintenance	2,500
Total Expenses	**$58,000**
NET OPERATING INCOME	$271,000
NET INCOME	$271,000

Figure 8.25 Budget vs. Actuals for January 2028

Case 05 - Student Name (ID Number)
Budget vs. Actuals: Budget 1 - FY28 P&L
January 2028

	TOTAL			
	ACTUAL	BUDGET	OVER BUDGET	% OF BUDGET
▼ Income				
Consulting	79,500	75,500	4,500	106.00 %
Sales	615,000	500,000	115,000	123.00 %
Training	3,500	4,000	−500	88.00 %
Total Income	**$698,000**	**$579,000**	**$119,000**	**121.00 %**
▼ Cost of Goods Sold				
Cost of goods sold	298,000	250,000	48,000	119.00 %
Total Cost of Goods Sold	**$298,000**	**$250,000**	**$48,000**	**119.00 %**
GROSS PROFIT	**$400,000**	**$329,000**	**$71,000**	**122.00 %**
▼ Expenses				
Advertising & marketing	3,000	3,500	−500	86.00 %
Equipment rental	7,500	8,000	−500	94.00 %
Insurance		6,000	−6,000	
Interest Expense	3,000	4,000	−1,000	75.00 %
Payroll expenses	26,859	30,000	−3,141	90.00 %
Recruiting	6,300	4,000	2,300	158.00 %
Repairs & maintenance		2,500	−2,500	
Total Expenses	**$46,659**	**$58,000**	**$ −11,341**	**80.00 %**
NET OPERATING INCOME	$353,341	$271,000	$82,341	130.00 %
NET INCOME	$353,341	$271,000	$82,341	130.00 %

5. After a review of the company's most recent statement and a comparison with the company's checking account, you note that a $80,000 deposit on 1/26/28 and all checks written on 1/31/28 had not cleared the bank.

6. Print the resulting Reconciliation Report. Select **All dates** from the Report Period drop-down text box, then click **2028**, and then click **View Report** on the statement ending date 01/31/28 line. A partial view of that report should look like Figure 8.26.

7. Sign out of your company.

Figure 8.26 Bank Reconciliation as of 1/31/28 (partial view)

```
                        Case 05 - Student Name (ID Number)
                         Checking, Period Ending 01/31/2028

                              RECONCILIATION REPORT

                              Reconciled on: 12/15/2023

                              Reconciled by: Glenn Owen
```

Any changes made to transactions after this date aren't included in this report.

Summary   USD
Statement beginning balance..30,000.00
Checks and payments cleared (8)..–115,390.24
Deposits and other credits cleared (3)..279,500.00
Statement ending balance..194,109.76

Uncleared transactions as of 01/31/2028..42,686.06
Register balance as of 01/31/2028...236,795.82

Details

Checks and payments cleared (8)

Case 6

Now it is time to create a budget and reconcile a bank account. Based on what you learned in the text using the Wild Water Sports company, you are to make the following changes to the Case 6 company you modified in Chapter 7:

1. Create a new budget titled "Budget 1." Be sure to select FY 2023 (Jan 2023–Dec 2023) from the Fiscal Year drop-down list in the new budget window. Enter the following budgeted amounts for 2023: sales: 10,000, sales of product income: 300,000, cost of goods sold: 230,000, advertising & marketing: 15,000, contractors: 2,000, insurance: 3,000, interest expense: 500, payroll: 20,000, repairs: 500, and depreciation: 1,000. Amounts provided should be input for each month of 2023.

2. Create, customize (save customization as Budget Overview), and print a Budget Overview report for the month of January 2023 without cents showing accounts vs. totals. Your report should look like Figure 8.27.

3. Create, customize (save customization as Budget vs. Actuals), and print a Budget vs. Actuals report for the month of January 2023 without cents showing accounts vs. totals. Your report should look like Figure 8.28.

4. Reconcile your company's checking account. No service charges were incurred or interest earned. The ending bank statement balance on 1/31/23 was $65,196.03.

Figure 8.27 Budget Overview for January 2023

Case 06 - Student Name (ID Number)

BUDGET OVERVIEW: BUDGET 1 - FY23 P&L

January 2023

	TOTAL
▼ Income	
Sales	10,000
Sales of Product Income	300,000
Total Income	**$310,000**
▼ Cost of Goods Sold	
Cost of Goods Sold	230,000
Total Cost of Goods Sold	**$230,000**
GROSS PROFIT	$80,000
▼ Expenses	
Advertising & Marketing	15,000
Contractors	2,000
Insurance	3,000
Interest Expense	500
Payroll	20,000
Repairs	500
Total Expenses	**$41,000**
NET OPERATING INCOME	$39,000
▼ Other Expenses	
Depreciation	1,000
Total Other Expenses	**$1,000**
NET OTHER INCOME	$ −1,000
NET INCOME	$38,000

Figure 8.28 Budget vs. Actuals for January 2023

Case 06 - Student Name (ID Number)

BUDGET VS. ACTUALS: BUDGET 1 - FY23 P&L
January 2023

	TOTAL			
	ACTUAL	BUDGET	OVER BUDGET	% OF BUDGET
▼ Income				
Sales		10,000	−10,000	
Sales of Product Income	290,000	300,000	−10,000	97.00 %
Total Income	**$290,000**	**$310,000**	**$ −20,000**	**94.00 %**
▼ Cost of Goods Sold				
Cost of Goods Sold	232,000	230,000	2,000	101.00 %
Total Cost of Goods Sold	**$232,000**	**$230,000**	**$2,000**	**101.00 %**
GROSS PROFIT	**$58,000**	**$80,000**	**$ −22,000**	**73.00 %**
▼ Expenses				
Advertising & Marketing	14,000	15,000	−1,000	93.00 %
Contractors	1,800	2,000	−200	90.00 %
Insurance		3,000	−3,000	
Interest Expense	400	500	−100	80.00 %
Payroll	18,848	20,000	−1,152	94.00 %
Repairs		500	−500	
Total Expenses	**$35,048**	**$41,000**	**$ −5,952**	**85.00 %**
NET OPERATING INCOME	**$22,952**	**$39,000**	**$ −16,048**	**59.00 %**
▼ Other Expenses				
Depreciation		1,000	−1,000	
Total Other Expenses	**$0**	**$1,000**	**$ −1,000**	**0%**
NET OTHER INCOME	**$0**	**$ −1,000**	**$1,000**	**0.00 %**
NET INCOME	**$22,952**	**$38,000**	**$ −15,048**	**60.00 %**

5   After a review of the company's most recent statement and a comparison with the company's checking account, you note that a $10,000 deposit on 1/26/23 and checks 593, 594, 598, 599, and 600 had not cleared the bank.

6   Print the resulting Reconciliation Report.

7   Sign out of your company.

Analysis and Recording of Adjusting Entries

Student Learning Outcomes

Upon completion of this chapter, the student will be able to do the following:

- Prepare an unadjusted trial balance
- Make adjusting entries for the following:
    - Prepaid expenses
    - Accrued expenses
    - Unearned revenue
    - Accrued revenue
    - Depreciation

Overview

In Chapter 8 you added a budget, a Profit and Loss budget report, and a bank reconciliation to your Wild Water Sports company. In this chapter, you will add adjusting journal entries. At the end of this chapter, you will perform the similar tasks on the case assigned by your instructor.

Prior to the creation of periodic financial statements, generally accepted accounting principles (GAAP) require that accounting records be adjusted to reflect accrual accounting. This process ensures revenues are recorded in the period in which they are earned and that expenses are recorded in the period in which they were consumed. In the process, expenses will be matched in the same period to the revenues generated from incurring those expenses.

There are five types of adjusting entries. Expenses paid, prior to being consumed, should be deferred (supplies, rent, insurance, etc.) and recorded as assets (supplies asset, prepaid rent, prepaid insurance, etc.) until they are consumed. To defer is to postpone. Expenses incurred prior to being paid (payroll, rent, utilities, etc.) must be recorded and accrued as a liability. To accrue is to increase. Revenue collected prior to being earned must be deferred (sales, services, etc.) and recorded as liabilities (unearned revenue, etc.) until they are earned. Revenues earned prior to being collected (sales and services, etc.) must be recorded and accrued as a receivable. Lastly, fixed assets (buildings, furniture, equipment, vehicles, etc.) must be depreciated over their useful life to match costs with revenues.

Trial Balance

In this section, you will create a trial balance (before adjusting entries), which must be analyzed in light of end of the period business events to determine the required adjusting entries.

To create a trial balance for the Wild Water Sports company, do the following:

1. Open your Internet browser.
2. Open your QBO account and the Wild Water Sports company like you've done in previous chapters.
3. Click **Reports** from the navigation bar.
4. Click the **Custom reports** tab and then click **Trial Balance** shown in Figure 9.1.

Figure 9.1 Trial Balance report

Wild Water Sports - Student Name (ID Number)
Trial Balance
As of January 31, 2027

	DEBIT	CREDIT
Checking	99,358.88	
Accounts receivable (A/R)	120,770.00	
Inventory	223,350.00	
Payments to deposit	70,000.00	
Prepaid expenses	17,500.00	
Equipment:Accumulated depreciation		10,000.00
Equipment:Original Cost	53,000.00	
Furniture:Original cost	10,000.00	
Investments	3,000.00	
Accounts Payable (A/P)		190,250.00
Mastercard		1,600.00
Florida Department of Revenue Payable		9,915.00
Payroll wages and tax to pay		2,944.66
Long-term business loans		155,000.00
Common stock		11,000.00
Opening balance equity		0.00
Retained Earnings		204,300.00
Sales		164,000.00
Service Revenue		2,000.00
Cost of goods sold	131,200.00	
Interest paid	2,500.00	
Payroll expenses	10,930.78	
Rent:Equipment rental	6,000.00	
Utilities:Phone service	1,800.00	
Vehicle expenses:Vehicle gas & fuel	1,600.00	
TOTAL	$751,009.66	$751,009.66

Analysis and Recording of Adjusting Entries **Chapter 9** **249**

Adjusting Journal Entries: Prepaid Expenses

Further investigation of this trial balance and period end business activities indicates that $500 of Vehicle gas & fuel were recorded as an expense but should have been deferred as a supplies asset until consumed in some future period. Thus, an adjusting entry is necessary.

To record an adjusting entry for supplies in the Wild Water Sports company, do the following:

1. Continue from where you left off.
2. Click the **+ New** icon and then click **Journal Entry**.
3. Type **1/31/27** as the Journal date, then accept 6 as the Journal no.
4. Type **Supplies asset** on line 1 of the Account column, and click **+ Add new Supplies asset** as shown in Figure 9.2. (This is another way to add a new account in QBO.)

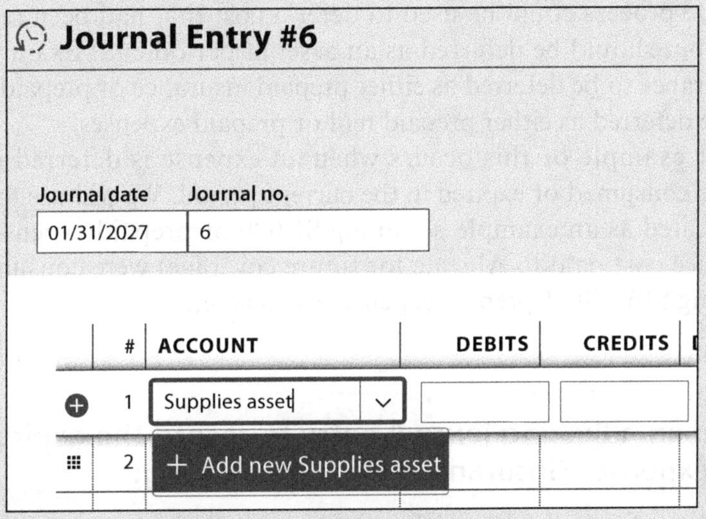

Figure 9.2

Journal Entry (adding a new account)

5. Select **Other Current Assets** from the drop-down list in the Account Type text box.
6. Select **Other Current Assets** from the drop-down list in the Detail Type text box.
7. Click **Save and close**.
8. Type **500** into the Debits column of line 1.
9. Select **Vehicle gas & fuel** from the drop-down list in line 2 of the Accounts column.
10. Accept **500** into the Credits column of line 2 and then press **[Tab]** to view the journal entry as shown in Figure 9.3.

Figure 9.3

Journal Entry #6 (to defer supplies)

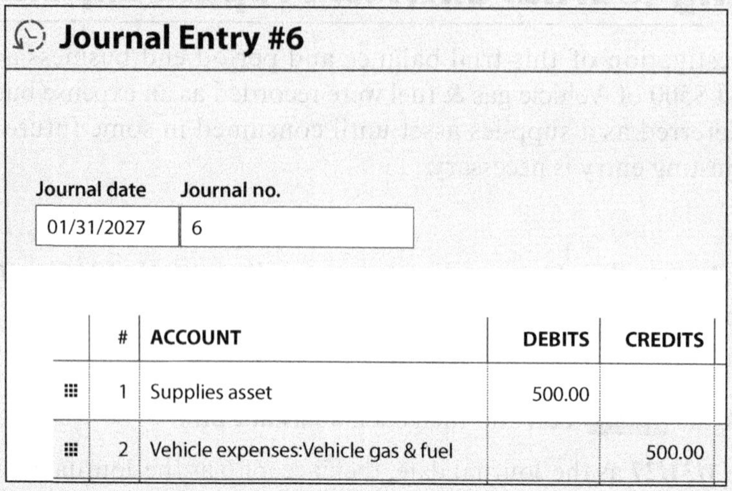

Journal Entry #6

Journal date: 01/31/2027
Journal no.: 6

#	ACCOUNT	DEBITS	CREDITS
1	Supplies asset	500.00	
2	Vehicle expenses:Vehicle gas & fuel		500.00

11 Click **Save and close**.

The same process could be used to defer a cost that had been recorded as an expense but should be deferred as an asset at period end. Examples might include insurance to be deferred as either prepaid insurance or prepaid expenses, or rent to be deferred as either prepaid rent or prepaid expenses.

Another example of this occurs when an expense is deferred in a prior period but is consumed or expired in the current period. We will use the Prepaid expenses created as an example assuming $1,000 of prepaid expenses (in this case insurance cost paid to Allstate for future coverage) were consumed in the month leaving $16,500 of prepaid expenses as an asset.

To record an adjusting journal entry to record the expiration of prepaid expenses (insurance), do the following:

1 Continue from where you left off.

2 Click the ⊕ New icon and then click **Journal Entry**.

3 Accept **1/31/27** as the Journal date and **7** as the Journal no.

4 Select **Insurance** from the drop-down list in line 1 of the Account column. (This is an expense account already in the Company's chart of accounts.)

5 Type **1000** into the Debits column of line 1.

6 Select **Prepaid expenses** from the drop-down list in line 2 of the Accounts column.

7 Accept **1000** into the Credits column of line 2 to view the journal entry as shown in Figure 9.4.

8 Click **Save and close**.

Analysis and Recording of Adjusting Entries Chapter 9 251

Journal Entry #7

Journal date: 01/31/2027

Journal no.: 7

#	ACCOUNT	DEBITS	CREDITS
1	Insurance	1,000.00	
2	Prepaid expenses		1,000.00

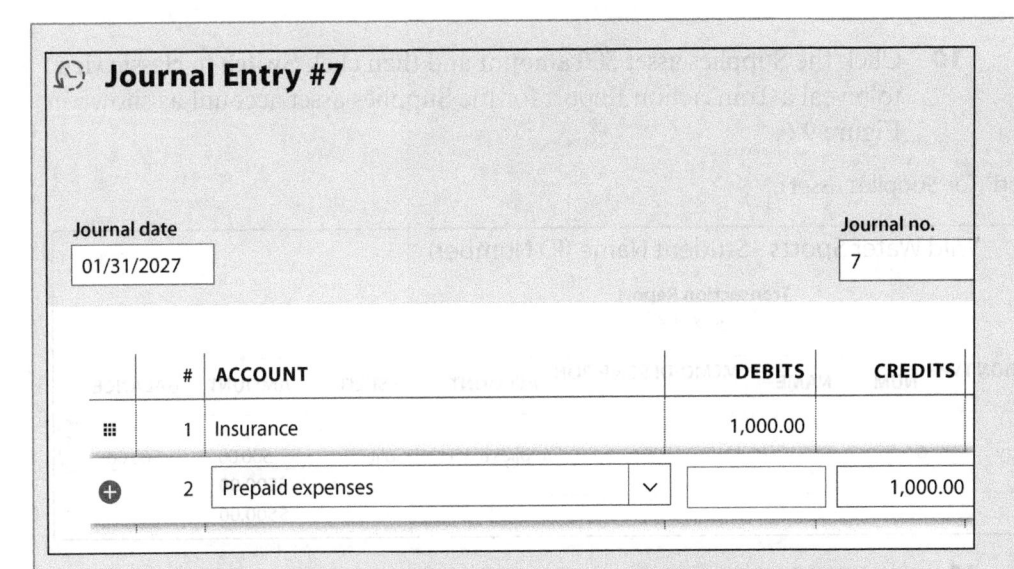

Figure 9.4

Journal Entry (recording the expiration of insurance)

9 Closing the journal entry should reveal the trial balance created before. The trial balance has now been updated to reflect the supplies asset account as shown in Figure 9.5.

Wild Water Sports - Student Name (ID Number)
Trial Balance
As of January 31, 2027

	DEBIT	CREDIT
Checking	99,358.88	
Accounts receivable (A/R)	120,770.00	
Inventory	223,350.00	
Payments to deposit	70,000.00	
Prepaid expenses	16,500.00	
Supplies asset	500.00	
Equipment:Accumulated depreciation		10,000.00
Equipment:Original Cost	53,000.00	
Furniture:Original cost	10,000.00	
Investments	3,000.00	
Accounts Payable (A/P)		190,250.00
Mastercard		1,600.00
Florida Department of Revenue Payable		9,915.00
Payroll wages and tax to pay		2,944.66
Long-term business loans		155,000.00
Common stock		11,000.00
Opening balance equity		0.00
Retained Earnings		204,300.00
Sales		164,000.00
Service Revenue		2,000.00
Cost of goods sold	131,200.00	
Insurance	1,000.00	
Interest paid	2,500.00	
Payroll expenses	10,930.78	
Rent:Equipment rental	6,000.00	
Utilities:Phone service	1,800.00	
Vehicle expenses:Vehicle gas & fuel	1,100.00	
TOTAL	**$751,009.66**	**$751,009.66**

Figure 9.5

Trial Balance after adjustments

> **10** Click the Supplies asset **500** amount and then click **Switch to classic view** to reveal a Transaction Report for the Supplies asset account as shown in Figure 9.6.

Figure 9.6 Transaction Report (for Supplies asset)

\multicolumn{9}{c}{**Wild Water Sports - Student Name (ID Number)**}
\multicolumn{9}{c}{**Transaction Report**}
\multicolumn{9}{c}{January 2027}
DATE	TRANSACTION TYPE	NUM	NAME	MEMO/DESCRIPTION	ACCOUNT	SPLIT	AMOUNT	BALANCE
▾ Supplies asset								
01/31/2027	Journal Entry	6			Supplies asset	-Split-	500.00	500.00
Total for Supplies asset							$500.00	
TOTAL							$500.00	

> **11** Click **Back to report summary** to return to the Trial Balance report. Click the Prepaid expenses **16,500** amount to reveal a Transaction Report for the Prepaid expense account.

The first entry deferred $500 from Vehicle expense; the second entry recorded the expiration of insurance reducing the Prepaid expenses account.

Adjusting Journal Entries: Accrued Expenses

Further investigation of this trial balance and period end business activities indicates that a bill for $2,500 was received and recorded in the next month for advertising consumed in the current month. Thus, an adjusting journal entry needs to be made to accrue this expense. For our purposes, we will create a new accrued liabilities account to keep track of these accruals and keep them separate from accounts payable.

> **To record an adjusting journal entry to record the accrual of advertising expense, do the following:**
>
> **1** Continue from where you left off.
>
> **2** Click the [+ New] icon and then click **Journal Entry**.
>
> **3** Accept **1/31/27** as the Journal date and **8** as the Journal no.
>
> **4** Select **Advertising & Marketing** from the drop-down list in line 1 of the Account column.
>
> **5** Type **2500** into the Debits column of line 1.
>
> **6** Type **Accrued liabilities** on line 2 of the Account column and then click **+ Add new Accrued liabilities**.
>
> **7** Select **Other Current Liabilities** from the drop-down list in the Account Type text box.

8   Select **Other Current Liabilities** from the drop-down list in the Detail Type text box.

9   Click **Save and close**.

10 Accept **2,500** into the Credits column of line 2 to view the journal entry as shown in Figure 9.7.

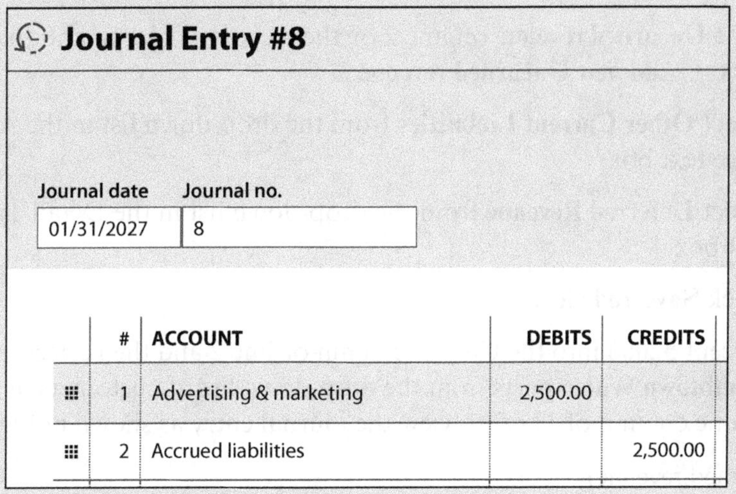

Figure 9.7
Journal Entry (accruing advertising & marketing expense)

Journal Entry #8

Journal date: 01/31/2027
Journal no.: 8

#	ACCOUNT	DEBITS	CREDITS
1	Advertising & marketing	2,500.00	
2	Accrued liabilities		2,500.00

11 Click **Save and close**.

12 Closing the journal entry should reveal the trial balance created before, but now updated to reflect the accrual of advertising & marketing expense to the accrued liabilities account.

13 Click the Accrued liabilities **2,500** amount to reveal a Transaction Report showing Journal entry 8.

14 Click **Back to report summary** or **Back** to return to the Trial Balance report.

Adjusting Journal Entries: Unearned Revenue

Further investigation of this trial balance and period end business activities indicates that the sale of a boat recorded on sales receipt #1001 for $55,145 to Southtown Watersports had not been delivered even though cash had been received. Thus, the revenue had not been earned. Delivery is expected to occur next month; thus, this amount of revenue and related sales tax must be deferred and set up as an unearned revenue liability.

To record an adjusting journal entry to reflect unearned revenue, do the following:

1   Continue from where you left off. From the Trial Balance as of 1/31/27 click the Sales amount **164,000** then click sales receipt **1001**. Note that this receipt recorded cash received of $55,145, sales of $52,000, and sales tax payable of $3,145. Now close this sales receipt.

2   Click the **+ New** icon and then click **Journal Entry**.

3. Accept **1/31/27** as the Journal date and **9** as the Journal no.
4. Select **Sales** from the drop-down list in line 1 of the Account column.
5. Type **52000** into the Debits column of line 1.
6. Select **Southtown Watersports** from the drop-down list of customers in the Name column of line 1.
7. Type **Unearned revenue** on line 2 of the Account column and then click **+ Add new Unearned revenue**.
8. Select **Other Current Liabilities** from the drop-down list in the Account Type text box.
9. Select **Deferred Revenue** from the drop-down list in the Detail Type text box.
10. Click **Save and close**.
11. Accept **52000** into the Credits column of line 2 and then select **Southtown Watersports** from the drop-down list of customers in the Name column of line 2 to view the journal entry as shown in Figure 9.8.

Figure 9.8 Journal Entry (recording unearned revenue)

Journal Entry #9

Journal date: 01/31/2027
Journal no.: 9

#	ACCOUNT	DEBITS	CREDITS	DESCRIPTION	NAME
1	Sales	52,000.00			Southtown Watersports
2	Unearned revenue		52,000.00		Southtown Watersports

12. Click **Save and close**.
13. Closing the journal entry should reveal the trial balance created before, but updated to reflect the deferral of revenue to the unearned revenue liability account.
14. Click the Unearned revenue **52,000.00** amount to reveal a Transaction Report.
15. Click **Back to report summary** or **Back** to return to the Trial Balance report.

Adjusting Journal Entries: Accruing Revenue

Further investigation of this trial balance and period end business activities indicates that a Tige 25 zx boat was sold and delivered to a new customer High Flyer Sports on 1/31/27 on net 30 terms, but not invoiced until the next month. Sales tax on that sale amounted to $13,525 and the boat was sold for $225,000. Thus, you will need to record an adjusting journal entry to accrue revenue and an accrued receivable.

To record an adjusting journal entry to reflect earned revenue, do the following:

1. Continue from where you left off.
2. Click the **+ New** icon and then click **Journal Entry**.
3. Accept **1/31/27** as the Journal date and **10** as the Journal no.
4. Type **Accrued receivable** on line 1 of the Account column and then click **+ Add new Accrued receivable**.
5. Select **Other Current Assets** from the drop-down list in the Account Type text box.
6. Select **Other Current Assets** from the drop-down list in the Detail Type text box.
7. Click **Save and close**.
8. Type **238525** into the Debits column of line 1.
9. Type **High Flyer Sports** in the Name column of line 1. Add this as a new customer.
10. Select **Sales** from the drop-down list in line 2 of the Account column.
11. Type **225000** in the Credits column of line 2.
12. Select **High Flyer Sports** from the drop-down list of customers in the Name column of line 2.
13. Select **Sales tax to pay** from the drop-down list in line 3 of the Account column.
14. Type **13525** in the Credits column of line 3.
15. Select **High Flyer Sports** from the drop-down list in line 3 of the Name column. Your journal should look like Figure 9.9.
16. Click **Save and close**.
17. Closing the journal entry should reveal the trial balance created before but updated to reflect the accrual of revenue to the accrued receivable account.

Figure 9.9 Journal Entry (recording accrued revenue)

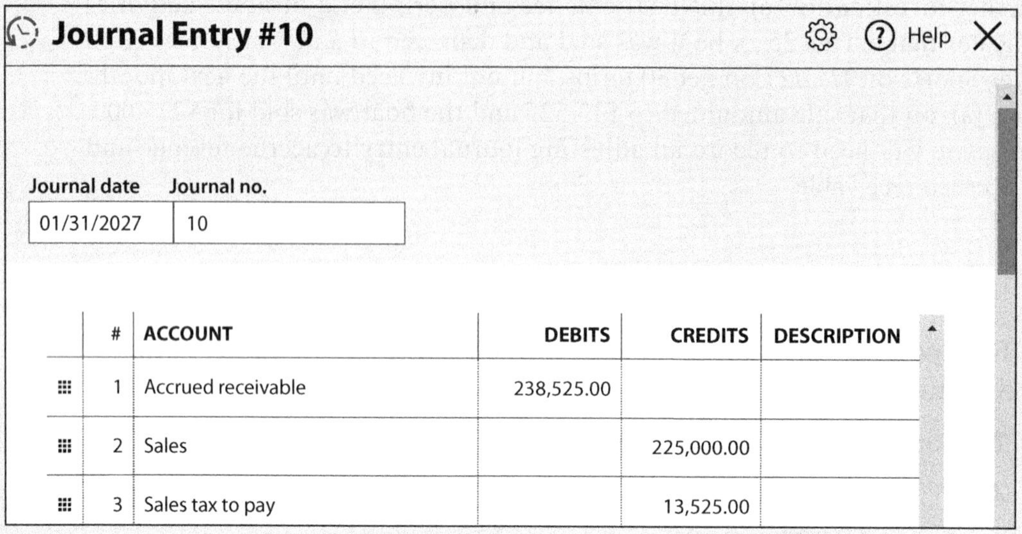

Journal Entry #10

Journal date: 01/31/2027
Journal no.: 10

#	ACCOUNT	DEBITS	CREDITS	DESCRIPTION
1	Accrued receivable	238,525.00		
2	Sales		225,000.00	
3	Sales tax to pay		13,525.00	

18 Click the Accrued Receivable **238,525** amount to reveal a Transaction Report.

19 Click **Back to report summary** or **Back** to return to the Trial Balance report.

Adjusting Journal Entries: Depreciation

Further investigation of this trial balance and period end business activities indicates the company's fixed assets need to be depreciated for the month. Monthly depreciation for equipment and furniture is $1,000 and $250, respectively. Normally, the adjusting entry would debit depreciation expense and credit accumulated depreciation. However, the accounts set up in the chart of accounts need to be edited. Thus, you decide to change the account names first and then record the depreciation adjusting journal entry.

To edit account names and then record an adjusting journal entry to record depreciation, do the following:

1 Continue from where you left off.

2 Click the **Gear** and then click **Chart of Accounts**.

3 Click **Edit** from the drop-down arrow next to the words View Register on the Depreciation line listed under the Furniture account.

4 Type **Accumulated** *in front* of Depreciation in the Account name text box and then click **Save**.

5 Scroll down to the bottom of the chart of accounts and select **Edit** from the drop-down arrow next to the words Run report on the Depreciation line.

6. Type **expense** *after* Depreciation in the Account name text box and then click **Save**.
7. Click the [+ New] icon and then click **Journal Entry**.
8. Type **1/31/2027** in the journal date text box and accept 11 as the journal no.
9. Select **Depreciation expense** from the drop-down list in line 1 of the Account column.
10. Type **1250** into the Debits column of line 1.
11. Select **Accumulated depreciation** listed as the Sub-account of the Equipment account from the drop-down list in line 2 of the Account column.
12. Type **1000** as the Credits column amount.
13. Select **Furniture: Accumulated Depreciation** from the drop-down list in line 3 of the Account column.
14. Accept **250** as the Credits column amount. Your screen should look like Figure 9.10.

Figure 9.10 Journal Entry (recording depreciation)

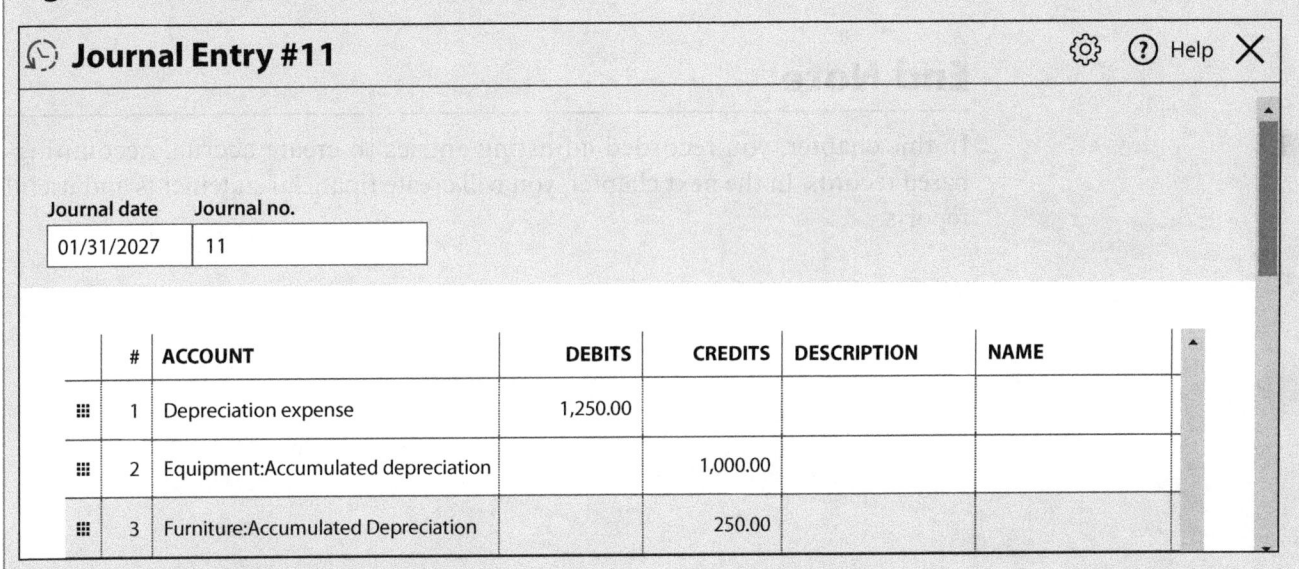

Journal Entry #11

Journal date: 01/31/2027
Journal no.: 11

#	ACCOUNT	DEBITS	CREDITS	DESCRIPTION	NAME
1	Depreciation expense	1,250.00			
2	Equipment:Accumulated depreciation		1,000.00		
3	Furniture:Accumulated Depreciation		250.00		

15. Click **Save and close**.
16. Click **Reports** from the navigation bar, then click the **Custom reports** tab, and then select **Trial Balance** to view the trial balance shown in Figure 9.11.

Figure 9.11

Revised Trial Balance report (partial view)

Wild Water Sports - Student Name (ID Number)
Trial Balance
As of January 31, 2027

Checking	99,358.88	
Accounts receivable (A/R)	120,770.00	
Accrued receivable	238,525.00	
Inventory	223,350.00	
Payments to deposit	70,000.00	
Prepaid expenses	16,500.00	
Supplies asset	500.00	
Equipment:Accumulated depreciation		11,000.00
Equipment:Original Cost	53,000.00	
Furniture:Accumulated Depreciation		250.00
Furniture:Original cost	10,000.00	
Investments	3,000.00	
Accounts Payable (A/P)		190,250.00

End Note

In this chapter, you recorded adjusting entries to create accrual accounting-based records. In the next chapter, you will create financial statements and useful reports.

Chapter 9 Questions

1. What is an unadjusted trial balance?
2. What is an adjusted trial balance?
3. Why accrue an expense?
4. Why defer an expense?
5. Why accrue revenues?
6. Why defer revenues?
7. What QBO task is used to record accruals and deferrals?
8. Why depreciate a fixed asset?
9. Describe the new method you learned in this chapter to add a new account from within a journal entry.
10. Describe the method you learned in this chapter to add a customer to a transaction within a journal entry.

Chapter 9 Matching

a. Prepaid Expenses   _____ Debit this account when recording depreciation
b. Accrue   _____ Credit this account when accruing an expense
c. Unearned Revenue   _____ Debit this account when accruing revenue
d. Defer   _____ Supplies consumed
e. Depreciation Expense   _____ Credit this account when recording depreciation
f. Supplies Asset   _____ Expenses not yet consumed
g. Supplies Expense   _____ Revenue not yet earned
h. Accrued Receivables   _____ To increase
i. Accrued Liabilities   _____ Supplies not yet consumed
j. Accumulate Depreciation _____ To postpone

Chapter 9 Cases

The following cases require you to open the company you updated in Chapter 8. Each of the following cases continues throughout the text in a sequential manner. For example, if you are assigned Case 01, you will use the file you modified in this chapter in all following chapters. Each of the following cases is similar in concepts assessed but differs in amounts and transactions.

To reopen your company, do the following:

1. Open your Internet browser.
2. Type **https://qbo.intuit.com** into your browser's address text box.
3. Type your user ID and password into the text boxes as you've done before.

Case 1

Now it is time to make some adjusting journal entries. Based on what you learned in the text using the Wild Water Sports company, you are to make the following changes to the Case 1 company you modified in Chapter 8:

1. Open and review your previously customized report named Trial Balance 1/31/24.

2. Record the appropriate adjusting journal entries on 1/31/24 based on the following:

    a. An inventory of supplies reveals that only $75 of supplies remain as of 1/31/24. (You'll need to add a new Supplies account—Account Type: Expenses, Detail Type: Supplies & Materials, Name: Supplies.)

    b. Prepaid expenses of $800 expired (representing prepaid rent) in the month of January.

    c. A bill for $150 was received and recorded in the next month for repairs and maintenance consumed in the current month. Create a new liability account as you did earlier in the chapter.

    d. Consulting services recorded on sales receipt #1004 for $2,500 to Surf Rider Foundation were never performed even though cash had been received. Thus, the revenue had not been earned. Create a new liability account as you did earlier in the chapter.

    e. Consulting services of $8,500 were performed on the last day of the month for a new customer Blazing Boards but not invoiced to the customer or recorded into the accounting records until a few days into the next month. Create a new asset account as you did earlier in the chapter.

    f. Depreciation Expense of $575 ($75 and $500 for Equipment and Furniture & Fixtures, respectively) needed to be recorded for the month. Before recording this journal entry, edit the "Depreciation" expense account so that the new name is "Depreciation Expense." Also, change the account title for Furniture & Fixtures accumulated depreciation from "Depreciation" to "Accumulated Depreciation" as you did earlier in the chapter. This also needs to be done for the Equipment accumulated depreciation account.

3. Open, print, and export to Excel your previously customized report named Trial Balance 1/31/24, which should now reflect your adjusting journal entries.

4. Open, print, and export to Excel your previously customized report named Transaction Detail by Account, which should now reflect your adjusting journal entries.

Case 2

Now it is time to make some adjusting journal entries. Based on what you learned in the text using the Wild Water Sports company, you are to make the following changes to the Case 2 company you modified in Chapter 8:

1. Open and review your previously customized report named Trial Balance 1/31/25.

2. Record the appropriate adjusting journal entries on 1/31/25 based on the following:

   a. An inventory of supplies reveals that only $200 of supplies remain as of 1/31/25. (You'll need to add a new Supplies account—Account Type: Expenses, Detail Type: Supplies & Materials, Name: Supplies.)

   b. Prepaid expenses of $1,800 expired (representing prepaid insurance) in the month of January.

   c. A bill for $750 was received and recorded in the next month for legal fees performed in the current month. Create a new liability account as you did earlier in the chapter.

   d. Custom painting services recorded on invoice #1003 for $4,500 to Hagen's toys were never performed even though invoiced. Thus, the revenue had not been earned. Create a new liability account as you did earlier in the chapter.

   e. Repair services of $6,298 were performed on the last day of the month for a new customer Kelly's Awesome Copters but not invoiced to the customer or recorded into the accounting records until a few days into the next month. Create a new asset account as you did earlier in the chapter.

   f. Depreciation Expense of $1,000 ($375 and $625 for Furniture and Machinery & Equipment, respectively) needed to be recorded for the month. Before recording this journal entry, edit the "Depreciation" expense account so the new name is "Depreciation Expense." Also, change the account title for Machinery & Equipment accumulated depreciation from "Depreciation" to "Accumulated Depreciation" like you did earlier in the chapter. This also needs to be done for the Furniture accumulated depreciation account.

3. Open, print, and export to Excel your previously customized report named Trial Balance 1/31/25, which should reflect your adjusting journal entries.

4. Open, print, and export to Excel your previously customized report named Transaction Detail by Account, which should reflect your adjusting journal entries.

Case 3

Now it is time to make some adjusting journal entries. Based on what you learned in the text using the Wild Water Sports company, you are to make the following changes to the Case 3 company you modified in Chapter 8:

1. Open and review your previously customized report named Trial Balance 1/31/26.

2. Record the appropriate adjusting journal entries on 1/31/26 based on the following:

   a. An inventory of supplies reveals that only $200 of supplies remain as of 1/31/26. (You'll need to add a new Supplies expense account—Account Type: Expenses, Detail Type: Supplies & Materials, Name: Supplies.)

   b. Prepaid expenses of $1,500 expired (representing prepaid insurance) in the month of January.

   c. A bill for $350 was received and recorded in the next month from Supreme Marketing (new vendor) for repairs & maintenance performed in the current month. Create a new liability account like you did earlier in the chapter.

   d. Phone Consulting services recorded on invoice #1003 for $210 to Diamond Girl, Inc. and recorded as Service income were never performed even though invoiced. Thus, the revenue had not been earned. Create a new liability account like you did earlier in the chapter.

   e. Phone Consulting services of $1,800 were performed on the last day of the month for a new customer Graham Engineering, Inc. but not invoiced to the customer or recorded into the accounting records until a few days into the next month. Create a new asset account like you did earlier in the chapter.

   f. Depreciation Expense of $1,200 ($850 and $350 for Computers and Machinery & Equipment, respectively) needed to be recorded for the month. Before recording this journal entry, edit the "Depreciation" expense account so that the new name is "Depreciation Expense." Also change the account title for the Machinery & Equipment accumulated depreciation from "Depreciation" to "Accumulated Depreciation" like you did earlier in the chapter. This also needs to be done for the Computers accumulation depreciation account.

3. Open, print, and export to Excel your previously customized report named Trial Balance 1/31/26, which should now reflect your adjusting journal entries.

4. Open, print, and export to Excel your previously customized report named Transaction Detail by Account, which should now reflect your adjusting journal entries.

Case 4

Now it is time to make some adjusting journal entries. Based on what you learned in the text using the Wild Water Sports company, you are to make the following changes to the Case 4 company you modified in Chapter 8:

1. Open and review your previously customized report named Trial Balance 1/31/27.
2. Record the appropriate adjusting journal entries on 1/31/27 based on the following:
   a. An inventory of supplies reveals that only $200 of supplies remain as of 1/31/27. (You'll need to create a new Supplies Expense account—Account Type: Expenses, Detail Type: Supplies & Materials, Name: Supplies Expense.)
   b. Prepaid rent of $1,500 expired (a new expense account called Rent and Lease) in the month of January.
   c. A bill for $675 was received and recorded in the next month from FixIt, Inc. (a new vendor) for advertising placed in the current month. Create a new liability account like you did earlier in the chapter.
   d. Training services recorded on invoice #1003 for $3,750 to Flyer Corporation were only partially performed even though invoiced. Thus, the $2,000 of sales had not been earned. Create a new liability account like you did earlier in the chapter.
   e. Training services of $750 were performed on the last day of the month for a new customer Jules, Inc. but not invoiced to the customer or recorded into the accounting records until a few days into the next month. Create a new asset account like you did earlier in the chapter and record additional sales.
   f. If necessary, create a new account titled Depreciation Expense. Depreciation Expense of $1,500 ($500, $1,000 for Vehicles, and Furniture, respectively) needed to be recorded for the month.
3. Print your Trial Balance 1/31/27 report that should now reflect your adjusting journal entries.

Case 5

Now it is time to make some adjusting journal entries. Based on what you learned in the text using the Wild Water Sports company, you are to make the following changes to the Case 5 company you modified in Chapter 8:

1. Open and review your previously customized report named Trial Balance 01/31/28.
2. Record the appropriate adjusting journal entries on 01/31/28 based on the following:
   a. Prepaid expenses of $8,000 expired (representing prepaid insurance) in the month of January.
   b. A bill for $2,800 was received and recorded in the next month from Indeed for recruiting services consumed in the current month. Create a new liability account like you did in the chapter.

c. Consulting services recorded on invoice #1003 for $32,000 to Boeing were only 50% complete as of 01/31/28 even though invoiced in the current month. Thus, $16,000 of consulting services had not been earned. Create an unearned revenue liability account like you did in the chapter.

d. Training services of $6,700 were performed on the last day of the month for a new customer Raonic but not invoiced to the customer or recorded into the accounting records until a few days into the next month. Create a new asset account like you did in the chapter.

e. Depreciation Expense of $11,000 ($6,000, $2,000, and $3,000 for Computers, Copiers, and Furniture, respectively) needed to be recorded for the month. Before recording this journal entry, edit the "Depreciation" expense account so that the new name is "Depreciation Expense." Also change the account title for the Computers, Copiers, and Furniture accumulated depreciation from "Depreciation" to "Accumulated Depreciation" like you did in the chapter.

3 Print your Trial Balance 01/31/28 report that should now reflect your adjusting journal entries.

Case 6

Now it is time to make some adjusting journal entries. Based on what you learned in the text using the Wild Water Sports company, you are to make the following changes to the Case 6 company you modified in Chapter 8:

1 Open and review your previously customized report named Trial Balance 1/31/23.

2 Record the appropriate adjusting journal entries on 1/31/23 based on the following:

a. An inventory of supplies reveals that only $400 of supplies remain as of 1/31/23 and $1,000 of supplies were mistakenly recorded as Contractors (an expense). You'll need to create a new Supplies Asset account and journalize $1,000 of Contractors (expense) to the newly created Supplies Asset account. (Note: This a correction of an error journal entry.) Then you'll need to create a new Supplies Expense account (Account Type: Expenses, Detail Type: Supplies & Materials) and journalize $600 of Supplies Asset to the newly created Supplies Expense account. (Note: This requires an adjusting journal entry.)

b. Prepaid expenses of $2,400 expired (representing prepaid insurance) in the month of January. (Note: This requires an adjusting journal entry.)

c. A bill for $1,800 was received and recorded in the next month from Pacific Marketing for advertising placed in the current month. Create a new liability account like you did in the chapter. (Note: This requires an adjusting journal entry.)

d. A Transmission Service of $350 and a Sewer System Repair of $600 were performed on the last day of the month for an existing customer (Deja Smith) but not invoiced to the customer or recorded into the accounting records until a few days into the next month. Create a new asset account like you did in the chapter and then record this as Sales. (Note: This requires an adjusting journal entry.)

e. Depreciation Expense of $2,100 ($1,000, $300, and $800 for Buildings, Computers, and Machinery & Equipment, respectively) needed to be recorded for the month. Before recording this journal entry, edit the "Depreciation" expense account so that the new name is "Depreciation Expense." Also change the account title for the Buildings, Computers, and Machinery & Equipment accumulated depreciation from "Depreciation" to "Accumulated Depreciation" like you did in the chapter. (Note: This requires an adjusting journal entry.)

3 Print your Trial Balance 1/31/23 report that should now reflect your adjusting journal entries.

chapter 10

Preparing Financial Statements and Reports

Student Learning Outcomes

Upon completion of this chapter, the student will be able to do the following:

- Create an income statement
- Create a balance sheet
- Create a statement of cash flows
- Create an accounts receivable aging summary
- Create an accounts payable aging summary
- Create an inventory valuation summary
- Customize and save reports

Overview

In Chapter 9, you added adjusting journal entries to your Wild Water Sports company. In this chapter, you will add several new reports. At the end of this chapter, you will perform similar tasks on the case assigned by your instructor.

Four standard reports exist in financial accounting: the income statement, the statement of stockholders' equity, the balance sheet, and the statement of cash flows. QBO does not have a report for stockholders' equity. It does have the others, along with a host of other reports so you can understand the underlying business events that have occurred during a particular accounting period. You will be exploring the A/R Aging Summary, A/P Aging Summary, and Inventory Valuation Summary reports. You will also be customizing them by adding columns and removing cents.

Income Statement

In this section, you will create an income statement. Intuit decided years ago to call this report Profit and Loss rather than an Income Statement. Even though this may confuse the accounting professional and accounting student, it resonates with the small business user that uses QBO. This report is designed to communicate the revenues earned and expenses incurred for a business over a month, quarter, or year.

Intuit defines this report as follows: "Shows money you earned (income) and money you spent (expenses), so you can see how profitable you are." That is not exactly how an accounting professional or accounting student was taught, but is close enough. Accountants define the income statement as a report reflecting revenues less expenses to derive net income. Intuit is not about to change its wording to accommodate us, so we will accept it at face value. Thus, revenues are the same as income in the Profit and Loss report. For simplicity, we will refer to this as the Profit and Loss report.

To create a Profit and Loss report for the Wild Water Sports company, do the following:

1 Open your Internet browser.

2 Open your QBO account and the Wild Water Sports company like you've done in previous chapters.

3 Click **Reports** from the navigation bar.

4 Type **Profit and Loss** in the Find report by name search box and then select the **Profit and Loss** text, which appears below the search text box.

5 Scroll to the top of the report to reveal the report period information. Type **1/1/2027** and **1/31/2027** as the new from and to dates then click **Run Report** as seen in the Report period text boxes at the top of Figure 10.1.

Figure 10.1 Profit and Loss report

Wild Water Sports - Student Name (ID Number)
Profit and Loss

January 2027

	TOTAL
Income	
Sales	337,000.00
Service Revenue	2,000.00
Total Income	**$339,000.00**
Cost of Goods Sold	
Cost of goods sold	131,200.00
Total Cost of Goods Sold	**$131,200.00**
GROSS PROFIT	**$207,800.00**
Expenses	
Advertising & marketing	2,500.00
Insurance	1,000.00
Interest paid	2,500.00
Payroll expenses	10,930.78
Rent	
Equipment rental	6,000.00
Total Rent	**6,000.00**
Utilities	
Phone service	1,800.00
Total Utilities	**1,800.00**
Total Expenses	**$24,730.78**
NET OPERATING INCOME	$183,069.22
Other Expenses	
Depreciation expense	1,250.00
Vehicle expenses	
Vehicle gas & fuel	1,100.00
Total Vehicle expenses	**1,100.00**
Total Other Expenses	**$2,350.00**
NET OTHER INCOME	$ -2,350.00
NET INCOME	$180,719.22

6 Click **Collapse** to view the report shown in Figure 10.2.

Figure 10.2 Profit and Loss report (collapsed)

Wild Water Sports - Student Name (ID Number)
Profit and Loss

January 2027

	TOTAL
Income	
Sales	337,000.00
Service Revenue	2,000.00
Total Income	**$339,000.00**
Cost of Goods Sold	
Cost of goods sold	131,200.00
Total Cost of Goods Sold	**$131,200.00**
GROSS PROFIT	$207,800.00
Expenses	
Advertising & marketing	2,500.00
Insurance	1,000.00
Interest paid	2,500.00
Payroll expenses	10,930.78
Rent	6,000.00
Utilities	1,800.00
Total Expenses	**$24,730.78**
NET OPERATING INCOME	$183,069.22
Other Expenses	
Depreciation expense	1,250.00
Vehicle expenses	1,100.00
Total Other Expenses	**$2,350.00**
NET OTHER INCOME	$ -2,350.00
NET INCOME	$180,719.22

By defining the accounting period as the month of January 2027, the only events reported are those recorded during that period. All reports in QBO allow you to drill down to specific transactions recorded in that period. You drill down by clicking an account on a report. That reveals a transactions report for that account for that period. Double-clicking a specific transaction in the transactions report reveals a specific source document, such as an invoice, sales receipt, cash receipt, and bill.

7 Click the **337,000.00** amount next to the Sales account as shown in Figure 10.2 to view the Transaction report for the Sales account for the month of January shown in Figure 10.3, remembering that this figure illustrates the details behind the number you just clicked.

Figure 10.3 Transaction Report (for the sales account)

Wild Water Sports - Student Name (ID Number)
Transaction Report
January 2027

DATE	TRANSACTION TYPE	NUM	NAME	MEMO/DESCRIPTION	ACCOUNT	SPLIT	AMOUNT	BALANCE
▾ Sales								
01/04/2027	Sales Receipt	1001	Southtown Watersports	Malibu Sportster LX	Sales	Payments to deposit	52,000.00	52,000.00
01/06/2027	Invoice	1002	Performance Rentals	Malibu Sportster LX	Sales	Accounts receivable (A/R)	52,000.00	104,000.00
01/06/2027	Invoice	1002	Performance Rentals	Malibu Sunset LX	Sales	Accounts receivable (A/R)	60,000.00	164,000.00
01/31/2027	Journal Entry	9			Sales	-Split-	−52,000.00	112,000.00
01/31/2027	Journal Entry	10			Sales	-Split-	225,000.00	337,000.00
Total for Sales							**$337,000.00**	
TOTAL							**$337,000.00**	

8 Click on the **Performance Rentals** text to view invoice #1002 shown in Figure 10.4.

9 Click **X** to return to the transaction report, and click **Back to report summary** or **Back** to return to the Profit and Loss report.

Figure 10.4 Invoice #1002 (partial view)

INVOICE

Wild Water Sports - Student Name (ID Number) samplestudent2024@gmail.com
5500 E Colonial Dr
Orlando, FL 32807

Edit company

Performance Rentals

Bill to

James Rogers
Performance Rentals
15 Hwy 22
Orlando, FL 32807
United States

Invoice no. 1002
Terms Net 30
Invoice date 01/06/2027
Due date 02/05/2027

Edit customer

Tags (hidden):

Start typing to add a tag

Product or service

	#	Product/Service	Description	Qty	Rate	Amount
⋮⋮	1	Boats:Malibu Sportster LX	Malibu Sportster LX	1	52,000.00	$52,000.00
⋮⋮	2	Boats:Malibu Sunset LX	Malibu Sunset LX	1	60,000.00	$60,000.00

10   Click the drop-down arrow in the Rows/Columns title and then select **% of income**.

11   Click **Customize**.

12   Check the **Without cents** check box.

13   Click **Run report** to view the report shown in Figure 10.5.

Figure 10.5 Customized Profit and Loss report

Wild Water Sports - Student Name (ID Number)

Profit and Loss
January 2027

	TOTAL	
	JAN 2027	**% OF INCOME**
▼ Income		
Sales	337,000	99.00 %
Service Revenue	2,000	1.00 %
Total Income	**$339,000**	**100.00 %**
▼ Cost of Goods Sold		
Cost of goods sold	131,200	39.00 %
Total Cost of Goods Sold	**$131,200**	**39.00 %**
GROSS PROFIT	$207,800	61.00 %
▼ Expenses		
Advertising & marketing	2,500	1.00 %
Insurance	1,000	0.00 %
Interest paid	2,500	1.00 %
Payroll expenses	10,931	3.00 %
Rent	6,000	2.00 %
Utilities	1,800	1.00 %
Total Expenses	**$24,731**	**7.00 %**
NET OPERATING INCOME	$183,069	54.00 %
▼ Other Expenses		
Depreciation expense	1,250	0.00 %
Vehicle expenses	1,100	0.00 %
Total Other Expenses	**$2,350**	**1.00 %**
NET OTHER INCOME	$ −2,350	−1.00 %
NET INCOME	$180,719	53.00 %

14   Click **Save customization**.

15   Type **Profit and Loss Custom** as the report name.

16   Click **Save**.

17   Click the **Export** button and then select **Export to Excel** as shown in Figure 10.6.

Figure 10.6 Exporting a report to Excel

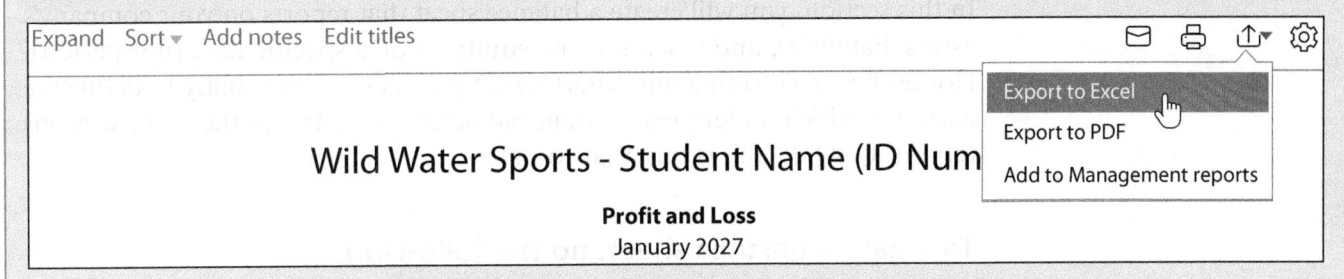

Expand Sort ▼ Add notes Edit titles

Wild Water Sports - Student Name (ID Num

Profit and Loss
January 2027

- Export to Excel
- Export to PDF
- Add to Management reports

18 Click **Save** after you've specified where you'd like to save the Excel worksheet naming the file WWS Profit and Loss.

19 Open the Excel file you just saved and click **Enable Editing** to view the Excel file shown in Figure 10.7.

Figure 10.7 Exported Excel File

	A	B	C
1	**Wild Water Sports - Student Name (ID Number)**		
2	**Profit and Loss**		
3	January 2027		
4			
5		Total	
6		Jan 2027	% of Income
7	Income		
8	Sales	337,000	99.41%
9	Service Revenue	2,000	0.59%
10	Total Income	$ 339,000	100.00%
11	Cost of Goods Sold		
12	Cost of goods sold	131,200	38.70%
13	Total Cost of Goods Sold	$ 131,200	38.70%
14	Gross Profit	$ 207,800	61.30%
15	Expenses		
16	Advertising & marketing	2,500	0.74%
17	Insurance	1,000	0.29%
18	Interest paid	2,500	0.74%
19	Payroll expenses	10,931	3.22%
20	Rent	6,000	1.77%
21	Utilities	1,800	0.53%
22	Total Expenses	$ 24,731	7.30%
23	Net Operating Income	$ 183,069	54.00%
24	Other Expenses		
25	Depreciation expense	1,250	0.37%
26	Vehicle expenses	1,100	0.32%
27	Total Other Expenses	$ 2,350	0.69%
28	Net Other Income	–$ 2,350	–0.69%
29	Net Income	$ 180,719	53.31%

Balance Sheet

In this section, you will create a balance sheet that reports on your company's assets, liabilities, and stockholders' equity as of a specific date (not period). However, when creating this report, QBO provides you the ability to define the period in which underlying account balances will reflect in their transactions reports. QBO default is this Year-to-date.

To create a balance sheet, do the following:

1 Continue from where you left off.

2 Click **Reports** from the navigation bar.

3 Type **Balance Sheet** in the Find report by name search box, and then select the **Balance Sheet** text. Type **1/1/2027** and **1/31/2027** in the from and to report dates text boxes, respectively, then click **Run report**. Then click **Collapse** to view a modified balance sheet shown in Figure 10.8.

Figure 10.8 Balance Sheet (partial view)

Wild Water Sports - Student Name (ID Number)

Balance Sheet

As of January 31, 2027

	TOTAL
▼ ASSETS	
▼ Current Assets	
▼ Bank Accounts	
Checking	99,358.88
Total Bank Accounts	**$99,358.88**
▼ Accounts Receivable	
Accounts receivable (A/R)	120,770.00
Total Accounts Receivable	**$120,770.00**
▼ Other Current Assets	
Accrued receivable	238,525.00
Inventory	223,350.00
Payments to deposit	70,000.00
Prepaid expenses	16,500.00
Supplies asset	500.00
Total Other Current Assets	**$548,875.00**
Total Current Assets	**$769,003.88**
▼ Fixed Assets	
Equipment	42,000.00
Furniture	9,750.00
Total Fixed Assets	**$51,750.00**
▼ Other Assets	
Investments	3,000.00
Total Other Assets	**$3,000.00**
TOTAL ASSETS	**$823,753.88**

4. Click the Accounts Receivable (A/R) balance **120,770.00** and then click **Switch to classic view** to view a transaction report for Accounts Receivable (A/R) for the month of January 2027 as shown in Figure 10.9.

Figure 10.9 Transaction Report for Accounts Receivable (A/R)

Wild Water Sports - Student Name (ID Number)
Transaction Report
January 2027

DATE	TRANSACTION TYPE	NUM	NAME	MEMO/DESCRIPTION	ACCOUNT	SPLIT	AMOUNT	BALANCE
▼ Accounts receivable (A/R)								
Beginning Balance								70,000.00
01/06/2027	Invoice	1002	Performance Rentals		Accounts receivable (A/R)	-Split-	118,770.00	188,770.00
01/10/2027	Invoice	1003	Florida Ski School		Accounts receivable (A/R)	Service Revenue	2,000.00	190,770.00
01/12/2027	Payment		Refugio		Accounts receivable (A/R)	Payments to deposit	−70,000.00	120,770.00
Total for Accounts receivable (A/R)							$50,770.00	
TOTAL							**$50,770.00**	

5. Note the ending balance of 120,770.00 which matches the Balance Sheet report shown in Figure 10.8.

6. Click **−70,000.00** (a payment from Refugio) to view the Receive Payment window shown in Figure 10.10.

Figure 10.10 Payment received (from Refugio)

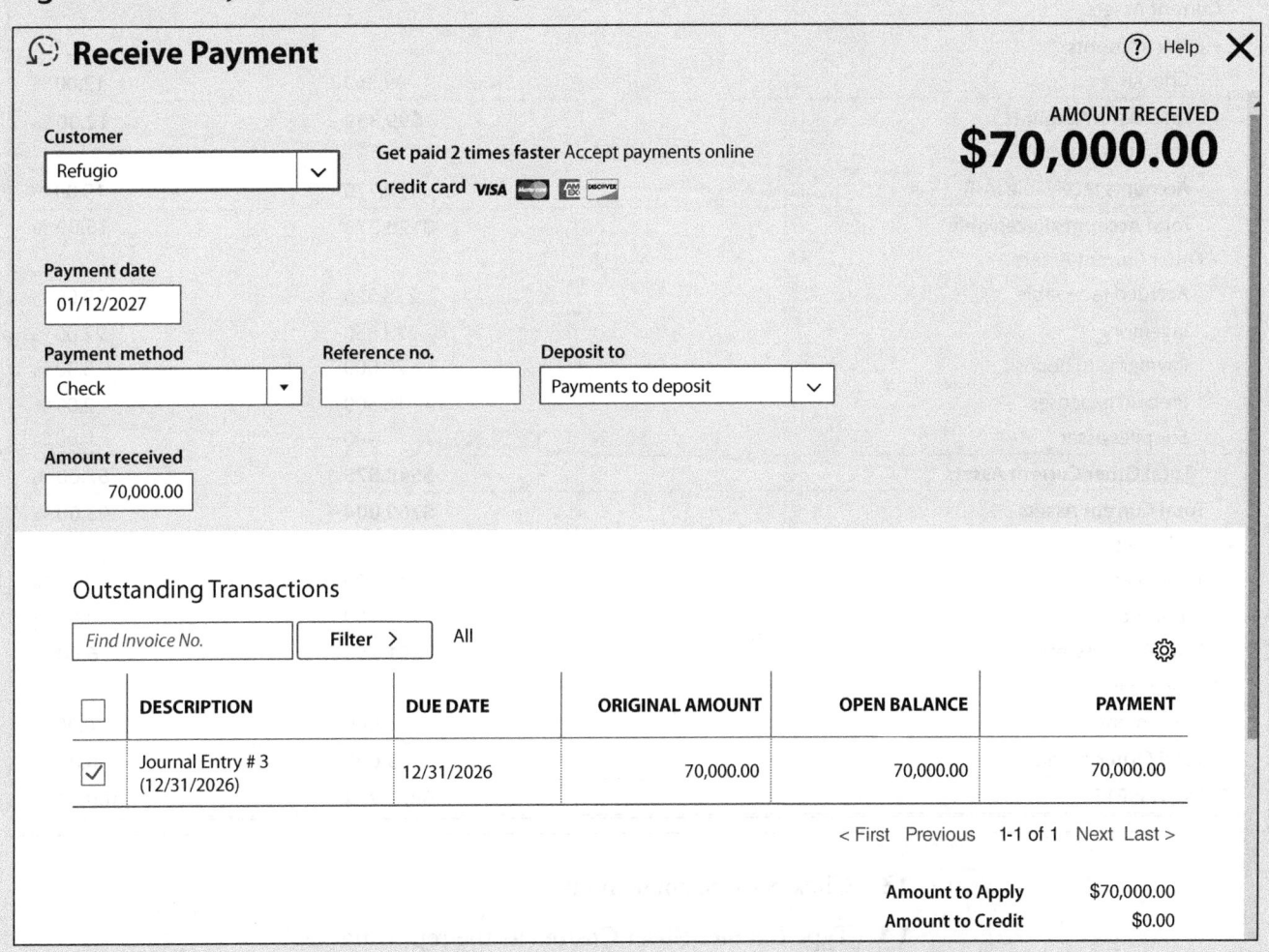

⊙ **Receive Payment**   ⑦ Help   ✕

AMOUNT RECEIVED
$70,000.00

Customer
Refugio

Get paid 2 times faster Accept payments online
Credit card VISA [MC] [AMEX] [DISCOVER]

Payment date
01/12/2027

Payment method   **Reference no.**   **Deposit to**
Check   Payments to deposit

Amount received
70,000.00

Outstanding Transactions

Find Invoice No.   Filter >   All   ⚙

☐	DESCRIPTION	DUE DATE	ORIGINAL AMOUNT	OPEN BALANCE	PAYMENT
☑	Journal Entry # 3 (12/31/2026)	12/31/2026	70,000.00	70,000.00	70,000.00

< First   Previous   1-1 of 1   Next Last >

Amount to Apply $70,000.00
Amount to Credit $0.00

274　Chapter 10　　*Preparing Financial Statements and Reports*

7　Click **X** to return to the transaction report, and click **Back to report summary** to return to the Balance Sheet.

8　Click **Customize**.

9　Check the **Without cents** check box.

10　Click the **Rows/Columns** drop-down arrow and then click the **Change columns** text.

11　Check the **% of Column** check box.

12　Click **Run report** to view the report shown in Figure 10.11.

Figure 10.11 Customized balance sheet report (partial view)

Wild Water Sports - Student Name (ID Number)
Balance Sheet
As of January 31, 2027

	TOTAL	
	AS OF JAN 31, 2027	% OF COLUMN
▾ ASSETS		
▾ Current Assets		
▾ Bank Accounts		
Checking	99,359	12.00 %
Total Bank Accounts	**$99,359**	**12.00 %**
▾ Accounts Receivable		
Accounts receivable (A/R)	120,770	15.00 %
Total Accounts Receivable	**$120,770**	**15.00 %**
▾ Other Current Assets		
Accrued receivable	238,525	29.00 %
Inventory	223,350	27.00 %
Payments to deposit	70,000	8.00 %
Prepaid expenses	16,500	2.00 %
Supplies asset	500	0.00 %
Total Other Current Assets	**$548,875**	**67.00 %**
Total Current Assets	**$769,004**	**93.00 %**
▾ Fixed Assets		
Equipment	42,000	5.00 %
Furniture	9,750	1.00 %
Total Fixed Assets	**$51,750**	**6.00 %**
▾ Other Assets		
Investments	3,000	0.00 %
Total Other Assets	**$3,000**	**0.00 %**
TOTAL ASSETS	**$823,754**	**100.00 %**

13　Click **Save customization**.

14　Type **Balance Sheet Custom** as the report name.

15　Click **Save**.

16. Click the **Export** button and then select **Export to Excel** as you've done before.

17. Click **Save** after you've specified where you'd like to save the Excel worksheet naming the file WWS Balance Sheet.

18. Open the Excel file you just saved and click **Enable Editing** to view the Excel file shown in Figure 10.12.

Figure 10.12 Exported Excel File

	A	B	C
1	**Wild Water Sports - Student Name (ID Number)**		
2	**Balance Sheet**		
3	As of January 31, 2027		
4			
5		Total	
6		As of Jan 31, 2027	% of Column
7	ASSETS		
8	Current Assets		
9	Bank Accounts		
10	Checking	99,359	12.06%
11	Total Bank Accounts	$ 99,359	12.06%
12	Accounts Receivable		
13	Accounts receivable (A/R)	120,770	14.66%
14	Total Accounts Receivable	$ 120,770	14.66%
15	Other Current Assets		
16	Accrued receivable	238,525	28.96%
17	Inventory	223,350	27.11%
18	Payments to deposit	70,000	8.50%
19	Prepaid expenses	16,500	2.00%
20	Supplies asset	500	0.06%
21	Total Other Current Assets	$ 548,875	66.63%
22	Total Current Assets	$ 769,004	93.35%
23	Fixed Assets		
24	Equipment	42,000	5.10%
25	Furniture	9,750	1.18%
26	Total Fixed Assets	$ 51,750	6.28%
27	Other Assets		
28	Investments	3,000	0.36%
29	Total Other Assets	$ 3,000	0.36%
30	TOTAL ASSETS	$ 823,754	100.00%

Statement of Cash Flows

In this section, you will create a statement of cash flows, which reports on a company's operating, investing, and financing activities.

To create a statement of cash flows, do the following:

1. Continue from where you left off.
2. Click **Reports** from the navigation bar.
3. Type **Statement of Cash Flows** in the Find a report by name search box, and then select the **Statement of Cash Flows** text.
4. Type **1/1/2027** and **1/31/2027** in the from and to report dates text boxes, respectively, then click **Run report** to view Statement of Cash Flows shown in Figure 10.13.

Figure 10.13 Statement of Cash Flows

Wild Water Sports - Student Name (ID Number)
Statement of Cash Flows
January 2027

	TOTAL
OPERATING ACTIVITIES	
Net Income	180,719.22
Adjustments to reconcile Net Income to Net Cash provided by operations:	
Accounts receivable (A/R)	−50,770.00
Accrued receivable	−238,525.00
Inventory	−50,550.00
Prepaid expenses	−1,500.00
Supplies asset	−500.00
Equipment:Accumulated depreciation	1,000.00
Furniture:Accumulated Depreciation	250.00
Accounts Payable (A/P)	134,250.00
Mastercard	1,600.00
Accrued liabilities	2,500.00
Florida Department of Revenue Payable	9,915.00
Payroll wages and tax to pay	2,944.66
Sales tax to pay	13,525.00
Unearned revenue	52,000.00
Total Adjustments to reconcile Net Income to Net Cash provided by operations:	−123,860.34
Net cash provided by operating activities	**$56,858.88**
INVESTING ACTIVITIES	
Equipment:Original Cost	−13,000.00
Furniture:Original cost	−10,000.00
Investments	−3,000.00
Net cash provided by Investing activities	**$ −26,000.00**
FINANCING ACTIVITIES	
Long-term business loans	105,000.00
Common stock	10,000.00
Opening balance equity	0.00
Retained Earnings	−1,500.00
Net cash provided by financing activities	**$113,500.00**
NET CASH INCREASE FOR PERIOD	**$144,358.88**
Cash at beginning of period	25,000.00
CASH AT END OF PERIOD	**$169,358.88**

5 Scroll down the report and click the Common stock amount **(10,000.00)** and then click **Switch to classic view** to view a transaction report for Common stock as shown in Figure 10.14.

Figure 10.14 Transaction Report (for Common stock)

\multicolumn{9}{c}{Wild Water Sports - Student Name (ID Number)}
\multicolumn{9}{c}{Transaction Report}
\multicolumn{9}{c}{January 2027}
DATE	TRANSACTION TYPE	NUM	NAME	MEMO/DESCRIPTION	ACCOUNT	SPLIT	AMOUNT	BALANCE
▼ Common stock								
01/21/2027	Deposit		WB Investments		Common stock	Checking	10,000.00	10,000.00
Total for Common stock							$10,000.00	
TOTAL							$10,000.00	

6 Click **10,000.00** in the Common Stock Transaction Report to view Bank Deposit (the source of the entry shown in Figure 10.15).

Figure 10.15 Bank deposit to record $10,000 received from WB Investments for the purchase of common stock

▼ Add funds to this deposit

#	RECEIVED FROM	ACCOUNT	DESCRIPTION	PAYMENT METHOD	REF NO.	AMOUNT	
1	WB Investments	Common stock		Check	56000	10,000.00	🗑

7 Click **X** to return to the transaction report, and click **Back to report summary** or **Back** to return to the Statement of Cash Flows.

8 Click **Customize**.

9 Check the **Without cents** check box.

10 Click **Run report**.

11 Click the **down arrow** next to the text Adjustments to reconcile.... to collapse the detail. Your screen should look like Figure 10.16.

12 Click **Save customization**.

13 Type **Statement of Cash Flows Custom** as the report name.

14 Click **Save**.

Figure 10.16 Customized Statement of Cash Flows

Wild Water Sports - Student Name (ID Number)

Statement of Cash Flows

January 2027

	TOTAL
OPERATING ACTIVITIES	
Net Income	180,719
Adjustments to reconcile Net Income to Net Cash provided by operations:	−123,860
Net cash provided by operating activities	**$56,859**
INVESTING ACTIVITIES	
Equipment:Original Cost	−13,000
Furniture:Original cost	−10,000
Investments	−3,000
Net cash provided by investing activities	**$ −26,000**
FINANCING ACTIVITIES	
Long-term business loans	105,000
Common stock	10,000
Opening balance equity	0
Retained Earnings	−1,500
Net cash provided by financing activities	**$113,500**
NET CASH INCREASE FOR PERIOD	$144,359
Cash at beginning of period	25,000
CASH AT END OF PERIOD	$169,359

Accounts Receivable Aging Summary

In this section, you will create an accounts receivable aging summary, which reflects unpaid invoices for the current period and for the last 30, 60, and 90+ days as of a specific date. Aging summaries assist with finding customers who may be delinquent in their payments, and help a company estimate the need for an allowance for uncollectible accounts. Aging information must take into consideration the company's normal terms for a customer. For example, it would not be an issue if many customers are in the 60+ category, but the normal terms for those customers are net 60. However, it would be an issue if the normal terms are net 30 and the same situation existed.

To create an accounts receivable aging summary report, do the following:

1 Continue from where you left off.

2 Click **Reports** from the navigation bar.

3 Type **Accounts receivable aging summary** in the Find a report by name search box, and then select the **Accounts receivable aging summary** text, which appears below the search text box to view the accounts receivable (A/R) aging report. Type **1/31/2027** in the as of report date text box, then click **Run report** to view the A/R Aging Summary report shown in Figure 10.17. Save this customized report as A/R Aging Summary 1/31/27.

Figure 10.17 A/R Aging Summary

Wild Water Sports - Student Name (ID Number)

A/R Aging Summary
As of January 31, 2027

	CURRENT	1 – 30	31 – 60	61 – 90	91 AND OVER	TOTAL
Florida Ski School	2,000.00					$2,000.00
Performance Rentals	118,770.00					$118,770.00
TOTAL	$120,770.00	$0.00	$0.00	$0.00	$0.00	$120,770.00

4 Click on the **118,770.00** owed by Performance Rentals shown in Figure 10.17 to view A/R Aging Detail report shown in Figure 10.18.

Figure 10.18 Accounts Receivable (A/R) Aging Detail report (partial view)

Wild Water Sports - Student Name (ID Number)

A/R Aging Detail
As of January 31, 2027

DATE	TRANSACTION TYPE	NUM	CUSTOMER	DUE DATE	AMOUNT	OPEN BALANCE
▾ Current						
01/06/2027	Invoice	1002	Performance Rentals	02/05/2027	118,770.00	118,770.00
Total for Current					$118,770.00	$118,770.00
TOTAL					$118,770.00	$118,770.00

5 Click **118,770.00** to view invoice #1002 shown in Figure 10.19.

6 Click **X** to return to the detail report, and click **Back to report summary** to return to the A/R Aging Summary report.

Figure 10.19 Invoice #1002 to Performance Rentals (partial view)

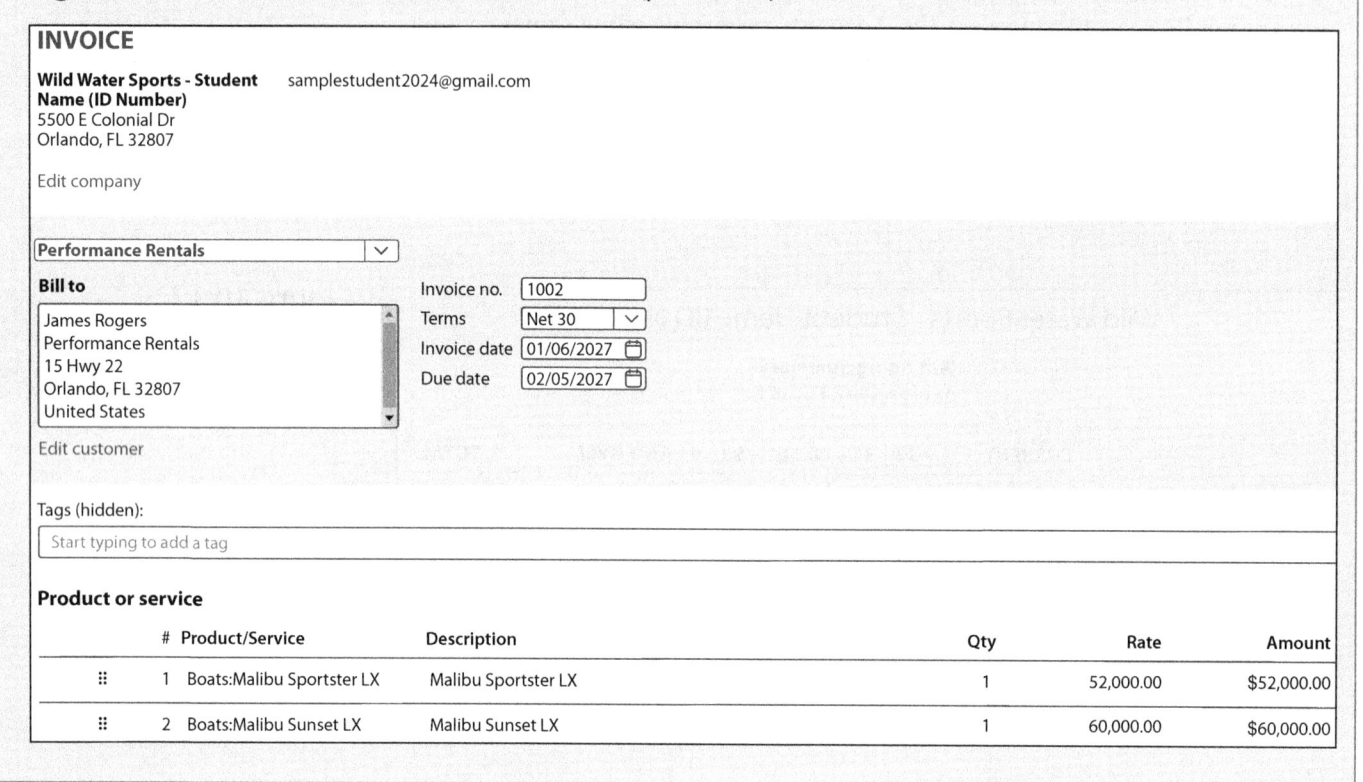

	#	Product/Service	Description	Qty	Rate	Amount
	1	Boats:Malibu Sportster LX	Malibu Sportster LX	1	52,000.00	$52,000.00
	2	Boats:Malibu Sunset LX	Malibu Sunset LX	1	60,000.00	$60,000.00

Accounts Payable Aging Summary

In this section, you will create an accounts payable aging summary, which reflects unpaid bills for the current period and for the last 30, 60, and 90+ days as of a specific date. Aging summaries help to prioritize the payment of bills. Aging information must take into consideration the company's normal terms from a vendor. For example, it would not be an issue if a large amount of vendors bills are in the 60+ category, but the normal terms for those vendors are net 60. However, it would be an issue if the normal terms are net 30, and the same situation existed.

To create an accounts payable aging summary report, do the following:

1 Continue from where you left off.

2 Click **Reports** from the navigation bar.

3 Type **Accounts payable aging summary** in the Find a report by name search box, and then select the **Accounts payable aging summary** text, which appears below the search text box to view the accounts payable aging report. Type **1/31/2027** in the as of report date text box, then click **Run report** to view the A/P Aging Summary report shown in Figure 10.20. Save this customized report as A/P Aging Summary 1/31/27.

Figure 10.20

Accounts Payable (A/P) Aging Summary

Wild Water Sports - Student Name (ID Number)
A/P Aging Summary
As of January 31, 2027

	CURRENT	1 – 30	31 – 60	61 – 90	91 AND OVER	TOTAL
Allstate Insurance	2,500.00					$2,500.00
Best Buy Geek Squad	6,000.00					$6,000.00
Malibu Boats	1,750.00					$1,750.00
Tige	180,000.00					$180,000.00
TOTAL	$190,250.00	$0.00	$0.00	$0.00	$0.00	$190,250.00

4 Click on the **6,000.00** owed to Best Buy Geek Squad shown in Figure 10.20 to view A/P Aging Detail report shown in Figure 10.21.

Figure 10.21 Accounts Payable (A/P) Aging Detail report

Wild Water Sports - Student Name (ID Number)
A/P Aging Detail
As of January 31, 2027

DATE	TRANSACTION TYPE	NUM	VENDOR	DUE DATE	PAST DUE	AMOUNT	OPEN BALANCE
Current							
01/19/2027	Bill		Best Buy Geek Squad	02/18/2027	–1489	6,000.00	6,000.00
Total for Current						**$6,000.00**	**$6,000.00**
TOTAL						**$6,000.00**	**$6,000.00**

5 Click **6,000.00** to view the bill shown in Figure 10.22.

6 Click **X** to return to the detail report, and click **Back to report summary** to return to the A/P Aging Summary report.

Figure 10.22 Bill (from Best Buy Geek Squad)

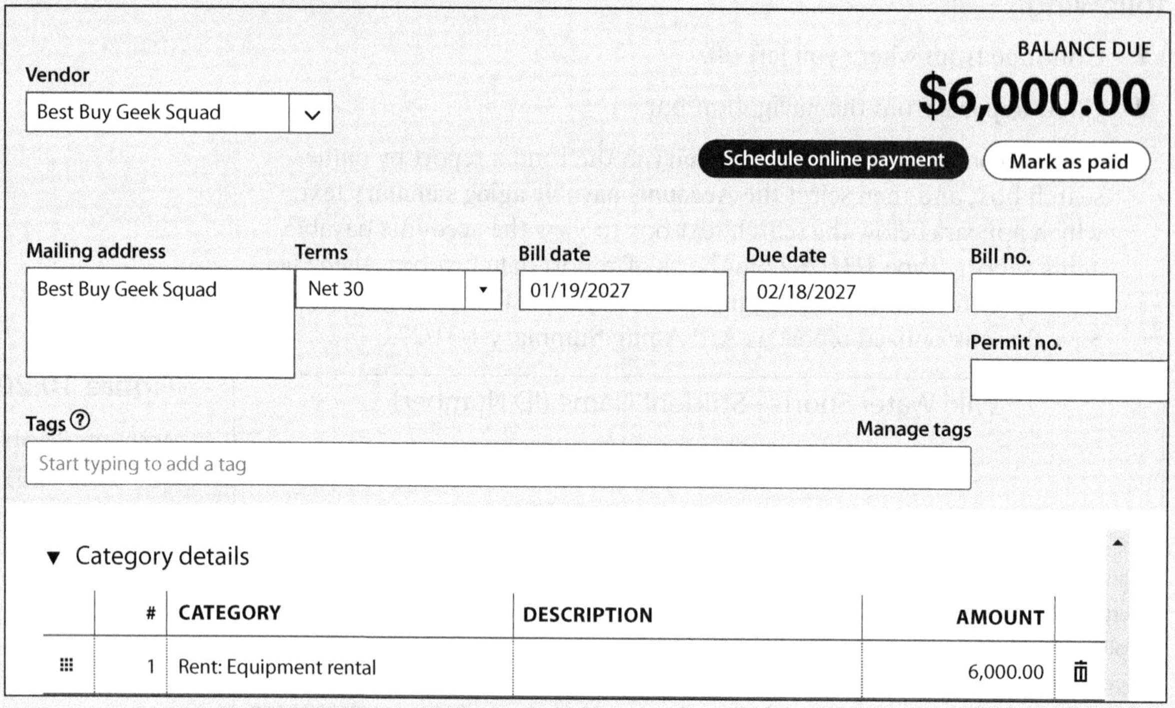

Vendor Best Buy Geek Squad				**BALANCE DUE** **$6,000.00**

Schedule online payment | Mark as paid

Mailing address	Terms	Bill date	Due date	Bill no.
Best Buy Geek Squad	Net 30	01/19/2027	02/18/2027	

Permit no.

Tags Manage tags
Start typing to add a tag

▼ Category details

#	CATEGORY	DESCRIPTION	AMOUNT
1	Rent: Equipment rental		6,000.00

Inventory Valuation Summary

In this section, you will create an inventory valuation summary that reflects each inventory item's quantity on hand, its average cost, and the resulting valuation as of a specific date.

To create an inventory valuation summary report, do the following:

1. Continue from where you left off.
2. Click **Reports** from the navigation bar.
3. Type **Inventory** in the Find a report by name search box, and then select the **Inventory Valuation Summary**. Change the as of date to **1/31/2027**. Then click **Run report** to view the report shown in Figure 10.23.

Figure 10.23 Inventory Valuation Summary

Wild Water Sports - Student Name (ID Number)
Inventory Valuation Summary
As of January 31, 2027

	SKU	QTY	ASSET VALUE	CALC. AVG
2023 Vi22		0.00	0.00	
▼ Boats				
Malibu Sunset LX		0.00	0.00	
Total Boats			0.00	
Malibu Sportster LX		1.00	41,600.00	41,600.00
Tige 25 zx		1.00	180,000.00	180,000.00
Tige Thruster Control Package		0.00	0.00	
Wake Accessory Package		5.00	1,750.00	350.00
TOTAL			**$223,350.00**	

4 Click on the **5.00** representing the number of wake accessory packages on hand shown in Figure 10.23 to view an Inventory Valuation Detail report shown in Figure 10.24.

Figure 10.24 Inventory Valuation Detail

Wild Water Sports - Student Name (ID Number)
Inventory Valuation Detail
As of January 31, 2027

DATE	TRANSACTION TYPE	NUM	NAME	QTY	RATE	FIFO COST	QTY ON HAND	ASSET VALUE
▼ Wake Accessory Package								
01/18/2027	Bill		Malibu Boats	5.00	350.00	1,750.00	5.00	1,750.00
01/18/2027	Inventory Starting Value	START		0.00	350.00	0.00	5.00	1,750.00
Total for Wake Accessory Package				**5.00**		**$1,750.00**	**5.00**	**$1,750.00**

5 Click **Bill** reflecting the purchase of five wake accessory packages shown in Figure 10.24 to view the bill shown in Figure 10.25.

6 Click **Cancel** to return to the detail report, and click **Back to report summary** to return to the Inventory Valuation Summary report. Save this report customization as Inventory Summary 1/31/27.

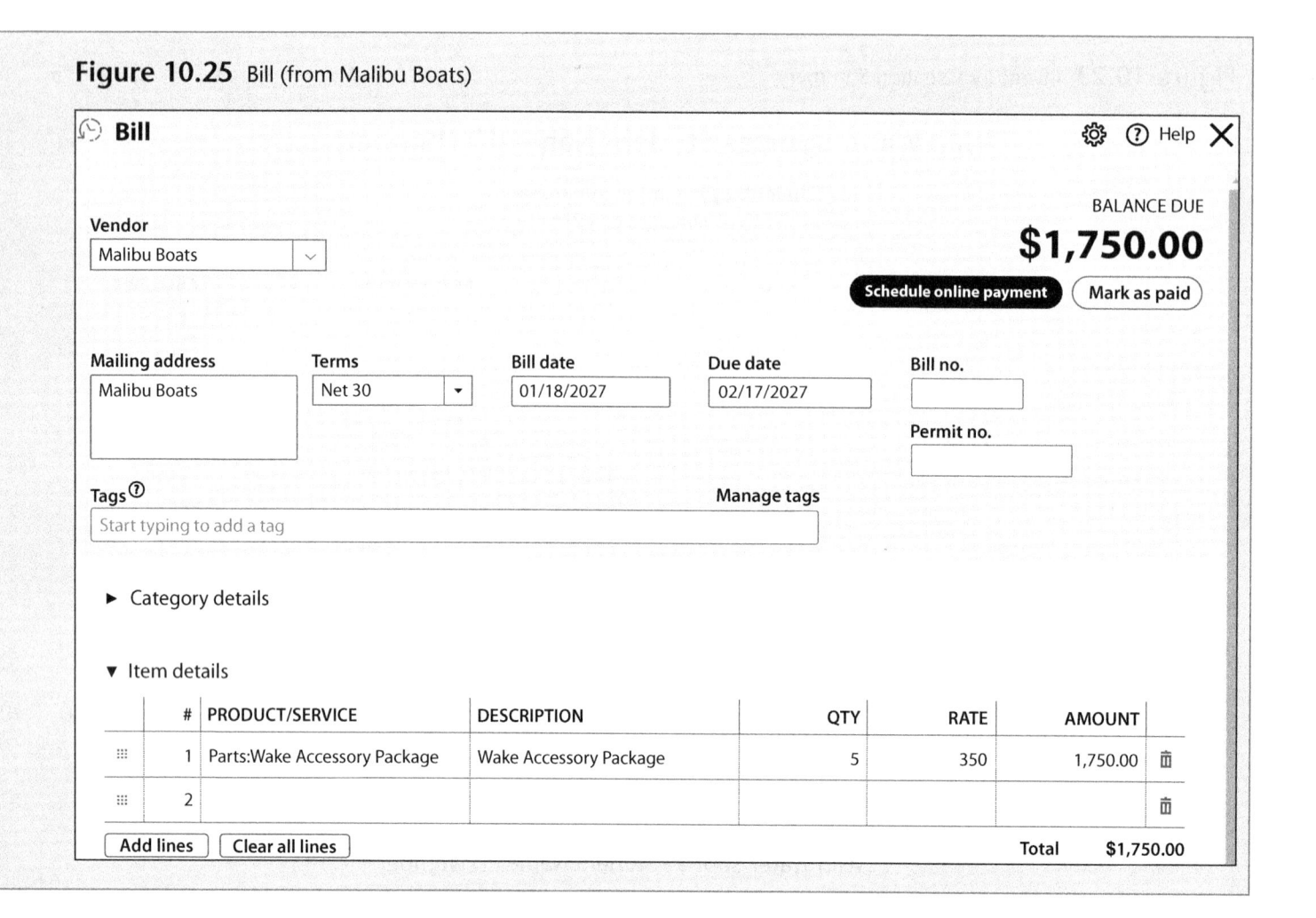

Figure 10.25 Bill (from Malibu Boats)

	Bill						
							Help ✕

BALANCE DUE

$1,750.00

Schedule online payment Mark as paid

Vendor
Malibu Boats

Mailing address
Malibu Boats

Terms
Net 30

Bill date
01/18/2027

Due date
02/17/2027

Bill no.

Permit no.

Tags Manage tags
Start typing to add a tag

▶ Category details

▼ Item details

#	PRODUCT/SERVICE	DESCRIPTION	QTY	RATE	AMOUNT	
1	Parts:Wake Accessory Package	Wake Accessory Package	5	350	1,750.00	🗑
2						🗑

Add lines   Clear all lines   Total $1,750.00

End Note

In this chapter, you did not add business events, but you did create the basic financial statement reports: profit and loss, balance sheet, and statement of cash flows. In addition, you drilled down beyond those reports to transaction detail reports and to source documents like payments, invoices, bills, and so on. You created some analytical reports to learn more about accounts receivable, accounts payable, and inventory.

Chapter 10 Questions

View the Wild Water Sports company QBO file to answer these questions by creating reports:

1. Invoice 1002 was created for which customer?
2. What was the first item sold on invoice 1002?
3. What document created an Advertising & Marketing expense?
4. Who did you send a check to for phone service?
5. How many Malibu Sunset LX boats are currently on hand?
6. What is the average cost per unit of a Wake Accessory Package?
7. How much cash was used for purchase equipment?
8. When is the bill from Allstate Insurance due?
9. When is the invoice to Florida Ski School due?
10. What amount of cash was provided by financing activities?

Chapter 10 Matching

a.	Income statement	_____ Click on an event in any transaction report
b.	Balance sheet	_____ Click an account on any report
c.	Statement of cash flows	_____ Click to add a new column in a report
d.	AR aging report	_____ Reflects unpaid bills for the current period
e.	AP aging report	_____ Reports revenues and expenses
f.	Inventory valuation report	_____ Includes operating, investing, and financing activities
g.	Profit and Loss report	_____ Reports inventory quantities on hand
h.	To view a transaction report	_____ Reports assets, liabilities, and equities
i.	To view a source document	_____ Another name for the income statement
j.	% of income check box	_____ Reflects unpaid invoices for the current period

Chapter 10 Cases

The following cases require you to open the company you updated in Chapter 9. Each of the following cases continues throughout the text in a sequential manner. Each of the following cases is similar in concepts assessed but differs in amounts and transactions.

> **To reopen your company, do the following:**
>
> 1. Open your Internet browser.
> 2. Type **https://qbo.intuit.com** into your browser's address text box.
> 3. Type your user ID and password into the text boxes as you have done earlier.

Case 1

Now it is time to create, customize, and print some new reports. Based on what you learned in the text using the Wild Water Sports company, you are to make the following changes to the Case 1 company you modified in Chapter 9:

1. Create, print, and export to Excel a Profit and Loss report for January 2024. Customize this report by adding a percent of income column and saving and by sharing your customization as Profit and Loss Jan 2024.

2. Using the Profit and Loss report created above, drill down to a Transactions Report for the Sales account. Print and export this report to Excel. Save and share this report as a Sales Transaction Report.

3. Create, print, and export to Excel a Balance Sheet report as of 1/31/24. Customize this report by adding a percent of column and saving and sharing your customization as Balance Sheet Jan 2024.

4. Using the Balance Sheet report created above, drill down to a Transactions Report for the Checking account. Print and export this report to Excel. Save and share this report as Checking Report.

5. Create, print, and export to Excel a Statement of Cash Flows report as of 1/31/24. Save and share your customization as Statement of Cash Flows Jan 2024.

6. Using the Statement of Cash Flows report created above, drill down to a Transactions Report for the Accounts Receivable account. Print and export this report to Excel. Save and share this report as an A/R SCF Report.

7. Create, print, and export to Excel an A/R Aging Summary report for the month of January 2024. Save and share your customization as A/R Aging Summary Jan 2024.

8. Create, print, and export to Excel an A/P Aging Summary report for the month of January 2024. Save and share your customization as A/P Aging Summary Jan 2024.

9. Create, print, and export to Excel an Inventory Valuation Summary report for the month of January 2024. Save and share your customization as an Inventory Valuation Summary Jan 2024.

Case 2

Now it is time to create, customize, and print some new reports. Based on what you learned in the text using the Wild Water Sports company, you are to make the following changes to the Case 2 company you modified in Chapter 9:

1. Create, print, and export to Excel a Profit and Loss report for January 2025. Customize this report by adding a percent of income column. Save and share your customization as Profit and Loss Jan 2025.

2. Using the Profit and Loss report created above, drill down to a Transactions Report for the Insurance account. Print and export this report to Excel. Save and share this report as an Insurance Transaction Report.

3. Create, print, and export to Excel a Balance Sheet report as of 1/31/25. Customize this report by adding a percent of column. Save and share your customization as Balance Sheet Jan 2025.

4. Using the Balance Sheet report created above, drill down to a Transactions Report for the Inventory Asset account. Print and export this report to Excel. Save and share this report as Inventory Report.

5. Create, print, and export to Excel a Statement of Cash Flows report as of 1/31/25. Save and share your customization as Statement of Cash Flows Jan 2025.

6. Using the Statement of Cash Flows report created above, drill down to a Transactions Report for the Prepaid Expenses account. Print and export this report to Excel. Save and share this report as PPE SCF Report.

7. Create, print, and export to Excel an A/R Aging Summary report for the month of January 2025. Save and share your customization as an A/R Aging Summary Jan 2025.

8. Create, print, and export to Excel an A/P Aging Summary report for the month of January 2025. Save and share your customization as an A/P Aging Summary Jan 2025.

9. Create, print, and export to Excel an Inventory Valuation Summary report for January 2025. Save and share your customization as Inventory Valuation Summary Jan 2025.

Case 3

Now it is time to create, customize, and print some new reports. Based on what you learned in the text using the Wild Water Sports company, you are to make the following changes to the Case 3 company you modified in Chapter 9:

1. Create, print, and export to Excel a Profit and Loss report for the month of January 2026. Customize this report by adding a percent of income column and saving and sharing your customization as Profit and Loss Jan 2026.

2 Using the Profit and Loss report created earlier, drill down to a Transactions Report for the Advertising & Marketing account. Print and export this report to Excel. Save this report as Advertising & Marketing Transaction Report.

3 Create, print, and export to Excel a Balance Sheet report as of 1/31/26. Customize this report by adding a percent of column and saving your customization as Balance Sheet Jan 2026.

4 Using the Balance Sheet report created earlier, drill down to a Transactions Report for the Accounts Receivable (A/R) account. Print and export this report to Excel. Save this report as AR Report.

5 Create, print, and export to Excel a Statement of Cash Flows report for the month of January 2026. Save your customization as Statement of Cash Flows Jan 2026.

6 Using the Statement of Cash Flows report created earlier, drill down to a Transactions Report for the Payroll Tax Payable to pay account. Print and export this report to Excel. Save this report as Payroll Tax SCF Report.

7 Create, print, and export to Excel an A/R Aging Summary report for the month of January 2026. Save your customization as A/R Aging Summary Jan 2026.

8 Create, print, and export to Excel an A/P Aging Summary report for the month of January 2026. Save your customization as A/P Aging Summary Jan 2026.

9 Create, print, and export to Excel an Inventory Valuation Summary report for the month of January 2026. Save your customization as Inventory Valuation Summary Jan 2026.

Case 4

Now it is time to create, customize, and print some new reports. Based on what you learned in the text using the Wild Water Sports company, you are to make the following changes to the Case 4 company you modified in Chapter 9:

1 Create and print a Profit and Loss report for the month of January 2027. Customize this report by adding a percent of income column and saving your customization as Profit and Loss Jan 2027.

2 Using the Profit and Loss report you just created, drill down to a Transactions Report for the Advertising & Marketing account. Print and save this report as Advertising Transaction Report.

3 Create and print a Balance Sheet report as of 1/31/27. Customize this report by adding a percent of column. Collapse, print, and save this report as Balance Sheet Jan 2027.

4. Using the Balance Sheet report you just created, drill down to a Transactions Report for the Accounts Receivable (A/R) account. Print and save this report as AR Report.

5. Create and print a Statement of Cash Flows report as of 1/31/27. Save your customization as Statement of Cash Flows Jan 2027.

6. Using the Statement of Cash Flows report you just created, drill down to a Transactions Report for the Payroll wages and tax to pay account. Print and save this report as Payroll Tax SCF Report.

7. Create and print an Accounts Receivable Aging Summary report for the month of January 2027. Save your customization as A/R Aging Summary Jan 2027.

8. Create and print an Accounts Payable Aging Summary report for the month of January 2027. Save your customization as A/P Aging Summary Jan 2027.

9. Create and print an Inventory Valuation Summary report for the month of January 2027. Save your customization as Inventory Valuation Summary Jan 2027.

Case 5

Now it is time to create, customize, and print some new reports. Based on what you learned in the text using the Wild Water Sports company, you are to make the following changes to the Case 5 company you modified in Chapter 9:

1. Create and print a Profit and Loss report for the month of January 2028. Customize this report by adding a percent of income column and saving your customization as Profit and Loss Jan 2028.

2. Using the Profit and Loss report you just created, drill down to a Transactions Report for the Advertising & Marketing account in classic view. Print and save this report as Advertising Transaction Report.

3. Create and print a Balance Sheet report for the month of January 2028. Customize this report by adding a percent of row column. Collapse, print, and save this report as Balance Sheet Jan 2028.

4. Using the Balance Sheet report you just created, drill down to a Transactions Report for the Accounts Receivable (A/R) account in classic view. Collapse, print, and save this report as AR Transaction Report.

5. Create and print a Statement of Cash Flows report as of 01/31/28. Save your customization as Statement of Cash Flows Jan 2028.

6 Using the Statement of Cash Flows report you just created, drill down to a Transactions Report for the Payroll wages and tax to pay account in classic view. Print and save this report as Payroll Tax SCF Report.

7 Create and print an Accounts Receivable Aging Summary report for the month of January 2028. Save your customization as AR Aging Summary Jan 2028.

8 Create and print an Accounts Payable Aging Summary report for the month of January 2028. Save your customization as AP Aging Summary Jan 2028.

9 Create and print an Inventory Valuation Summary report for the month of January 2028. Save your customization as Inventory Valuation Summary Jan 2028.

Case 6

Now it is time to create, customize, and print some new reports. Based on what you learned in the text using the Wild Water Sports company, you are to make the following changes to the Case 6 company you modified in Chapter 9:

1 Create and print a Profit and Loss report for the month of January 2023. Customize this report by adding a % of income column and saving your customization as Profit and Loss Jan 2023.

2 Using the Profit and Loss report you just created, drill down to a Transactions Report for the Payroll account. Print and save this report as Payroll Transaction Report.

3 Create and print a Balance Sheet report as of 1/31/23. Customize this report by adding a % of row column. (This is done in a similar manner to adding a % of income column done for the Profit and Loss report.) Collapse, print, and save this report as Balance Sheet Jan 2023.

4 Using the Balance Sheet report you just created drill down to a Transactions Report for the Prepaid Expenses account. Collapse, print, and save this report as Prepaid Expenses Transaction Report.

5 Create and print a Statement of Cash Flows report as of 1/31/23. Save your customization as Statement of Cash Flows Jan 2023.

6 Create and print an Accounts Receivable Aging Summary report for the month of January 2023. Save your customization as A/R Aging Summary Jan 2023.

7 Create and print an Accounts Payable Aging Summary report for the month of January 2023. Save your customization as A/P Aging Summary Jan 2023.

8 Create and print an Inventory Valuation Summary report for the month of January 2023. Save your customization as Inventory Valuation Summary Jan 2023.

appendix 1

Sales Tax

Some companies are required to collect sales tax from customers depending on the state(s) in which they do business. Collecting sales tax in QBO has gotten easier! Through the new Automated Sales Tax experience, you just need to answer a few simple questions and QBO will know what taxes apply to your business, set them up, and automatically track your sales taxes.

This means you no longer need to select a tax rate when you create an invoice or other transaction. As long as your Sales Tax Center and all applicable tax agencies are set up, the system will automatically do it for you!

Be advised that end-of-chapter Cases 1 and 2 do not require the collection of sales tax. Cases 3 through 6 do require the collection of sales tax using the new Automated Sales Tax system. Keep in mind that sales tax rates change year to year, state to state. The solutions provided by the author for each case were based on tax rates in effect for that particular year. If a rate changes, your answers for sales tax payable and related accounts may be different.

At the time of publication, Intuit had two different procedures for setting up sales tax. The first works for regular companies students and instructors. This is the process used in prior editions of QBO and this text. The second works for the Sample Company and is the new process used going forward. At some point this new process will be implemented and work for both types of companies.

The following are steps to set up the new Automated Sales Tax system. The following example assumes the company is in California. That is not true in all cases. Your case may be in a different state, and thus, your steps to create a company's sales tax will be different.

VIDEO LINK

Navigate your browser to the Video Tutorials provided by Intuit (See web site address specified in the Preface to this text) and then search on How to Set Up and use Automatic Sales Tax.

To set up a company's sales tax (QBO regular companies):

1. Click **Taxes** and then click **Sales tax** from the navigation bar.
2. Click the **Use Automatic Sales Tax** button (assuming you've already entered your company's address during the setup process).

3 Select **Quarterly** from the Filing Frequency drop down list shown in Figure A1 and then click **Next**.

Figure A.1 Tax agencies

| ✓ Address | 2 Tax agencies | 3 Review and finish |

You have to pay sales tax to these tax agencies

Based on your business address, you have to pay sales tax to these tax agencies. Tell us how often you file so we can track your deadlines and how much you owe. Your filing frequency is on your sales tax business registration.

TAX AGENCY	FILING FREQUENCY
California Department of Tax and Fee Administration > Contact info	Quarterly

Back   Next

4 Select **No** when asked if you registered for sales tax in any other state, then click **Next**.
5 Click **Finish** to end the set up sales tax process, then click **Take a look**.
6 From the Sales Tax Center click **Sales Tax Settings**.
7 Click **Edit** from the Agency Action column.

VIDEO LINK
Navigate your browser to the Video Tutorials provided by Intuit (see website address specified in the Preface to this text) and then search on How to Set Up and use Automatic Sales Tax.

Appendix 1   *Sales Tax*

8   Type **01/01/20XX** replacing XX with the start date of your company. See example shown in Figure A.2.

Figure A.2

Example of changing the start date for the sales tax center

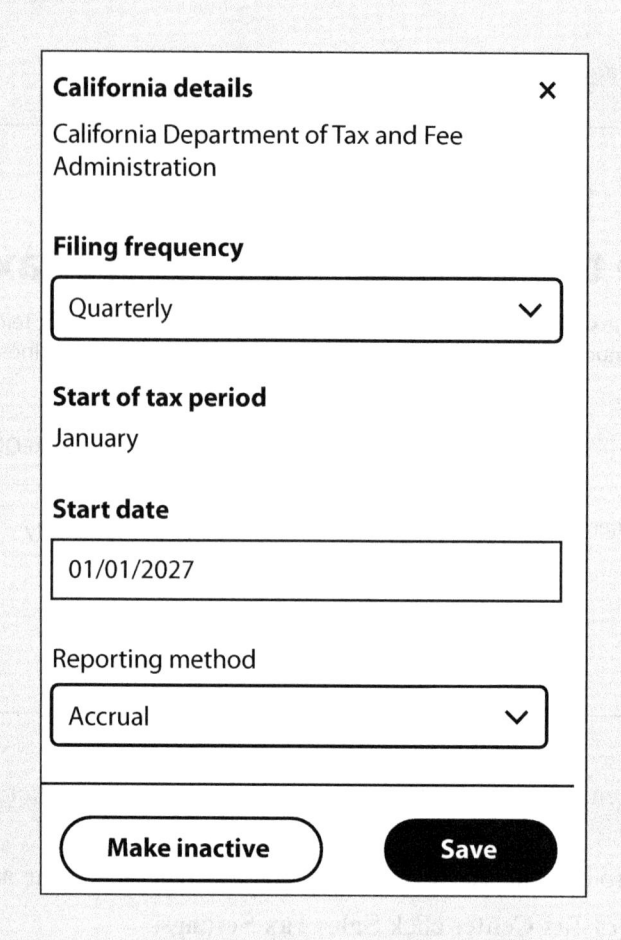

California details   ✕

California Department of Tax and Fee Administration

Filing frequency

Quarterly

Start of tax period

January

Start date

01/01/2027

Reporting method

Accrual

Make inactive   Save

9   Click **Save** and then click **Back to sales tax center**.
10 Click **Dashboards** and then click **Getting things done** to return to the Dashboard.

Comprehensive Case Problems

appendix 2

Your instructor may assign you these comprehensive case problems after you complete all 10 chapters of the text. These are an *extension* of the cases assigned at the end of Chapters 3 to 10 of the *QuickBooks Online for Accounting*, eighth edition, text. Case 1 can be used by students only if they have *successfully completed* Case 1 through Chapter 10, Case 2 can be used by students only if they have *successfully completed* Case 2 through Chapter 10, Case 3 can be used by students only if they have *successfully completed* Case 3 through Chapter 10, Case 4 can be used by students only if they have *successfully completed* Case 4 through Chapter 10, Case 5 can be used by students only if they have *successfully completed* Case 5 through Chapter 10, and Case 6 can be used by students only if they have *successfully completed* Case 6 through Chapter 10.

Case 1 Comprehensive Problem

Case 1, which begins in Chapter 3, is a company that distributes surfboards and is in La Jolla, California. Business events in Case 1 occurred from 12/31/23 to 1/31/24 when presented in Chapters 3 to 10. The following is a description of business events that occurred in the month of February 2024.

Date	Description of Event	Chapter	Event
2/1/24	Add a new product	4	Add a new product with quantity tracked – Biscuit Bonzer, initial quantity on hand: 0, as of date: 2/1/24, price: $1,000, cost: $675, income account: Sales, expense account: Cost of Goods Sold. Vendor: Channel Islands.
2/1/24	Edit the chart of accounts	3	Change the name of the account Notes Payable to Notes Payable – Bank of CA.
2/1/24	Add a new service	4	Add a new service – Repairs, rate: $85, income account: Services.
2/1/24	Modify budget	8	Modify the following monthly budgeted amounts (Budget 1) for February 2024 through December 2024 as follows: sales: $35,000, services: $2,000, cost of goods sold: $21,500, interest expense: $800, payroll: $13,000, rent or lease: $2,500, travel: $500, utilities: $300.
2/1/24	Add a new employee	7	Add a new employee – Jane Price, 65 Ocean View Lane, La Jolla, CA 92037, Employee ID No.: 555-15-3537.
2/1/24	Add a new customer	4	Add a new customer – Awesome Surf, 501 Boardwalk Place, Santa Cruz, CA 95060.
2/5/24	Add a sales receipt	4	Add a new sales receipt #1005 for $2,810 – Customer: Awesome Surf, payment method: Check, reference no.: 984, deposit to: Undeposited Funds, product: The Water Hog, quantity: 1, and product: Rook 15, quantity: 3.
2/6/24	Add a new invoice	4	Add a new invoice #1006 for $820 – Customer: Surf Rider Foundation, terms: Net 30, service: Repairs, quantity: 2, and product: Rook 15, quantity: 1.
2/7/24	Add a cash receipt	4	Add a new cash receipt – Customer: Blondie's Boards, payment method: Check, reference no.: 1003, deposit to: Undeposited Funds, amount received: $8,000, applied to invoice #1003.
2/8/24	Make a bank deposit	4	Add a bank deposit to the checking account in the amount of $15,810, which represents payments from Blondie's Boards for $5,000 and $8,000 and Awesome Surf for $2,810.
2/9/24	Add a new vendor	5	Add a new vendor – BoardsWest, 36 Anacapa St., Santa Barbara, CA 93101, terms: Net 30.

Date	Action		Description
2/9/24	Add a new product	5	Add a new product with quantity tracked – Wiley One, initial quantity on hand: 0, as of date: 2/9/24, price: $4,000, cost: $2,400, income account: Sales, expense account: Cost of Goods Sold. Vendor: BoardsWest.
2/9/24	Add a new account	3	Add a new account – Account type: Other Current Assets, detail type: Other Current Assets, name: Employee Loans.
2/9/24	Add a new purchase order	5	Add a new purchase order #1003 for $9,600 to purchase 4 Wiley One boards from vendor BoardsWest.
2/10/24	Use credit card	5	Add a credit card charge – Vendor: Village Travel, using credit card: VISA, category Travel, amount: $775.
2/11/24	Record a check	5	Add check no. 1013 – Vendor: Office Depot, amount: $575, category: Supplies Asset.
2/11/24	Add a new purchase order	5	Add a new purchase order #1004 for $12,400 – Vendor: Channel Islands, ordered 10 Fred Rubbles, 6 Rook 15, and 8 The Water Hog boards.
2/12/24	Add a new bill	5	Add a new bill based on a purchase order #1002 for $4,700 – Vendor: Stewart Surfboards, terms: Net 30. All items ordered were received.
2/13/24	Add a new bill	5	Add a new bill without a purchase order – San Diego Gas & Electric, terms: Net 15, category: Utilities, amount: $150.
2/14/24	Add a new bill	5	Add a new bill without a purchase order – Prime Properties, terms: Net 15, category: Rent or Lease, amount: $2,500.
2/14/24	Pay a bill with a check	5	Pay bill $7,500 due to Prime Properties using check no. 1012.
2/15/24	Add new fixed asset accounts	6	Create four new fixed asset accounts – Account type: Fixed Assets, detail type: Buildings and Accumulated Depreciation (where appropriate), account names: Original Cost (a sub account of Building) and Accumulated Depreciation (a sub account of Building), and Land with Account type: Fixed Asset, detail type: Land.
2/15/24	Purchase land and building	6	Add the purchase of land and a warehouse building from Prime Properties, check no. 1014, amount: $2,000, as a down payment on land $5,000 and a building $15,000. The balance was paid by signing a long-term note for $18,000 (create a new account called Notes Payable – Chase, Account type: Long-Term Liabilities, detail type: Notes Payable).
2/19/24	Sell common stock	6	Add the sale of common stock to shareholders as a deposit of a $15,000 check.
2/19/24	Pay dividends	6	Add the payment of dividends to shareholders on 2/19/24, check no. 1015, in the amount of $500.
2/20/24	Make a loan payment	6	Add the payment of $339.68 to Chase Bank (a new vendor) as an installment on the land and building purchase made on 2/15/24, which included interest expense of $75 and principal amount of $264.68 using check no. 1016.
2/20/24	Make a loan payment	6	Record the payment of $1,132.27 to Bank of CA on 2/20/24 (as an installment on a loan received last month), which included interest expense of $250 and principal amount of $882.27 using check no. 1017.
2/20/24	Pay first payroll	7	Add payroll (as you did in the chapter) based on the information shown in Figure 1. (This payroll covers work through 2/15/24 but wasn't paid until 2/20/24.)
2/27/24	Add a new bill	6	Add a new bill based on purchase order #1003 on 2/9/24 – Vendor: BoardsWest, terms: Net 30. All items ordered were received.
2/27/24	Add a new invoice	4	Add invoice #1007 for $12,000 to Blazing Boards, terms: Net 30, for 3 Wiley One boards.
2/28/24	Pay second payroll	7	Add payroll (as you did in the chapter) based on the information shown in Figure 2 as follows.
2/28/24	Add a new bill	5	Add a new bill based on purchase order #1004 for $12,400 – Vendor: Channel Islands, terms: Net 15. All items ordered were received. (*Hint:* First clear all lines in the Item details section of the bill that are left over from a previous bill from Channel Islands.)
2/28/24	Add a new invoice	4	Add an invoice #1008 for $12,990 to Blondie's Boards, terms: Net 30, for 8 Fred Rubble, 3 Rook 15, and 4 The Water Hog boards.

Comprehensive Case Problems **Appendix 2** 297

Date	Action		Description
2/28/24	Add a sales receipt	4	Add a sales receipt #1009 for Sarah Hay at Hey Hays Surf for $12,210 to record their check no. 988, which was deposited to the checking account, for 1 California Nose Rider, 3 Fred Rubble, 1 Wiley One, 1 Water Hog, and 2 Rook 15 boards.
2/28/24	Reconcile bank account	4	Reconcile your company's checking account. No service charges or interest were incurred or earned. The ending bank statement balance on 2/28/24 was $39,896.91. All checks cleared the bank except check nos. 1021 to 1023. All deposits cleared the bank except a check from Sarah Hay for $12,210.
2/28/24	Adjust supplies	9	$250 of supplies were used in February. Use journal entry 10.
2/28/24	Adjust prepaid rent	9	$800 of prepaid expenses expired (representing prepaid rent) in the month of February. Use journal entry 11.
2/28/24	Accrue expenses	9	A bill for $450 was received and recorded in the next month for travel consumed in the current month. Use journal entry 12. In January, you accrued $150 in maintenance costs, which remains unpaid. No adjustment is necessary, but payment needs to be made next month.
2/28/24	Defer revenue	9	Consulting services recorded on invoice #1004 for $2,500 to Surf Rider Foundation were unearned as of 1/31/24 but were performed in February 2024. Thus, the revenue was earned. This requires the reversal of journal entry 7 recorded on 1/31/24. (*Hint:* Look at journal entry 7, and use journal entry 13 to reverse it on 2/28/24.)
2/28/24	Accrue revenue	9	Consulting services of $8,500 (340 hours) were performed as of 1/31/24 for Blazing Boards but not invoiced to the customer or recorded into the accounting records. Revenue was accrued using journal entry 8. Add invoice #1010 to bill Blazing Boards for this service. This also requires reversal of journal entry 8 recorded on 1/31/24. (*Hint:* Look at journal entry 8, and use journal entry 14 to reverse it on 2/28/24.)
2/28/24	Accrue depreciation	9	Depreciation Expense of $675 ($100, $75, and $500 for Building, Equipment, and Furniture & Fixtures, respectively) needs to be recorded for the month. Use journal entry 15 to record this depreciation.
2/28/24	Accrue revenue	9	Consulting services of $10,200 were performed on 2/28/24 for a new customer, Kyle Hain, but not invoiced or recorded into the accounting records. Use journal entry 16 to accrue this revenue.

Pay/Tax/Withholding	Ben	Betsy	Jane	Total
Hours if applicable	n/a	62	60	
Annual salary or hourly rate	95,000.00	21.50	20.00	
Gross pay	3,958.33	1,333.00	1,200.00	5,291.33
Federal withholding	542.29	182.62	164.40	724.91
Social security employee (6.2%)	245.42	82.65	74.40	328.07
Medicare employee (1.45%)	57.40	19.33	17.40	76.73
Employee withholding	845.11	284.60	256.20	1,129.71
Social security employer (6.2%)	245.42	82.65	74.40	328.07
Medicare employer (1.45%)	57.40	19.33	17.40	76.73
Employer payroll tax expense	302.82	101.98	91.80	404.80
Net Check amount	3,113.22	1,048.40	943.80	5,105.42
Check number	1018	1019	1020	

Figure 1

First semimonthly payroll

Figure 2

Second semimonthly payroll

Pay/Tax/Withholding	Ben	Betsy	Jane	Total
Hours if applicable	n/a	52	45	
Annual salary or hourly rate	95,000.00	21.50	20.00	
Gross pay	**3,958.33**	**1,118.00**	**900.00**	**5,076.33**
Federal withholding	542.29	153.17	123.30	695.46
Social security employee (6.2%)	245.42	69.32	55.80	314.74
Medicare employee (1.45%)	57.40	16.21	13.05	73.61
Employee withholding	**845.11**	**238.70**	**192.15**	**1,083.81**
Social security employer (6.2%)	245.42	69.32	55.80	314.74
Medicare employer (1.45%)	57.40	16.21	13.05	73.61
Employer payroll tax expense	**302.82**	**85.53**	**68.85**	**388.35**
Net Check amount	3,113.22	879.30	707.85	3,992.52
Check number	**1021**	**1022**	**1023**	

Requirements:

1. Create, save, and print a Profit and Loss report for February 2024.
2. Create, save, and print a Sales Transaction report for February 2024.
3. Create, save, and print a Balance Sheet report for February 28, 2024, with a % of column.
4. Create, save, and print a Checking report for February 2024.
5. Create, save, and print a Statement of Cash Flows report for February 2024.
6. Create, save, and print an A/R Aging Summary report for February 2024.
7. Create, save, and print an A/P Aging Summary report for February 2024.
8. Create, save, and print an Inventory Valuation Summary report for February 2024.
9. Create, save, and print a Transactions List by Date report for February 2024.
10. Create, save, and print a Budget vs. Actuals report for February 2024.

Case 2 Comprehensive Problem

Case 2, which begins in Chapter 3, is a company that distributes remote controlled toys and is in La Jolla, California. Business events in Case 2 occurred from 12/31/24 to 1/31/25 when presented in Chapters 3 to 10. The following is a description of business events that occurred in the month of February 2025.

Date	Description of Event	Chapter	Event
2/1/25	Add a new product	4	Add a new product – Speedy Whit, initial quantity on hand: 0, as of date: 2/1/25, price: $1,500, cost: $925, income account: Sales, expense account: Cost of Goods Sold.

Date	Action		Description
2/1/25	Add a new vendor	5	Add a new vendor – 3D Robotics, 36 Anacapa St., Santa Barbara, CA 93101, terms: Net 30.
2/1/25	Edit the chart of accounts	3	Change the name of the account Notes Payable to Notes Payable – Bank of San Diego.
2/1/25	Add a new service	4	Add a new service – Consulting, rate: $105, income account: Services.
2/1/25	Modify budget	8	Modify the following monthly budgeted amounts (Budget 1) for February 2025 through December 2025 as follows: sales: $22,000, services: $4,800, cost of goods sold: $11,000, interest expense: $400, payroll: $10,000, rent or lease: $2,500, travel: $500, utilities: $300. All other accounts remain the same.
2/1/25	Add a new employee	7	Add a new employee – Juan Perez, 65 Ocean View Lane, La Jolla, CA 92037, Employee ID No.: 555-15-3537.
2/1/25	Add a new customer	4	Add a new customer – Briggs Construction, 501 Boardwalk Place, Santa Cruz, CA 95060.
2/5/25	Add a sales receipt	4	Add a new sales receipt #1005 for $3,300 – Customer: Briggs Construction, payment method: Check, reference no.: 984, deposit to: Undeposited Funds, product: Broon F830 Ride, quantity: 1, and product: Sport Cub S, quantity: 3.
2/6/25	Add a new invoice	4	Add a new invoice #1006 for $2,250 – Customer: Hagen's Toys, terms: Net 30, service: Consulting, quantity: 10, and product: Sport Cub S, quantity: 2.
2/7/25	Add a cash receipt	4	Add a new cash receipt – Customer: Hagen's Toys, payment method: Check, reference no.: 5841, deposit to: Undeposited Funds, amount received: $1,425 (related to invoice #1002).
2/8/25	Make a bank deposit	4	Add a bank deposit to the checking account in the amount of $5,650 (Benson's RC $925, Brigg's Construction $3,300, and Hagen's Toys $1,425).
2/9/25	Add a new product	4	Add a new product – Pro View, initial quantity on hand: 0, as of date: 2/9/25, price: $2,500, cost: $1,200, income account: Sales, expense account: Cost of Goods Sold.
2/9/25	Add a new account	3	Add a new account – Account type: Other Current Assets, detail type: Other Current Assets, name: Security Deposits.
2/9/25	Add a new purchase order	5	Add a new purchase order #1003 for $11,550 to purchase 6 Speedy Whit and 5 Pro View drones from vendor 3D Robotics.
2/9/25	Use credit card	5	Add a credit card charge, new vendor: Village Travel, using credit card: AMEX, category: Travel, amount: $1,800.
2/11/25	Record a check	5	Add check no. 1011, vendor: Staples, Inc., amount: $750, account: Supplies Asset.
2/11/25	Add a new purchase order	5	Add a new purchase order #1004 for $3,695 – Vendor: E-flite for 5 Sport Cub S and 4 Mystique RES drones.
2/12/25	Add a new bill	5	Add a new bill based on a purchase order #1002 for $8,820 – Vendor: Kyosho, terms: Net 30. All items ordered were received.
2/13/25	Add a new bill	5	Add a new bill without a purchase order – San Diego Gas & Electric (a new vendor), terms: Net 15, category: Utilities, amount: $150.
2/13/25	Add a new bill	5	Add a new bill without a purchase order – Deluxe Properties (a new vendor), terms: Net 15, category: Rent & Lease, amount: $3,500.
2/13/25	Add new fixed asset accounts	6	Create four new fixed asset accounts – Account type: Fixed Assets, detail type: Buildings and Accumulated Depreciation (where appropriate), account names: Original Cost (a sub account of Building) and Accumulated Depreciation (a sub account of Building), and Land with Account type: Fixed Asset, detail type: Land.
2/13/25	Purchase land and building	6	Add the purchase of land and a warehouse building from Deluxe Properties, check no. 1012, amount: $10,000, as a down payment on land $15,000 and a building $35,000. The balance was paid by signing a long-term note for $40,000 to the Bank of San Diego (a new vendor).

Date	Action	#	Description
2/15/25	Pay first payroll	7	Add payroll (as you did in the chapter) based on the information shown in Figure 1.
2/19/25	Sell common stock	6	Add the sale of common stock to shareholders as a deposit of a $10,000, check no. 3009.
2/19/25	Pay dividends	6	Add the payment of dividends to shareholders on 2/19/25, check no. 1016, in the amount of $500.
2/20/25	Make a loan payment	6	Add the payment of $1,216.88 to the Bank of San Diego as an installment on the land and building purchase made on 2/15/25, which included interest expense of $200 and principal amount of $1,016.88, using check no. 1017.
2/22/25	Add a new bill	5	Add a new bill based on a purchase order #1003 – Vendor: 3D Robotics, terms: Net 30, amount: $11,550. All items ordered were received.
2/25/25	Add a new invoice	4	Add invoice #1007 for $10,500 to Kelly's Awesome Copters, terms: Net 30, for 4 Speedy Whit and 3 Broon F830 Ride drones.
2/25/25	Pay a bill with a check	5	Pay bill $3,500 due to Deluxe Properties using check no. 1018.
2/26/25	Receive payment	4	Receive payment on account from Hagen's Toys of $4,500 for invoice #1003 using check no. 938 and deposited to the Undeposited Funds account.
2/27/25	Add a new invoice	4	Add an invoice #1008 for $4,755 to A+ Engineering (a new customer), terms: Net 30, for 15 hours of consulting, 2 Speedy Whit drones, and 4 hours of custom painting.
2/27/25	Add a new bill	5	Add a new bill based on purchase order #1004 for $3,695 – Vendor: E-flite, terms: Net 15. All items ordered were received. (*Hint:* First clear all lines in the Item details section of the bill that are left over from a previous bill from E-flite.)
2/27/25	Add a sales receipt	4	Add a sales receipt #1009 for Fly by Night (a new customer) for $2,700 to record cash received, which was deposited to the checking account for 3 Sport Cub S and 2 Mystique RES drones.
2/27/25	Make a deposit	4	Deposited Hagen's Toys check for $4,500 into the checking account.
2/28/25	Add a new invoice	4	Add invoice #1010 to record repair services performed for Kelly's Awesome Copters. This transaction had been accrued on 1/31/25 via journal entry 8. (A variety of rates were used on this repair; thus, just enter $6,298 as the Rate for this invoice and 1 as the QTY.)
2/28/25	Add a bill	5	Add a bill for legal services rendered by Galas & Associates (new vendor) for $750. This had been accrued on 1/31/25 using journal entry 6.
2/28/25	Pay second payroll	7	Add payroll (as you did in the chapter) based on the information shown in Figure 2 as follows.
2/28/25	Reconcile bank account	8	Reconcile your company's checking account. No service charges or interest were incurred or earned. The ending bank statement balance on 2/28/25 was $29,835.47. All checks cleared the bank except check nos. 1019 to 1021. All deposits cleared the bank except a deposit from Hagen's Toys for $4,500.
2/28/25	Adjust supplies	9	$250 of supplies were used in February. Use journal entry 10.
2/28/25	Adjust prepaids	9	$1,800 of prepaid expenses expired (representing prepaid insurance) in the month of February. Use journal entry 11.
2/28/25	Accrue expenses	9	A bill for $850 was received and recorded in the next month for travel consumed in the current month. Use journal entry 12.
2/28/25	Reverse accrual	9	Legal fees accrued on 1/31/25 for $750 via journal entry 6 were properly recorded in February. Use journal entry 13 to reverse it.
2/28/25	Defer revenue	9	Consulting services recorded on invoice #1008 for $1,575 to A+ Engineering were not yet performed and thus were unearned as of 2/28/25. Use journal entry 14 to defer this revenue.
2/28/25	Accrue depreciation	9	Depreciation Expense of $1,125 ($125, $375, and $625 for Building, Furniture, and Machinery & Equipment, respectively) needs to be recorded for the month. Use journal entry 15 to record this depreciation.

2/28/25	Reverse accrual	9	$6,298 of revenue had been accrued on 1/31/25 via journal entry 8 for services rendered but not yet invoiced. These were then invoiced using invoice #1010 to Kelly's Awesome Copters. (*Hint:* Reverse journal entry 8 via a new journal entry 16.)
2/28/25	Accrue revenue	9	Consulting services of $15,000 were performed on 2/28/25 for a new customer, Wesley Ray, but not invoiced or recorded into the accounting records. Use journal entry 17 to accrue this revenue.

Figure 1

First semimonthly payroll

Pay/Tax/Withholding	Frank	Sara	Juan	Total
Hours if applicable	n/a	80	65	
Annual salary or hourly rate	72,000.00	18.75	17.00	
Gross pay	**3,000.00**	**1,500.00**	**1,105.00**	**4,500.00**
Federal withholding	411.00	205.50	151.39	616.50
Social security employee (6.2%)	186.00	93.00	68.51	279.00
Medicare employee (1.45%)	43.50	21.75	16.02	65.25
Employee withholding	**640.50**	**320.25**	**235.92**	**960.75**
Social security employer (6.2%)	186.00	93.00	68.51	279.00
Medicare employer (1.45%)	43.50	21.75	16.02	65.25
Employer payroll tax expense	**229.50**	**114.75**	**84.53**	**344.25**
Net Check amount	2,359.50	1,179.75	869.08	3,539.25
Check number	1013	1014	1015	

Figure 2

Second semimonthly payroll

Pay/Tax/Withholding	Frank	Sara	Juan	Total
Hours if applicable	n/a	75	70	
Annual salary or hourly rate	72,000.00	18.75	17.00	
Gross pay	**3,000.00**	**1,406.25**	**1,190.00**	**4,406.25**
Federal withholding	411.00	192.66	163.03	603.66
Social security employee (6.2%)	186.00	87.19	73.78	273.19
Medicare employee (1.45%)	43.50	20.39	17.26	63.89
Employee withholding	**640.50**	**300.24**	**254.07**	**940.74**
Social security employer (6.2%)	186.00	87.19	73.78	273.19
Medicare employer (1.45%)	43.50	20.39	17.26	63.89
Employer payroll tax expense	**229.50**	**107.58**	**91.04**	**337.08**
Net Check amount	2,359.50	1,106.01	935.93	3,465.51
Check number	1019	1020	1021	

Requirements:

1. Create, save, and print a Profit and Loss report for February 2025.
2. Create, save, and print a Total Income Transaction report for February 2025. (*Hint:* Click the **Total Income amount** in the Profit and Loss report for February 2025.)
3. Create, save, and print a Balance Sheet report for February 28, 2025.
4. Create, save, and print a Checking report for February 2025.
5. Create, save, and print a Statement of Cash Flows report for February 2025.
6. Create, save, and print an A/R Aging Summary report for February 2025.
7. Create, save, and print an A/P Aging Summary report for February 2025.
8. Create, save, and print an Inventory Valuation Summary report for February 2025.
9. Create, save, and print a Transactions List by Date report for February 2025.
10. Create, save, and print a Budget vs. Actuals report for February 2025.

Case 3 Comprehensive Problem

Case 3, which begins in Chapter 3, is a company that sells and services cell phones to consumers (retail business) and is in La Jolla, California. Business events in Case 3 occurred from 12/31/25 to 1/31/26 when presented in Chapters 3 to 10. The following is a description of business events that occurred in the month of February 2026.

Date	Description of Event	Chapter	Event
2/2/26	Add new products	4	Add two new taxable products – iPhone 8, initial quantity on hand: 0, as of date: 2/1/26, inventory asset account: Inventory Asset, price: $850, cost: $650, income account: Sales of Product Income, expense account: Cost of Goods Sold (taxable) and iPhone 8 Plus, initial quantity on hand: 0, as of date: 2/1/26, inventory asset account: Inventory Asset, price: $1,050, cost: $850, income account: Sales of Product Income, expense account: Cost of Goods Sold (taxable).
2/2/26	Change the name of a product	4	Change the name of the Apple iPhone 7 to iPhone 7.
2/2/26	Add a new vendor	5	Add a new vendor – LG Baker Distributing Company, 36 Sequoia St., Redlands, CA 92374, terms: Net 30.
2/2/26	Add a new product	4	Add a new taxable product – LG V30, initial quantity on hand: 0, as of date: 2/2/26, inventory asset account: Inventory Asset, price: $830, cost: $600, income account: Sales of Product Income, expense account: Cost of Goods Sold (taxable).
2/3/26	Add a new service	4	Add a new service – LG Repairs, rate: $95, income account: Services (not taxable).
2/3/26	Modify budget	8	Modify the following monthly budgeted amounts (Budget 1) for February 2026 through December 2026 as follows: sales of product income: $25,000, services: $9,000, cost of goods sold: $18,000, advertising and marketing: $2,000, insurance: $750, interest paid: $200, meals: $0, payroll: $11,000, utilities: $300.
2/3/26	Add a new employee	7	Add a new employee – Obi-Wan Kenobi, 65 Ocean View Lane, La Jolla, CA 92037, Employee ID No.: 555-22-9741.

Figure 1
First semimonthly payroll

Pay/Tax/Withholding	Kira	Jedi	Obi-Wan	Total
Hours if applicable	n/a	72	80	
Annual salary or hourly rate	48,000.00	17.00	22.00	
Gross pay	**2,000.00**	**1,224.00**	**1,760.00**	**4,984.00**
Federal withholding	274.00	167.69	241.12	682.81
Social security employee (6.2%)	124.00	75.89	109.12	309.01
Medicare employee (1.45%)	29.00	17.75	25.52	72.27
Employee withholding	**427.00**	**261.33**	**375.76**	**1,064.09**
Social security employer (6.2%)	124.00	75.89	109.12	309.01
Medicare company employer (1.45%)	29.00	17.75	25.52	72.27
Employer payroll tax expense	**153.00**	**93.64**	**134.64**	**381.28**
Net Check amount	1,573.00	962.67	1,384.24	3,919.91

Figure 2
Second semimonthly payroll

Pay/Tax/Withholding	Kira	Jedi	Obi-Wan	Total
Hours if applicable	n/a	65	85	
Annual salary or hourly rate	48,000.00	17.00	22.00	
Gross pay	**2,000.00**	**1,105.00**	**1,870.00**	**4,975.00**
Federal withholding	274.00	151.39	256.19	681.58
Social security employee (6.2%)	124.00	68.51	115.94	308.45
Medicare employee (1.45%)	29.00	16.02	27.12	72.14
Employee withholding	**427.00**	**235.92**	**399.25**	**1,062.17**
Social security employer (6.2%)	124.00	68.51	115.94	308.45
Medicare company employer (1.45%)	29.00	16.02	27.12	72.14
Employer payroll tax expense	**153.00**	**84.53**	**143.06**	**380.59**
Net Check amount	1,573.00	869.08	1,470.75	3,912.83

Requirements:

1. Create, save, and print a Profit and Loss report for February 2026 that includes a % of income column.
2. Create, save, and print a Total Income Transaction report for February 2026. (*Hint:* Click the **Total Income amount** in the Profit and Loss report for February 2026.)
3. Create, save, and print a Balance Sheet report for February 28, 2026.
4. Create, save, and print a Checking report for February 2026.
5. Create, save, and print a Statement of Cash Flows report for February 2026.
6. Create, save, and print an A/R Aging Summary report for February 2026.
7. Create, save, and print an A/P Aging Summary report for February 2026.
8. Create, save, and print an Inventory Valuation Summary report for February 2026.
9. Create, save, and print a Transactions List by Date report for February 2026.
10. Create, save, and print a Budget vs. Actuals report for February 2026.

Case 4 Comprehensive Problem

Case 4, which begins in Chapter 3, is a sports gym that sells month-to-month memberships and related merchandise. Business events in Case 4 occurred from 12/31/26 to 1/31/27 when presented in Chapters 3 to 10. The following is a description of business events that occurred in the month of February 2027.

Date	Description of Event	Chapter	Event
2/2/27	Add new product	4	Add a new taxable product – Bowflex Xtreme Home Gym, initial quantity on hand: 0, as of date: 2/1/27, inventory asset account: Inventory Asset, price: $1,199, cost: $700, income account: Sales of Product Income, expense account: Cost of Goods Sold (taxable).
2/2/27	Change the name of a product	4	Change the name of the Yoga pants to Xtreme Yoga pants.
2/2/27	Add a new vendor	5	Add a new vendor – Sole Fitness LLC, 1844 Raven Rd., Diana, TX 75640, terms: Net 30.
2/2/27	Add a new product	4	Add a new taxable product – Sole E98 Elliptical, initial quantity on hand: 0, as of date: 2/1/27, inventory asset account: Inventory Asset, price: $2,300, cost: $1,500, income account: Sales of Product Income, expense account: Cost of Goods Sold (taxable).
2/3/27	Add a new service	4	Add a new service – Annual Fee – Individual, rate: $1,620, income account: Sales (not taxable).
2/3/27	Modify budget	8	Modify the following monthly budgeted amounts (Budget 1) for February 2027 through December 2027 as follows: sales of product income: $6,000, sales: $60,000, cost of goods sold: $3,000, advertising & marketing: $3,000, insurance: $2,100, interest expense: $325, payroll: $16,000, repairs & maintenance: $700.
2/3/27	Add a new employee	7	Add a new employee – Sammy Watkins, 300 Westwood Blvd., Westwood, CA 90037, Employee ID: 555-22-9741.
2/3/27	Add a bill	5	Add a bill from Supreme Marketing, terms: Net 15, for advertising performed last month for $675. This bill was accrued as of 1/31/27. You will reverse this accrual at the end of this month.
2/4/27	Add a new customer	4	Add a new customer – Fox Broadcasting Company, 10201 West Pico Blvd., Los Angeles, CA 90064, terms: Net 30.

Date	Action	Ch	Details
2/5/27	Add a sales receipt	4	Add a new sales receipt #1005 for $6,480 – New customer: Harrison Ford, payment method: Check, reference no.: 1987, deposit to: Payments to deposit, service: Annual Fee – Individual, quantity: 4.
2/5/27	Add a new purchase order	5	Add a new purchase order #1003 for $2,100 to purchase 3 Bowflex Xtreme Home Gyms from vendor Bowflex, Inc.
2/5/27	Add a new purchase order	5	Add a new purchase order #1004 for $7,500 to purchase 5 Sole E98 Elliptical machines from vendor Sole Fitness LLC.
2/8/27	Add a new invoice	4	Add a new invoice #1006 for $29,453.10 – Customer: Fox Broadcasting Company, terms: Net 30, service: Monthly Fee – Corporate Membership 50 Employees, quantity: 4, and product: Bowflex Dumbbells, quantity: 20.
2/9/27	Add a new invoice	4	Add a new invoice #1007 for $12,000 – Customer: ABC Studios, terms: Net 30, service: Monthly Fee – Corporate Membership 50 Employees, quantity: 2.
2/10/27	Add a new invoice	4	Add a new invoice #1010 for $750 – Customer: Jules, Inc., terms: Net 30, service: Training – Individual, quantity: 10.
2/11/27	Receive payment	4	Receive payment – Customer: ABC Studios, payment method: Check, reference no.: 98745, deposit to: Payments to deposit, amount received: $7,368.75 (related to invoice #1002).
2/11/27	Pay bills	5	Pay $6,800 in bills from Bowflex, Inc. and Supreme Marketing, using check nos. 25511 and 25512.
2/11/27	Make a bank deposit	4	Add a bank deposit to the checking account in the amount of $13,848.75 to deposit previously received payments from ABC Studios ($7,368.75) and Harrison Ford ($6,480).
2/12/27	Record a credit card purchase	5	Purchase supplies from Wal-Mart (a new vendor) using the VISA credit card $1,800. (Be sure to use the Supplies asset account.)
2/12/27	Record a check	5	Add check no. 25513 to Barber Investments, Inc. for $10,000 in long-term investments.
2/12/27	Record a check	5	Add check no. 25514 to Leaseco, Inc. (a new vendor) for $6,000 to prepay one-year rent on a storage facility (Prepaid Rent).
2/12/27	Add a new purchase order	5	Add a new purchase order #1005 for $25,000 – Vendor: NordicTrack, Inc. for 5 new treadmills for use in the facility and not for resale. (You will need to create 3 new Fixed Asset accounts; Equipment, Original Cost, and Accumulated Depreciation like you did in Chapter 3. Be sure to record this purchase to the Original Cost account.)
2/15/27	Add a new bill	5	Add a new bill based on a purchase order #1003 for $2,100 – Vendor: Bowflex Inc., terms: Net 15. All items ordered were received. Be sure to delete any other items from this bill other than the 3 Bowflex Xtreme Home Gym.
2/15/27	Add a new bill	5	Add a new bill without a purchase order – LADWP (a new vendor), terms: Net 15, category: Utilities, amount: $900.
2/15/27	Add new fixed asset accounts	6	Create 3 new Fixed Asset accounts; Computers, Original Cost, and Accumulated Depreciation like you did in Chapter 3.
2/15/27	Record a credit card purchase and bank loan using a journal entry	6	Add the purchase of $45,000 in computers from Best Buy (a new vendor) for which $10,000 was charged to the VISA credit card and the $35,000 balance was paid by signing a long-term business loan using journal entry 11. (Be sure to indicate Coast Bank in the Name section of the notes payable entry and to record the purchase in the original cost sub account of Computers.)
2/15/27	Pay first payroll	7	Using recurring transactions (as you did in the chapter), pay Graham, Beckett, and Allegra based on the information shown in Figure 1. Using the Check function, pay Sammy based on the information shown in Figure 1. Be sure to indicate that Sammy's check is a recurring transaction. (Use check nos. 25515 to 25518.) Note: There may be rounding differences in the withdrawal amounts.
2/17/27	Sell common stock	6	Add the sale of common stock as a deposit of $25,000, check no. 1974, from shareholders.
2/17/27	Pay dividends	6	Add the payment of dividends to shareholders, check no. 25519, in the amount of $1,000.
2/18/27	Make a loan payment	6	Add the payment of $2,000 made to Coast Bank as an installment on long-term business loans, which included interest expense of $300 and principal amount of $1,700, using check no. 25520.

Date	Action	Ch	Description
2/19/27	Add a new bill	5	Add a new bill of $2,985 based on a purchase order #1002 – Vendor: Precor, terms: Net 30. All items ordered were received.
2/25/27	Pay bills	5	Pay bills from LADWP ($900) and Supreme Marketing ($675) using check nos. 25521 and 25522.
2/26/27	Add a bill	5	Add a new bill of $7,500 based on purchase order #1004 – Vendor: Sole Fitness LLC, terms: Net 30.
2/27/27	Add a new invoice	4	Add invoice #1008 for $7,555.50 to Jules, Inc., terms: Net 30, for 3 Sole E98 Elliptical machines plus tax.
2/27/27	Receive payment	4	Receive payment on account from ABC Studios of $12,000 from invoice #1007 using check no. 19981 into the Payments to deposit account.
2/27/27	Add a new bill	5	Add a new bill of $25,000 based on purchase order #1005 – Vendor: NordicTrack Inc., terms: Net 30.
2/27/27	Add a sales receipt	4	Add a new sales receipt #1009 for $3,280.62 to Taylor Swift (a new customer), product: Bowflex Xtreme Home Gym, quantity: 2, and product: Power Block Elite Dumbbells, quantity: 2, deposit check 948 to: Payments to deposit. (Click **See the math** to update amounts.)
2/27/27	Make a deposit	4	Deposited ABC Studios check for $12,000 into the checking account.
2/28/27	Pay second payroll	7	Add payroll (as you did in the chapter) based on the information shown in Figure 2 as follows. (Use check nos. 25523 to 25526.) Note: There may be rounding differences in the withdrawal amounts.
2/28/27	Reconcile bank account	8	Reconcile your company's checking account. No service charges or interest were incurred or earned. The ending bank statement balance on 2/28/27 was $19,173.16. All checks cleared the bank except check nos. 25524 and 25526 for $1,671.31 and $1,286.41, respectively. All deposits cleared the bank except a deposit from ABC Studios for $12,000.
2/28/27	Adjust supplies	9	Supplies worth $1,700 were used in February. Use journal entry 12.
2/28/27	Adjust prepaids	9	Prepaid rent of $3,000 expired in the month of February (rent & lease). Use journal entry 13.
2/28/27	Reverse accrual	9	Reverse journal entry 7 made on 1/31/27 to accrue advertising & marketing expenses of $675 to Supreme Marketing using journal entry 14.
2/28/27	Accrue expenses	9	A bill for $1,300 was received and recorded in the next month for legal & professional services consumed in the current month from a new vendor Legal Beagles. Use journal entry 15.
2/28/27	Reverse accrual	9	Sales accrued on 1/31/27 for $750 via journal entry 9 were properly recorded in February. Use journal entry 16 to reverse this accrual.
2/28/27	Defer revenue	9	Sales of product income recorded on sales receipt #1009 for $2,996 to Taylor Swift were deemed unearned as of 2/28/27. Use journal entry 17 to defer this revenue.
2/28/27	Reverse deferral	9	Training services recorded on invoice #1003 for $3,750 to Flyer Corporation were only partially performed even though invoiced. Sales of $2,000 had not been earned and thus were deferred in the prior month. Use journal entry 18 to reverse journal entry 8 recorded on 1/31/27.
2/28/27	Accrue depreciation	9	Record Depreciation Expense of $1,600 ($500, $600, $400, and $100 for Vehicles, Furniture, Equipment, and Computer, respectively). Use journal entry 19 to record this depreciation.
2/28/27	Accrue revenue	9	Training (Sales) of $2,500 was performed for ABC Studios on 2/28/27 but not invoiced or recorded into the accounting records. Use journal entry 20 to accrue this revenue.

Pay/Tax/Withholding	Graham	Allegra	Beckett	Sammy	Total
Hours if applicable	n/a	70	80	90	
Annual salary or hourly rate	75,000.00	25.00	22.00	20.00	
Gross pay	**3,125.00**	**1,750.00**	**1,760.00**	**1,800.00**	**8.435.00**
Federal withholding	428.13	239.75	241.12	246.60	1,155.60
Social security employee (6.2%)	193.75	108.50	109.12	111.60	522.97
Medicare employee (1.45%)	45.31	25.38	25.52	26.10	122.31
Employee withholding	**667.19**	**373.63**	**375.76**	**384.30**	**1,800.87**
Social security employer (6.2%)	193.75	108.50	109.12	111.60	522.97
Medicare company employer (1.45%)	45.34	25.38	25.52	26.10	122.34
Employer payroll tax expense	**239.09**	**133.88**	**134.64**	**137.70**	**645.31**
Net Check amount	2,457.81	1,376.37	1,384.24	1,415.70	5,218.42

Figure 1

First semi-monthly payroll

Pay/Tax/Withholding	Graham	Allegra	Beckett	Sammy	Total
Hours if applicable	n/a	85	72	83	
Annual salary or hourly rate	75,000.00	25.00	22.00	20.00	
Gross pay	**3,125.00**	**2,125.00**	**1,584.00**	**1,660.00**	**8,494.00**
Federal withholding	428.13	291.13	217.01	246.60	1,182.86
Social security employee (6.2%)	193.75	131.75	98.21	102.92	526.63
Medicare employee (1.45%)	45.31	30.81	22.97	24.07	123.16
Employee withholding	**667.19**	**453.69**	**338.18**	**373.59**	**1,832.65**
Social security employer (6.2%)	193.75	131.75	98.12	102.92	526.63
Medicare company employer (1.45%)	45.34	30.81	22.97	24.07	123.19
Employer payroll tax expense	**239.09**	**162.56**	**121.18**	**126.99**	**649.82**
Net Check amount	2,457.81	1,671.31	1,245.82	1,286.41	6,661.35

Figure 2

Second semimonthly payroll

310   Appendix 2   *Comprehensive Case Problems*

Requirements:

1. Create, save, and print a Trial Balance report for February 2027.
2. Create, save, and print a Profit and Loss report for February 2027.
3. Create, save, and print a Budget vs. Actuals report for February 2027 without cents and reflecting accounts vs. total.
4. Create, save, and print a Balance Sheet report for February 28, 2027.
5. Create, save, and print a Checking report for February 2027.
6. Create, save, and print a Statement of Cash Flows report for February 2027.
7. Create, save, and print an A/R Aging Summary report for February 2027.
8. Create, save, and print an A/P Aging Summary report for February 2027.
9. Create, save, and print an Inventory Valuation Summary report for February 2027.
10. Create, save, and print a Transactions List by Date report for February 2027.

Case 5 Comprehensive Problem

Case 5, which begins in Chapter 3, is a software engineering firm that develops training materials and computer workstations for government and commercial enterprises. Business events in Case 5 occurred from 12/31/27 to 1/31/28 when presented in Chapters 3 to 10. The following is a description of business events that occurred in the month of February 2028.

Date	Description of Event	Chapter	Event
2/1/28	Add new product	4	Add a new taxable product – Computer Workstation 800, initial quantity on hand: 0, as of date: 2/1/28, Inventory asset account: Inventory, Income account: Sales, Price/rate: $43,750, Purchase cost: $21,250, Expense account: Cost of goods sold (taxable).
2/2/28	Change the name of a product	4	Change the name of Computer Workstation 800 to Computer Workstation 750.
2/2/28	Add a new vendor	5	Add a new vendor – Southside Equipment, 1218 Ellis Blvd., Las Vegas, NV 89102, terms: Net 30
2/2/28	Add a new product	4	Add a new taxable product – Training Materials – Volume 3, initial quantity on hand: 0, as of date: 2/2/28, Inventory asset account: Inventory, Income account: Sales, Price/rate: $19,000, Purchase cost: $9,000, Expense account: Cost of goods sold (taxable).
2/2/28	Add a new service	4	Add a new service – Technical Solutions – Government, Price/rate: $350, Income account: Consulting (not taxable).
2/3/28	Receive payment	4	Receive payment – Customer: NASA, payment method: Check, reference no. 18843, deposit to: Payments to deposit, amount received: $80,000 (related to Journal Entry #1).
2/3/28	Modify budget	8	Modify the following monthly budget amounts (Budget 1) for February 2028 through December 2028 as follows: consulting: 70,000, sales: 510,000, training: 4,500, cost of goods sold: 275,000, advertising & marketing: 3,700, equipment rental: 7,500, insurance: 5,900, interest expense: 4,500, payroll: 35,000, recruiting: 4,100, and repairs & maintenance: 2,700.
2/3/28	Add a new employee	7	Add a new employee – Dylan Lucas, 322 Stockholm Blvd., Huntsville, AL 35805, Employee ID: 555-63-1803.

Date	Action	Ch.	Description
2/3/28	Add a bill	5	Add a bill from Indeed, terms: Net 30, for recruiting services performed last month for $2,800. This bill was accrued as of 1/31/28. You will reverse this accrual at the end of this month.
2/4/28	Add a new customer	4	Add a new customer – Traver Solutions, 1055 East Kennedy Rd., Seattle, WA 98106, terms: Net 30.
2/4/28	Add a bill	5	Add a new bill based on purchase order #1002 dated 1/17/28 for $180,000 – Vendor: Wild Research, Inc., terms: Net 30. All items ordered were received. (Be sure to first remove any products/services listed from previous purchase orders.)
2/5/28	Add a sales receipt	4	Add a new sales receipt #1006 for $3,500 – New customer: KC Enterprises, payment method: Check, reference no.: 5010, deposit to: Payments to deposit, service: Consulting, quantity: 10.
2/5/28	Add a new purchase order	5	Add a new purchase order for $90,000 to purchase 10 Training Materials – Volume 3 from vendor Wild Research, Inc. (Be sure to remove any product/services listed from previous purchase orders.)
2/5/28	Add a new purchase order	5	Add a new purchase order for $425,000 to purchase 25 Computer Workstation 500 from vendor HP Computers.
2/6/28	Add a new invoice	4	Add a new invoice #1007 for $167,500 including sales tax, Customer: Traver Solutions, terms: Net 30, service: Technical Solutions – Commercial, quantity: 10, products: Computer Workstation 100, quantity: 5, and Training Materials – Volume 1, quantity: 5.
2/6/28	Receive payment	4	Receive payment – Customer: Boeing, payment method: Check, reference no.: 7008, deposit to: Payments to deposit, amount received: $48,350.00 (related to invoice #1003).
2/7/28	Receive payment	4	Receive payment – Customer: US Department of Defense, payment method: Check, reference no.: 12008, deposit to: Payments to deposit, amount received: $30,000.00 (related to invoice #1002).
2/7/28	Record a credit card purchase	5	Purchase supplies from Walmart (a new vendor) using the AMEX credit card $2,100. (Be sure to use the Supplies Asset account.)
2/8/28	Make a bank deposit	4	Add a bank deposit to the checking account in the amount of $161,850 to deposit previously received payments from US Department of Defense ($30,000), Boeing ($48,350), NASA ($80,000), and KC Enterprises ($3,500).
2/9/28	Record a check	5	Add check no. 3020 to Fleet Investments, Inc. for $15,000 in long-term investments.
2/10/28	Record a check	5	Add check no. 3021 to Showcase (a new vendor) for $6,500 to prepay one-year rent on a storage facility (Prepaid Expenses).
2/10/28	Add a new invoice	4	Add a new invoice #1008 for $197,150 including sales tax – Customer: KC Enterprises, terms: Net 30, products: Computer Workstation 100, quantity: 5, Training Materials – Volume 2, quantity: 5, and service: Technical Solutions – Commercial, quantity: 16.
2/11/28	Add a new invoice	4	Add a new invoice #1009 for $1,500 – Customer: Northrup, terms: Net 15, service: Training, quantity: 15.
2/12/28	Add a new bill	5	Add a new bill based on purchase order #1003 dated 2/5/28 for $90,000 – Vendor: Wild Research, Inc., terms: Net 30. All items ordered were received. (Be sure to remove any products/services listed that were not ordered on purchase order #1003.)
2/13/28	Add a new bill	5	Add a new bill without a purchase order – Brighton Energy (a new vendor), terms: Net 15, category Utilities, amount: $750.
2/13/28	Add new fixed asset accounts	3 & 6	Create 3 new Fixed Asset accounts: Equipment, Original Cost, and Accumulated Depreciation like you did in Chapter 3.
2/14/28	Record a credit card purchase and bank loan using a journal entry	6	Record the purchase of equipment for $52,000 from Southside Equipment for which $12,000 was charged to the AMEX credit card and the $40,000 balance was paid by signing a long-term business loan (note payable) using journal entry no. 9. (Be sure to indicate Gold Coast Bank in the Name section of the notes payable entry and to record the purchase in the original cost sub account of Equipment.)
2/14/28	Pay bills	5	Pay bills from HP Computers ($350,000), State Farm Insurance ($12,000), and Brighton Energy ($750) using check nos. 3022 to 3024.

Date	Action	#	Description
2/14/28	Receive payment	4	Receive payment – Customer: Northrup, payment method: Check, reference no.: 98745, deposit to: Payments to deposit, amount received: $492,000 (related to invoice nos. 1005 and 1009).
2/15/28	Pay first payroll	7	Using recurring transactions (as you did in the chapter), pay Jamal, Rebecca, and Sarah based on the information shown in Figure 1. Using the Check function, pay Dylan based on the information in Figure 1. Be sure to indicate that Dylan's check is a recurring transaction. (Use check nos. 3025 to 3028.) Note: There may be rounding differences in the withdrawal amounts.
2/18/28	Add a new bill	5	Add a new bill of $425,000 based on purchase order #1004 dated 2/5/28 – Vendor: HP Computers, terms: Net 30. All items ordered were received. (Be sure to remove any products/services in the Item details section not related to purchase order #1004.)
2/19/28	Add a sales receipt	4	Add a new sales receipt #1010 for $525,000 plus $47,250 sales tax to Northrup, product: Computer Workstation 500, quantity: 15, deposit check #4005 to Payments to deposit. (Click **See the math** to show sales tax.)
2/19/28	Make a bank deposit	4	Add a bank deposit to the checking account in the amount of $1,064,250 to deposit previously received payments ($492,000 and $572,250) from Northrup.
2/20/28	Make a loan payment	6	Add the payment of $20,907 made to Gold Coast Bank as an installment on long-term business loans (notes payable), which included interest expense of $2,725 and principal amount of $18,182, using check no. 3029.
2/24/28	Pay bills	5	Pay bills from Indeed ($2,800) and Wild Research Inc. ($180,000) using check nos. 3030 and 3031.
2/28/28	Pay second payroll	7	Add payroll (as you did in the chapter) based on the information shown in Figure 2 as follows. (Use check nos. 3032 to 3035). Note: There may be rounding differences in the withdrawal amounts.
2/28/28	Reconcile bank account	8	Reconcile your company's checking account. No service charges or interest incurred or earned. The ending bank statement balance on 2/28/28 was $862,783.46. All checks cleared the bank except check nos. 3032, 3033, 3034, and 3035 for $4,096.35, $3,277.09, $2,516.80, and $2,240.74. All deposits cleared the bank.
2/28/28	Adjust supplies	9	Supplies worth $1,500 were used in February. Use journal entry 10.
2/28/28	Adjust prepaids	9	Prepaid insurance of $3,000 expired in the month of February. Use journal entry 11.
2/28/28	Reverse accrual	9	Reverse journal entry 5 made on 1/31/28 to accrue recruiting services of $2,800 to Indeed using journal entry 12.
2/28/28	Accrue expenses	9	A bill for $1,700 was received and recorded in the next month for legal services consumed in the current month from Legal Sharks (a new vendor). Use journal entry 13.
2/28/28	Defer revenue	9	Some consulting services recorded on sales receipt #1006 for $1,500 to KC Enterprises were deemed unearned as of 2/28/2028. Use journal entry 14 to defer this revenue.
2/28/28	Reverse deferral	9	Consulting services recorded on invoice #1003 for $32,000 to Boeing were only partially performed even though invoiced. Consulting of $16,000 had not been earned and thus were deferred in the prior month. Use journal entry 15 to reverse journal entry 6 recorded on 1/31/28.
2/28/28	Accrue depreciation	9	Record Depreciation Expense of $3,000 ($900, $750, $500, and $850 for Computers, Copiers, Furniture, and Equipment, respectively). Use journal entry 16 to record this depreciation.
2/28/28	Accrue revenue	9	Training of $3,000 was performed for KC Enterprises on 2/28/28 but not invoiced or recorded into the accounting records. Use journal entry 17 to accrue this revenue.

Pay/Tax Withholding	Jamal	Rebecca	Sarah	Dylan	Total
Hours if applicable	n/a	n/a	78	80	
Annual salary or hourly rate	125,000.00	100,000.00	40.00	37	
Gross pay	**5,208.33**	**4,166.67**	**3,120.00**	**2,960.00**	**15,455.00**
Federal withholding	713.54	570.83	427.44	405.52	2,117.33
Social security employee (6.2%)	322.92	258.33	193.44	183.52	958.21
Medicare employee (1.45%)	75.52	60.42	45.24	42.92	224.10
Employee withholding	**1,111.98**	**889.58**	**666.12**	**631.96**	**3,299.64**
Social security employer (6.2%)	322.92	258.33	193.44	183.52	958.21
Medicare company employer (1.45%)	75.55	60.45	45.24	42.92	224.16
Employer payroll tax expense	**398.47**	**318.78**	**238.68**	**226.44**	**1,182.37**
Net check amount	4,096.35	3,277.09	2,453.88	2,328.04	12,155.36

Figure 1

First semimonthly payroll

Pay/Tax Withholding	Jamal	Rebecca	Sarah	Dylan	Total
Hours if applicable	n/a	n/a	80	77	
Annual salary or hourly rate	125,000.00	100,000.00	40.00	37	
Gross pay	**5,208.33**	**4,166.67**	**3,200.00**	**2,849.00**	**15,424.00**
Federal withholding	713.54	570.83	438.40	390.31	2,113.08
Social security employee (6.2%)	322.92	258.33	198.40	176.64	956.29
Medicare employee (1.45%)	75.52	60.42	46.40	41.31	223.65
Employee withholding	**1,111.98**	**889.58**	**683.20**	**608.26**	**3,293.02**
Social security employer (6.2%)	322.92	258.33	198.40	176.64	956.29
Medicare company employer (1.45%)	75.55	60.45	46.40	41.31	223.71
Employer payroll tax expense	**398.47**	**318.78**	**244.80**	**217.95**	**1,180.00**
Net check amount	4,096.35	3,277.09	2,516.80	2,240.74	12,130.98

Figure 2

Second semimonthly payroll

Requirements:

1. Create, save, and print a Trial Balance report for February 2028.
2. Create, save, and print a Transaction Detail by Account report for December 2027 through February 2028.
3. Create, save, and print a Profit and Loss report for February 2028 that includes a percent of income column.
4. Create, save, and print a Budget vs. Actuals report for February 2028 without cents and reflecting accounts vs. total.
5. Create, save, and print a Balance Sheet report for February 28, 2028 that includes a percent of column.
6. Create, save, and print a Checking report for February 2028.
7. Create, save, and print a Statement of Cash Flows report for February 2028.
8. Create, save, and print an A/R Aging Summary report for February 2028.
9. Create, save, and print an A/P Aging Summary report for February 2028.
10. Create, save, and print an Inventory Valuation Summary report for February 2028.
11. Create, save, and print a Transactions List by Date report for February 2028.

Case 6 Comprehensive Problem

Case 6, which begins in Chapter 3, is a Recreational Vehicle (RV) dealership in the state of Washington. They sell new RVs and related accessories to individuals and businesses. In addition, they repair and service RVs. Business events in Case 6 occurred from 12/31/22 to 1/31/23 when presented in Chapters 3 to 10. The following is a description of business events that occurred in the month of February 2023.

Date	Description of Event	Chapter	Event
2/1/23	Add a new vendor	5	Add a new vendor – R-Pod, 888 SE Sheridan Road, Sheridan, OR 97378, terms: Net 30.
2/2/23	Add new product	4	Add a new product – Name/Description/Purchasing information: RP-171, initial quantity on hand: 0, as of date: 2/2/23, inventory asset account: Inventory, Sales price: $26,900, cost: $21,520, income account: Sales of Product Income, expense account: Cost of Goods Sold, Sales tax category: Taxable – standard rate, Preferred vendor: R-Pod.
2/2/23	Change the name of a product	4	Change the name/description of the service Basic 6,000-mile service to Basic 8,000-mile service.
2/2/23	Add a new product	4	Add a new product – Name/Description/Purchasing information: RP-179, initial quantity on hand: 0, as of date: 2/2/23, inventory asset account: Inventory, Sales price: $22,800, cost: $18,240, income account: Sales of Product Income, expense account: Cost of Goods Sold, Sales tax category: Taxable – standard rate, Preferred vendor: R-Pod.
2/3/23	Add a new service	4	Add a new service – Detailing, rate: $50, income account: Sales, Sales tax category: Nontaxable.
2/3/23	Modify budget	8	Modify the following monthly budgeted amounts (Budget 1) for February 2023 as follows: sales of product income: $400,000, sales: $15,000, cost of goods sold: $320,000, advertising & marketing: $18,000, contractors: $3,000, insurance: $4,000, interest expense: $600, payroll: $22,000, repairs: $700, utilities: $5,000, and depreciation: $1,200. Leave budgets for March through December as is.

Date	Action	#	Description
2/3/23	Add a new employee	7	Add a new employee – Anastasia Quinn, 507 N 169th St., Shoreline, WA 98133, Social Security No.: 555-54-1111.
2/3/23	Add a bill	5	Add a bill from Pacific Marketing, terms: Net 15, for advertising performed last month, for $1,800. This bill was accrued as of 1/31/23. You will reverse this accrual at the end of this month.
2/4/23	Add a new customer	4	Add a new customer – Apple Travel, terms: Net 30.
2/6/23	Add a sales receipt	4	Add a new sales receipt #1003 – New customer: Rose Ski, 241 St., Andrews Way, Santa Maria, CA 93454, payment method: Check, reference no.: 355, deposit to: Undeposited Funds, product: 2022 Winnebago Revel 44E, price: $150,000, quantity: 1, amount received: $163,950.
2/7/23	Add a new purchase order	5	Add a new purchase order #1003 to purchase two RP-171 and three RP-179 trailers from vendor R-Pod for a total cost of $97,760.
2/8/23	Add a new purchase order	5	Add a new purchase order #1004 to purchase two 2023 Thor Motor Coach Palazzo 33.2 motorhomes from vendor Thor Motor Coach for a total cost of $288,000.
2/8/23	Add a new invoice	4	Add a new invoice #1004 for $108,207 – Customer: Apple Travel, terms: Net 30, product: one 2023 Airstream Flying Cloud 27FB TWIN. (Click **See the math** to update amounts.)
2/10/23	Add a new invoice	4	Add a new invoice #1005 for $700 – Customer: Rose Ski, terms: Net 30, service: one Basic 8,000-mile service and five hours of Detailing.
2/13/23	Receive payment	4	Receive payment – Customer: Deja Smith, payment method: Check, deposit to: Undeposited Funds, amount received: $153,020 (related to invoice: #1002).
2/14/23	Pay bills	5	Pay $322,000 in bills from Winnebago, Inc., and Pacific Marketing, using check nos. 601 and 602.
2/15/23	Make a bank deposit	4	Add a bank deposit to the checking account in the amount of $316,970 to deposit previously received payments from Deja Smith and Rose Ski.
2/15/23	Record a credit card purchase	5	Purchase supplies from Best Buy using the AMEX credit card $3,000. (Be sure to use the Supplies Asset account.)
2/15/23	Record a check	5	Add check no. 603 to McConnel Investments, Inc. for $20,000 in additional investments.
2/15/23	Record a check	5	Add check no. 604 to Global Leasing (a new vendor) for $24,000 to prepay one-year rent on a warehouse (Prepaid Expenses).
2/15/23	Add a new bill	6	Add a new bill without a purchase order – Seattle City Light (a new vendor), terms: Net 15, category: Utilities, amount: $3,000.
2/15/23	Add new fixed asset accounts	6	Create new fixed asset accounts – Account type: Fixed Assets, detail type: Vehicles, name: Vehicles. Track depreciation of this asset. Be sure to change the name of the Vehicles accumulated depreciation account from Depreciation to Accumulated Depreciation.
2/15/23	Record a vehicle purchase and bank loan using a journal entry	6	Add the purchase of a truck for $95,000 from Seattle Ford (a new vendor) and the signing a note payable to Seattle Bank for the full purchase price using journal entry 10.
2/15/23	Pay first payroll	7	Using recurring transactions (as you did in the chapter), pay Rhett, Oliver, and Emelia based on the information shown in Figure 1. Using the check function, pay Anastasia. Be sure to indicate that Anastasia's check is a recurring unscheduled transaction. (Use check nos. 605 to 608.)
2/17/23	Sell common stock	6	Add the sale of common stock as a deposit of $20,000 from shareholders (Common stock: $200, Paid-In Capital: $19,800).
2/20/23	Pay dividends	6	Add the payment of dividends to shareholders, check no. 609, in the amount of $500.
2/21/23	Make a loan payment	6	Add the payment of $3,542.88 made to Seattle Bank as an installment on notes payable, which included interest expense of $390 and principal amount of $3,152.88, using check no. 610.
2/22/23	Add a new bill	5	Add a new bill of $97,760 based on a purchase order #1003 – Vendor: R-Pod, terms: Net 30. All items ordered were received.

Date	Action	Ref	Description
2/25/23	Pay bills	5	Pay bills from State Farm Insurance ($18,000), National Covers ($4,000), and Airstream, Inc. ($180,000) using check nos. 611 to 613.
2/27/23	Add a new invoice	4	Add invoice #1006 for $29,401.70 to Donald Biden, terms: Net 30, for one RP-171 plus tax. (Click **See the math** to update amounts.)
2/27/23	Receive payment	4	Receive payment on account from Apple Travel of $108,207 from invoice #1004 recorded into the Undeposited Funds account.
2/27/23	Add a sales receipt	4	Add a new sales receipt #1007 for $153,020 to Ebony Williams for one 2022 Winnebago View 24G deposited to Undeposited Funds. (Click **See the math** to update amounts.)
2/27/23	Add a new invoice	4	Add invoice #1008 for $950 to Deja Smith, terms: Net 30, for a transmission service ($350) and sewer system inspection and repair ($600).
2/28/23	Make a deposit	4	Deposited Apple Travel and Ebony William's checks for a total of $261,227 into the checking account.
2/28/23	Add a new bill	5	Add a new bill without a purchase order, vendor: Pacific Marketing, terms: Net 15, category: Advertising & Marketing, amount: $1,800.
2/28/23	Pay second payroll	7	Add payroll using recurring transactions for Rhett, Oliver, Emelia, and Anastasia based on the information shown in Figure 2. (Use check nos. 614 to 617.)
2/28/23	Reconcile bank account	8	Reconcile your company's checking account. No service charges or interest were incurred or earned. The ending bank statement balance on 2/28/23 was $182.49. All checks cleared the bank except check nos. 613 through 617. All deposits cleared the bank except a deposit made on 2/28/23 for $261,227.
2/28/23	Adjust supplies	9	Supplies worth $1,200 were used in February. Use journal entry 11.
2/28/23	Adjust prepaids	9	Prepaid expenses of $4,400 expired in the month of February ($2,400 related to insurance and $2,000 related to rent & lease). Use journal entry 12.
2/28/23	Reverse accrual	9	Reverse journal entry 7 made on 1/31/23 to accrue advertising & marketing expenses of $1,800 to Pacific Marketing using journal entry 13.
2/28/23	Accrue expenses	9	A bill for $2,500 was received from Elite Events and recorded in March 2023 for contractors expense consumed in the current month. Use journal entry 14 to accrue this liability.
2/28/23	Reverse accrual	9	Sales accrued on 1/31/23 for $950 via journal entry 8 were properly recorded in February. Use journal entry 15 to reverse this accrual.
2/28/23	Defer revenue	9	The sale of a motorhome to Donald Biden on 2/27/23 for $29,401.70 was deemed unearned as of 2/28/23 since it wasn't delivered until March. Use journal entry 16 to defer this revenue to a new Unearned Revenue account and reduce sales tax payable. You'll need to review invoice #1006 to determine amounts by account.
2/28/23	Accrue depreciation	9	Record Depreciation Expense of $3,000 ($1,000, $300, $800, and $900 for Buildings, Computers, Machinery & Equipment, and Vehicles, respectively). Use journal entry 17 to record this depreciation.
2/28/23	Accrue revenue	9	Services of $16,000 were performed for Sam Ski on 2/28/23 but not invoiced or recorded into the accounting records until the next month. Use journal entry 18 to accrue Sales and Accrued Receivables.

Pay/Tax/Withholding	Oliver	Rhett	Emelia	Anastasia	Total
Hours if applicable	n/a	n/a	83	65	
Annual salary or hourly rate	85,000.00	60,000.00	35.00	40.00	
Gross pay	**3,541.67**	**2,500.00**	**2,905.00**	**2,600.00**	**8,946.67**
Federal withholding	485.22	342.50	397.99	356.20	**1,225.70**
Social security employee (6.2%)	219.58	155.00	180.11	161.20	**554.69**
Medicare employee (1.45%)	51.35	36.25	42.12	37.70	**129.73**
Employee withholding	**756.15**	**533.75**	**620.22**	**555.10**	**1,910.11**
Social security employer (6.2%)	219.59	155.00	180.11	161.20	**554.70**
Medicare company employer (1.45%)	51.38	36.28	42.12	37.70	**129.79**
Employer payroll tax expense	**270.97**	**191.28**	**222.23**	**198.90**	**684.48**
Net Check amount	2,785.52	1,966.25	2,284.78	2,044.90	7,036.55

Figure 1

First semimonthly payroll

Pay/Tax/Withholding	Oliver	Rhett	Emelia	Anastasia	Total
Hours if applicable	n/a	n/a	73	72	
Annual salary or hourly rate	85,000.00	60,000.00	35.00	40.00	
Gross pay	**3,541.67**	**2,500.00**	**2,555.00**	**2,880.00**	**8,596.67**
Federal withholding	485.22	342.50	350.04	394.56	**1,177.75**
Social security employee (6.2%)	219.58	155.00	158.41	178.56	**532.99**
Medicare employee (1.45%)	51.35	36.25	37.05	41.76	**124.65**
Employee withholding	**756.15**	**533.75**	**545.49**	**614.88**	**1,835.39**
Social security employer (6.2%)	219.59	155.00	158.41	178.56	**533.00**
Medicare company employer (1.45%)	51.38	36.28	37.05	41.76	**124.71**
Employer payroll tax expense	**270.97**	**191.28**	**195.46**	**220.32**	**657.71**
Net Check amount	2,785.52	1,966.25	2,009.51	2,265.12	6,761.27

Figure 2

Second semimonthly payroll

Requirements:

1. Create, save, and print a Bank Reconciliation report as of 2/28/23 (click **Hide additional information** when generating this report).
2. Create, save, and print a Trial Balance report as of 2/28/23.
3. Create, save, and print a Profit and Loss report for the month of February 2023 with a % of income column.
4. Create, save, and print a Balance Sheet report as of 2/28/23 with a % of row column.
5. Create, save, and print a Statement of Cash Flows report for February 2023.
6. Create, save, and print an A/R Aging Summary report as of 2/28/23.
7. Create, save, and print an A/P Aging Summary report as of 2/28/23.
8. Create, save, and print an Inventory Valuation Summary report as of 2/28/23.
9. Create, save, and print a Transactions Detail by Account report for all dates.
10. Create, save, and print a Budget vs. Actuals report for the two months ended 2/28/23.

Overview—Do I Need to Become QuickBooks Online Certified?

appendix 3

There are two schools of thought here. The first is that becoming certified provides employers/clients independent confirmation of an individual's skill and proficiency in using QBO. Thus, certification is a good résumé builder. The second is that any employer/client that relies solely on certification to assure competency in using QBO will eventually find themselves looking for a new QBO professional.

Does it hurt? No. Does it help? Maybe. Is it necessary? No. What is important is the knowledge, skill, and proficiency in using QuickBooks as a tool to help businesses better understand the financial implications of their decisions.

In the author's opinion, certification takes a back seat to accounting education and experience. Thus, it is in the student's best interest to gain accounting knowledge (the more, the better) through courses at accredited institutions in the topics of bookkeeping, financial accounting, managerial accounting, cost accounting, and tax accounting, as well as the application of QuickBooks to different business situations. The next step is to gain experience through internships or part-time jobs working under a QuickBooks/Accounting professional. Add that to certification and you're ready for gainful employment.

The following is a summary overview of the topics covered by the QuickBooks certified user online exam.

What Topics Are Covered in the QBO Accountant Certification?

1. QuickBooks Online solutions
2. Configuring a QBO company
3. Sales and customers
4. Expenses and vendors
5. Banking
6. Reports
7. Managing your work, team, and clients
8. Year end

Links to QuickBooks Certification Information

https://certiport.pearsonvue.com/Certifications/QuickBooks/Certified-User/Overview

https://quickbooks.intuit.com/accountants/training-certification/

Index

A

account(s). *See also* charts of accounts
   Accounts Payable
      create, 64–65
      establishing beginning balance, 53–56, 64–65
      Transaction Report, 143
   Accounts Receivable
      create, 64–65
      establishing beginning balance, 53–56, 64–65
      reports, 22
      Transaction Report, 273
   charts of, 16–18
   Checking account
      Transaction Report, 142
   creating, 2–3, 29
   Inventory account
      Transaction Report, 143
   Opening Balance Equity, 68–70
   Payroll (expense), 190–191
   Payroll Tax Payable (liability), 191
Account and Settings section, 35
Account and Settings window, 16
Account Quickreport, 18
Accounts Payable (A/P) account
   create, 64–65
   establishing beginning balance, 53–56, 64–65
   Transaction Report, 143
Accounts Payable (A/P) Aging Detail Report, 281
Accounts Payable (A/P) Aging Summary report, 280–282
Accounts Payable (A/P) Register page, 17
Accounts Receivable (A/R) account, 64–65
   create, 64–65
   establishing beginning balance, 53–56, 64–65
   reports, 22
   Transaction Report, 273
Accounts Receivable (A/R) Aging Detail Report, 279
Accounts Receivable (A/R) Aging Summary reports, 278–280
accrued expenses, 252–253

accruing revenue, 255–256
adjusting entries, 247–258
   accrued expenses, 252–253
   accruing revenue, 255–256
   analysis of, 247–258
   creating trial balance, 248
   depreciation, 256–258
   overview, 247
   prepaid expenses
      deferring supplies as asset, 249–252
      recording consumption of supplies, 249–250
      recording expiration of, 250–252
   recording of, 247–258
   types of, 247
   unearned revenue, 253–254
Advanced settings, 25
aging summaries
   Accounts Payable Aging Summary report, 280–282
   Accounts Receivable Aging Summary reports, 278–280
A/P (Accounts Payable) Aging Detail Report, 281
A/P (Accounts Payable) Aging Summary report, 280–282
A/P (Accounts Payable) Register page, 17
A/R (Accounts Receivable) Aging Detail Report, 279
A/R (Accounts Receivable) Aging Summary reports, 278–280
Automated Sales Tax system, 292

B

balance sheet
   creating, 68–70, 272–275
   customizing, 68–70
   exporting, 68–70
   printing, 68–70
   saving, 68–70
Balance Sheet page, 69
Balance Sheet reports, 20–21
Bank and Credit Cards page, 10
bank deposit, inputting, 107

bank deposits, 11
banking transactions, 9–12
   recognizing, 9
   viewing, 10–11
bank reconciliations, 226–230
   creating, 227–230
   overview, 226–227
   preparing, 217–230
   Summary Reconciliation Report, 230
Bank Register (partial view), 11
bill(s). *See also* invoices
   adding purchase order information, 134
   after adding purchase order information, 135
   credit card, 139–141
   entering, 133
   paying, 138–139
   payment, 137–141
   for prepaid expenses, 137
   for services, 136
   from vendors for receipt of products or services, 133–137
budget(s)
   Budget Overview reports, 222–224
   Budget *vs.* Actual reports, 226
   creating, 218–221
   establishing, 217–230
   overview, 217
   reports, 221–226
   viewing, 222–226
Budgeting window, 219
Budget Overview reports, 222–224
Budget *vs.* Actual reports, 226
Budget worksheet, 220
   for annual Income, 221
business
   main role in, 31
   name, 30
   set up, 31
   type of, 30
   works, 32
Business Overview reports, 20

C

case studies, 295–318
   adjusting entries, 259–265
   budgets and bank reconciliations, 231–246
   financial statements and reports, 285–291
   investing and financing activities, 173–186
   operating activities, purchases and cash payments, 145–160
   operating activities, sales and cash receipts, 111–126
   payroll, 200–216
   setting up company, 73–94
Cash Flows report, statement of, 22
cash receipts, 106–108
charts of accounts, 16–18. *See also* account(s)
   modifying, 53–67
      adding checking accounts, 54–56
      adding Common stock accounts, 61–63
      adding Long-term business loans accounts, 61–63
      adding Prepaid expenses accounts, 61–63
      adding products and services, 57–61
   viewing, 16–18
checking account
   chart of accounts, 56
check payments, 139–141
common stock
   definition of, 166
   recording deposit of funds from sale of, 166–168
Common stock accounts, 61–63
companies
   closing Opening Balance Equity account, 68–70
   establishing beginning balances, 53–67
   modifying chart of accounts, 53–67
   setting for, 23–25, 51–53
Company dashboard, 34
Company settings, 23–25, 51–53
Company Settings window, 15
create
   Accounts Payable (A/P) account, 64–65
   Accounts Receivable (A/R) account, 64–65
   balance sheet, 68–70
   purchase orders, 130–132
   trial balance, 70–71
Create (+) menu, 2
Create window, 101, 107
credit card
   payment, 139–141
   use of, 137–141
Credit card charge, 140
Customer information window, 42, 99
customers, 3–9
   accessing information about, 3–5, 41–42
   adding, 96–100

Customers window, 3–4
customizing
   balance sheet report, 274
   Budget Overview report, 223–224
   Budget *vs.* Actuals report, 225–226
   Profit and Loss report, 270
   Statement of Cash Flows, 278

D
dashboard, 2
deferring
   definition of, 247
   supplies as asset, 249–250
Deposit window, 108
depreciation, 162, 256–258
depreciation account, 65–67
dividends
   definition of, 166
   payment of cash, 166–168
due on receipt, 139

E
Employee Information, 8–9, 189
employees, 3–9
   accessing information about, 8–9, 43–44
   adding, 188–190
   paying, 191–199
      recording payment, 192–199
      Recurring Transactions, 196
      Transaction Report, 195, 199
      Trial Balance, 194, 198
   semi-monthly payroll information, 191, 196
equipment, purchase of, 163–164
equity accounts, 12
equity transactions, 166–168
Expenses settings, 24
expense transactions, viewing, 12–14
Expense window, 14

F
financial reports, 266–284
financial statements
   balance sheet, 272–275
   income statements, 266–271
      creating, 267–271
      definition of, 266
      Invoice, 269
      Profit and Loss Report, 266–271
      Transaction Report, 269
   overview, 266
   Statement of Cash Flow, 275–278
fixed assets
   acquisition of in exchange for long-term debt, 170–172
   definition of, 162
   depreciation, 162
   recording purchase of, 163–164, 171

G
Gear icon, 15–16, 19, 23
Gear window, 15–16, 44
generally accepted accounting principles (GAAP), 247

H
Help feature
   adding account in QBO, 40
   QuickBooks Online, 39
   set up sales tax in QBO, 40

I
Income Statement report, 20–21
income statements, 266–271
   creating, 267–271
   definition of, 266
   Invoice, 269
   Profit and Loss Report, 266–271
   Transaction Report, 269
Intuit, 1, 25, 27–28, 45–48, 139
Inventory account, 143
Inventory Valuation Detail, 283
Inventory Valuation Summary report, 282–284
investing and financing activities, 161–172
   acquisition of fixed assets in exchange for long-term debt, 170–172
   common stock and dividends, 166–168
   fixed assets, 162–164
   long-term debt, 168–170
   long-term investments, 164–165
   owner investments/withdrawals, 166–168
investments
   long-term, 164–165
   owner, 166–168
invoices
   Accounts Payable Aging Summary, 282
   Accounts Receivable Aging Summary, 280

adding, 102–105
income statements, 269
Inventory Valuation Summary, 284
sales, 100–105

J

journalizing
    Accounts Payable (A/P) account, 64–65
    Accounts Receivable (A/R) account, 64–65
    accruing advertising and marketing expense, 253
    adding new account, 249
    closing Opening Balance Equity, 68
    recording accrual of advertising expense, 252–253
    recording depreciation, 256–258
    recording expiration of prepaid expenses, 250–252
    recording purchase of fixed asset in exchange for long-term debt, 171
    recording reflect earned revenue, 255–256
    recording reflect unearned revenue, 253–254

L

lists
    of products and services, 99
    in QBO, 18
    viewing
        list of lists, 19
        list of terms, 19
Long-term business loans accounts, 61–63
    establishing beginning balances, 62
long-term debt, 168–170
    acquisition of fixed assets in exchange for, 170–172
    payment of, 168–170
    recording receipt of funds from borrowing, 168–170
    repayment with interest, 170
long-term investments
    definition of, 164
    recording purchase of, 165

M

Medicare taxes, 191

N

+ New menu, 41
+ New window, 133, 138

O

Opening Balance Equity account, 68–70
operating activities
    paying bills, 138–139
    purchases and cash payments, 127–144
        adding vendors, 128–129
        purchase orders, 129–132
        recording bills, 133–137
        recording check payments, 139–141
        recording credit card payments, 139–141
        Trial Balance reports, 141–144
    sales and cash receipts, 95–110
        adding services, products, and customers, 95–100
        recording cash receipts, 106–108
        sales invoices, 100–105
        sales receipts, 100–105
        Transaction Detail by Account reports, 108–110
        Trial Balance reports, 108–110
owner investments, 166–168
owner withdrawals, 166–168

P

payments
    bill, 137–141
    check, 139–141
    credit card, 139–141
    receipts of, 106–108
    recording, 192–199
payroll, 187–199
    adding employees, 188–190
    adding payroll-related accounts, 190–191
    paying employees, 191–199
        recording payments, 192–199
        Recurring Transactions, 196
        semi-monthly payroll information, 191, 196
        Transaction Report, 195, 199
        Trial Balance, 194, 198
Payroll (expense) account, 190–191
Payroll Tax Payable (liability) account, 191
Performance Rentals customer window, 100
prepaid expenses
    bills for, 137
    deferring supplies as asset, 249–252
    recording consumption of supplies, 249–250
    recording expiration of, 250–252
Prepaid expenses accounts, 61–63

products
    adding, 96–100, 129–132
    lists of, 99
    purchase orders, 129–132
    from vendors for receipt of, 133–137
Product/Service information window, 58–59
Profit and Loss budget, 218–221
    creating, 219–221
Profit and Loss report, 20–21. *See also* income statements
    creating, 267–271
purchase
    of computer, 163–164
    of furniture, 164
    of a long-term investment, 165
    of network equipment, 163–164
purchase orders, 129–132
    creating, 130–132
    uses, 129
purchases and cash payments, 127–144
    adding vendors, 128–129
    paying bills, 138–139
    purchase orders, 129–132
    recording bills, 133–137
    recording check payments, 139–141
    recording credit card payments, 139–141
    trial balance, 141–144

Q

QuickBooks Accountant (QBDT), 28–29
QuickBooks/Accounting professional, 319
QuickBooks certified user online exam objectives, 319
QuickBooks Online (QBO)
    adding account, 40
    assigning instructor as company's "accountant", 45–46
    creating accounts, 28–29
    dashboard, 39
    definition of, 27
    vs. desktop version of QuickBooks Accountant, 28–29
    navigating, 38–45
    overview, 27
    setup guide, 33
    set up sales tax in, 40
    signing in of, 29, 38
    signing out of, 38
    video tutorials for, 46–48

R

receipts of payment (cash receipts), 106–108. *See also* sales and cash receipts
Receive Payment window, 108
Reconcile—Checking form, 229
    partial view of, 228
Reconcile window, 228
reconciliation process, 227
Recurring Transactions, 196
report(s)
    accessing customers information, 3–5
    accessing employee information, 8–9
    accessing vendor information, 6–7
    account and settings window, 16
    Accounts Payable Aging Detail, 281
    Accounts Payable Aging Summary, 280–282
    accounts receivable, 22
    Accounts Receivable Aging Detail Report, 279
    Accounts Receivable Aging Summary, 278–280
    Balance Sheet, 21
    banking transactions, viewing, 10–11
    budget, 221–226
    Business Overview, 20
    chart of accounts, viewing, 16–18
    expense transactions, viewing, 12–14
    financial, 266–284
    Income Statement, 20–21
    Inventory Valuation Summary, 282–284
    Profit and Loss, 20–21, 266–271
    sales transactions, viewing, 12–14
    Statement of Cash Flows, 20, 22
    Transaction
        for Accounts Receivable (A/R), 273
        income statements, 269
    Transaction Detail by Account
        creating, 71–72
        exporting, 71–72
        printing, 71–72
    Transaction Detail by Account reports, 108–110
        creating, 108–110
        exporting, 108–110
        printing, 108–110

revenue
    accruing, 255–256
    unearned, 253–254
Revised Trial Balance report, 258

S

sales and cash receipts, 95–110
    adding services, products, and customers, 96–100
    recording cash receipts, 106–108
    sales invoices
        adding, 101–105
        definition of, 100
    sales receipts
        adding, 101–105
        definition of, 100
    Transaction Detail by Account reports, 108–110
sales invoices
    adding, 101–105
    definition of, 100
Sales Receipt, 102
sales receipts
    adding, 101–105
    definition of, 100
sales tax, 292–294
Sales tax calculations, 103
Sales Tax Center, 292–294
sales transactions, viewing, 12–14
Sample Company
    accessing customer information, 41–42
    accessing employee information, 43–44
    accessing vendor information, 42–43
    accuracy of, 127–128, 161–162, 187–188, 217–218
    adding customers, 96–100
    adding new employees, 188–190
    adding new services, 96–100
    adding products, 96–100
    adding sales invoices, 101–105
    adding sales receipts, 101–105
    address, 37
    banking transactions, viewing, 10–11
    cash receipts, 106–108
    changing name, 36
    chart of accounts, viewing, 16–18
    choosing type, 36
    expense transactions, viewing, 12–14
    list of lists, viewing, 19
    list of terms, viewing, 19
    opening, 2
    payroll for, 192–199
    receipts of payment, 106–108
    recording deposit of funds from refinancing, 169
    recording purchase of long-term investment, 165
    recording purchase of new computer and network equipment, 163–164
    sales tax, 292–294
    sales transactions, viewing, 12–14
    settings management
        Advanced settings, 25
        Company settings, 23–25
        Expenses settings, 23
    switching, 45
Sample Company Dashboard, 2
Sample Company Home page, 10
Save Report Customizations, 70
saving
    balance sheet, 68–70
semi-monthly payroll information, 191, 196
services
    adding, 96–100
    lists of, 99
    paying bills for, 136
    settings management
        Advanced settings, 25
        Company settings, 23–25
        Expenses settings, 23
    from vendors for receipt of, 133–137
Settings menu, 34
Settings window, 15–16
Sign In window, 74
social security, 191
Statement of Cash Flows, 20, 22, 275–278
    creating, 276–278
Summary Reconciliation Report, 230

T

taxes
    Medicare, 191
    sales, 292–294

Time settings, 24
Transaction
   for Accounts Payable account, 143
   for Checking account, 142
   for Inventory account, 143
   for supplies asset, 252
Transaction Detail by Account, 108–110
   creating, 71–72, 108–110
   exporting, 71–72, 108–110
   printing, 71–72, 108–110
Transaction Detail by Account Report, 72, 110
Transaction reports
   for Accounts Payable account, 143
   for Accounts Receivable (A/R), 273
   for Checking account, 142, 195, 199
   for common stock, 277
   income statements, 269
   for Inventory account, 142
   for sales account, 269
   for supplies asset, 252
trial balance, 70–71, 108–110, 141–144
   adjustments, 251
   creating, 108–110, 141–144, 172, 248
   exporting, 108–110
   investigating, 141–144
   printing, 108–110
Trial Balance report, 109, 194, 198, 248

U
unearned revenue, 253–254
U.S. Treasury, 191

V
Vendor Information window, 43, 129
vendors, 3–9
   accessing information about, 6–7, 42–43
   adding, 128–129
   recording bills from vendors for receipt of products or services, 133–137
Vendors information, 6
video tutorials
   online navigating QuickBooks, 46–48
   for QuickBooks Online, 46–48

W
Welcome window, 29